China's Global Political Economy

Much has been written about China's economy, as well as its business management system. *China's Global Political Economy*, however, is designed to bring together these two perspectives, serving to enhance our understanding of China's growing global role.

Examining changes in the management strategies of foreign companies investing in China and Chinese enterprises doing business overseas, this book analyses China's political economy in the context of the Communist Party's changing policies. The introductory section begins by studying the aspects of Chinese economic growth as it impacts on domestic social issues and the projection of Chinese power abroad. Within this overall framework, it then goes on to critically assess the effects of foreign investment, business management strategies, human resource management, corporate social responsibility and the financial services sector. Arguing that the encouragement of consumption is a significant objective of the Chinese leadership, the last section is concerned with the importance of the food industry.

This book will be of interest to students and scholars of Chinese business, management and international political economy, as well as policymakers and business practitioners.

Robert Taylor was formerly Director of the Centre for Chinese Studies and Reader in Modern Chinese Studies at the University of Sheffield, UK. His publications include *The Globalization of Chinese Business* (2014) and *International Business in China* (Routledge, 2012).

Jacques Jaussaud is Professor of Management Sciences at University of Pau, France. He has co-edited several books, including *Economic Change in Asia: Implications for Corporate Strategy and Social Responsibility* (Routledge, 2017).

Routledge Studies on Comparative Asian Politics

Books in this series will cover such areas as political institutions and systems, political economy, political culture, political thought, political psychology, public administration, law, and political histories of Asia. The studies may deal with Asia as a whole, a single country, or a group of countries in Asia. Those studies that have a clear comparative edge are especially welcome.

The series is edited by Shiping Hua, the Calvin and Helen Lang Distinguished Chair in Asian Studies, Director of the Asian Studies Program and Professor of Political Science at the University of Louisville, USA.

The Authoritarian Public Sphere
Legitimation and Autocratic Power in North Korea, Burma, and China
Alexander Dukalskis

An East Asian Challenge to Western Neoliberalism
Niv Horesh and Kean Fan Lim

China's Global Political Economy
Managerial Perspectives
Robert Taylor and Jacques Jaussaud

China's Global Political Economy

Managerial Perspectives

Edited by Robert Taylor and Jacques Jaussaud

Routledge
Taylor & Francis Group

LONDON AND NEW YORK

First published 2018 by Routledge

2 Park Square, Milton Park, Abingdon, Oxfordshire OX14 4RN
52 Vanderbilt Avenue, New York, NY 10017

Routledge is an imprint of the Taylor & Francis Group, an informa business

First issued in paperback 2019

British Library Cataloguing-in-Publication Data
A catalogue record for this book is available from the British Library

Library of Congress Cataloging-in-Publication Data
A catalog record for this book has been requested

ISBN: 978-1-138-10373-3 (hbk)
ISBN: 978-0-367-42415-2 (pbk)

DOI: 10.4324/9781315102566

Contents

Figures and tables

Figures

Tables

Acknowledgements

This volume includes a selection of original papers presented at the 21st International Euro-Asia Research Conference on Asia-Europe Strategic Partnership in a Dynamic World, Business, Economic Linkages and Political Interdependence, held at Pukyong National University, Busan, Republic of Korea from the 22 to 24 June 2016. The editors wish to acknowledge the contributions to discussions of all participants at the seminar. We also extend our thanks to the conference organizers at Pukyong National University.

Abbreviations

AFC	Asian Financial Crisis
AIIB	Asian Infrastructure Investment Bank
ASEAN	Association of Southeast Asian Nations
AVIC	Aviation Industry Corporation of China
BOISEE	Unified Basic Old Age Insurance for Enterprise Employees
BOPSCS	Old Age Pension System for Civil Servants
BSR	Business for Social Responsibility
BT	British Telecom
CAP	Common Agricultural Policy
CAPM	Capital Asset Pricing Model
CCP	Chinese Communist Party
CEMs	Companies from Emerging Markets
CEO	Chief Executive Officer
CNOOC	China National Offshore Oil Company
CNPC	China National Petroleum Organization
COMAC	Commercial Air Corporation of China
CSA	Country Specific Advantage
CSR	Corporate Social Responsibility
CSRP	Corporate Social Responsibility Plan
DB	Di Bao Minimum Income Guarantee
DG	Director General
DJSI	Dow Jones Sustainability Index
EAP	16th Environmental Action Programme
EFTA	European Free Trade Association
FAO	Food and Agricultural Organization
FDI	Foreign Direct Investment
FGS	Five Guarantee Schemes
FSA	Firm Specific Advantage
FTAs	Free Trade Agreements
GAC	Guangdong Automobile
GAIM	General Aviation Inner Mongolia
GFC	Global Financial Crisis
GIs	Global Indications

GM	General Manager
GMP	Good Manufacturing Practice
HRM	Human Resource Management
HS	Harmonized System
ICT	Information and Communication Technologies
ILO	International Labour Organization
IMF	International Monetary Fund
IPM	Integrated Pest Management
IPPC	International Plant Protection Convention
IPR	Intellectual Property
ISO	International Standards Organization
ISPMS	International Standards for Phytosanitary Measures
IT	Information Technology
JV	Joint Ventures
LLL	Linkage, Leverage, Learning
LSG	Leading Small Groups
M&A	Merger and Acquisition
MEAs	Multilateral Environmental Agreements
MES	Market Economy Status
MNCs	Multinational Corporations
MOA	Ministry of Agriculture of China
MOCA	Ministry of Civil Affairs
MOFA	Ministry of Foreign Affairs
MOFCOM	Ministry of Commerce
MOU	Memorandum of Understanding
MRL	Maximum Residue Levels
MRSI	Maritime Silk Road Initiative
NAPs	National Action Plans
NCMS	New Cooperative Medical Scheme
NDRC	National Development and Reform Commission
NGOs	Non-Governmental Organizations
NORINCO	China North Industries
NPC	National People's Congress
NRSPS	New Rural Social Pension Scheme
OBOR	One Belt One Road
ODI	Overseas Direct Investment
OECD	Organization for Economic Cooperation and Development
OEM	Original Equipment Manufacturer
OLI	Ownership, Localization and Internationalization
PBR	Price Book Ratio
PER	Price Earnings Ratio
PIC	Prior Informed Consent
PRC	People's Republic of China
QS	Quality Supervision
RDF	Registration Document Fiscal

RMB	Renminbi
R&D	Research and Development
ROE	Return on Equity
RSCA	Responsible Supply Chain Association
SAFE	China State Administration of Foreign Exchange
SASAC	State Owned Assets Supervision and Administration
SDR	Sustainable Development Report
SEPA	State Environmental Protection Administration
SHZ300	Shanghai Shenzhen 300
SITC	Standard International Trade Classification
SMEs	Small and Medium Sized Enterprises
SOEs	State-Owned Enterprises
SPS	Application of Sanitary and Phytosanitary Products
SPSS	Statistical Package for Social Scientists
UN	United Nations
WB	World Bank
WHO	World Health Organization
WTO	World Trade Organization
WWF	World Wildlife Fund
YTO	China First Tractor Group Corporation

Contributors

Bruno Amann is a Professor of Management Science at Paul Sabatier University in Toulouse, France. His research relates to family business, corporate governance and international management. He has presented papers at academic conferences focused on Asia and has published widely in the above fields.

Bernadette Andreosso-O'Callaghan holds the Jean Monnet Chair of Economic Integration at the Kemmy Business School at the University of Limerick (Ireland) where she co-founded the first research centre dealing with contemporary Asian Studies in Ireland in 1997. She is also Visiting Professor of East Asian Economics at the Ruhr University, Bochum, Germany. She has taught in various Asian universities, including Seoul National University and Chulalongkorn University, Bangkok. She has published extensively in the following areas: comparative Europe-Asia economic integration in addition to economic growth and structural change in Asian countries, with a focus on East Asia. One of her latest publications is a co-edited book (with Robert Taylor) entitled *Emerging Asian Economies and MNCs Strategies* (Edward Elgar, 2016).

Isabelle Barth is at the HUMANIS Research Centre of the EM Strasbourg Business School, conducting research relating to gender equality, life-work balance, religion as a cultural and social phenomenon and female entrepreneurship. In her research she has sought to promote diversity management as a strategic area and has published widely in the above fields.

Romain Belz received his Master's degree in International Business from the Kedge Business School. His research interests are international trade and the supply chain. His Master's dissertation investigated the phenomenon of Chinese foreign direct investment in Europe. He is currently working in an international food and beverage company.

Agar Brugiavini is Professor of Economics at the Ca' Foscari University of Venice, Italy. She obtained her PhD in Economics from the London School of Economics and has been a lecturer at the City Business School, London. She was a Fulbright Fellow at Northwestern University, USA. She is currently responsible for the Ca' Foscari node of SHARE (Survey of Health, Ageing and

Retirement in Europe). She is also part of the National Bureau of Economic Research and a Research Associate of the IFS (Institute of Fiscal Studies, UK.).

Matilde Cassin graduated from Ca'Foscari University of Venice and has a PhD in the Environmental Sciences. She has collaborated with scholars in research centres and universities, focusing in particular on the integration of environmental issues into European cooperation programmes. She currently works in the Veneto region, as project manager within the Joint Secretariat of the 2014–2020 Italy-Croatia Cross Border Programme.

Danilo Cavapozzi is Assistant Professor of Economic Policy at the Ca'Foscari University of Venice, Italy, and a NETSPAR(Network for Studies on Pensions, Aging and Retirement) Research Fellow. He holds a Lurea degree in Statistics and Economics and a PhD in Economics and Management from the University of Padua, Italy. His research interests cover applied microeconomics, microeconometrics, labour economics, household economics and the economics of aging.

Claire Etienne, after practising as a business lawyer, has since taught in universities in the fields of management, marketing, law and economics. She holds a doctorate in management from the Sorbonne Business School. She has participated in academic conferences, discussing issues related to corporate social responsibility.

Fan Yunxin received her Master of Science degree in Economics and Statistics from the Georgia Institute of Technology in December 2016. She worked as a research assistant for Professor Richard. B.Freeman at Harvard University for his China Gazateer Project. Fan Yunxin also focuses on artificial intelligence and the intersection between art, technology and the social sciences.

Gao Ni is a doctoral student at the University of Pau et des Pays de l'Adour, France. In 2017 she completed her PhD dissertation on the organization and strategy of Chinese multinational companies setting up subsidiaries in France. She is also a lecturer at the Kedge Business School where she teaches International Business, Strategic Diagnostics and case studies to French and international students at the Master's degree level.

Jörn-Carsten Gottwald is Professor of East Asian Politics at the Ruhr University Bochum. Earlier he held positions in Political Science and Chinese Studies at the Free University of Berlin, the University of Trier, Germany and the University of Ireland, Cork. He holds a PhD (FU Berlin) and a habilitation (University of Trier) in Political Science. With his background in Chinese Studies and political economy he has published in the areas of financial services regulation, China's political economy and global economic governance.

Guo Yugang is a Research Associate at the Institute of Economics of the Chinese Academy of Social Sciences (CASS) in Beijing and has been a Senior Lecturer at Nanchang University. His main research interests are in the areas of bank risk and financial market return, especially in the Chinese financial system. He has published more than 30 scientific papers, books and book chapters in these fields.

Bhumika Gupta holds a PhD in Human Resource Management from the University of Pau, France. She is Associate Professor of Human Resource Management in the Department of Management, Marketing and Strategy at the Telecom Ecole de Management, Evry, France. Her research concerns corporate culture and psychological contracts in the workplace. She has published widely in academic journals.

Sajjad Haider is a doctotal student at the School of Management, Lanzhou University and a Research Scholar at the Mark. O. Hatfield School of Government, Portland State University, USA. He attended the International MBA Programme at Lanzhou University. His primary research areas are human resource management, public service motivation, performance based governance, leadership and cross-cultural management. He has work experience ranging across corporate sectors and non-profit international organizations. He served on the Faculty of Business Management at Karakoram International University (KIU).

Jacques Jaussaud is Professor of Management and vice-Dean of the Doctoral School in the Social Sciences and Humanities, University of Pau, France. His research interests are in the areas of business strategy, organization, control and human resource management, with a particular focus on Japan, China and other Asian countries. He has published widely in academic journals, including the Management International Review, the Journal of International Management and the International Journal of Human Resource Management. He has co-edited several books, including the recent volume, Economic Change in Asia: Implications for Corporate Strategy and Social Responsibility (Routledge, 2017).

Cuiling Jiang is an Assistant Professor at the Kedge Business School. She holds a PhD in Management Science from the University of Pau, France. She teaches International Human Resource Management, Cross-Cultural Management, Human Resource Management in Asia and Change Management. Her research interests include French MNCs and their internationalization in Asia, Chinese companies in Europe and international human resource management.

Li Junshi obtained a Bachelor's degree in Law from Sichuan Normal University, China in 2014 as well as a Master's degree in Business Management from the Kemmy Business School of the University of Limerick, Ireland, in 2015. He is currently a PhD candidate at the Kemmy Business School. His research area is the EU-China trade relationship and his PhD research topic deals with the evolving agricultural trade relationship between China and the EU.

Gildas Lusteau is currently Director of the Confucius Institute at Pays de la Loire, Angers, France. He received his PhD from the EM Strasbourg Business

School, University of Strasbourg. His research interests include international business ethics, corporate social responsibility, intercultural management, China's youth and Chinese education.

Ilda Mannino is Scientific Coordinator of the Ten Programme on Sustainability at the Venice International University. She took a PhD in Environmental Science at Ca'Foscari University of Venice and spent a post-doctoral period at the Centre of Industrial Ecology of Yale University. Her current research interests focus on Sustainable Development, Environmental Policy and Economics, Industrial Ecology, Green Economy and Integrated Coastal Zone Management. She is involved in research and education projects on these themes at national and international levels.

Lucia Morales holds Bachelor's and Master's degrees in the fields of Economics, Finance, Education and Time Series Analysis. She has published in areas related to international economics and finance, emerging markets, economic and financial crises, financial market integration, contagion energy economics, commodity markets, international capital markets, education, critical thinking and learning. Her main interests concern the application of her research output in the context of her teaching and learning strategies. She thus aims to contribute to the development of teaching in higher education by examining how traditional theories need to be updated in the light of current economic and financial dynamics.

Sophie Nivoix is an Associate Professor of Finance at the University of Poitiers, France, and has been a visiting Professor at Warsaw and Nanchang Universities. Her research interests include stock market return and risk, econometrics and international management, with a special focus on China and Japan. She has published research papers in academic journals and written several books and book chapters.

Pan Yao is currently a PhD student in Economics at the Ca'Foscari University of Venice, Italy. She holds a Research Master's degree in Global Economics and Management and a degree in International Economics and Business from the University of Groningen, the Netherlands. She worked as a research assistant for one year during her Master's programme at the University of Groningen. Her research interests cover welfare economics, health economics and the economics of aging, with a special focus on China.

Robert Pauls is a Lecturer in East Asian Politics in the Faculty of East Asian Studies, Ruhr University Bochum, where he received his PhD for a dissertation related to capitalist development in the People's Republic of China. His research focuses on the comparative and international political economy of China.

Jan Schaaper is Associate Professor at the Institute of Business Administration at the University of Poitiers, France. He holds a PhD degree in Economics and a Research Accreditation in Management Science. His research interests are in the field of international management, with a special focus on Asian markets. He has published widely in French and English in academic journals, including the International Journal of Human Resource Management, the Management International Review, the Journal of Asian Pacific Economies, the Journal of International Management and the Asia Pacific Business Review. He has professional experience in the Netherlands, France, Lebanon, China and Japan, thus enriching his perception of international management issues.

Robert Taylor was formerly Director of the Centre for Chinese Studies and Reader in Modern Chinese Studies at the University of Sheffield. His research interests focus on China's domestic and foreign policy, especially Chinese business management and foreign economic relations as well as Sino-Japanese relations. He has published widely in such academic journals as the Asia-Pacific Business Review and Asian Business and Management. He has contributed to media programmes relating to contemporary Asia. His publications include *China's Intellectual Dilemma* (University of British Columbia, 1981) and *Greater China and Japan* (Routledge,1996). He edited *International Business in China* (Routledge,2012), *The Globalisation of Chinese Business* (Chandos, 2014) and (with Bernadette Andreosso-O'Callaghan) *Emerging Asian Economies and MNCs Strategies* (Edward Elgar, 2016). He also engages in management consultancy.

Zhang Boqi is a Chinese PhD student in Management Science at the University of Pau. His PhD dissertation concerns strategies of internationalization for emerging multinationals, especially Chinese enterprises. He earlier received his Bachelor's and Master's degrees in management from the 3rd University of Toulouse. He is also a Junior Lecturer at the University of Lorraine.

Zhu Yanru received her Master of Science degree in Marketing from Imperial College, London, in October 2016. She has been engaged in branding and digital marketing. She has been an entrepreneur in Sweden and has worked in the marketing analysis sector in London. She now works for AB InBev, focusing on innovation.

M. Bruna Zolin is Professor of Economics-Rural Development and Commodity Markets- at Ca'Foscari University of Venice. Her academic research focuses primarily on agricultural and food products, the economics of rural development, international trade, the environment and business development, and European policy. She has been Deputy Head of the School of Asian Studies and Business Management at Ca'Foscari University. She has served as an expert for the FAO in Rome and a Visiting Professor in several universities. She has published mainly in the areas of agricultural markets and rural development policies.

1 Introduction and overview

Robert Taylor

Introduction and overview

Recent decades have witnessed the emergence of China as a global power and its leaders are a major force in decision-making. The action of the International Monetary Fund (IMF) to designate the RMB as a reserve currency, involving special drawing rights, from 1 October 2016 is but one indication of China's global ascent. The following chapters, mainly derived from papers presented at the 21st Euro-Asia Research Conference, held at Pukyong National University in Busan, the Republic of Korea in June 2016, reflect these concerns, focusing on ongoing key issues in China's political economy. There are, however, constraints on China's continuing ascent. In the wake of the Western economic crisis in 2008 supply and demand in the Chinese market was seen as a saviour of American and European economies. China's economic growth in previous decades was based largely on labour intensive exports, a competitive low wage structure, facilitated in part by the influx of rural migrants to the cities of the country's Southeastern seaboard and a cheap currency. But demand for Chinese goods like steel has slowed in Western markets and China's importation of minerals in the context of the Chinese economic slowdown has impacted upon producers in developing countries. In addition, Chinese labour intensive goods have become less competitive in the face of lower wage economy producers like the Vietnamese. Moreover heavy industrial sectors like steel, largely the province of China's state enterprises, are over-manned, resulting in the overcapacity of plant discussed below. Additionally, the Chinese leadership is concerned with rising regional and social inequality which threatens national stability, forcing debates concerning policy direction in CCP leadership circles. Most importantly, China's emerging market economy operates in a one party state which could to a degree constrain the kind of innovation and entrepreneurship demanded by competitive global markets.

Chinese Communist Party (CCP) leadership relationships will necessarily have a bearing on economic change. The rule of Xi Jinping, CCP leader since 2012, has been distinctly authoritarian, in line with Chinese tradition, and there has been a tightening of party control under his leadership, with evidence of a power struggle over differences regarding policy direction. In general, it could be said that the leadership as a whole believes that only their monopoly of power

DOI: 10.4324/9781315102566-1

can provide the discipline needed for national unity and thus economic advance; a pluralistic political system could invite disunity and dissidence. Factionalism within the CCP leadership seems to be centred around Xi Jinping and the Premier, Li Kejiang; the former representing the princeling faction of offspring of early revolutionaries and the latter leading those whose power base has included those promoted through the Communist Youth League. While Li Kejiang has appeared more committed to the market economy, Xi Jinping has been more concerned with the consolidation of CCP power in his own hands, witness his policymaking shift to leading groups which he chairs. Some observers have suggested that Xi is also exploiting nationalist fervour, especially over disputed islands in the East China Sea, to distract attention from the party's internal battles. (Sheridan, 2015; Laurence and Sheridan, 2016; Ferguson, 2015). It might be argued that Xi Jinping and his close associates are more committed to the idea of the state as the one locus of power and influence; any market forces are at its service and must be controlled. There are resonances here of Imperial China. Socialism is like feudalism; both assign social status, even though the latter term must be used advisedly in the traditional Chinese context.

Undoubtedly linked to the campaign against corruption within the CCP itself, which has brought down a number of provincial casualties, Xi Jinping has embarked on a drive to censor social media when they do not reflect CCP views. Targets are social and entertainment news which should be dominated by 'positive energy', a pseudonym for only reporting an optimistic appraisal of ongoing developments and furthering the party line (Reuters, 2016). Potential sources of dissent are Non-Government Organisations (NGOs) which are to be subject to new rules stated in a document released by China's State Council and CCP in August 2016. These guidelines follow a foreign NGO management law imposed earlier in the year and are designed to strengthen party guidance or control in such bodies through CCP representatives and Youth League branches. In addition the police are to be granted extensive powers to regulate foreign NGOs which must obtain the former's approval (Li, 2016).

As stated, the CCP leaders see the strengthening of party control as a prerequisite for achieving the goals necessary to eliminate the constraints on economic growth. These impediments are addressed in the targets of China's 13th Five Year Plan (2016–2020), outlined at the 5th Plenum of the CCP in 2015. In a later elucidation Xi Jinping outlined the objectives of medium to high rates of economic growth, a sine qua non for building a moderately prosperous society by 2020. The objectives of the plan may be summarized under two headings: innovation and entrepreneurship designed to avoid the 'middle income trap' and achieve the elimination of poverty by 2020.

Both these objectives are reflected in the plan to achieve an annual economic growth rate of 6.5% during the period from 2016–2020, indispensable for doubling 2010 GNP and per capita income for both urban and rural residents by 2020. To solve the problem of industrial overcapacity, especially prevalent in the state sector, the economy must be restructured through emphasis on innovation. In other words industries must become more efficient, with a premium placed on quality. This should take place in tandem with plans to reduce environmental degradation.

Such economic restructuring necessarily impacts on measures to reduce social inequality, particularly the urban-rural divide. The Chinese leaders have staked their legitimacy on achieving higher living standards for the population at large and, to contain rising expectations, seek to make consumption more affordable. Consumption rather than excessive investment in industrial plant is thus seen as a driver of economic growth. The plan is to lift all China's poor out of poverty by 2020. Xinhua, China's official news agency, has stated that the country had 70.2 million people in rural areas below the poverty line, that is, below an income of 2,300 yuan per annum, equivalent to US$376 at the 2010 rate of exchange. It is acknowledged that there is a dire need to improve rural services like infrastructure, electric power and the Internet. Rural facilities like education and healthcare lag behind those of the cities. Through both fiscal expenditure and private investment the aim is to take ten million people out of poverty each year from 2016 to 2020. If these goals are to be achieved, planners must factor in demographic change; the one child policy is being abandoned in the wake of a continuing decrease in the number of the working age population, since 15% of the population is aged sixty or over (Zhang, ed., 2015).

Demographic change together with industrial overcapacity, the latter a target for economic reform, have implications for employment structure. At the onset of the global financial crisis in 2008 the level of Chinese exports was drastically reduced as a result of economic retrenchment in Western countries. This resulted in industrial overcapacity in China, that is, an increasing differential between production capacity and actual production, an issue raised in a report by the European Chamber. The Chinese government's response was a fiscal stimulus package, focusing on investment in infrastructure and increased lending to SOEs which then expanded industrial capacity. Thus inefficient manufacturing was subsidized and this led to only a short-term effect in stimulating the economy. Efforts since to reduce overcapacity have been hampered by the fact that China is not a unified market but a series of regional markets. This has a concomitant, barriers to trade and investment, engendering provincial particularism. Local governments, mindful of the dangers of social instability, are reluctant to cause bankruptcies and lose tax revenues (European Chamber and Roland and Berger Consultants, 2016).

An example of overcapacity is the steel industry where the main players are SOEs which, receiving official support, have less need to respond to market signals than private enterprises which reduce production when prices fall. As of 2016, China accounted for 50% of total global steel output, as compared to 15% at the turn of the century (Liu and Song, 2016). The solution is to reduce excess capacity but, in spite of central government plans to do so, China still produces as much steel as the rest of the world combined, and in 2014 exports of that product rose by 50.5% (Mananquil and Wagley, 2015). An unintended consequence of this overcapacity is to inhibit the movement of underemployed workers to service jobs, where labour demand is growing (Bloomberg News, 2016). It has been suggested that a Chinese initiative, the One Belt One Road (OBOR), designed to provide infrastructure linking Asian and European markets and financed by the Asian Infrastructure Investment Bank, could help solve the incapacity problems. In the short term, however, the markets of central Asian countries linked to China by the scheme would surely prove too small to absorb excess production on any scale (European Chamber and Roland Berger, 2016).

A long-term solution to the problem of overcapacity is innovation. Companies in overcapacity industries, however, suffer from low profit margins; this discourages investment in research and development (R&D) projects. As the Boston Consulting Group has been quoted as stating, the greatest income returns have been shifting 'from commodity products to focused specialties'. Perhaps nowhere is the issue of overcapacity discussed above better demonstrated than in the EU countries dispute with China over steel imports (ibid).

Accordingly, the Chinese leaders are adopting more focused measures to reduce overcapacity, one palliative being the offer of 100 billion RMB in additional funding for social security, designed to cushion the effects of unemployment among laid-off workers (He, 2016). In the longer term, of course, a better structured social security net will be crucial.

Strategically, however, the solution to overcapacity lies in innovation and its concomitant, R&D. In 2010 China's State Council launched the Strategic and Emerging Industries Concept, identifying innovative development in such priority industries as energy efficient and environmental technologies, high end equipment manufacturing and biotechnology as drivers of China's future economic development (Marro, 2015).

As a key role will be played by small and medium sized enterprises (SMEs), often privately owned, they should be afforded greater protection through intellectual property (IPR) laws. Lack of protection potentially inhibits R&D in China, whether by foreign or domestic companies (European Chamber and Roland Berger Consultants, 2016). In fact, the private sector may well prove a driver of economic growth through innovation and entrepreneurship, a linkage defined as 'innopreneurship' by Professor Ying Lowrey of Qinghua University, constituting the Alibaba model, after the Chinese enterprise. This is said to facilitate increasingly efficient production leading to higher productivity, that is, in terms of the amount of output produced per unit. China is replete with examples like Haier, the latter investing in technologies like 3D printing (Kenyatta, 2016; Armstrong, 2015).

Nevertheless a constraint on achieving innovation, whether by the state or the private sector, is the shortage of professional and managerial cadre, essential for adapting to changing corporate demands and adjusting to fluctuating market conditions (Lawrence, 2015).

Educational attainment and retraining are crucial factors in enabling innovation, and one criterion is the ranking of innovative countries. While China's commitment to innovation is relatively recent, the following gives some indication of the country's success to date. According to Bloomberg's 2015 listing of the world's most innovative countries which is based on six measures, R&D

expenditure per capita, gross value added by manufacturing, number of high tech companies, research personnel per capita and patents per capita, in addition to post-secondary education levels, China was placed 22nd out of more than 200 states (Chen, 2015).

Innovation is a key to addressing domestic consumption, a Chinese government policy which also demands increasing levels of personal income, as China moves to a high wage economy. A highly skilled labour force will need to be paid more. Currently, however, China suffers from significant regional disparities and income inequalities. In terms of GDP per capita China averages US$ 12,900 per person, ranking alongside low income countries, in contrast with the United States figure of US$ 54,800 per capita. Additionally, China has a GINI index of 47.3, making it the twenty-sixth most unequal country in the world (ibid). This, in part, reflects, the urban-rural divide in China, and Chinese economic planners see urbanization as a driver of consumption. Therefore one of the objectives in the current Five Year Plan is to increase the urbanization ratio based on the number of registered residents; this is to reach approximately 45% by 2020 (Zhang, ed., 2015). The number of people who currently live in cities has reached 55% of China' population but this figure masks regional variations in urbanization; in the East the ratio increased from 53.6% in 2005 to 62.2% in 2012, contrasting with equivalent figures of 39.1% and 48.5% for the central region, 34.5% and 44.7% for the West (Cao and Wu, 2015). In addition, included in the above urbanization figure of 55% are rural migrants who do not have hukou or official residence status and are thus denied equal education, employment rights and social security entitlement. Thus urbanization will not automatically achieve the desired increase in consumption. There are, however, various measures in train to reform the hukou system and retrain rural migrants to help satisfy the need for the highly qualified personnel demanded by an increasingly high-tech economy (Zhang, ed., 2015; Wang and Cai, 2015). It was announced in September 2016 that the Chinese government was ending the distinction between urban and rural residents in the cities' household registration system, with both groups in future to have the same access to public services. But, in practice, it will take time for such a measure to reduce the urban-rural gap. Additionally, an effective way of raising consumption is through increasing income in the countryside itself. This may also help to lessen the urban-rural divide. One key to this is developing rural technical training as an aid to employability outside agriculture. Facilitating land transfer will make possible such greater mobility, raise wage levels and thus boost consumption. Finally, distribution needs to be improved, one way being e-commerce, as briefly discussed below (Li, 2015; Zou, 2015).

There is also other potential for increasing personal consumption, especially in the cities. While SOEs are likely to offload employees, the private sector created 64 million jobs between 2011 and 2015 and recruitment continues. In tandem with employment growth in private enterprises, the affluent middle class is increasing, with the number of households earning over the equivalent of US$ 24,000 expected to double to 100 million, constituting 30% of the urban total (The Economist, 2016).

This affluence is in turn reflected in greater discretionary income and consumer discernment, causing retail sales in China to grow between 10% and 11% from 2015 to 2016. (Asian Equities Team, 2016). In recent years wealthy Chinese consumers have engaged in conspicuous consumption, a feature which, recalling Thorstein Veblen's study of New York's upper classes in the late nineteenth and early twentieth centuries, characterizes a nation's ascent to great power status. For several decades there has been a market for luxury items but now, with the assistance of foreign investors, Hermes clothing being an example, Chinese native brands are being designed (Arlidge, 2016). China's car market may be cited as an example of luxury brands; it is the world's largest, with total sales of its passenger vehicles rising by nearly 10% between 2015 and 2016. Sales of sports-utility vehicles (SUVs) increased by 46% over the same period. There have been similar increases in consumption as a whole, with retail sales, taking account of inflation, rising by 9.6% during the first quarter of 2016 as compared to the same period in 2015 (The Economist, 2016).

A spur to both urban and rural consumption has been e-commerce which has enjoyed spectacular growth, with online shopping accounting for 3% of total private consumption in 2010 but 15% in 2016. In 2015 Alibaba's Chinese revenues grew to US$ 9.7 billion in 2015, rising 40% over the total for 2014. The expansion in e-commerce has no doubt been aided by sales of consumer devices like smartphones, China's telecom giant, Huawei, predicting that revenues from such sales would rise by about 50% in 2016 (ibid).

Thus, in summary, consumption in China is being stimulated by the discretionary income of the expanding middle class, especially in China's coastal area, contributing substantially to the country's economic growth in 2015 (Jin and Li, 2016).

This selectivity is reflected in the priorities of the 13th Five Year Plan, briefly referred to earlier, and which is informed by the focus on consumption, in turn demanding increased service provision in areas like the legal determination of consumer rights and financial instruments. Consequently, the 13th Five Year Plan invites foreign investment in finance, law, accounting, consultancy, education and training, healthcare, entertainment and tourism. Significantly, the service sector's share of GDP grew by 44% in 2010 to 48% in 2014, currently growing at a faster pace than manufacturing and agriculture (Jin and Li, 2016; Cooper, 2015). But the caveat must be added that, while Chinese planners seek to encourage investment in the service sector, some areas remain closed to foreign companies or are heavily protected on security grounds (Magnus, 2016). Moreover the censorship mentioned earlier is impacting on service provision; there are restrictions on the foundation of private schools, especially by foreigners, and rules are being imposed governing films. In fact, there is also an emphasis on indigenous innovation, and regulations regarding cyber security and insurance are designed to favour local suppliers. The Chinese wish to acquire knowledge and data without risking foreign control, even though they made a commitment to the liberalization of services at their country's accession to the WTO. Failure to open services could, however, adversely impact on China's economic growth; the country's banks are familiar with servicing state-owned industries but have often failed to lend to private small and medium sized enterprises (SMEs) which could emerge as key players in innovation (Mananquil, 2015).

Nevertheless foreign investment is encouraged in other priority sectors like advanced engineering, high and new technologies, energy conservation and environmental protection (Jin and Li, 2016).

The targets relating to indigenous innovation are informed by the 2025 Made in China Strategy, China's First Ten Year Plan for Transforming Manufacturing, which offers opportunities for those foreign companies with innovative technologies, including information technology, advanced machinery and new materials, in addition to bio-medical and environment related research. A major vehicle for the achievement of these objectives, especially that of innovation, is Merger and Acquisition (M&A), both by Chinese enterprises and foreign companies. Whereas formerly foreign entities often initiated a brand new venture or plant in China, with a delay in the inception of production, domestically produced inputs from the Chinese partner may now be utilized. Likewise Chinese enterprises may acquire foreign ventures which transfer technology (ibid).

In summary, FDI in China is shifting from labour intensive processing to the higher value added and advanced manufacturing sectors. In 2015 US$ 77.2 billion or 61.1% of FDI went to the service sector. In addition, almost a quarter of FDI in manufacturing was invested in high-tech and new manufacturing, an increase of 9.5% over that of 2014 (ibid).

If Chinese planners' inward investment policies have changed, so have foreign investors begun to adjust to the new economic reality in China. In past decades the attraction was cheap labour and low production cost which advantaged foreign investors in exporting to their home or secondary markets. But the coming of age of Chinese consumers has meant that foreign companies are seeking to tailor their products to Chinese tastes, which are evolving. Accordingly, they are employing local innovative R&D personnel who can help create products attuned to the local market. The cultivation of such talent has been an objective of the National Plan for Science and Technology Talent Development, launched by the State Council in 2010; government incentives also offer tax reductions, there being preferential rates for R&D (Marro, 2016).

The commitment to innovation is also a feature of China's outward foreign direct investment (ODI). In fact, this may well already have exceeded the country's inward (FDI), when the use of offshore intermediaries such as Hong Kong and Caribbean tax havens are taken into account (Garcia-Herrero, 2015). Chinese government policy has been a driver of ODI in simplifying significantly the scrutiny of proposed investments of Chinese enterprises, thereby balancing the need to ensure the appropriate deployment of foreign currency reserves with the desire to ease the complexity of the negotiation process for company investors (Wang and Pooley, 2011). Necessarily guided by official policy, by the end of 2012, most of China's ODI was invested in services: 33% related to leasing and business services, 18% to finance, 13% to wholesale and retail trade, in addition to 6% in transportation and storage. Moreover, to satisfy the needs of Chinese industry, 14% was invested in mining, while 6% was devoted to manufacturing which domestically was undergoing restructuring (World Resources Institute, 2015). Rebalancing of China's economy has meant that China's corporate leaders are seeking to globalize production in order to boost productivity and reduce excessive capacity. Thus, as of 2013, most of China's ODI stock was invested, where, especially in ASEAN countries, demand is rising. Excessive capacity, particularly in labour intensive industry, may be outsourced, thereby benefitting from lower labour costs and improved profit margins (Garcia-Herrero, 2015).

In contrast, a different pattern emerges in China's ODI in Europe, accounting for 8% of the country's total, where Chinese investors have targeted services and innovation in manufacturing. In services Chinese investors have bought into healthcare and finance, an example being a stake in Barclays Bank (European Parliament Research Service, 2014; Anderson, 2015). Investment in media and entertainment is exemplified by Dalian Wanda's purchase of Britain's Odeon Cinemas in 2016 (Evans, 2016). In manufacturing, innovative skills have been sought to improve brand recognition and reputation, in addition to gaining market access. The automobile sector, notably Sweden's Volvo has been targeted. Huawei, the information technology giant, has sought involvement in financial services. Moves into the development of infrastructure have been designed to exert control over distribution channels, witness interest in the Greek port of Piraeus (European Parliamentary Research Service, 2014). Chinese investment in certain sectors and infrastructure may, however, be contentious, given national security considerations. Into this category fall Britain's Thames Water and China's controversial investment in the nuclear power plant at Hinkley Point, the latter approved in late 2016 (Anderson, 2015; Brown, 2016).

Thus, despite a slowing domestic economy, China's growing global role is indicated by increasing ODI, which grew from US$ 20 billion to US$ 171 billion in 2014 (Anderson, 2015).

The foregoing has outlined ongoing developments in China's global political economy and forms the background against which discussion in the following chapters may be viewed. In their contribution at the beginning of the political economy section Morales and O'Callaghan discuss the global implications of a prolonged Chinese economic meltdown, given the country's lower level of growth. They conclude, however, that the main challenge for the CCP leaders lies in gradual measured economic reform, in order to prevent global contagion impacting, for instance, on China's stock markets.

Continuing the theme of China's global economic role, in their research Pauls and Gottwald envisage the Maritime Silk Road as supporting domestic reform by facilitating the development of China's Western provinces. In addition, in the maritime context, the project will help further the establishment of Southeast Asian economic integration, with China as a major player.

A prerequisite, however, for China's increasing global influence is the nation's economic health which necessarily depends on the maintenance of national unity, potentially threatened by social and economic inequality, as exemplified by disparity in living standards between the cities and the countryside. Brugiavini, Cavapozzi and Yao Pan discuss a key determinant, the hukou system of household registration, now ripe for reform, since it governs access to education, social security, housing and pensions.

In their chapter Haida, Gupta, Zhu and Fan examine the changing face of China's government. The internet, through social media, is shaping peoples' lives and, in China, as elsewhere, it is also being used for organisational purposes in the workplace. This is a pioneering study, examining the impact of social media on the leadership style of bureaucrats in the city of Lanzhou.

The second section highlights China's emergence as a global investor. In their study Amann, Jaussaud and Zhang examine the outward investment of Chinese companies in a number of industrial sectors, enjoying state support through such incentive measures as those of the 'going out' policy, initiated in 1999. Their research concludes that the Chinese firms studied have acted in a global environment different from that in which earlier Western investors initiated operations, thus challenging earlier theory.

In their chapter Li and Schaaper, on the basis of interviews, consider the motivation of Chinese companies investing in France, revealing two complementary goals: increasing sales on European and Francophone African countries and competing on the Chinese market, the latter meeting the needs of Chinese consumers, in line with government policy. Additionally and, as importantly, Chinese companies seek to improve their overall global competitiveness.

Jiang and Belz in their study similarly focus on Chinese investment in France. Their aim, however, is to provide an understanding of motives behind China's overseas investment in France and top manager staffing practices. They conclude that entry mode, whether brownfield or greenfield investment, and the motives for internationalisation, largely determine the staffing of management. Generally, French managers conversant with Chinese culture are preferred.

A greater consumer consciousness of environmental standards and the safety of food products have highlighted awareness of corporate social responsibility. In their chapter Lusteau, Barth and Jaussaud examine the emergence of corporate social responsibility in China which has implications for access to foreign markets. In contrast with Western countries, corporate social responsibility is mainly government rather than Non-Governmental Organization driven, as civil society remains weak in China. The main focus of corporate social responsibility is also environmental, given that the subject of human rights is politically sensitive.

Similarly, Etienne's research investigates the corporate social responsibility of a French multinational, in this case operating in China itself. The study is based on qualitative content analysis of interviews of leaders at group and subsidiary levels and concludes that, while the strategy must be locally adapted, this should not conflict with the development of a global corporate social responsibility model.

The chapter by Nivoix and Guo begins the section relating to services and consumption, both Chinese government priorities. They conducted research into the operations of the Shanghai and Shenzhen stock markets, indicating that the PBR ratio seems to be far more relevant than that of the PER as part of an investment strategy in the Chinese market, with implications for consumer income.

Food supply, a crucial area, given the diversification of diet in China, is the concern of Zolin and Cassin in their chapter. Focusing on areas like food production, distribution, consumption and trade, they identify policies and constraints bearing on the development of the food industry, the evolution of companies and the nature of supply and demand.

In their study the objective of Zolin, Cassin and Mannino is to explore the relationship between food security and food safety, given the need for increased production due to population increase. They compare the respective approaches of China and the EU to legislation regarding sustainability and pesticides. Such issues are key to food trade relationships between China and the EU.

In the concluding chapter to this section Andreosso-O'Callaghan and Li note the dearth of literature relating to China-EU trade in agricultural products. They employ a number of descriptive statistics to analyse future trading potential: while the EU could profit from trade expansion in meat and dairy produce, China could gain market share in, for instance, fish, vegetables and fruit.

Concluding remarks

The studies summarized above reflect the major themes discussed in this volume. China's economic restructuring is necessitated by the ongoing global recession and the falling competitiveness of labour intensive Chinese exports. Consequently, as China becomes a developed economy, a premium is placed on innovation, given overcapacity in smokestack industries like steel and a move into high-tech sectors. Economic strategy now emphasises domestic consumption rather than over-investment in production, with a growing role for services. It is, however, an open question whether new consumption patterns will alleviate social inequality, which itself has potential for social instability. In turn, these policies will affect the nature of management; highly skilled employees, in their display of initiative, demand more sophisticated means of control, as witnessed in China's companies at home and those engaged in outward investment overseas. This also brings into play corporate social responsibility in areas like environmental sustainability, an increasing concern of both government and populace. In addition, the chapters also suggest that China's economic strategy impacts on the nation's foreign policy, especially in relation to central and Southeast Asian countries. Thus the ensuing studies, within the framework of China's political economy, highlight managerial change, simultaneously underlining the country's ascent as a global economic and diplomatic player.

References

Anderson, R. (2015). *What does China own in the UK?* 20 October, www.bbc.co.uk/news/business-34542147, accessed 23 August 2016.

Arlidge, J. (2016). What's happened to the great malls of China? *Sunday Times*, 24 January.

Armstrong, S. (2015) Boosting China's consumption,7 December, www.Eastasiaforum.org, Weekly Digest.

Asian Equities Team. (2016). Tailwinds of the Asian consumer. *Invesco Perpetual Investor Magazine*, April.

Bloomberg News. (2016). China is grappling with hidden unemployment, 21 August, www. bloomberg.Com/news/articles/2016-08-21, accessed 22 August.

Brown, K. (2016). *Erase and Rewind: Britain's Relations With China*. Ultima: Australia-China Relations Institute.

Cao, Z. P., and Wu, S. S. (2015). A study on the internal relevance between the evolution of industrial structure and the process of urbanization in China. *Shanghai Xingzheng Xueyuan* Xuebao *(Journal of Shanghai Administration Institute)*, 16(1), 45–53.

Chen, B. (2015). Where does China rank in the world? 24 July, www.chinabusinessreview. com, accessed 6 January 2016.

Chinability (2016). *FDI inflows into China, 1984–2015: The rise of foreign direct investment (FDI)*, 7 April, www.chinability.com/FDI.htm, accessed 25 August.

Cooper, K. (2015). Enter the shopper: China's answer to slowing growth. *Sunday Times*, 1 November.

The Economist (2016). Still kicking: Despite China's economic slowdown, consumption is resilient, 30 April, www.economist.Com/news/business-and-finance/21697597, accessed 16 August.

European Chamber of Commerce in China (2016). *Overcapacity in China: An impediment to the party's reform agenda*, www.european.chamber.com.cn.

European Parliamentary Research Briefing (2014). 23 May.

Evans, P. (2016). Chinese bid to score at Anfield part of long term national goal. *Sunday Times*, 28 August.

Ferguson, N. (2015). We fret as China slips but the real tremors are inside Emperor Xi's palace. *Sunday Times*, 6 September.

Garcia-Herrero, A. (2015). *China's outward foreign direct investment*, 28 June, breugel. org/2015/06, accessed 23 August.

He, L. (2016). *China's plan to kill zombie firms faces resistance at local level*, 29 August, www.scmp.com/business/companies/article/2010664, accessed 30 August.

Jin, I., and Li, X. G. (2016). *China's inward FDI flowing to service and advanced manufacturing sectors*, 27 June, www.asiapacific.ca/blog, accessed 25 August.

Kenyatta, S. (2016). *China's new normal: An indispensable locomotive of global growth*, 20 May, www.chinabusinessreview.com, accessed 2 June.

Laurence, B., and Sheridan, S. (2016). Breaking China. *Sunday Times*, 10 January.

Lawrence, J. (2015). *What scarce labour means for talent development in China*, 1 June, www.chinabusinessreview.com, accessed 6 January 2016.

Li, J. (2016). *China tightens grip over social groups through greater Chinese Communist Party presence*, 22 August, www.scmp.com/news/china/policies-politics/article/2007359, accessed 22 August.

Li, Z. L. (2015). The influence of urbanization development on farmer's income growth in Wuhan City. *Asian Agricultural Research*, 7(6), 85–89, 93, www.cnki.net, accessed at *China Academic Journal Electronic Publishing House*.

Liu, H. M., and Song, L. G. (2016). *Reconstructing China's steel industry*, 18 August, www. Eastasiaforum.org, accessed 22 August.

Magnus, G. (2016). The world is now ours- shame it's in such a mess. *Sunday Times*, 21 August.

Mananquil, K., and Wagley, R. (2015). *An interview with Malcolm. R. Lee: The 2015 US-China strategic and economic dialogue in review*, 18 August, nbr.org/research/activity. Aspx? id=594, accessed 27 August.

Marro, N. (2015). *Foreign company R&D in China, for China*, 1 June 2015, www.chinabusiness review.com, accessed 6 January 2016.

Reuters (2016). *China regulator to curb news that promotes 'Western lifestyles'*, 30 August, www.reuters.com/article/us-china-media-id USKCN11509M, accessed 30 August.

Sheridan, M. (2015). Chinese whispers grow against Xi. *Sunday Times*, 30 August.

Wang, M. Y., and Cai, F. (2015). *Migrant workers key driver of consumption*, 6 December, www.esastasiaforum.org, accessed 7 December.

Wang, Y., and Pooley, J. (2011). *Outward Chinese equity investments, understanding the regulatory approval process*, November, www.nortonrosefulbright.com/knowledge/ publications/62023, accessed 24 August 2016.

World Resources Institute (2015). *China's overseas investments, explained in 10 graphics*, www.wri.org/blog/2015/01/china%E2%80%99s, accessed 23 August.

Zhang, J. F. (ed.) (2015). *Xi expounds on guideline for 13th Five Year Plan*, 11 March, Cntv. cn/2015/11/03/ ART1144559744633822.SHTML, accessed 23 August 2016 at English.

Zou, X. F. (2015). Empirical analysis of the role of urbanization in driving the growth of rural residents' consumption. *Asian Agricultural Research*, 7(3), 1–3, 7.

Part 1

Political economy

2 China's 'new normal' growth trajectory

Regional and global implications

Lucia Morales and Bernadette Andreosso-O'Callaghan

Introduction

The world economy remains fragile and its recovery process from the Global Financial Crisis (GFC) is not quite settled as yet since commodity and stock markets are showing signs of overtiredness and frail progress (World Bank, 2015). The situation is well illustrated by recent economic data from China and Japan: the Japanese economy contracted during the second-quarter of the year 2015, at the time when corporate investment registered a weak performance; Chinese trade showed a significant reduction with exports falling by 6.1% during the third quarter of the year 2015, and imports slumping 14.3% (Bloomberg View, 2015). These indicators suggest that the surprise currency devaluation by the Chinese central government during the summer of 2015, to boost exports, as well as a slow-moving economic growth did not manage to create the desired effects (The Washington Post, 2015). In addition, private sector companies have seen their positions deteriorate (Fabre, 2017). Chinese manufacturing performance has experienced a sharp fall over a period of six years, as companies responded to a slowing economy by laying off workers and cutting output at faster rates since those registered in 2009, when the world economy was facing the first direct effects of the Global Financial Crisis. Besides, the country's services sector has barely managed to stay afloat due to reductions in prices motivated by a weaker customer demand in the East Asian region. Growth in the region is slowing more sharply than was anticipated, and China's ability to fuel the global economy is therefore under serious questioning. After three decades of rapid economic growth, the Chinese economy is slowing down and the country's economic leaders, while trying to implement some policy measures that strengthen its macroeconomic fundamentals, have been resorting to a 'new' – low growth – 'normal'.

With China's efforts to liberalise the financial sector, analysts' eyes are turning to China for explanations regarding the potential of sharp spillover effects (Gorrie, 2013). Questions regarding the potential of spillover effects turning into a contagion wave are being asked due to the fact that Asia-Pacific nations are closely tied to the fortunes of the world's second-biggest economy. There is no doubt that a continuous weakening of China's growth rates would have detrimental effects in the region. For example, Japan's performance would be badly affected and its

DOI: 10.4324/9781315102566-3

nascent recovery, after years of economic stagnation, would be threatened. On the other hand, Australia could be thrown into recession and countries like South Korea, Indonesia and India would be badly hit, as would also any commodity-exporting nations around the world (New York Times, 2015a). Therefore, recent events in the Asian region need to be carefully considered, analysed and put into an appropriate context; the question as to whether current signs of economic distress could lead to a new economic meltdown regionally or worldwide needs to be addressed. In the case of the 1997 Asian Financial Crisis (AFC), which was a regionally isolated episode, China managed to escape unscathed from the regional turmoil thanks to its financial isolation. However, the current situation is somewhat different, as China could have a more prominent role. Asian economies' levels of integration with the world economy and across the region have increased since the AFC, and recent events are proving that instability in the region could lead towards major distress at both the regional and international levels.

Consequently, an important issue of concern that needs to be considered is the extent to which China would be the country that might trigger a new financial and economic meltdown in the Asian region. For all the outlined reasons, investors are monitoring closely the situation that is unfolding in the Asian region, and government officials are – once more – core players in the financial and economic arena, as it happened during the Global Financial Crisis. Market instability and sustained levels of uncertainty are putting a pressure on governments that do not seem to be able to put in place the necessary policy measures that help prevent the occurrence of another economic and financial turmoil of significant dimension at the global level.[1] Therefore, the focus of this research is on two main issues:

1   China's economic and financial integration in the region since the AFC is briefly studied with the aim of identifying how its economic and financial ties have evolved.
2   The role of commodity and financial markets is considered in order to illustrate the implications of China's economic slowdown for the region and for the global economy; this will help analyse the way in which the Chinese slowdown might contribute to an economic meltdown.

This study starts with a review of the existing literature analysing the increasing role of China in the Asian and global contexts through the examination of the country's level of integration in the world main commodity and stock exchange markets (Section 2). The analysis proceeds with an econometric framework that looks into China's economic integration through the analysis of China's top commodity imports, and into the world major stock markets that aid illustrate China's linkages with these markets; the econometric analysis will be useful in detecting how spillover effects might affect both the region and the global economy. As a result, Section 3 presents the sample under study and the proposed research framework. Section 4 outlines the main research findings, and Section 5 concludes the analysis and offers some notes for further research.

Brief overview of China's economic and financial performance in the regional and global contexts

After more than three decades of high growth underpinned by a number of structural reforms (Yueh, 2013; OECD, 2015), the Chinese economy is facing a challenging economic transition with slower GDP growth rates. Real GDP growth fell to 7.4% in 2014, whereas the latest figure recorded for 2015 indicate a 6.9% growth, a twenty-five years historical low; forecasts indicates that the growth rate would be even lower during the coming years (IMF, 2015). The new behaviour and conditions of the Chinese economy – summarised euphemistically by President Xi's 'new normal' expression – reflect a changing growth trajectory (World Bank, 2013, 2015; Bank of China, 2016). The country's traditional growth model focused on export-led growth, on an unlimited supply of cheap labour, on subsidised finance, and on large volumes of investment in low-end manufacturing (Yueh, 2013; Goodman and Parker, 2015; Fabre, 2017). The important drop in imported energy resources and raw materials led to the current economic climate characterised by deflationary pressures that are pushing GDP down. Global economic performance is affected by a general decline in investment that has dramatically impacted upon imports in emerging and developing economies. Given this economic climate, the Chinese authorities are trying to rebalance the economy towards a new consumption-led growth model in order to avoid falling into the middle-income trap; however, major challenges lie ahead, such as the shrinking size of China's labour force connected with an ageing population. Furthermore, the productivity gains arising from the reallocation of labour from agricultural to industrial activities have been materialised already (IMF, 2015).

In the background of these major challenges, commodity and financial markets take a prominent role. In this regard, lower commodity and energy prices coupled with China's increasing role in these markets create concerns regarding the potential of spillover effects from China towards other regional and global economies. In its global economic outlook, the IMF (2015) indicates that global economic activity will remain subdued over the next few years, a state that is accompanied by increased levels of volatility on financial markets. China's difficulty to transition smoothly towards more balanced and stable growth rates might have significant implications for international trade and commodity price stability. An increase of the level of market risk aversion, due to the lack of confidence among international players could enhance and exacerbate financial markets' instability and currency valuations; this could lead to increased levels of risk aversion that might end up translating into contagion effects at the global level.

Consequently, the analysis of commodity markets and their connection to China's economic growth performance is an issue that requires attention. The Chinese economic slowdown might be one among several broader issues that need to be considered by the world economies in their attempt to recover from the recent financial crisis. During 2015, commodity prices suffered a severe adjustment as China's slower performance ended up affecting a range of commodity imports; as a result, emerging and developing economies with heavy ties to commodity markets performance have been badly hit (KPMG, 2015). China's major role in worldwide commodity markets has been noted with the country's coal consumption representing for example twice the OECD coal consumption in 2015 (World Bank, 2016). Over the past few years, China's demand for commodities has grown to the point that the country moved from being a major exporter of commodities to becoming an importer. In the area of agricultural commodities, the country's top agricultural imports reflect its relative scarcity of land resources, with its most prominent agricultural imports being oilseeds, oils, soybeans and cotton – products that have high land requirements per unit of output (Gale et al., 2015). China's heavy industry suffered a downward adjustment with a significant reduction in terms of imports of iron ore and coking coal. As a result, developing economies have been severely affected, in particular those heavily dependent on commodity exports to China such as for example: Mauritania, Turkmenistan, Sierra Leone, Gambia, Mongolia, Mali and the Solomon Islands. There are also examples in the Asia-Pacific region; countries such as Japan, South Korea and Australia might see their economies affected if the Chinese slowdown continues, as they export a mix of products to China (Barone and Bendini, 2015).

In terms of commodity performance, the cotton market has significantly been affected over the past few years. The price spike in 2011 triggered actions from the Chinese government that started buying much of its domestic output with the aim of increasing its reserves and supporting its farmers; the resulting increase in prices did not however end up with the desired effects. On the contrary, the cotton world market experienced a year-on-year excess of supply. On the other hand, the government actions in 2014 to offload some of its stockpiles back onto the world markets at reduced prices, just exacerbated the downward pressure that has caused a significant damage to the country's cotton producers as well as to emerging and developing economies that have ties to this commodity. The case of precious metals and metals in general also requires some attention, as these markets have also been significantly affected by the downward trend experienced on commodity markets. The case of gold is noteworthy; between 2013 and 2014, the Chinese demand for gold fell substantially, causing China to drop below India as the world's top gold consumer, and helping to further push down gold prices. During 2014, iron ore, copper, lead and tin prices also fell, with the declines experienced in the iron ore and tin markets mainly driven by supply issues. On the other hand, the case of downward price movements in the copper and lead markets was dominated by a weak demand the origin of which can be linked to China's weak economic performance (World Bank, 2015; IMF, 2015).

Slower economic growth has also hit the energy sector, with crude oil prices declining by 55% from June 2014 to January 2015. During the second-half of 2014, oil prices fell sharply and with their fall their brought to an end a four-year period of high and more stable prices (World Bank, 2015). Coal production and imports also fell in a significant manner; again, this was explained by the economic slowdown experienced by the Chinese economy together with the need of implementing actions that combat excessive levels of pollution such as the increasing usage of hydropower contributing ultimately to bring coal prices to a six-year low. Moreover, and as hinted at earlier, China is heavily dependent on the use of coal as its main energy resource; it still represents around 70% of the country's energy usage and half of the total of the world consumption, followed by petroleum consumption that accounts for nearly 20% of the country's total energy consumption (EIA, 2015). While the country has the world's second largest proven coal reserves after the USA, several factors have contributed to the country's entrance into the coal import markets. Issues in terms of transportation bottlenecks, environmental and safety considerations and, above all, concerns about depleting national coking coal reserves need to be highlighted (Jianjun Tu and Johnson-Reiser, 2012).

A brief review of the world commodity markets and of China's role therein has shown so far that, as the world's most populous country and the largest energy consumer in the world, China has become very influential in these world markets (EIA, 2015). The behaviour of commodity prices since their peak in early 2011 has been characterised by a downward spiral that has ended up affecting commodity exporting countries.

Many of the national champions created by the Chinese government in its 'going global' strategy are precisely reformed State-Owned-Enterprises (SOEs) involved in commodity markets. Consequently, China's thirst for commodities coupled with the expansion of its SOEs has an impact on its stock exchange markets. Market capitalisation on the Chinese stock exchange has more than doubled during 2014, despite an economy that was affected by a significant slowdown and declining profit growth (IMF, 2015). An influx of new but less informed investors and increases in the levels of corporate leverage could be fuelling the rise of Chinese equities; as a result, this increases both the level of risk on these stock markets and an expected disorderly correction. The financial market turmoil recorded in the summer 2015 stemmed from both poor economic news and policy miscommunication, especially regarding the country's exchange rate (Islam and Subran, 2015). As a result, in August 2015, the Shanghai Composite Index fell by more than 20% representing a significant drop in less than two months, as a similar development took place in July (Barone and Bendini, 2015a; Barone and Bendini, 2015b). On the other hand, the limited impact that sudden adjustments on Chinese financial markets have on the real economy of China is explained by: (i) the nature of investors exposed to losses, with households having less than 10% of the shares; and (ii) by the limited level of integration of the three Chinese stock markets with international major markets. The Chinese financial sector is still affected by strong state intervention, making China one of the world's most tightly controlled countries in terms of finance (Andreosso-O'Callaghan and Gottwald, 2013). A gradual opening and liberalisation of the stock exchange markets have nevertheless meant for example that foreign investors can trade in the A-share market since December 2002, denominated in RMB, albeit to a limited extent. However, the main international connection between China's stock markets and the global stock exchanges is still through the Hong Kong stock exchange. Although the instability of China's stock markets in 2007 led to a short-lived storm, the unfolding situation since 2007 suggests that a weak stock market seems to be flashing some initial signs of concern for those countries that share strong export links with China.

Data and research methodology

The interaction between the developing Chinese stock markets and the world major stock markets is the core question in our econometric analysis. The analysis is supported by daily data relating to the following indexes: Shanghai Composite, FTSE 100, DAX 30, Nikkei 225, the Chinese currency – Renminbi, and China's main commodity imports: cotton, gold coal, crude oil, iron ore, soybeans and copper for the period January 2013 to December 2015. The data range is limited to three years of study to limit the impact of the Global Financial Crisis, and to concentrate on the variables' latest performance that help identify the potential causal effects between the variables; these causal effects will ultimately signal the global impact that changes on the Chinese currency markets and that fluctuations in its main stock market might have on the world leading stock exchanges and on China's top commodity imports. The natural logarithms of selected series are worked out over a period of five days. Then, the series' first differences of the logged data are representing continuously compound growth rates/returns. The research framework considers the traditional Granger causality approach combined with the Granger causality in mean and variance model developed by Cheung and Ng (1996). The authors propose estimating univariate GARCH models for stationary variables. Through the univariate GARCH estimation, the conditional means and variances (μ_t, σ_t^2) are estimated. The analysis' main strength lies in the estimation of three causality models that allow crosschecking the main findings and identifying consistencies across the model estimations. Therefore, the causality analysis is supported by three main estimations: (i) the traditional Granger Causality test; (ii) The well-known GARCH model as suggested by Cheung and Ng (1996); and (iii) the EGARCH model that would help accounting for asymmetric effects of positive and negative shocks on volatility.

The methodological framework is complemented by the implementation of two well-known tests: (i) the traditional Johansen cointegration test; (ii) and the familiar Granger causality test on the estimated returns. The main goal is to identify the long run relationship between the selected variables and to look at the existence of significant unidirectional or bidirectional effects running from the Shanghai stock exchange and the Renminbi towards the world leading stock exchanges and top commodity imports in China. Analysing the level of integration between the selected markets/variables and their causal links helps indeed understand the current role of China at the global level. Additionally, the selected research framework helps identify potential effects of the shock faced by the Chinese stock market during the summer of 2015, and its ramifications. In order to check for consistency in the obtained results, the traditional Granger causality test based on a bidirectional VAR model was applied. The model is as follows:

$$RCr_t = k_1 + \sum_{s=1}^{\partial} \emptyset_{11} RCr_{t-s} + \sum_{s=1}^{\partial} \emptyset_{12} EVr_{t-s} + \varepsilon_{1t} \tag{1}$$

$$EVr_t = k_2 + \sum_{s=1}^{\partial} \emptyset_{21} EVr_{t-s} + \sum_{s=1}^{\partial} \emptyset_{22} RCr_{t-s} + \varepsilon_{2t} \tag{2}$$

$$R_t = \mu_{t+} \varepsilon_t; \varepsilon_{t\sim} N(0, \sigma_t^2) \tag{3}$$

$$h_t = \omega + \alpha \varepsilon_{t-1}^2 + \beta h_{t-1} \tag{4}$$

$$\log(\sigma_t^2) = \omega + \beta \log(\sigma_{t-1}^2) + \gamma \frac{\varepsilon_{t-1}}{\sqrt{\sigma_{t-1}^2}} + \alpha \left[\frac{|\varepsilon_{t-1}|}{\sqrt{\sigma_{t-1}^2}} - \sqrt{\frac{2}{\pi}} \right] \tag{5}$$

Where RCr_t signifies the Shanghai index returns and the Renminbi at time t; Evr represents the explanatory variables including selected commodities and the world market leading stock exchanges. R_t denotes the stationary series (the compound returns for each one of the selected variables), μ_t is a constant, and ε_t are the normally distributed error terms. The standardised residuals ($\hat{\varepsilon}_{it} = R_{it} - \hat{\mu}_{it})/\hat{h}_{it}$) are obtained from the GARCH and EGARCH models and the sample residual cross correlation functions $-\hat{\rho}_{e1e2}(k)-$ are derived to test for causality. For the Granger causality in variance test, the squared standardized residuals are obtained, and the sample residual cross-correlation functions between the squares of the two standardized results are derived. The Granger causality in mean and variance tests are based on the statistic $\sqrt{T}\hat{\rho}_{e1e2}(k)$. The test statistic follows a normal distribution asymptotically.[2] Overall, the combination of different causality tests offers the opportunity to cross check the findings and to identify consistency or potential inconsistency in terms of market performance and causal relationships that is useful when understanding markets dynamics across the selected countries and particularly when considering the role of China.

Research findings

Series basic properties

The analysis of the series prices as illustrated in Figure 2.1 shows evidence of a significant downturn in the Shanghai stock market towards the second-quarter of 2015 with magnifying effects that lasted until the end of that year. Meanwhile, there are clear differences in terms of behaviour between the Shanghai stock market and the main commodity and world selected stock exchange markets. In

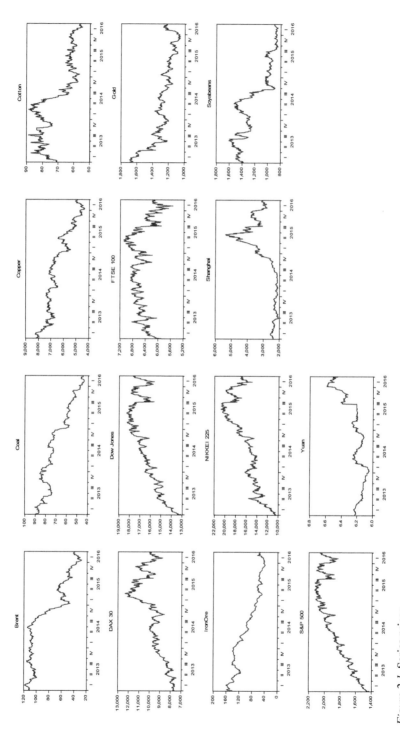

Figure 2.1 Series prices

general terms, commodity markets faced a downward trend that is quite consistent during the years 2014 and 2015, while the world stock markets' major indexes registered an upward performance over the years of study particularly up to the mid-2015. This type of trend is confirmed by the descriptive statistics on returns that showed high values on the Shanghai stock market up until the summer of 2015. This stock market was the most volatile with a 1.63% daily variation, with only copper registering more volatility over the period (Table 2.1). The average values on returns were negative in the following cases: Shanghai index, FTSE 100, DAX 30, Dow Jones and gold, whereas in the remaining cases, the mean values were all positive. In most of the cases, the series exhibited negative skewness and were leptokurtic and non-normal. The basic testing was followed by the implementation of a VAR(p) that helped identify the appropriate number of lags to be used in the subsequent econometric testing, in order to avoid over-parameterising the econometric estimations; the Hannan-Quinn and Schwarz Information Criterion were considered for the lag selection process. Three main tests for stationarity were considered to ensure that our series showed mean reverting properties and that the three tests offered consistent outcomes. The tests under consideration were: the traditional Augmented Dickey Fuller test, the Phillip-Perron test and the Unit Root with break test. The main findings show strong results indicating that the series returns were stationary in all cases, allowing then the implementation of the cointegration and causality tests outlined in the methodology section (see Table 2.2).

Cointegration and causality findings

The results from the Johansen test indicate that there is no evidence of any long run relationship between the series under study. This interesting outcome implies that the Shanghai stock exchange and the Chinese currency are not moving together in the long run with the world major stock markets and with China's top imports. These findings are in line with the views and suggestions that indicate that any negative shock affecting the Chinese stock market would have only but a limited impact at the global scale, and that the crisis of confidence that followed China's stock market shock was misplaced (Godement, 2015). In this regard, it would be most likely that any shocks from the Shanghai stock exchange would have a limited impact and should be considered as a sign of the shift that is taking place in China towards a market economy model that is more service-based and consumption driven. Therefore, any shocks arising from this economic transition would be felt only at the national level and with limitations at both the regional and international levels. Therefore, the described situation is not that new, as it seems to mirror the behaviour of markets during the Asian Financial Crisis, when the international implications of the regional downturn was quite limited. It should be noted that the causality framework was quite constrained due to the following issues:

- Cotton had to be removed from the research sample as the GARCH and EGARCH models were not working; the coefficients were insignificant and there were issues regarding stationarity in variance.

Table 2.1 Descriptive statistics – series returns

Statistics/Variable	Shanghai	Yuan	FTSE 100	DAX 30	NIKKEI 225	Brent	Coal	Gold	IronOre	Soyabeans	Copper	Dow Jones	S&P 500	Cotton
Mean	-0.001208	-0.000819	-0.00057	-0.000275	0.000318	0.000354	5.42E-05	-0.00035	-0.001116	0.000564	0.00033	-0.00055	0.000434	4.27E-05
Std. Dev.	1.63%	0.92%	1.20%	1.28%	1.20%	0.80%	0.91%	1.06%	1.54%	1.47%	1.72%	1.38%	0.82%	0.14%
Skewness	0.380195	-1.220974	0.114527	-0.27334	-0.227436	-0.2482	-0.25802	-0.97952	1.306157	-0.22552	-1.167298	-1.297168	-0.320511	2.236415
Kurtosis	7.153149	23.09609	5.042314	5.863445	4.16515	4.88118	5.338392	14.92003	19.52994	6.199361	8.390315	14.61632	5.039387	44.24439
Jarque-Bera	629.1389	14463.09	149.0548	299.9148	55.21327	133.5875	202.3758	5149.938	9883.891	368.4222	1217.768	4999.751	161.2831	60740.69

Table 2.2 Tests for stationarity

	Returns		
	ADF	*PP*	*Unit Root with Break*
Shanghai	−27.115	−27.093	−27.85524
FTSE 100	−29.6954	−29.6954	−30.58668
DAX 30	−30.0921	−30.0852	−30.61201
NIKKEI 225	−31.9157	−31.8841	−32.44019
Dow Jones	−30.0131	−30.0194	−30.78058
S&P 500	−29.5188	−29.6011	−30.35447
Yuan	−25.1915	−25.2056	−28.08645
Brent	−19.8887	−23.234	−24.14801
Coal	−27.5256	−27.5917	−29.03426
Gold	−30.1601	−30.1391	−33.09288
IronOre	−21.9538	−21.7562	−23.58987
Soyabeans	−29.3298	−29.3287	−31.29324
Copper	−32.7005	−32.7006	−33.41193
Cotton	−30.3384	−30.3384	−31.0953

- In the case of gold, the model had to be adjusted to account for an ARCH coefficient that was insignificant.
- For the Chinese currency, the outcomes for the GARCH and EGARCH models were found to be insignificant implying that the RMB is a variable that had to be excluded from the econometric analysis. This might ultimately be due to the heavy political manipulations exercised in relation to the RMB exchange rate.
- The outcomes for the GARCH and EGARCH models were also found to be insignificant in the case of Brent Oil returns.
- The EGARCH model could not be estimated in the case of Copper as the coefficients were found to be insignificant and negative. In the case of Coal, DAX 30, Gold, Iron ore, Nikkei 225, Soybeans, Standard and Poor's 500 and Renminbi, the EGARCH coefficients were negative and insignificant.

The final research framework considered the estimation of Granger Causality in mean and variance using a GARCH (1,1) model, in the case of the Shanghai stock market returns with the following stock market returns: Dow Jones Industrials, Standard and Poor's 500, FTSE 100 and Nikkei 225. In the case of commodities, the ones included in the study were: crude oil Brent, copper, gold, iron ore and soybeans.

An important finding is that the Granger Causality test highlighted the existence of a causal relationship running from the world top stock markets towards the Shanghai stock exchange (see Table 2.3). This relationship was found to be unidirectional implying again that the Chinese stock market did not have a major impact on the performance of the world top markets during the period. However in the case of the Nikkei 225, the result indicated also a unidirectional causal relationship, but this time it did run from the Chinese stock market towards the

Table 2.3 Causality tests

Granger Causality

Shanghai and FTSE 100	Shanghai and Dax	Shanghai and Nikkei	Shanghai and Dow Jones	Shanghai and SP500	Shanghai and Brent	Shanghai and Gold	Shanghai and Iron Ore	Shanghai and SoyBeans	Shanghai and Copper
←*	←*	→**	←*	←*	→**	insignificant	→*	insignificant	←**

Granger Causality in Mean

Shanghai and FTSE 100	Shanghai and Dax	Shanghai and Nikkei	Shanghai and Dow Jones	Shanghai and SP500	Shanghai and Brent	Shanghai and Gold	Shanghai and Iron Ore	Shanghai and SoyBeans	Shanghai and Copper
↔*	↔*	↔*	↔*	↔*	↔*	insignificant	↔*	↔*	↔*

Granger Causality in Variance

Shanghai and FTSE 100	Shanghai and Dax	Shanghai and Nikkei	Shanghai and Dow Jones	Shanghai and SP500	Shanghai and Brent	Shanghai and Gold	Shanghai and Iron Ore	Shanghai and SoyBeans	Shanghai and Copper
↔*	↔*	↔*	←**	↔*	←**	insignificant	←*	insignificant	→***

Table 2.4 Granger causality in mean and variance – statistics

Granger Causality in Mean

	Shanghai and Brent		Shanghai and Copper		Shanghai and Dax		Shanghai and Dow Jones		Shanghai and Gold		Shanghai and Iron Ore		Shanghai and Nikkei		Shanghai and SoyBeans		Shanghai and SP500		Shanghai and FTSE100	
	Lag	Lead	Lag	Lead	Lag	Lead	Lag	Lead	Lag	Lead	Lag	Lead	Lag	Lead	Lag	Lead	Lag	Lead	Lag	Lead
0	2.36	2.36	4.15	4.15	3.25	3.25	2.02	2.02	0.02	0.02	1.95	1.95	6.34	6.34	2.75	2.75	2.32	2.32	4.88	4.88
1	1.07	2.80	2.42	-2.24	2.98	-1.66	3.07	-0.33	-0.34	0.32	-1.73	4.55	0.86	1.83	-0.83	-0.58	3.48	-0.50	2.25	-1.52
2	-1.19	-1.49	-0.13	0.36	0.87	-0.03	1.18	-0.85	1.58	-0.20	-2.31	2.68	0.24	-0.89	-0.58	-1.02	1.60	-0.85	0.72	-0.08
3	-0.04	-0.18	-1.10	0.93	1.36	-0.93	1.66	-1.39	-0.66	0.31	-1.24	1.67	-0.30	1.03	-1.82	0.02	1.44	-1.59	0.99	-1.36
4	-0.87	-0.20	-1.62	0.90	0.43	-0.74	-1.20	0.52	-0.90	0.38	-0.68	0.67	1.95	-1.57	0.84	0.05	-1.36	0.33	0.04	-0.38
5	0.07	-1.59	-0.19	-1.29	1.71	-0.43	1.44	0.10	-0.85	-0.10	-1.89	-1.38	-1.62	1.24	0.05	-0.19	1.24	0.11	0.09	0.25
6	1.20	-0.74	-1.06	0.21	0.49	0.27	0.64	-0.40	-0.34	0.01	-0.97	-0.44	1.38	-1.15	0.78	-0.38	0.93	-0.17	1.10	-0.88
7	0.99	0.38	2.07	-0.27	1.12	0.56	-0.67	0.56	-0.18	0.66	-1.37	-2.57	1.35	-0.14	0.15	0.51	-0.93	0.95	0.93	0.24

Granger Causality in Variance

	Shanghai and Brent		Shanghai and Copper		Shanghai and Dax		Shanghai and Dow Jones		Shanghai and Gold		Shanghai and Iron Ore		Shanghai and Nikkei		Shanghai and SoyBeans		Shanghai and SP500		Shanghai and FTSE100	
	Lag	Lead	Lag	Lead	Lag	Lead	Lag	Lead	Lag	Lead	Lag	Lead	Lag	Lead	Lag	Lead	Lag	Lead	Lag	Lead
0	1.25	1.25	1.31	1.31	3.81	3.81	1.32	1.32	1.36	1.36	-0.03	-0.03	2.22	2.22	0.95	0.95	1.60	1.60	4.04	4.04
1	0.33	1.68	0.08	-0.69	-0.14	1.58	0.07	0.34	-0.58	-0.74	0.19	0.23	-0.88	-0.18	-0.50	0.10	0.41	0.22	-0.26	0.29
2	-0.90	0.24	0.84	-0.66	1.40	-0.83	1.30	0.55	3.04	-0.44	-0.75	-0.13	-1.12	-0.08	-0.24	0.33	1.70	0.11	2.24	-0.97
3	0.27	0.81	3.03	0.41	-0.50	0.98	-0.30	4.52	-1.10	0.32	0.80	0.56	0.85	0.70	-0.36	-0.58	-0.45	4.16	0.51	2.07
4	1.44	0.66	0.66	-0.64	1.00	0.80	0.14	0.34	0.25	-1.62	-0.15	0.20	-0.69	1.19	0.09	-0.50	-0.17	-0.18	0.27	0.36
5	-1.51	-0.22	-0.11	1.67	0.85	1.59	-1.03	0.09	-0.22	2.49	-0.17	-0.30	-0.30	-0.20	-0.04	-0.66	-1.02	-0.03	-0.45	1.46
6	0.73	2.14	-1.09	0.39	-1.07	-0.06	0.33	1.41	1.54	-1.21	-0.28	-0.97	-0.03	0.87	-0.50	0.35	0.16	1.24	-0.94	0.07
7	0.29	1.74	0.75	0.56	0.87	-1.05	0.80	0.20	-0.18	-1.30	0.89	3.71	-0.82	0.01	-0.04	-0.25	1.35	0.74	0.03	-0.67

Japanese market. This suggests that the Shanghai stock market – and therefore China's financial sector despite it being underdeveloped – becomes an important actor at the regional level. When looking at commodity markets, the results show that in two cases the Shanghai stock market impacted on the behaviour of crude oil and iron ore, with insignificant results recorded for gold and soybeans. These results are also consistent when looking at the outcomes of the Granger Causality in Mean and Variance. On the other hand, copper is found to be impacting on the performance and behaviour of the Chinese stock market. The research findings from the causality in mean confirm the existence of a bidirectional relationship between the Shanghai stock market and all the variables under study, with the exception of gold. The outcomes from the Granger causality in variance test looking at market volatility identify a bidirectional causal relationship between Shanghai and the world top exchange markets, with the only exception being the Dow Jones where a unidirectional relationship was identified. Crude oil is having an impact on the Shanghai stock market, as does iron ore. However, in the case of copper, volatility in the Shanghai market has a weak effect on this commodity, while gold and soybeans were found to be insignificant.

Conclusions

The slowdown of the Chinese economy epitomised by a 'new normal' growth path, and the market shocks that the economy and its financial system are facing seem to be signalling the difficulty of devising a new (more sustainable) economic model, rather than major problems that could lead towards a global economic and financial meltdown, as feared by some analysts. This situation highlights a temporary failure in terms of adequate measures to accompany the transition process towards a new growth model. There is no doubt however that the increasing economic and financial ties between the Chinese economy and the world most developed, emerging and developing economies lead today to different scenarios. Our analysis based on a Granger Causality test in mean and variance between the Shanghai stock market returns and other stock market returns such as the Dow Jones Industrials, Standard and Poor's 500, FTSE 100 and Nikkei 225 shows a causal unidirectional relationship running from the world top stock markets towards the Shanghai stock exchange. This suggests that the Chinese stock markets (proxied by Shanghai) are not sheltered any more from a shock happening elsewhere. Results relating to the Nikkei 225 indicate also a unidirectional causal relationship, but from the Chinese stock market towards the Japanese market denoting that China is becoming a noteworthy financial actor in the region. With regard to commodity markets, the results show that the Shanghai stock market does have an impact on the behaviour of crude oil and iron ore. On the other hand, copper is found to be impacting on the performance and behaviour of the Chinese stock market.

These findings reinforce the view that the Beijing authorities, and their vision of a 'new normal' economic growth model, are facing two conflicting challenges: on the one hand, the implementation of deeper reforms (including financial reforms) so as to help the Chinese economy embark upon a sustainable level of economic growth; and on the other hand, a slow liberalization so as to avoid too much contagion, at both the regional and international levels.

Notes

1 The Chiang Mai Initiative devised shortly after the AFC and expanded since the global financial crisis into what is now known as the Chiang Mai Multilateral is one of the few financial cooperation mechanisms that can respond, albeit in an insufficient manner, to a new problem of lack of liquidity in the region.
2 For further details regarding the derivation of the sample cross-correlations functions, the interested reader can refer to Cheung and Ng (1996).

References

Andreosso-O'Callaghan, B., and Gottwald, J. C. (2013). How red is China's red capitalism? Continuity and change in China's financial services sector during the global crisis. *Asia Pacific Business Review*, 19, 4, Special Issue 'Demystifying Chinese Management: Issues and Challenges', 444–460.

Bank of China (2016). *China's economic and financial outlook.* Institute of International Finance, 2016 Annual Report, Issue 25.

Barone, B. (2015). *In depth analysis – exceptional measures: The Shanghai stock market crash and the future of the Chinese economy.* Directorate-General for External Policies, Policy Department, European Parliament.

Barone, B., and Bendini, R. (2015). *In depth analysis – China: Economic outlook, 2015.* Directorate-General for External Policies, Policy Department, European Parliament.

Barone, B., and Bendini, R. (2015). *Protectionism in the G20.* Directorate-General for External Policies. Policy Department. European Parliament.

Bloomberg View (2015). *China's economic troubles start to spread,* www.bloombergview.com/articles/2015-07-14/china-s-economic-troubles-start-to-spread.

Cheung, Y.-W., and L.K. Ng (1996). A Causality-in-Variance Test and its Application to Financial Market Prices, *Journal of Econometrics 72,* 33–48.

The Diplomat (2015). Asia's biggest worry isn't Grexit, http://thediplomat.com/2015/07/asias-biggest-worry-isnt-grexit/

EIA (2015). *U.S. Energy Information Administration: China – international energy data and analysis.* Full Report.

Fabre, Guilhem (2017). The lion's share: What's behind China's economic slowdown? in: Zolin, B., Andreosso-O'Callaghan, B., and Jaussaud, J. (eds.), *Economic Change in China – Implication for Corporate Strategy and Social Responsibility.* London: Routledge.

Gale, F., Hansen, J., and Jewison, M. (2015). *China's Growing Demand for Agricultural Imports.* Washington, DC: United States Department of Agriculture.

Godement, F. (2015). *China's economic downturn: The facts behind the myth.* European Council of Foreign Relations, http://www.ectfr.eu.

Goodman, M. P., and Parker, D. (2015). *Navigating choppy water. China's economic decision-making at a time of transition.* CSIS (Center for Strategic and International Studies), http://csis.org/files/publication/150327_navigating_choppy_waters.pdf

Gorrie, J. R. (2013). *The China Crisis: How China Economic Collapse Will Lead to a Global Recession.* Hoboken: Wiley, July.

International Business Times (2015). China's manufacturing sector sees sharpest fall in over 6 years, but economists see hope for rebound, www.ibtimes.com/chinas-manufacturing-sector-sees-sharpest-fall-over-6-years-economists-see-hope-2122161.

International Monetary Fund (IMF) (2015). *World economic outlook: Update: Cross currents*, January.

International Monetary Fund (2015). *People's Republic of China*. IMF Report no. 15/234/2015

Islam, M., and Subran, L. (2015). China: Monkey forces for the year of the monkey. *Eurler Hermes Economic Research. Economic Insight*.

Jianjun Tu, K., and Johnson-Reiser, S. (2012). *Understanding China's rising coal imports*. Carnegie Endowment for International Peace, Policy Outlook.

KPMG (2015). *China Outlook*. Beijing: China Global Practice.

New York Times (2015a). China, Japan and Europe are flashing economic warning signs, www.nytimes.com/2015/08/25/opinion/china-japan-and-europe-are-flashing-economic-warning-signs.html?

New York Times (2015b). A plunge in China rattles markets across the globe, www.nytimes.com/2015/08/25/business/dealbook/daily-stock-market-activity.html?_r=0.

OECD (2015). *OECD Economic Surveys China Overview*. Paris: OECD.

The Washington Post (2015). What China's surprise currency devaluation means for its economy and the world, www.washingtonpost.com/news/wonkblog/wp/2015/08/11/china/ (accessed: 13th May 2016).

World Bank (2015). *China Economic Update, Macroeconomic and Fiscal Management Global Practice*. Wasington, DC: World Bank.

World Bank (2016). *Commodity Markets Outlook – Resource Development in an Era of Cheap Commodities*. Washington, DC: World Bank.

World Bank and Development Research Center of the State Council, People's Republic of China (2013). *China 2030: Building a Modern, Harmonious, and Creative Society*. Washington, DC: World Bank, www.worldbank.org/content/dam/Worldbank/document/China-2030-complete.pdf.

Yueh, Linda (2013). *China's Growth: The Making of an Economic Superpower*. Oxford: Oxford University Press.

3 Origins and dimensions of the Belt and Road Initiative

Experimental patch-work or grand strategy?

Robert Pauls and Jörn-Carsten Gottwald

Introduction

At the time of China's great Han-Dynasty (206 BC–220 CE), important trade routes between the Middle Kingdom and its central Asian neighbours were opened up. Chinese silk in particular was highly coveted in regions as far as the Roman Empire. A few centuries later, Chinese ports became market places for goods from India and South East Asia establishing an interregional trade network aptly coined the 'Maritime Silk Road'. For the one-party state in the People's Republic of China, history and its official interpretation is an important device in legitimizing its policies. Thus, when the leadership under Xi Jinping announced a new regional policy initiative in two distinctive speeches in 2013, the reference to the ancient trade and exchange between imperial China and countries near and far was by no means coincidental: the '21st Century Maritime Silk Road' (*ershiyi shiji haishang sichou zhi lu*, 二十一世纪海上丝绸之路; MSRI) initiative and its complementary 'Silk Road Economic Belt' (*sichou zhi lu jingji dai*, 丝绸之路经济带) initiative represent a resuscitation of ancient economic and civilizational ties in and between Asia, Africa and Europe. Both initiatives have been brought together under the label of 'One Belt, One Road' (*yi dai yi lu*, 一带一路, or OBOR for short), more recently translated as the Belt and Road Initiative (BRI). History generally plays an important role in Chinese political discourse as its distinctive and centralized interpretation by the CCP transports specific images of China's role in a regional as well as in a global context (Harnisch et al., 2015). Thus the recurrence on ancient relations between Imperial China and neighbouring countries or distant empires in Europe and Africa reasserts Chinese contemporary claims of a civilizational power pursuing policies not to its particularistic advantage but rather to the benefit of everyone who joins in – independent of the historical correctness of the argument (Glahn, 2016: 154ff, 197ff). Accordingly, the BRI is said to provide principles and opportunities for 'win-win cooperation' among China and other participants.

In contrast, Western academia are more critical of the potential geopolitical and regional impact of the BRI (Arase, 2015; Beeson and Li, 2016; Callahan, 2016; Ferdinand, 2016) and view it as an attempt at devising a strategy not only primarily aligned to its own economic interests in Asia and beyond, but also geared

DOI: 10.4324/9781315102566-4

towards supporting its interests in the struggle for regional global dominance by providing alternatives to and even replacing established principles and institutions of regional and global governance. One can infer from these interpretations that the BRI is a grand strategy designed to establish China as the dominant power in its neighbouring regions, including South East and East Asia.

The exact nature of the BRI, however, remains difficult to determine, not least because the initiative is still young and implementation of relevant policies in their early stages. The official academic Chinese discourse stresses the significance of the BRI as a new foreign policy paradigm (Fu and Lou, 2015; Su, 2016; Sun, 2016) and as domestic and foreign economic policy (Bao, 2015a; Bao, 2015b; Wang, 2015). The multi-facetted discussion among Chinese observers, however, also reflects the variety of interests and interpretations regarding the initiative (Swaine, 2015: 7–8). With the emphasis of the BRI's relevance under Xi Jinping, the terms and ideas linked to it have become pervasive in Chinese foreign policies and politics – in bilateral relations with its neighbours, as part of the revision of the EU-China Strategic Partnership or in China's policies in the G20. Similarly, Chinese academia face a flood of events linked to BRI themes. In the international realm, Chinese money and influence is pushing the agenda at international conferences often resembling propaganda events to sell the concept. While these developments amplify the buzz surrounding the BRI, they do not exactly contribute to sharpening the picture.

Furthermore, the BRI incorporates a number of diverse policy elements formulated at different times and at different levels of government and party. The idea, for example, that the development of trade and investment with Central Asian neighbours may help to curb the increasing asymmetry of socio-economic development between China's coastal areas and its western regions, predates the announcement of the initiative. Likewise, the need to boost economic growth by internationalization of the Chinese economy is not new and has been formulated as the 'Going Out' policy. Finding outlets for massive overcapacities in certain industries and attempts to preserve nominal growth rates with the help of huge state investment programs also form tried and true elements of the initiative. Earlier reform experiments such as the Free Trade Experimental Zones have also been incorporated ex-post into the strategy (Wang Yiwei according to Xinhua, 2015c). Other ideas affecting the formulation of the BRI include regional economic diplomacy or the search for a new development model.

Additionally, the BRI also seems to be strongly influenced by power struggles within the Chinese leadership (Johnson, 2016; Lam, 2015) and seems to reinforce the ongoing centralization of decision-making power in the hands of General Secretary and President Xi Jinping. As 'an economic planner's delight' (Lam, 2015) it presents another case of top-down economic policy-making geared towards China's SOE sector stretching the influence of central administrators into the activities of provincial governments, enterprises, and social organisations: 'large multinational companies which are officially listed as private but do enjoy close ties with the central leadership are also to gain from the projects, among them the likes of Huawei, ZTE, or Lian Wen'gen's SANY Group' (Lam, 2015).

The apparent relevance of diverse and divergent interests with regard to the BRI is contrasted by Xi Jinping's attempts to centralize control over the initiative under his leadership, giving it credibility as a key project in Chinese politics. For example, organizationally, the party leadership seeks to exert centralized control by setting up a new Leading Small Group to implement the Belt and Road. Besides, three leading ministerial units – the National Development and Reform Commission (NDRC), the Ministry of Foreign Affairs (MOFA) and the Ministry of Commerce (MOFCOM) – published a detailed program 'with authorization by the State Council' (National Development and Reform Commission, 2015a), the Chinese cabinet. By taking these steps, the Chinese leadership presents the initiative as a central (and centralized) strategy encompassing foreign, economic, and regional policies.

Summarized, the Belt and Road is a policy initiative that connects to a broad range of policy fields with relevance to domestic economic and political reform, foreign economic policy, regional economic integration in South East, East and Central Asia and beyond, regional and global governance, and foreign grand strategy. The BRI has its origins in pre-existing policies and appears to involve a number of actors and interests, while at the same time Xi Jinping claims centralized leadership over the policy.

In China's domestic policy-making, recent studies have emphasized the significance of a new type of coordinative planning (Heilmann, 2008; Heilmann, 2009; Heilmann and Melton, 2013; Heilmann and Perry, 2011). Today's role of planning in the Chinese policy-making process has been studied mostly in relation to economic policy-making. Here, its role is quite different today from what it was in the command economy. Whereas until the 1980s planning referred to a process of top-down resource allocation, it should today be understood as 'a set of coordinated policies designed to achieve an operational outcome' (Naughton, 2013: 643), achieving developmental outcomes while fundamentally preserving market mechanisms. In this sense, developmental planning in China today aims to achieve its goals through '*strategic policy coordination* (prioritizing and coordinating state policies from an anticipatory, long-term, cross-sectoral perspective); *resource mobilization* (mobilizing and pooling limited resources to bring about structural changes identified by policy-makers as necessary to achieve sustained economic and social development); and *macroeconomic control* (controlling the level and growth of principal economic variables to achieve a predetermined set of development objectives, prevent severe cyclical fluctuations, and contain the effects of external shocks)' (Heilmann and Melton, 2013: 4, original emphasis).

The Chinese one-party-state officially denies the existence of factions within the Communist Party of China (CPC) which is still following Leninist principles of the revolutionary cadre-party and its democratic centralism. Numerous studies, however, have shown the extent to which inner-party negotiations effect the decision-making process and the implementation of policies. While still significantly different from pluralistic societies with legally competing interests, the Chinese polity has developed its own mechanisms for dealing with different interest groups within the party-state. In this context, one significant characteristic of

China's policy-making is experimentalism or 'foresighted tinkering' (Heilmann, 2008, 2009; Heilmann and Melton, 2013; Heilmann and Perry, 2011). In this distinctive policy-making process, top-down central planning is conjoined with bottom-up entrepreneurial activities by cadres, enterprises or social organisations.

Regarding the relationship of the central and provincial governments, policy planning is combined with a specific method of experimentation within hierarchy, in which the interests of central government and provincial governments are aligned through individual contracts, giving provincial governments space to devise their own plans for implementation of a policy devised by the center. More recently, however, 'a much more comprehensive initiative for aligning central and regional development policies through joint programs has been made by launching a series of macro- regional, cross-provincial plans' (Heilmann and Melton, 2013: 11).

As most of the literature dealing with the particular style of policy planning in China deals with economic policy, Heilmann and Melton (2013: 37–38) advise scrutiny when transferring the concept to other policy areas. Accepting substantial differences in the institutional set-up and configuration of actors in domestic and foreign policy-making, the literature on experimental policy-making yet calls for a deeper analysis of different ideas, their revision and amalgamation into China's foreign policy as a dualistic process of both bottom-up interest articulation and policy innovation and top down grand design by the central authorities. Furthermore, while the particular style of Chinese policy-making may be well-suited to implement central policies while accommodating domestic interests, attempts to re-define China's *foreign policy* strategy have in the past created serious issues due to the lack of China's partners (and rivals) willingness to simply follow the one-sided innovation (see Harnisch et al., 2015).

Against the background of the wide array of policy fields and actors involved in the BRI on the one hand, and the particularities of policy making in the party-state on the other outlined above, we will evaluate the significance of the Belt and Road Inititative by analyzing its policy-making process as well as the contents of the initiative. Given that the actual effects 'on the ground' of the still young initiative are, as of yet, limited, an analysis of the policy-making process and content should provide insight to the question, whether a coherent strategy has emerged under the Belt and Road label, or whether a more or less uncoordinated patch-work of actors and policies have gathered under the BRI label.

The policy-making process of the Belt and Road Initiative

As highlighted above, policy-making in China usually exhibits a combination of top-down central planning with bottom up entrepreneurialism. Due to the shadow of hierarchy and the capacity of the one-party state to conduct and reign in (local) policy experiments, the People's Republic of China has developed a distinctive decision-making process which incorporates a multitude of diverse interests in spite of the unified organisation of the Leninist party-state.

When Xi Jinping assumed supreme power within the Chinese party-state in 2012/2013, he wasted little time to announce a flurry of ideological and political initiatives ranging from his 'Chinese Dream' to the short-lived and misunderstood call for a 'New Constitutionalism' and the consistent call for 'Rejuvenation of the Chinese Nation'. Under his predecessor's steering, China had started a 'charm offensive' investing heavily in soft power and presenting itself as a reliable partner in global economic governance. Yet relations with China's Eastern and South-Eastern neighbours were fraught with tensions. Similarly, relations with Russia and Central Asian nations were difficult while the strategic partnership with the European Union called for new impetus. Domestically, Xi ascended to power among substantial uncertainty following the Bo Xilai-affair and infighting between various factions inside the party-state. Finally, the economic situation of the PRC following the massive stimulus package of 2008 showed troubling signs of exhaustion and an emerging structural crisis.

Against this background emerged the ideas of The Silk Road Economic Belt in Central Asia and Europe and the 21st Maritime Silk Road in Southeast Asia. What resembles a sophisticated foreign and geopolitical strategy in hindsight started off as little more than a series of speeches by a new leader consolidating his power trumpeted into the world by China's efficient propaganda-system. Yet the Belt and Road initiative developed into a bundle of domestically and outward oriented policies, underscored by an increasingly dense base of new or re-developed institutions and turning into a major frame for various policy-debates and politics within and outside the PRC.

The Belt and Road's provincial pedigree

In proposing the two new silk roads, Xi referred not only to a distant imperial history but also to more recent attempts to provide a new impetus for China's Western and interior provinces lagging behind coastal China in terms of socio-economic development and integration into the global economy. In this regard, the origins of the new Silk Roads can be traced back to sub-national initiatives (Summers, 2016: 1632–1633) from as early as the 1980s. Structurally disadvantaged interior provinces, such as Yunnan and Xinjiang, used the Silk Road metaphor as reference to policies proposing intra-provincial and cross-border economic and trade hubs. Arguably, and without reference to the Silk Road name, these initiatives were later integrated into the central initiative of 'Opening the West' (*xibu da kaifang*, 西部大开放), launched in the late 1990s by then General Secretary Jiang Zemin. Opening the West was again taken up as a high-level policy under the slogan of a 'New Round of Develop the West' in 2010, both emphasizing the building of cross-border economic linkages. Similar policy statements can be found in the 12th Five-Year Plan. 'In short, the ideas and practices of linking up China's western border provinces with neighbouring economies has been an idea at the provincial level since the 1980s, even though the early focus of reform and opening up was on the coastal regions' (Summers, 2016: 1633). Yet the success of the

Opening the West policies were far from obvious and its contribution to the development of the BRI was seen critically by some observers (Huang, 2015). The gaps in socio-economic development between China's richest, predominantly coastal areas and the less advanced regions were further exacerbated by the lacklustre implementation of various attempts of reforming China's state-owned industries and the effects of the stimulus package of 2008.

Yet the relations between local authorities and the central leadership as well as among local authorities continue to be complicated. With provincial leaders being one significant reservoir for the appointment of top positions at the centre, balancing competing regional and local interests in the aftermath of Xi's appointment continued to be challenging. This affected Xi's ability to define the way of how to integrate the interests of the western provinces and the SOE sector into his ideas of the new Silk Roads: Whereas originally, the Silk Road Economic Belt was to focus on connecting China's western provinces with Central Asia, some commentators argue that it was lobbying by China's southern coastal provinces that has led to the inclusion of the Maritime Silk Road and the commitment of significant resources expanding the initiative towards ASEAN countries (Godement and Kratz, 2015: 9–10).

The origins of the Silk Roads idea in provincial politics as well as the suggestion that the scope of OBOR has been widened due to provincial lobbying, at first glance limit its credibility of being a coherent strategy under control of the central leadership and that instead it is designed to cater to the particular material interests of provincial governments. On the other hand, as Summers proposes, 'the fact that the Silk Roads vision builds on these local policy frameworks and practice suggests that it has an increased chance of successful implementation' (Summers, 2016: 1634).

From innovative slogans to official policy under Xi

Even though the origin of the Silk Roads idea may be traced back to the provinces and earlier initiatives with similar goals, their inauguration under Xi appears as a clear case of top-down policy-making. Xi Jinping himself introduced the basic idea in 2013, shortly after formally assuming the positions of General Secretary of the Communist Party of China, President of the People's Republic and Chairman of the Central Military Commission. In his April 2013 keynote speech at the Bo'ao Forum, he announced China's intention to promote regional cooperation in Asia and around the world, to increase connectivity with its neighbouring countries, to build a regional financing platform, and to advance economic integration within the region and increase its competitiveness (Xi, 2013b). The following September, in a speech at Nazarbayev University Kazakhstan, Xi proposed the building of a 'Silk Road Economic Belt' in continental Asia, promoting policy cooperation, construction of lines of communication, trade, financial integration and people-to-people exchanges between the countries involved (Xi, 2013c). In October, the president announced the '21st Century Maritime Silk Road' proposal together with the intention to found the

Asian Infrastructure Investment Bank in a speech at the Indonesian parliament. He called for increasing bilateral trade between ASEAN and China to US$ 1 trillion until 2020 and for strengthening the construction of connections between ASEAN and China, supported by the AIIB, which should focus its activities in the region (Xi, 2013a). These speeches were the first open declaration of the intention of the new leadership for China to take on a leadership role in the region and confirmed the departure from Deng Xiaoping's paradigm of taking a low profile in international politics as long as the domestic process of reform and opening up was underway.[1]

In 2013, Xi also 'formally presented the new strategy *fenfayouwei* (striving for achievement [. . .]) signalling a transformation of China's foreign strategy' (Yan, 2014: 154) at a special conference of the Chinese leadership on international affairs. In November, at the 3rd Plenary Session of 18th CPC congress, Li in a speech on 'comprehensively deepening reform', stated that this required the acceleration of building connections with peripheral countries, building the Silk Road Economic Belt and the Maritime Silk Road, for 'a new pattern of all-round opening' of the Chinese economy (Lu et al., 2015: 13).

These meetings fed the concept into a top-down planning process. In late 2013, the MOFA and the NDRC – the latter in charge of economic development planning – held a work meeting on the Belt and Road, followed by at least three meetings between relevant ministries and the State Council in 2014 to elaborate its policy content (Lu et al., 2015: 13). In November 2014, the powerful Leading Small Group for Finance and Economics also held a study session chaired by Xi Jinping (Lu et al., 2015: 14; Zhongguo Xinwen Wang, 2014). Leading Small Groups (LSG) are a key device in the Chinese party-state of coordinating the policies of various party- and state organs. Under Xi, they have become a key instrument in overcoming resistance by entrenched interest groups within the state-bureaucracy and a mechanism to centralize decision-making in the hands of Xi Jinping and trusted allies. During the meeting, Xi reportedly confirmed that the AIIB, with funds from a number of participating countries, would be used to support infrastructure projects for building the BRI. Additionally, a Silk Road Fund, capitalized in full by the Chinese state, was to be established. It is remarkable, that contrary to tradition, Xi took on the role as director of the LSG on Finance and Economics. This position had usually been held by the prime ministers who previously, under Jiang Zemin and Hu Jintao, were in charge of economic policies. Now the President and General Secretary, Xi Jinping, assumed responsibility for this area.[2]

One outcome of this policy-making process, initiated by Xi and coordinated among the top party leadership and the relevant state ministries, is the 'Vision and Actions on Jointly Building Silk Road Economic Belt and 21st-Century Maritime Silk Road' document, jointly published by MOFA the NDRC, and MOFCOM with State Council authorization on 28 March 2015 (National Development and Reform Commission, 2015a). So far, it appears to be the most authoritative policy document released to the public in conjunction with the BRI. While not a term used in the document itself, both the Chinese government (National Development and Reform Commission, 2015b) as well as academic commentators have characterized the 'Vision and Actions' as the 'top-level design' (*dingceng sheji*, 顶层设计) (An, 2016) for the Belt and Road, a term coined by Xi Jinping in relation to his foreign policy initiatives (Callahan, 2016: 4), outlining the aims and tasks of the policy for the subsequent process of implementation.

The transformation of the BRI from a proposal of party leader Xi Jinping into official policy is further documented in the work reports of the Chinese government to the National People's Congress. In the official government report to the 1st session of the 12th NPC by Prime Minister Li Keqiang (Li, 2013) these new initiatives are not yet taken up; only a year later, the official work report refers to the establishment of the China (Shanghai) Free Trade Zone and the work on the Silks Roads (Li, 2014). Another 12 months later, great progress in the BRI is announced as well as the setting up of the Silk Road Fund (Li, 2015). One year on, the Silk Roads are further linked with the industrial-capacity cooperation (Li, 2016b). The initiative is also portrayed as a means for regional development within China: 'Work continued to promote the coordinated development of the eastern region, the central region, the western region, and the northeast; priority was placed on moving forward with the Three Initiatives-the Belt and Road Initiative, the Beijing-Tianjin-Hebei integration initiative, and the Yangtze Economic Belt initiative' (Li, 2016b: 6). Later on, the initiative is again called an important element to foster peace and cooperation (Li, 2016b: 27). Thus, within a short period of time, the ideas presented by Xi find their way into the official work reports of the Chinese government.

Integrating the Belt and Road into foreign policy

The BRI forms part of a general drive by the Chinese leadership under Xi to develop a more coherent and more assertive foreign policy (Schmidt, 2012). It is another indicator on how China is redevising key concepts of its global and regional policies (Huotari, 2015). Instructive in this regard is the initiative's relationship to China's 'neighbourhood diplomacy' or 'peripheral diplomacy' (*zhoubian waijiao*, 周边外交),[3] a new foreign policy program developed under Xi, moving the focus of China's diplomacy away from its relations on the United States towards the neighbouring countries. Neighbourhood diplomacy became a corner stone of foreign policy under Xi Jinping and Li Keqiang in the first months of assuming office. An early official commentary stresses the efforts the new leaders invested in improving relations with central Asian Countries, Russia, and Mongolia describing, among other things, how 'Chinese leaders (sic!) also proposed a series of strategic concepts aimed at promoting regional prosperity and development, including a Silk Road Economic Belt with Central Asian countries, an SCO development bank and a 21st-century maritime Silk Road with Southeast Asian countries' (Ping, 2013). Peripheral diplomacy was the topic of a special Work Conference in 2013 and further discussed at the 2014 Central Work Conference on Foreign Affairs.

The 2013 Neighbourhood Diplomacy Work Conference (*zhoubian waijiao gongzuo zuotan*, 周边外交工作座谈) expressed the significance it attached to redeveloping China's regional relations (Su, 2015). In his speech, Xi already highlighted the importance of the three areas of economic exchange, security, and culture for China's regional policy (Chen, 2016). Internationally, Xi presented a new concept for regional security at the 4th Summit Conference on Interaction and Confidence Building Measures in Asia. While he proposed comprehensive measures for security building, he referred to the idea of re-establishing the Silk Roads as a means to improve and institutionalize cooperation with China's neighbours (Xi, 2014). This process of policy-revision was followed by a Central Work Conference on Foreign Affairs (*zhongyang waishi gongzuo huiyi*, 中央外事工作会议) in 2014, the first under the new leadership of Xi Jinping and, presumably, Li Keqiang.[4] In his speech, Xi referred to the need to revise China's foreign policy according to the changes in the relation between China and the international system; the idea to implement the new Silk Roads is mentioned, but is not yet as central as other key concepts presented by the General Secretary (Xinhua, 2014). In those months, however, the idea of the 'One Belt One Road' was 'integrated into the foreign policy lay-out, became a new essential factor' (Su, 2015).

Both conferences sought to unite the various actors involved in foreign policy-making in China. With professionalization of China's expert community progressing fast, the integration of academia, think tanks, ministries and the party-apparatus in the field has become more complex. Among the representatives were the party and military leadership, the Ministry of Foreign Affairs, the Ministry of Commerce and the Ministry of Culture, key cities and provinces as well as financial institutions and state-owned enterprises to lay the direction for a coordinated and comprehensive foreign policy (Callahan, 2016: 4).

Institutionalization of the new program: the One Belt, One Road Leading Small Group

To facilitate the implementation of the Belt and Road, China's leadership set up a new specialized Leading Small Group in February 2015. Zhang Gaoli, Vice Premier and member of the Politburo Standing Committee, was appointed head of the 'Leading Small Group on Implementing One Belt, One Road construction' (OBOR LSG) (Xinhua, 2015b). The appointments of Zhang Gaoli and of Wang Huning as two of four Vice-Chairs highlight the significance attached to the BRI and indicate the significance of the group for power relations inside the CCP: 'The OBOR initiative has also confirmed that the seventh-ranked member of the Politburo Standing Committee, Executive Vice-Premier Zhang Gaoli, wields more powers than his putative boss Premier Li (. . .) And regarding the division of labour within the central government cabinet, Zhang is in charge of heavyweight ministerial-units, including the National Development and Reform Commission and the Ministry of Finance' (Lam, 2015 with reference to <www.mingpaocanada.com/Van/htm/News/20150423/tcbm1_r.htm>, April 24; and <www.china.com.cn/news/txt/2013-03/22/content_28333632.htm>, March 22.).

The OBOR LSG composition reflects the main political bodies – the Central Committee and Politburo of the CCP, the Central Secretariat of the CCP, and the State Council, as well as the different policy areas that are involved in the policies: Wang Huning is a member of the Politburo and Head of the Central Policy Research Office considered 'one of the most influential figures in China today, a key architect of its domestic and foreign policy over the past decade' (Page, 2013). Wang's reputation as a very influential advisor and speech-writer for three successive Chinese leaders – Jiang Zemin, Hu Jintao, and Xi Jinping – indicate the central task of developing the idea of the new silk roads into a political programme. A former professor in political science and international relations at the prestigious Fudan University, Wang Huning is considered a leading expert on international politics. 'China has not had a Politburo-level official in charge of foreign policy for a decade, meaning that Wang can now act in that role as the only foreign affairs expert with a seat on the party's decision-making body' (Huang, 2013). As Vice-Chairmen of the OBOR LSG, Wang is particularly tasked with liaising with the National Development and Reform Commission (Xinhua, 2015c). Wang and fellow leading cadres are also members of the Finance and Economics LSG; Wang is also secretary of the LSG on Comprehensively Deepening Reforms, a group initiated and implemented by Xi Jinping as part of his consolidation of inner-party leadership and centralization of political power (Beijing Qingnianbao, 2016).

According to Cheng Li, He Lifeng 'is currently in charge of the strategic development of the "One Belt, One Road" initiative' (Li, 2016a: 362). He Lifeng was appointed Deputy Director of the NDRC and Vice-Secretary of the Party Branch of the NDRC. He had been working under Xi Jinping in Xiamen in the 1990s. He Lifeng was tasked with setting up the OBOR LSG's secretariat located in the NDRC with the assistance of fellow deputy director Wang Xiaotao (Caixin, 2015).[5] In Ou Xiaoli, the head of the NDRC office in charge of the Development of the West has also been appointed to the office of the new OBOR LSG (Xiu, 2015) thus indicating the link between the earlier strategy to Develop the West and the new Silk Roads.

Zhao Kejin emphasizes in his study that the composition of the LSG reflects the comprehensive approach of implementing the BRI both for domestic as well as foreign policies (Zhao, 2015). He interprets the LSG as a new mechanism for policy coordination among various ministries and the party-state. The OBOR LSG organises annual conferences to revise and coordinate the policies of ministries, commissions, provinces and all other organisations involved. In 2016, the BRI was again presented as a key concept of Xi Jinping whose contribution should guide the LSG in their work (Xinhua, 2016).

Other elements of institutionalisation of the BRI include the Silk Road Fund and the Asian Infrastructure Investment Bank (AIIB). The Silk Road Fund was set up by the State Administration of Foreign Exchanges (SAFE), holding 65%, China Investment Corporation (15%), China Export-Import Bank (15%) and the China Development Bank (5%). AIIB, a potential rival to the Asian Development Bank and a signature case of China's new regional and foreign economic policies has been closely linked with the BRI in the Chinese view, albeit its membership and official objectives are officially independent of China's initiative.

Initial implementation

The 'Vision and Actions' document as top-level design is fed by the government into a process where NGOs, think tanks, and other social actors are integrated into the process of implementation. SASAC (State-owned Assets Supervision and Administration Commission), the central government's body in charge of the SOEs of the central government, plays a crucial role in defining the contributions of – and securing the benefits for – several of the largest enterprises. The Silk Roads are thus deconstructed into various special areas such as transport Silk Road, construction Silk Road, information Silk Road and others (Zhao, 2015). Officially, more than 100 think tanks have been dedicated to study the Belt and Road (Xinhua Finance, 2016).

The 'Vision and Actions' document further highlights the role of 18 provinces, municipalities, and areas (*sheng shi qu*, 省市区), 8 cities (*chengshi*, 城市) and 15 ports (*gangkou*, 港口). 'Under the banner of the state, each province, municipality and area must base itself on its relative advantage, capture one's own position, and work equally according to the regulation of the central authorities and each unit's individual situation' (Zhao, 2015 transl. by authors). All lower administrative levels are required to link up with the central outline and develop matching plans (*fang'an*, 方案) to promote the initiative.

The formulation of Belt and Road policy led to provinces following up and competing with one another to participate in the policies and carve out a niche for them. Guangzhou became the first province to publish its own programme on how to link up with the central plan seeking to establish itself as a strategic hub, centre for trade and cooperation, and as a significant engine (Zhao, 2015).

According to one member of the OBOR LSG, all provinces were ordered to submit their own plans how to link with the OBOR actions and visions within a few months (21 Shiji Jingji Baogao, 2015). While all provinces were called upon to integrate their plans, and while some 18 were mentioned in the 'Vision and Actions', Xinjiang and Fujian were clearly designated as 'core areas', according to Ou Xiaoli (ibid.). Provinces like Hunan (Liu, 2016) and large SOEs like CNOOC (China National Offshore Oil Company) created internal leading groups (under the guidance of the party-committee within CNOOC) to organize their own business with regard to the BRI (Zhongguo Haiyang Shiyou Bao, 2015).

OBOR thus started as an initiative of the highest party leader, was fed into the internal discussion and decision-making mechanisms of LSGs, the State Council and special Central Work Conferences. The introduction of the LSG coincided with the announcement of a policy program for the implementation of OBOR called the 'Vision and Actions on Jointly Building the Silk Road Economic Belt and 21st-Century Maritime Silk Road'.[6]

Policy content of the Belt and Road Initiative

The previous chapter traced the origins of the BRI, the policy-making process and its initial implementation by various actors within China. The previous analysis already suggests that the initiative is indeed the centrally coordinated strategy that it has been advertised as by the party-state. Its successful design and initial implementation within the party-state, however, does not yet prove its feasibility as foreign policy. The fact that the Belt and Road is still a young initiative also prevents factual evaluation of its effects 'one the ground' for (China's role in) South East and East Asian regionalism. Instead, the following section will highlight some of the political content of OBOR and its relevance for Asian regionalism.

The Belt and Road as (foreign) economic policy

'OBOR also has immense significance for the future direction of the economy, especially the partial revival of central planning as well as boosting the pivotal role of state-owned enterprise (SOE) conglomerates' (Lam, 2015). In his 2015 work report, Premier Li officially links the BRI with the 'Go Global Strategy' for Chinese enterprises and the rebalancing of economic development between and within Chinese regions. According to some observers, the BRI's key significance lies in the link between domestic reforms and regional policy and constitutes a new stage in China's opening up policies (Xu, 2015: 27f.). The Silk Roads are presented as an element to promote the development of the western and southern regions and connects with the plans to form new regional centres, Beijing-Tianjin-Hebei and the Yangtze Economic Belt.

Economically, the Belt and Road may thus help to achieve a number of goals to further the development and reform of China's economy, which has been plagued by uneven development and, since the late 2000s, by a general slowdown accompanied by stagnating productivity, overinvestment, and rapid accumulation of debt. The initiative thus aims to support the development of China's western provinces, which have been left behind in the rapid economic development of the past couple of decades; furthermore, it may create foreign infrastructure investment opportunities for China's (state-owned) enterprises, support the general program of internationalization of China's economy. The focus on development of the western provinces has been blurred, however, by the initiative's inclusion of the Maritime Silk Road in addition to the Economic Belt, allowing the already well developed Southern and Eastern coastal provinces to also claim their stake in the initiative.

To support outward foreign direct investment of Chinese companies, a number of rules and regulations have been put into place by various agencies and compiled by the NDRC (for an overview, see National Development and Reform Commission, 2016b) who in general is required to approve major foreign investments (along with SAFE, the central bank's organization managing China's foreign exchange reserves). There is already some indication that the various policies may effect a shift of Chinese FDI towards Belt and Road countries (Summers,

2016: 1636). According to the Ministry of Commerce, in 2015 Chinese compa-nies made a total of US$ 14.82 billion direct investments in Silk Road countries, an increase of 18.2% year-on-year. Of these direct investments, US$ 11.66 billion were in traffic, electricity and communications and similar projects, an increase of 80.2% over the previous year, signaling a clear shift of Chinese FDI towards infra-structure. Chinese companies committed to almost 4,000 engineering projects in 60 Silk Road countries, with a value of US$ 92.64 billion, an increase of 44% over the previous year (Ministry of Commerce, 2016a). The Chinese government signed cooperation agreements to facilitate the projects pursued and conducted by Chinese enterprises. During the first half of 2016, Chinese companies have made direct investments related to OBOR amounting to US$ 6.82 billion, falling 2.7% year-on-year, with the most important receiving countries being Singapore, Indo-nesia, India, Malaysia, Laos and Russia. In the same period, Chinese companies have engaged in more than 3,000 engineering and construction projects in 61 Silk Road countries, with a value of US$ 51.45 billion, an increase of 37% year-on-year (Ministry of Commerce, 2016b).

Among a number of infrastructure projects being implemented along the '21st Century Maritime Silk Road', is the construction of railroads and highways con-necting China with the proposed deep sea port of Kyaukpyu in Myanmar. Rail-roads are proposed to be built between China and Laos as well as China and Thailand. In Cambodia, China is involved in the construction of the Shianook Harbor Development Zone. China won a competition for a HSR project in Indo-nesia against Japan. Thailand and China are developing an industrial park in Rayong (Su, 2016). The investment in railroads follows three economic principles of the initiative: that China should further develop its comparative advantages (railroad), use its financial muscle by providing credit and thereby create an inter-national valve for an industry that seem to have peaked within China where the high-speed rail network has grown dramatically in recent years. Besides, infra-structure is an area dominated by large central SOEs allowing for tighter control of activities by the state.

Supporting these infrastructure projects is the task of the Asian Infrastructure and Investment Bank (AIIB), a Chinese initiative which started operations in December of 2015 after 37 regional and 20 non-regional countries had signed the articles of agreement. Chinese commentators hail its establishment as one of China's greatest diplomatic successes in recent times, and notably against US opposition. While not originally part of the BRI, the AIIB has been quickly asso-ciated with the project by academic commentators and official statements. Xi Jin-ping stressed the importance of the AIIB for constructing the Belt and Road at the Bank's opening ceremony (Xi, 2016). The AIIB focuses its activities on South-East Asia. It will have US$ 100 billion in funds available, as well an additional US$ 50 billion pledged by China for a special infrastructure fund for developing countries. Moreover, the Silk Road Fund focuses on Central Asia and supplies an additional US$ 40 billion to projects associated with the BRI. Finally, another US$ 10 billion are supposed to be made available through the BRICS-led New Development Bank (Su, 2016: 3).

The Belt and Road as regional and geo politics

At its core, the 'Vision and Actions' document outlines five priority areas of international cooperation as part of the Belt and Road initiative, these being intergovernmental policy coordination, the promotion of interconnectivity through building of infrastructure, including roads, train lines, ports, energy, telco and IT; the promotion of trade and investment through free trade areas and customs cooperation, financial integration, supporting regional currency stability and investment banks and funds, such as the AIIB; and foster people-to-people bonds to provide cross-country public support for the initiative. These five priority areas of cooperation are contextualized by references linking the initiative to China's wider interpretation of the state of the international political economy and to its foreign policy.

Regarding foreign policy, the 'Vision and Actions' document cites the Five Principles of Peaceful Coexistence, a long-standing doctrine of China's foreign policy, evocative of South-South cooperation, including mutual respect for each other's sovereignty and territorial integrity, mutual non-aggression, mutual non-interference in each other's internal affairs, equality and mutual benefit, and peaceful coexistence. Furthermore, the Belt and Road is part of the new emphasis on 'peripheral diplomacy' or 'neighborhood diplomacy', as discussed above. During his November 2015 visit to Singapore, Xi Jinping stressed that under periphery diplomacy China is seeking 'peaceful and stable development' in a 'secure neighborhood and wealthy neighborhood' and 'comprehensive cooperation' in a 'China-ASEAN community of shared destiny', portraying the BRI as an invitation to jointly achieve these aims (Xinhua, 2015a).

Concerning the state of the international political economy, the document mentions the continuing impact of the international financial crisis, a slow economic recovery, uneven global development, and development challenges faced by many countries. Against the background of changes in the landscape and rules for international trade and investment, OBOR seeks to create 'an open, inclusive and balanced regional economic cooperation architecture that benefits all', as well as 'new models of international cooperation and global governance' (National Development and Reform Commission, 2015a). The document is careful to emphasize 'the decisive role of the market in resource allocation and the primary role of enterprises', but with 'due functions' for governments. It also emphasizes that 'China will take full advantage of the existing bilateral and multilateral cooperation mechanisms . . . to promote the development of regional cooperation' (National Development and Reform Commission, 2015a). But the document also emphasizes respect for 'the paths and modes of development chosen by different countries' (National Development and Reform Commission, 2015a).

What this means becomes more clear in the often more explicit interpretations of the carefully worded document by Chinese scholars. Here, the International Financial Crisis, emerging from the US, has brought to light diverging problems as well as approaches to managing economic recovery in the US, Europe and Japan, causing international economic governance to face unprecedented challenges.

Moreover, emerging economies have been unable to manage associated complex and difficult problems. These circumstances, in the words of one scholar, 'objectively require China as the second largest economy and largest emerging economy to achieve its own development by contributing to global economic development' (Wang, 2015: 49). Critique is also addressed to the existing global governance system, including international organizations, dominated by the developed countries, which reflect their governance concepts and interests and are unwilling or unable to address reform of the unequal economic order, uneven development, unfair resource allocation mechanisms, etc. to the benefit of developing economies (Su, 2016).

Thus, the wake of the financial crisis has shown that despite the global financial crisis, the institutions of the Washington Consensus and Bretton Woods have been slow or unable to reform, and are unable to formulate suitable development goals as development norms and programs are focused on individual poverty reduction rather than on state-level development in infrastructure, economic growth, social stability, effectively undermining UN development goals. Given the failure of US-led neo-liberalism, China and other developing countries would need to get out of the dependent and exploitative relationship with developed countries, so that they can catch up (Sun, 2016). These attempts to legitimize the Belt and Road as a part of global development efforts have been helped by the signing of a 'Memorandum of Understanding between the Government of the PRC and the UN Development Program on "jointly promoting construction of the Silk Road Economic Belt and the 21st Century Maritime Silk Road"' (National Development and Reform Commission, 2016a).

In the eyes of some Chinese scholars, the BRI will thus serve the common interests of China and its neighboring emerging economies, by addressing problems of economic development and international economic governance in new and alternative ways to those prescribed by the existing order dominated by the interests of developed countries (i.e. Washington Consensus). Following these interpretations, the respect for 'the paths and modes of development chosen by different countries' emphasized in the Vision and Actions document, is a rejection of the 'one size fits all' approach to development advocated by the Washington consensus, instead 'giving full consideration to the economic needs of countries at various stages of development' (Su, 2016: 7).

From the perspective of the Chinese government and Chinese academics, the Belt and Road is thus designed to provide an alternative program of economic development and alternative forms of international cooperation or governance (see also Beeson and Li, 2016). Both points, development and governance, are programmatically captured by regular reference to concepts such as 'interconnectivity' (*hulian hutong*, 互联互通) and 'docking' (*duijie*, 对接).

Wu Zelin highlights the significance of these concepts in Chinese policy discourse and for a 'Chinese' resp. 'Asian' understanding of regionalism, by contrasting it with the European experience. Wu describes the European process of regionalization as one of integration based on convergence whereas the (South East) Asian experience as one moving from diversity to commonality through 'interconnectivity'. 'Asian interconnectivity does not pursue the establishment of a new supranational political centre, its objective is to establish a "commonality" of the world, being a road from diversity towards commonality. At its core is the process of docking between sovereign states. That each country develops its own development strategies and plans, taking a path of development suited to their own national conditions, is a prerequisite for docking' (Wu, 2016: 69). Successful 'docking' depends on two factors, the first being shared visions and strategies of development, such as the Silk Road and its counterparts proposed by other countries in the region; secondly, it depends on comparative advantages/disadvantages to be exploited for common development (Wu, 2016: 69–70).

China has pursued a number of agreements and memoranda of understanding with countries, often in the context of state visits by leading Chinese politicians, that in line with the aim of 'policy coordination' outlined in the Vision and Actions document, many of these memoranda and agreements seek to 'dock' the Silk Road initiative with national and regional economic development initiatives. These include the Eurasian Economic Union, Kazakhstan's 'Shining Path' ('Nurly Zhol') program, Korea's Eurasia program, Mongolia's 'Prairie Road', and Russia's Trans-Eurasian Belt Development. In South East Asia, China agreed with Indonesia to coordinate their development strategies, while Vietnam and China agreed to coordinate the Belt and Road and the 'Two Corridors and One Ring' initiative. In South Asia, China and Pakistan have agreed on the development of a common economic corridor. In Eastern Europe, China has signed MOUs with nine countries, and seeks to coordinate its BRI under the 16+1 framework (Su, 2016).

From the standpoint of Chinese observers, the BRI thus is aimed at improving global economic governance, not seeking to replace existing institutions, but instead seeking to provide public goods in areas that have previously been neglected, such as the investment needs of developing countries in the Asian region (Su, 2016: 16). This is achieved by investment improving 'interconnectivity' in the region and by a mode of governance 'docking' various initiatives with one another, so as to address the divergent needs of countries at various stages of development. OBOR is thus suited to internationalize the Chinese development experience and provides policies and a mode of governance different from those of the 'West'.

Western observers share the assessment that the BRI seeks to propose alternative policies and mechanisms in global and regional governance but emphasize how China's own strategic interests and (geo) political ambitions come as part and parcel with the proposal. Against the background of an intensification of strategic competition between China and the United States in the Pacific, the tendency for their interdependent economic relationship to unravel, the tectonic shifts in global political economy that have become noticeable in the wake of the 2008 financial crisis, and the challenges to the Western-dominated system of global governance, Arase (2015), Callahan (2016), and Ferdinand (2016) all see OBOR as some part or another of wider changes towards a more assertive, coherent and strategic Chinese foreign policy under Xi Jinping that in the eye of observers of previous administrations often lacked direction.

To Peter Ferdinand (2016), the relevance of the One Belt One Road initiative needs to be interpreted as the foreign policy equivalent of the domestically oriented 'China Dream' (*zhongguo meng*, 中国梦). The term 'China Dream' emerged in public discourse in the late 2000s but has been adapted as doctrine by Xi Jinping. While its policy content remains ill-defined, ideologically, the China Dream under Xi may be interpreted as emphasizing China's national unity, and as reasserting the leading role of the CCP and particular a centralization of power around its centre, correcting for what has been perceived as the weak leadership of Hu Jintao and Wen Jiabao. The ideological assertiveness found in the China Dream under Xi is reflected in foreign policy discourse: 'Whereas 20 years ago China used to keep saying "no", or at best "maybe", to the international community, now it wants to say "yes", though without simply acquiescing in western hegemony' (Ferdinand, 2016: 955). Also, and most relevant in relation to the BRI, the China Dream emphasizes China's unique or even superior path of development (Ferdinand, 2016: 948). According to Ferdinand, the initiative's alternatives offered to the Washington Consensus-approach to economic development and global governance advocated by 'the West' 'demonstrates a Chinese concern to compete with the United States at least as much, if not more, through strategic economic policies as through military ones' (Ferdinand, 2016: 953).

Arase believes that the promotion of a particular mode of regional integration through the Belt and Road will increase China's political and economic leverage over neighboring countries. Instead of promoting multilateral treaties and international or supranational institutions of authority, the initiative seeks to promote cooperation through material incentives and on a case-by-case bilateral basis. Given the difference in economic scale between China and its neighbors, these 'will need to accommodate themselves to the values and interests of China in order to avoid the loss of rights and privileges in the community of common destiny' (Arase, 2015: 35), a sentiment shared by Callahan (2016: 3), who expects that with the help of the BRI China will apply its economic leverage 'to build a Sino-centric "community of shared destiny" in Asia, which in turn will make China a normative power that sets the rules of the game for global governance' (Callahan 2016:3).

At the Forum on China Africa Cooperation in 2015, Xi Jinping seemed to hint at a military dimension to the Maritime Silk Road Strategy: 'It has long been a topic of hot debate among Sinologists and pundits alike whether the "One Belt, One Road" $140 billion plan is in fact an elaborate cloak under which Beijing can disguise its military ambitions' (Kleven, 2015). The decision to lease a military base in Djibouti and Xi's reference to Djibouti's right way of handling China's Maritime Silk Road Initiative can be interpreted as a confirmation of military considerations in this regard. Ericson and Strange highlight the link between the PRC's participation in multi-lateral security off the coast of Somali and its regional and security policies. They note that 'there is a strong correlation between where Chinese antipiracy warships have docked ashore and Chinese-funded port development projects in South Asia, the Middle East and Africa' (Erickson and Strange, 2015). Clemens (2015) agrees that '(t)he Maritime Silk Road makes it unmistakably clear that China's strategic interests in and along the maritime routes leading to the west (as well as the number and vulnerability of Chinese citizens working in the adjacent countries) will only increase in coming years'. He further observes: 'The Maritime Silk Road already represents China's most vital sea lines of communication, both because it gives China access to three major economic zones (Southeast Asia, South Asia and the Middle East) and because it is the route for many of China's strategic materials, including oil, iron ore and copper ore imports. Moreover, active efforts to develop strategic and economic relationships along the Maritime Silk Road afford an opportunity (in the Chinese view) to escape the growing containment and encirclement embodied by the U.S. "pivot to Asia"' (Clemens, 2015). The geopolitical significance of the maritime silk road had early been emphasized by Chinese observers (Liang, 2015) stressing the link it establishes with Southeast and South Asia as well as Africa and Arabia.

Conclusion

The analysis of the policy-making process and the policy content of One Belt, One Road has shown that, on the one hand, the leadership under Xi Jinping has managed to transform the initiative from slogan into a centralized and coordinated policy framework, that has now entered the early stages in a top-down process of implementation, involving a range of actors at various levels of the party-state. Futhermore, regarding its content, the BRI does have the hallmarks of grand strategy, as it seeks to integrate domestic and foreign economic policy, as well as strategic goals by extending Chinese influence over economic governance and its modus in the region.

The policy-making process of the BRI exhibits many of the features and characteristics found by Heilmann and Melton (2013) in their study of development planning in China, where a 'set of coordinated policies designed to achieve an operational outcome' is devised at the centre, and hierarchically implemented by the organs of the party-state. The initiative involves policies coordinated among the Ministries of Foreign Affairs and Commerce and the National Development and Reform Commission, under the leadership of the highest party organs and the State Council. Central control over the process of implementation has been institutionalized by creating the Leading Small Group on One Belt One Road. The top-down initiative is now reaching the point where local interests and pre-existing policies are fed back into decision-making and implementation. The use of work conferences underscores the principle of democratic centralism: before turning an idea into policies, the views of a broad array of stake-holders are consulted by the top leadership who then defines the policy and the set-up of organisations in charge. To a certain extent, implementation of the policy on the provincial level or by State-owned enterprises follows the principle of 'experimentation within hierarchy', as these units are given some leeway in devising their own plans so as to adapt them to local circumstances. The provincial plans at least, however, have to be approved by the NDRC before implementation. It would be interesting to know whether the NDRC in conjunction with SASAC would have similar control over the foreign investment plans of enterprises. Furthermore, the concept of 'top-level design', devised by Xi Jinping in the context of foreign policy-making, suggests that under his leadership, the centre claims tighter control over policy-making and implementation than the previous administration. In any case, Xi Jinping's role in the policy-making process seems exceptional, taking leadership of work conferences and Leading Small Groups, tasks traditionally left to the Prime Minister. This, however, maybe a hallmark of Xi's reign, who has been ruthlessly consolidating and expanding power since his inauguration.

Regarding policy-content, the Belt and Road brings together domestic and foreign policy goals, uniting economic and strategic aims. In the process of reforming its economy, the massive investment drive associated with the BRI is designed to strengthen the connections with neighbouring economies, supporting the internationalization of China's economy. If successful, these policies may significantly shift the economic centre of the regional economies of South East and Central Asia towards China. The success of the BRI will crucially depend on the question, if the development recipes and governance principles attached to it find acceptance among China's neighbours. This will also determine the initiative's relevance for what form regional economic governance and regionalism may take in Asia in the future. Given the fallout of the 2008 financial crisis and the continued unevenness of global development, contrasted with the relative success of China's own development model, China's neighbours may find the proposals of the Belt and Road attractive and see it as an opportunity to shed the governance and development principles of the Washington Consensus. Of course, such a step might come at the price of increased dependence upon China in a new Sino-centric regional order.

Coming back to our lead-question, the analysis of the policy-making process and content of the initiative, appear to lend credibility to 'One Belt, One Road' as a comprehensive and centrally coordinated grand strategy. Of course, successful policy-making and domestic implementation cannot by themselves attest to the feasibility of the Belt and Road as grand strategy. It remains to be seen, whether or not the recipes advocated with it will be successful in providing remedies to the causes of China's continued economic slowdown, or whether the associated investment binge will just exacerbate and defer a solution to these problems to the future. Furthermore, regarding the foreign policy component of the BRI, it remains to be seen whether China's regional neighbours will be willing to accept China's ideas of regional and global governance as part and parcel of China's investment offensive.

Notes

1 The famous *taoguang yanghui* (韬光养晦).
2 This process is further reflected in Xi chairing the new LSG on Comprehensively Deepening Reform in addition to chairing the new LSGs on National Security, Internet Security, and Reform of the Military.

3 Authoritative Chinese sources such as government web sites and official news outlets usually translate 周边外交 as 'neighborhood diplomacy'. More literally, however, 周边 is translated as 'periphery', a term connoted with Sino-centrism.
4 Li Keqiang and Xi Jinping had been rivals for promotion to the top positions in China's party-state; in 2007, Xi came out on top of Li when both were first elevated into the PBSC as an indication that the two of them were groomed to take on Secretary-General and Prime Minister positions in 2012/2013. When exactly this happened, rumours continued to spread about uneasy working relations between the two. In either case, Xi managed to consolidate his superiority which included, among other things, the clear assignment of important new policies to him and not to 'central leaders' as referred to in the commentary above.
5 According to Caixin and the official NDRC website, He Lifeng ranks second among the 10 Deputy Directors of the NDRC (with Xi jinping's key economic policy advisor Liu He ranked first), well above Wang Xiaotao at rank 10.
6 The 'Vision and Actions' document is one of the first official English language documents referring to the *yi dai yi lu* as 'Belt and Road Initiative' and not as 'One Belt One Road'. (National Development and Reform Commission, 2015a), English version available at http://en.ndrc.gov.cn/newsrelease/201503/t20150330_669367.html.

References

21 Shiji Jingji Baogao (2015). 国务院推进"一带一路"工作领导小组办公室负责人欧晓理："一带一路"战略全国覆盖 (Ou Xiaoli, Head of Office of the Leading Group for the Promotion of Belt and One Road, State Council: National Strategy for Belt and One Road covering the whole country), http://finance.sina.com.cn/china/20150414/011921946699.shtml, accessed 23 September 2016.
An, Xiaoming (2016). 我国 "一带一路" 研究脉络与进展 (Venation and progress on "Belt and Road" research). 区域经济评论 *(Regional Economic Review)*, (2), 77–88.
Arase, David (2015). China's two silk roads initiative – what it means for Southeast Asia, in: Singh, Daljit (ed.), *Southeast Asian Affairs 2015*. Singapore: ISEAS YUsof IShak Institute, 25–45.
Bao, Jianyun (2015a). 论"一带一路"建设给人民币国际化创造的投融资机遇、市场条件及风险分布 (On the investment opportunities, market conditions and risk distribution created by RMB Internationalization through building "One Belt, One Road"). 天府新论, (1), 112–116.
Bao, Jianyun (2015b). 论海上丝绸之路建设与海上丝路人民币贸易圈的形成与发展 (On the building of maritime silk road and formation and development of RMB trade rim along maritime silk road). 江苏行政学院学报 *(Journal of Jiangsu Administration Institute)*, (2), 43–48.
Beeson, Mark, and Li, Fujian (2016). China's place in regional and global governance: A new world comes into view. *Global Policy*, 7(4), 491–499.
Beijing Qingnianbao (2016). *最高规格"领导小组"囊括多少部委?* (How many ministries are part of the highest ranking "leading small group"?), http://epaper.ynet.com/html/2016-05/03/content_195637.htm, accessed 23 September 2016.
Caixin (2015). *'"一带一路"领导小组办公室设在发改委* ("Belt and Road" leading small group office established at NDRC), http://economy.caixin.com/2015-03-30/100795962.html, accessed 23 September 2016.
Callahan, William A. (2013). China's harmonious world and post-western world orders: Official and citizen intellectual perspectives, in: Foot, Rosemary (ed.), *China Across the*

Divide: The Domestic and Global in Politics and Society. Oxford: Oxford University Press, 19–42.

Callahan, William A. (2016). Chinas "Asia Dream": The belt road initiative and the new regional order. *Asian Journal of Comparative Politics*, 1(3), 226–243.

Chen, Xiangyang (2016). 习近平以周边外交战略思想主动塑造周边新秩序 (Xi Jinping's neighborhood diplomacy strategic thought takes initiative to mold new peripheral order), http://news.china.com.cn/world/2016-01/12/content_37554548.htm, accessed 18 September 2016.

Clemens, Morgan (2015). *The maritime silk road and the PLA: Part one*, https://jamestown.org/program/the-maritime-silk-road-and-the-pla-part-one/, accessed 23 Septmber 2016.

Erickson, Andrew S., and Strange, Austin (2015). *China's global maritime presence: Hard and soft dimensions of plan antipiracy operations*, https://jamestown.org/program/chinas-global-maritime-presence-hard-and-soft-dimensions-of-plan-antipiracy-operations/, accessed 23 September 2015.

Ferdinand, Peter (2016). Westward ho – the China dream and 'One Belt, One Road': Chinese foreign policy under Xi Jinping. *International Affairs*, 92(4), 942–957.

Fu, Mengzi, and Lou, Chunhao (2015). 关于21世纪海上丝绸之路之建设的若干思考 (Some consideratons on building the 21st century Maritime Silk Road). Xiandai Guoji Guanxi, (3): 1–9.

Glahn, Richard von (2016). *The Economic History of China: From Antiquity to the 19th Century*. Cambridge: Cambridge University Press.

Godement, François and Kratz, Agatha (2015). *'One Belt, One Road': China's Great Leap Outward*, http://www.ecfr.eu/publications/summary/one_belt_one_road_chinas_great_leap_outward3055, accessed 22 January 2018.

Harnisch, Sebastian (2015). China's international role and its 'historical self', in: Harnisch, Sebastian, Bersick, Sebastian, and Gottwald, Jörn-Carsten (eds.), *China's International Roles: Challenging or Supporting International Order?* New York: Routledge, 38–58.

Heilmann, Sebastian (2008). Policy experimentation in China's economic rise. *Studies in Comparative International Development*, 43(1), 1–26.

Heilmann, Sebastian (2009). Maximum tinkering under uncertainty: Unorthodox lessons from China. *Modern China*, 35(4), 450–462.

Heilmann, Sebastian, and Perry, Elizabeth (eds.) (2011). *The Political Foundations of Adaptive Governance in China*. Cambridge, MA: Harvard University Press.

Heilmann, Sebastian, and Melton, Oliver (2013). The reinvention of development planning in China, 1993–2012. *Modern China*, 39(6), 580–628.

Huang, Cary (2013). *Think-tank Veteran Wang Huning to retain influence despite lack of portfolio*, www.scmp.com/news/china/article/1192583/think-tank-veteran-wang-huning-retain-influence-despite-lack-portfolio, accessed 23 September 2016.

Huang, Yiping (2015). 黄益平谈一带一路：希望不要成为国际版西部大开发 (Huang Yi-ping talks about the Belt and Road: I hope it won't become an international version of Developing the West), http://finance.sina.com.cn/hy/20150130/111621437403.shtml, accessed 15 September 2016.

Huotari, Mikko (2015). Finding a new role in the East Asian financial order: China's hesitant turn towards leadership, in: Harnisch, Sebastian, Bersick, Sebastian, and Gottwald, Jörn-Carsten (eds.), *China's International Roles: Challenging or Supporting International Order?* New York: Routledge, 145–168.

Johnson, Christopher K. (2016). *President Xi Jinping's 'Belt and Road' initiative – a practical assessment of the Chinese Communist Party's roadmap for China's global resurgence*. Report of the CSIS Freeman Chair in China Studies, www.uschina. org/sites/default/files/President%20Xi%20Jinping's%20Belt%20and%20Road% 20Initiative.pdf.

Kleven, Anthony (2015). *Is China's Maritime Silk Road a military strategy?* http:// thediplomat.com/2015/12/is-chinas-maritime-silk-road-a-military-strategy/, accessed 23 September 2016.

Lam, Willy (2015). 'One Belt, One Road' enhances Xi Jinping's control over the economy. *Jamestown China Brief*, 15(10), https://jamestown.org/program/one-belt-one-road-enhances-xi-jinpings-control-over-the-economy/, last accessed 22 January 2018.

Li, Cheng (2016a). *Chinese Politics in the Xi Jinping Era: Reassessing Collective Leadership*. Washington, DC: Brookings Institution.

Li, Keqiang (2013). 李克强作政府工作报告—回顾2013年工作 (Li Keqiang delivers government work report – reviewing work of 2013). www.chinanews.com/gn/2014/03-05/5912684.shtml, accessed 23 September 2016.

Li, Keqiang (2014). *Report on the work of the government*, www.china.org.cn/chinese/ 2014-03/17/content_31806665_3.htm, accessed 23 September 2016.

Li, Keqiang (2015). *Report on the work of the government*, www.china.org.cn/chinese/ 2015-03/17/content_35077119_3.htm, accessed 23 September 2016.

Li, Keqiang (2016b) *Report on the work of the government*, http://online.wsj.com/public/ resources/documents/NPC2016_WorkReport_English.pdf, accessed 23 September 2016.

Liang, Fang (2015). 今日 "海上丝绸之路" 通道风险有多大 (How risky is passage of today's "Maritime Silk Road"?), www.81.cn/jwgd/2015-02/11/content_6351319.htm, accessed 23 September 2016.

Liu, Yuxian (2016). 湖南成立' 一带一路' 建设领导小组　陈向群任组长 (Hunan establishes leading small group to build Belt and Road, Chen Xiangqun leader), http:// hn.rednet.cn/c/2016/01/11/3885131.htm, accessed 23 September 2016.

Lu, Feng et al. (2015). 为什么是中国? – "一带一路" 的经济逻辑 (Why is it China? – the economic logic Of "One Belt One Road"). 国际经济评论 (International Economic Review), (3), 9–34.

Ministry of Commerce (2016a). 商务部合作司负责人谈2015年我国对外投资合作情 况 (Head of Ministry of Commerce, Department of Cooperation, on China's Foreign Investment and Cooperation in 2015), www.mofcom.gov.cn/article/ae/ai/201601/ 20160101235603.shtml, accessed 10 August 2016.

Ministry of Commerce (2016b). 2016年上半年我对"一带一路"相关国家投资合作情况 (First half of 2016 investment cooperation circumstances towards "One Belt One Road" countries), http://fec.mofcom.gov.cn/article/fwydyl/tjsj/201607/20160701363205.shtml, accessed 22 January 2018.

National Development and Reform Commission (2015a) 推动共建丝绸之路经济带和 21世纪海上丝绸之路的愿景与行动 (Vision and actions on jointly building silk road economic belt and 21st-century Maritime Silk Road), www.ndrc.gov.cn/gzdt/201503/ t20150328_669091.html, accessed 23 September 2016.

National Development and Reform Commission (2015b) 标准联通 "一带一路" 行动计 划 (2015–2017) (Official standards connected to the One Belt One Road Action Plan, 2015–2017), www.ndrc.gov.cn/gzdt/201510/t20151022_755473.html.

National Development and Reform Commission (2016a) 中国政府与联合国开发计划 署签署《关于共同推进丝绸之路经济带和21世纪海上丝绸之路建设的谅解备忘 录》 (Chinese Government and UNDP Jointly Sign Memorandum of Understanding on Jointly Promoting Construction of the Silk Road Economic Belt and the 21st Century

Maritime Silk Road), www.sdpc.gov.cn/gzdt/201609/t20160920_818939.html, accessed 23 September 2016.

National Development and Reform Commission (2016b). 中国双向投资 – 政策指南 (China Bidirectional Investment – Policy Guide). Beijing: 机械工业出版社 (China Machine Press).

Naughton, Barry (2013). The return of planning in China: Comment on Heilmann-Melton and Hu Angang. *Modern China*, 39(6), 640–652.

Page, Jeremy (2013). *The Wonk with the ear of Chinese President Xi Jinping*, www.wsj.com/articles/SB10001424127887323728204578513422637924256, accessed 23 September 2016.

Ping, Xiong (2013). *Commentary: China's neighborhood diplomacy promotes regional peace*, http://news.xinhuanet.com/english/indepth/2013-11/03/c_132855402.htm, accessed 23 September 2016.

Schmidt, Dirk (2012). 'From the Charm to the Offensive': Hat China eine neue Außenpolitik? *ASIEN*, (122), 34–56.

Shambaugh, David (2013). *China Goes Global: The Partial Power*. Oxford: Oxford University Press.

Su, Ge (2016). 全球视野之"一带一路" (The Belt and Road initiative in global perspective). 国际问题研究 (International Topics Research), (2), 1–23.

Su, Xiaohui (2015). **立足周边，谋篇全球** (Standing on the periphery, set on the world), *CIIS Shishi Pinglun*, www.ciis.org.cn/chinese/2015-03/03/content_7715685.htm, accessed 23 September 2016.

Summers, Tim (2016). China's 'New Silk Roads': Sub-national regions and networks of global political economy. *Third World Quarterly*, 37(9), 1628–1643.

Sun, Yiran (2016). 亚投行、"一带一路"与中国的国际秩序观 (AIIB, "One Belt, One Road", and the Chinese international order). 外交评论: 外交学院学报 (Foreign Relations Commentary: Journal of the Foreign Relations Research Department), (1), 1–30.

Swaine, Michael D. (2015). Chinese views and commentary on the "One Belt One Road" initiative. *China Leadership Monitor*, (47), https://www.hoover.org/sites/default/files/research/docs/clm47ms.pdf, accessed 22 January 2018

Wang, Da (2015). 亚投行的中国考量与世界意义 (AIIB: China's considerations and global significance). 东北亚论坛 (Northeast Asia Forum), (3), 48–64.

Wu, Zelin (2016). '探析欧亚两种不同的区域合作模式 (Exploring Europe's and Asia's two different models of regional cooperation). 中国国情国力 (Aspets of China's National Power), (3), 69–71.

Xi, Jinping (2013a) *携手建设中国-东盟命-共同体* (Together Build China – ASEAN Community of Shared Destiny), Speech Before Indonesian Parliament, 3 October 2013, www.chinanews.com/gn/2013/10-03/5344133.shtml, accessed 23 September 2016.

Xi, Jinping (2013b) *共同创造亚洲和世界的美好未来* (Work Together to Create a Beautiful Future in Asia and the World), Keynote Speech At the Bo'ao Forum, 7 April 2013, http://news.xinhuanet.com/politics/2013-04/07/c_115296408.htm, accessed 23 September 2016.

Xi, Jinping (2013c) *弘扬人民友谊共创美好未来* (Promote Peoples' Friendship for a Beautiful Future), Speech at Nazarbayev University, 7 September 2013, http://news.xinhuanet.com/world/2013-09/08/c_117273079.htm, accessed 23 September 2016.

Xi, Jinping (2014). *New Asian security concept for new progress in security cooperation*, Speech at the 4th Cioca Summit, Shanghai, 20–21 May 2014, www.china.org.cn/world/2014-05/28/content_32511846.htm, accessed 20 September 2016.

Xi, Jinping (2016). 习近平在亚洲基础设施投资银行开业仪式上的致辞 (Speech of Xi Jinping at Asia Infrastructure Investment Bank Opening Ceremony), www.fmprc.gov.cn/web/zyxw/t1332258.shtml, accessed 23 September 2016.

Xinhua (2014). 习近平出席中央外事工作会议并发表重要讲话, http://cpc.people.com.cn/n/2014/1130/c64094-26119225.html, accessed 23 September 2016.

Xinhua (2015a) 习近平在新加坡国立大学发表重要演讲 (Xi Jinping Attends Central Foreign Affairs Working Conference and Delivers an Important Speech), http://news.xinhuanet.com/politics/2015-11/07/c_1117071632.htm, accessed 23 September 2016.

Xinhua (2015b) 张高丽：努力实现"一带一路"建设良好开局 (Zhang Gaoli: Trying to achieve a good start in building the "Belt and Road"), http://news.xinhuanet.com/politics/2015-02/01/c_1114209284.htm, accessed 23 September 2016.

Xinhua (2015c) 一带一路领导班子"一正四副"名单首曝光 (The One Belt One Road Leading Group, Leader and Members Revealed for the First Time), http://news.xinhuanet.com/city/2015-04/06/c_127660361.htm, accessed 23 September 2016.

Xinhua (2016). 张高丽：有力有序有效推进"一带一路"建设 (Zhang Gaoli: Vigorously, Orderly, and Effectively Promote Building "One Belt, One Road"), www.gov.cn/guowuyuan/2016-09/13/content_5108062.htm, accessed 23 September 2016.

Xinhua Finance (2016). *China's Belt and Road Initiative Brings Think Tank Boom*, http://en.xfafinance.com/html/OBAOR/Analysis/2016/200990.shtml, accessed 22 September 2016.

Xiu, Wen (2015). 为何由他们来领导"一带一路"小组(Why Do They Lead the "One Belt, One Road" Small Group?), www.shobserver.com/news/detail?id=4416, accessed 23 September 2016.

Xu, Gao (2015). '一带一路'中的三个关系 (The Three Relationships of "One Belt, One Road), in Lin, Yifu and Jin, Liqun (eds.), '一带一路'引领中国 ("One Belt, One Road"awaits China). Beijing: Zhongguo Wenshi Chubanshe, 27–31.

Yan, Xuetong (2014). From keeping a low profile to striving for achievement. *The Chinese Journal of International Politics*, 7(2), 153–184.

Zhao, Kejin (2015). "一带一路"应加强统筹领导 ("One Belt, One Road" Should Strengthen Leadership), http://opinion.china.com.cn/opinion_58_131358.html, accessed 23 September 2016.

Zhongguo Haiyang Shiyou Bao (2015). 总公司成立"一带一路"专项规划领导小组 (Head Office Establishes "One Belt, One Road" Special Dedicated Leading Small Group), www.cnooc.com.cn/art/2015/7/13/art_191_2047011.html, accessed 23 September 2016.

Zhongguo Xinwen Wang (2014). 习近平：要以创新思维办好亚洲基础设施投资银行 (Xi Jinping: Asian Infrastructure Investment Bank Should Be Set Up with Innovative Thinking), www.chinanews.com/gn/2014/11-06/6759286.shtml, accessed 23 September 2016.

4 Urban-rural differences in social policies

The case of the hukou system in China

Agar Brugiavini, Danilo Cavapozzi and Yao Pan

Introduction

In the second-half of the 1950s the People's Republic of China introduces a household registration system to keep under control the internal migration from rural to urban areas, which was rising disproportionately in view of the increasing industrialization of the urban areas in the country. In 1949 households living in the urban area account for 10.6% of the overall population, while in 1956 this percentage increased by more than one-third and reached 14.6% (China Statistical Yearbook, 2004). Due to an excess labor influx from rural agriculture sector to urban industrial sector, the State introduces a household registration system to establish a strict control over the migration from rural to urban areas in order to reduce unemployment in urban areas. This makes it possible to guarantee enough grain production from the agriculture sector to support urban workers through a strict food rationing system.

This registration system is called hukou system. Although it was formally introduced in 1951, it has been shaped as a strict regulation system in 1958 and its features remain overall unaltered at least until the beginning of the 2000s. According to the 1958 regulations, all Chinese citizens' are classified into either urban or rural hukou based on their place of residence at that time. Newborn babies' hukou status have to follow their mother's hukou status (Chan and Zhang, 1999). The State allowed the change in the hukou type only in very special cases. Even nowadays, changes of the hukou type are extremely uncommon and allowed by the State in limited circumstances. This classification is particularly relevant for Chinese citizens' well-being since it determines individual's entitlements to social policies, which are hukou-type specific.

Having a urban or rural hukou becomes a key determinant of the quality as well as the generosity of the social policies provided to citizens with respect to education, health care, income protection schemes, housing and pensions. Social policies designed for urban residents are based on the availability of higher resources, while rural hukou holders are only guaranteed to the basic services and infrastructures. The main reason for this is that the State takes the responsibility of financing urban hukou social policies and decentralizes the organization and the financing of the social policies for rural hukou households at the local level. Clearly, the

DOI: 10.4324/9781315102566-5

amount of resources and credit access that rural local communities have at their disposal are much lower than those that the State can invest to develop urban areas social infrastructures, such as schools and hospitals, or to finance pension systems for urban workers. This tremendous imbalance in available resources produces wide differentials in the effectiveness of social policy schemes and jeopardizes their inclusiveness. Official statistics describing the health care system in rural and urban areas provide a clear snapshot of this heterogeneity. In 2013 there were 33.45 beds in medical institutions in rural areas for every 10,000 individuals. This number more than doubles for urban citizens and it is equal to 73.58. Moreover, in the same year the per capita health expenditure amounts to 1,274.44 yuan in rural areas and to 3,234.12 yuan in urban areas (China Statistical Yearbook, 2015).

After almost 70 years from the introduction of the hukou system, China presents stark differences between rural and urban areas in well-being indicators with respect to a variety of dimensions and they always suggest a better quality of life in urban areas. In 2013 the newborn mortality rate is 3.7% in urban areas and 7.3% in rural areas (China Statistical Yearbook, 2015). On average, almost 15 children out of 1000 die before the age of five in rural areas, this number reduces to six in urban areas. In 2000 the life expectancy at birth is 75.21 years of age for those born in urban areas but it shrinks to 69.55 for those born in rural areas (Pan and Wei, 2016). In addition, the access to education appears to be higher in urban areas. As documented by Zhang et al. (2015), in the period 2010–2012, only 88% of rural children completed primary education, this percentage is equal to 100%. Of those who entered junior high schools in rural areas, only 70% completed this cycle of study. Likewise before, this percentage is equal to 100% for urban areas. Finally, only 2% of rural children access tertiary education (college or university). This is an extremely disappointing outcome as compared with the percentage of 54% found for the urban population. Analogous patterns are found when considering household income per capita. In 2013 its average for rural households is about one-third of that found for their urban counterparts (China Statistical Yearbook, 2015).

This chapter contributes to the literature that investigates the reasons underlying these wide differentials by summarizing the different social policies individuals with rural and urban hukou types are eligible to. We will offer an introduction to the main features of the social policy schemes with respect to education, health care, income protection schemes, housing and pensions that rural and urban individuals deal with. In particular, we will pay attention to the evolution of these schemes over time. Explaining current socioeconomic and health differences between individuals with rural and urban hukou types cannot neglect the social policies features that they have faced throughout their whole life.

The rest of the paper is structured as follows. First, we provide an overview of the hukou system over time. Then, in the next five sections, we will present the main features of the education system, health care system, income protection schemes, housing policies and pension systems available to rural and urban hukou holders. Finally, the last section discusses our main findings.

An overview of the hukou system

Since the mid-1950s, Communist party leaders in China introduced a strictly enforced residential permit (hukou) system to separate urban and rural residents as an important administrative tool for relieving demographic pressures in the course of rapid industrialization (Chan, 1994). Hukou system then has come into effect in China for more than half a century. It has influenced various aspects of life for hundreds of millions of Chinese people and is closely related to the Chinese economic development policies. Residents were classified into the 'rural' and 'urban' hukou (or 'agriculture' and 'non-agriculture' hukou).[1] Holding a different hukou type makes a pronounced distinction between rural and urban residents, determining the social-economic entitlements they are eligible to as well as invisibly shaping the order of social classes of the country. Social welfare policies a Chinese citizen is eligible to are designed differently according to whether she/ he is an urban or rural hukou holder. Urban hukou holders get the access to better education resources, health care, housing subsidies, unemployment insurance as well as pensions while rural counterparts are only guaranteed to basic services and infrastructures. Although the rural-urban distinction has characterized the hukou system since the beginning, the degree of rigidity of hukou conversion, referring to change from the rural to urban hukou, varies. One important aim of this chapter is to emphasize and document the evolution of the hukou system over time.

There is extensive literature that gives an explicit introduction to the history and development of hukou system in China. For instance, Cheng and Selden (1994) discuss the origins and social consequences of hukou system until 1990s into details Chan and Zhang (1999) study the role of hukou system in internal migration and how the policies have changed since the late 1970s. Chan (1994) reviews the history of hukou system from a socio-political point of view and examines its influence on the country's industrialization, urbanization, and social and spatial stratification. Many papers regard the hukou system as a barrier to development and modernization as well as an obstacle to social equality and the free flow of the labour market (i.e. Wang, 2003b; Liang, 2013).

The long history of hukou system can be broadly divided into three phases.

The first phase is before 1958 ('free mobility period'). Before the establishment of the People's Republic of China (PRC) in 1949, a similar population registration system collecting and managing demographic statistics for the purpose of taxation and conscription already existed in the Chinese history. With the exception of the years during the Second Sino-Japanese War (1937–1945), this system was used as an infrastructure to provide public certificates, such as citizen's cards (Liang-min zheng) in Japanese-occupied Shanghai (Wang, 2006) and identity cards (shenfen zheng) in Kuomintang-ruled post-war Shanghai (White, 1978). Generally, for the pre-1949 era, the system did not impose any rigid social-economic control between urban and rural people and its main function was to collect residents' data. After the establishment of the PRC, the hukou system was first introduced in 1951 to record urban population and was extended to rural areas in 1953. The main purpose was 'to maintain social peace and order, safeguard the people's security, and protect their freedom of residence and movement' (Cheng and Selden, 1994). The first Chinese constitution adopted in 1954 guaranteed the freedom of residence and movement for citizens.

The second phase was between 1958–1978 ('strict control period'). The 1958 regulations represent the only national legislation on migration and residence promulgated by the National People's Congress, which still remains in effect today. Each Chinese citizen is included in the hukou system since then (Zhu, 2003; Cheng and Selden, 1994) and classified as being either a rural or an urban hukou holder based on their place of residence at that time. This status cannot be changed easily during life. Newborn babies' hukou status have to follow their mother's hukou status (Chan and Zhang, 1999). Hukou type was linked to a variety of economic and social welfare policies to the greatest extent. Free mobility no longer existed. Instead, rigorous measures to prevent migration from rural to urban areas were imposed in order to reduce the pressures on urban cities. Regardless of being assigned to a rural or an urban hukou, the public services that the hukou system makes eligible to could be provided only in the place of residence. The hukou system crystallized the rural and the urban population by binding citizens to their place of residence and offering limited possibilities of changing their hukou type.

The reasons underlying the introduction of these mobility limitations were rooted in the consequences of Chinese economic policies implemented at that time. China followed the Marxist tradition and mimicked the Soviet-era's economic development, which put a higher emphasis on the heavy industry. The big push to industrialization (or 'traditional socialist development strategy') resulted in a considerable gap between urban-industrial and rural-agriculture sector (Chan, 1994). A large influx of rural people started to leave the villages to reach the cities at the beginning of the establishment of the PRC. This flows made the cities under a great demographic pressure. China's urban population increased from 10.6% in 1949 of total population to 14.6% in 1956, where rural migrants accounted for almost 60% of the total increase (Kirkby, 1985). Due to limited resources in cities and over-supply of the labour force, the State built up a great barrier on the rural-urban migrants through hukou system in order to preserve the demographic stability and reduce unemployment in urban areas. Moreover, this measure was needed to guarantee enough grain production in agriculture sector to support urban workers through a strict food rationing system.

The third phase is from 1979 until now ('opening-up period'). Since 1978, China has started to transfer from a planned to a market economy, characterized by the privatization of many State-owned companies. A more flexible hukou system has been adopted to facilitate rural-urban migration (Seeborg et al., 2000; Wu and Yao, 2003). One major change was the introduction of two special types of residential registration, administered by local governments. The first is the 'Interim Provisions on the Management of Transient Population in Cities Act' published in 1985, which supported the integration of rural workers in urban cities by allowing them registering as temporary residents in urban areas, but without assigning them any urban hukou and all related rights and benefits. The new provisions cancelled the rule that restricted temporary residents to stay no more than three months in urban cities but still did not allow them to change their hukou status (Yusuf and Saich, 2008).

For rural workers, job access in cities became easier than before. As a result, a large influx of rural workers into cities has been experimented. Noticeably, systematic abuses, such as selling false urban registration cards to rural peasants, have been detected (Yan, 2008). In response, the State published 'A Notice on Strictly Controlling Excessive Growth of "Urbanization"' in 1989 to manage migration flows towards urban areas, which again restricted rural people access to State-funded programs.

The second special type of residential registration is the so-called 'blue-stamp' hukou. The pool of blue-stamp hukou holders consists of investors, property buyers and professionals, who were originally assigned to a rural hukou. The 'blue-stamp' hukou makes them eligible to most of the social benefits of regular urban hukou holders, conditional on the payment of a very high one-time entry fee (Chan and Zhang, 1999). These two types of residential registration were temporary and have been faded away gradually after 2000.

In addition to these two acts, several reforms have been implemented to redesign the hukou system. Newborns can choose to follow their father's or mother's hukou status since 1998. Furthermore, the hukou conversion process (nong-zhuangfei process), which is needed to legally switch from rural hukou to urban hukou status, was much harder to obtain before the 1980s. Since the 1980s, the regular channels for rural-urban hukou conversion have been made more flexible and include the recruitment by State-owned enterprises (zhaogong), enrollment in higher education institutions (zhaosheng), promotion to senior administrative positions (zhaogan), joining the army (canjun), land acquisition by government and other personal migration reasons (Chan and Zhang, 1999; Chan, 2009). The quota of Chinese migrants allowed to switch their hukou from rural to urban is annually set by the central government. As an example, between 1989 and the beginning of the 2000s the annual quota of rural hukou holders allowed to switch their hukou to the urban type lied between 0.15 and 0.2% of the population of urban hukou holders in the city in which they want to live (Chan, 2009). These restrictions have been recently relaxed but remain strict. Overall, the government will allow 100 millions of rural hukou holders to change their hukou between 2014 and 2020 in order to promote urbanization.[2] This amounts to say that on average the annual quota of the current rural citizens allowed to change their hukou amounts to approximately 2%.[3] In general, current hukou conversion policy is clearly still strict, mainly allowing the rich and the highly educated people to change their hukou type (Zhang, 2010). As rural workers found it easier to move to cities for jobs, one important consequence is an increasing movement of rural peasants to urban areas. For the internal migration in China, movement and citizenship can be totally separated. For instance, someone can move to a new place but might not obtain the access to various social welfare policies supplied there.

People who move from rural areas to urban cities but do not obtain urban hukou are called 'floating population' or 'mobile population' (liudong renkou), meaning they are not de jure residents although they are de facto residents. Although they live in urban areas, these Chinese citizens face an administrative barrier that makes them impossible to exploit the public services supplied to urban hukou holders. Only those who can successfully convert to urban hukou through the above-mentioned channels are permitted to use the resources and services as the other urban hukou holders. The size of floating population has increased rapidly from a few million in the early 1980s to about 150 million in 2011 (Chan, 2012). In 2013, floating population reached 18% of total Chinese population[4]. Rural-urban migrants, usually low-skilled workers, move to cities in order to obtain a better job. They struggle to integrate into urban life but because of their rural hukou type they do not obtain the same entitlements as the urban hukou holders (Solinger, 1999). For example, they are not entitled to the subsidized education system, welfare programs, and community cultural activities. This barrier threatens their social inclusion. Knight and Gunatilaka (2010) find that rural-urban migrants report lower happiness score than rural and urban hukou holders. Furthermore, migrants children were assigned to privately-run migrants schools in urban areas, many of which have limited space, worse facilities and fewer certified teachers (Dong, 2010).

Urban and rural hukou holders are eligible to social policies that widely differ with respect to their design, financing and quality. In the following sections we will discuss in detail to what extent being assigned to a rural or an urban hukou type can lead to dramatic differences in the architecture of selected social policies individuals face in their lifetime. In particular, we will focus on the education system, health care system, income protection scheme, housing policy and pension system.

Education system

China pursues a two-track education system, referring to government-supported urban education track and family-supported rural education track since the pre-1949 era due to limited educational resources to guarantee full education access to the whole population (Fu, 2005). The new People's Republic of China adopted the same education model since its establishment. Hence, the State takes the main responsibility for urban education, while the management and financing of the rural education system are burdened on the local collectives[5] and rural families. Consistent with the goal of hukou system, two-track education system emphasized the importance of developing education in cities, industrializing and mining areas in order to cater for the needs of industrialization. Liu Shaoqi, chairman of the National People's Congress Standing Committee between 1954–1959, proposed the concept of 'two kinds of labor and two kinds of education system' in 1958 that further reaffirmed the pursuit of two different ways of education in rural and urban China.[6] In addition, the Education Minister, Yang Hsiu-feng stressed that the principle of 'selective development' in the education policy was an effective way of 'utilizing reasonably our limited strength' to 'popularize education simultaneously with raising standards' in 1959.[7] The reasons behind it were again due to the lack of sufficient resources and capital to fulfill the needs of the whole nation. According to the central government point of view, for a country with limited resources and capital, it was necessary to focus on a certain group of people to fast produce qualified elites for modernization and industrialization. In the case of China, public resources were mainly given to key schools[8] and urban schools to train a selected group of urban youth who was artificially chosen to be the future elites and manage the economic development. Rural children had to accept this kind of unequal education opportunity.

Two-track education system has been always in place except for a short period during the cultural revolution era (1966–1976). After the first two years of the cultural revolution, in which education at all levels was suspended, inequality between rural and urban education was eliminated radically. For example, both rural and urban children received the same primary school education (five years primary schooling) since 1968. Secondary and higher education attendance was determined on the basis of work experience and political activism, rather than education achievements, favoring workers and peasants instead of intelligentsia (Lo, 1984). After the cultural revolution, everything was recovered. The two-track system was characterized again by government-subsidized urban schools and people-run rural schools.

The difference between rural and urban education is reinforced especially when Chinese government formally switched from centralized towards decentralized fiscal system since 1980. The State remained the primary source for financing urban education like before, while in rural areas most of the expenditures was left to the sponsorship of townships or of the county-level governments replacing the local collectives. However, since local governments have limited fiscal capacity, some of education expenditures are left to the rural families to afford on their own.

In 1986 the first formal nine-year compulsory education law was promulgated in China, including six years of primary school and three years of junior high school. The law was implemented initially in urban cities and then gradually diffused to rural areas. National Bureau of Statistics of the PRC announced that in 2014 the coverage of nine-year compulsory law has reached almost the whole nation[9].

From late 1990s and onwards, education system has been modified in order to eliminate the stark educational inequality between rural and urban areas. For instance, the State tried to reduce and even dismantle the nine-year compulsory education fees (i.e. 'tax-for-fee reform', 'one-fee-system', 'no charge')[10] (Tsang, 1996; Sun, 2007; Fu, 2005). Nevertheless, the gap between rural and urban education remains substantial. Most of the rural educational funds are from the local government (county/township level), whose fiscal capacity is rather limited and much lower than the central government. Urban schools are equipped with better infrastructure and allocated to better teaching resources. For instance, Wang (2003a) calculated that in urban areas the student-teacher ratio[11] in 2001 is 19.7 for primary school and 17.9 for secondary school, while rural areas have higher ratios, 22.7 and 19.9 for primary and secondary school, respectively. Besides, the certified full-time teachers of junior secondary school in urban areas are about 92% of the total, while they are only around 85% in rural areas. Among certified teachers, 24% of those working in urban area obtained at least a university degree, while only 9% of those in rural areas did. Hence, the quality of teachers is expected to exhibit substantial variation between rural and urban areas.

Health care system

Health care system differs between rural and urban China in terms of health care policies, administration of health service and resources.

In urban areas, health care has been supported by the State from the beginning. Two major employment-related health schemes, which were the State labor insurance scheme and the public service medical scheme, were established in 1951 and 1952, respectively (Knight and Song, 1999). All the medical expenditures of government staff and workers at State-owned companies were supported by the State and State-owned enterprises (Shi, 1993). Their immediate relatives could enjoy 50% reduction on normal medical fees. Furthermore, for most of the private sector employees, their health-care schemes were organized by many private and public companies (Knight and Song, 1999). With the exception of employees in a few small private firms and the self-employed, all urban workers have been covered by health insurance schemes, which make medical expenditures free of charge. In order to cover all the urban employees, the 'Urban Employee Basic Medical Insurance' (UEBMI) was established in 1998 to replace previous working-unit based schemes and to cover the employees of both private and public sectors. As a complementary, the 'Urban Resident Basic Medical Insurance' (URBMI) was introduced in 2007 to include all non-employee urban residents, such as self-employed, retirees, children and other dependents.

Rural areas lack an effective health care system until the mid-1960s. Most of rural individuals were not covered by any scheme but mainly depend on private out-of-pocket expenses. In 1965, a cooperative medical system was launched. This system was ran and financed by the communes,[12] which were multifunctional organizations that directed local government and managed economic and social activities. The health care provision was based on the presence of 'barefoot doctors', who were trained by urban doctors and sent to rural health clinics in order to provide medical care to peasants. By 1970, 1.2 million barefoot doctors had been trained (Knight and Song, 1999). Medical expenditures that exceeded a higher level can be reimbursed up to a certain percentage (Shi, 1993).

The rural health care system changed dramatically during the post-Mao period (1979–1990s). One important change in the Chinese economic policy implemented at that time was the transfer of production responsibility system from the collectives to the household level. This was aimed at emphasizing the importance of individual efforts and responsibility in maintaining economic growth of China. Communes were no longer the cornerstone of local economic activities. The rural health care was influenced by such dissolution of the commune-centred management system. Government subsidies for health care system in rural areas became rather limited and the communes were no longer in the position of sustaining the cooperative health care system launched in the 1965 and paying barefoot doctors. As a result, cooperative health schemes collapsed and village clinics were shut down. The proportion of rural individuals covered by cooperative medical system fell from 90% in 1978 to 9.5% in 1986 (Shi, 1993). A fee-for-service system has replaced the previous system and barefoot doctors became private practitioners.

In addition, before 1978, the central government allotted a proportion of money to local government to support communes in financing the cooperative health care system. After 1978, due to the decentralized fiscal policy, local governments (county and township governments) are the solely responsible for managing and financing their own health care system, whereas the State only directly finances national hospitals, research institutions and medical schools in urban China (Liu et al., 1995).

After 2000, central government shifts more attention to the health care provided in rural areas. For instance, more generous subsidies were provided in order to reduce out-of-pocket expenses of rural citizens. In 2003, the government introduced the 'New Cooperative Medical Scheme' (NCMS) to provide universal health care coverage for rural residents. At the beginning, the pilot has been run in some cities. The NCMS was then extended to the whole nation since 2010.

China still remains underdeveloped when considering the provision of public long-term care services to individuals with permanent chronic disabilities, especially the elderly and the disabled. Although formal care (i.e. nursing homes, elder care homes, community service) exists, informal care provided by family members is currently the main source of health care in China (Zeng, 2010; Wu et al., 2009). Long-term health care facilities are more developed in urban areas, while very limited services are provided in rural areas (Chu and Chi, 2008). So far, most of formal care institutions are funded and operated by the government, whereas few of them are financed by non-government organization or private investors. The government recently started improving long-term care system and encouraging private investments in urban areas. However, the supply of these health care institutions are unable to meet the growing needs of long-term health care of Chinese population. In particular, there is not any publicly-funded national long-term care insurance program to cover long-term care expenditures in China (Feng et al., 2011). The long-term care expenditures of the elderly mainly depend on out-of-pocket expenses, pensions, family or other private resources. Long-term health care in China still has a long way to go.

Income support benefits

China has an unemployment insurance scheme available only to citizens with urban hukou. The first unemployment insurance system was the 'Interim Provisions on Workers' Job-Waiting Insurance in State-Owned Enterprises (SOE)' and was launched in China in 1986. The State-owned companies took full responsibility of the welfare of the unemployed workers and hence workers were not required to pay contributions. Provisions were extended slightly in 1993. In 1999, the latest 'Regulations on Unemployment Insurance' Act was introduced and it is still in place. These new regulations indicate that enterprises, individuals and government fiscal subsidies are the three main sources of contributions to the unemployed insurance scheme and the coverage was extended to all urban workers. No unemployment insurance scheme is available for individuals with rural hukou, except for some rural workers recruited by urban enterprises.[13]

Facing an increased unemployment, low wages, inadequate pensions, and rampant inflation, the number of urban poor in China grew fast in the early 1990s (Saunders and Shang, 2001; Gao, 2006). In order to support them, the minimum income guarantee (Di bao), also known as 'Minimum Living Standard Guarantee Scheme' was introduced in Shanghai in 1993 first and then became a national policy in 1999. The targeting population includes a mixed group of people in both chronic and temporary poverty, such as the unemployed, the elderly, as well as sick and disabled individuals. The aim of Di bao (DB) was to provide financial support to all registered[14] urban households whose income is below a threshold set at the municipal level (Ravallion et al., 2006). Before 1999, DB was financed by local government only. After 1999, the central government increasingly started to subsidize local government in financing the DB scheme.

According to the 1999 regulations on DB, only those households whose monthly income was below the threshold set by local government can apply for DB. Furthermore, only household members with an urban hukou who reside in the same local administrative unit in which the household applies for DB are eligible for this allowance and counted in the determination of the total benefits distributed to that family. Instead, family members with rural hukou or residing in other cities or provinces were not eligible to receive DB benefits from the local government. Di bao in rural areas was started only in 2003. Participation of local governments of rural areas to DB is voluntary and depends on the availability of enough financial resources to run the scheme. The minimum income rural hukou holders could receive every month is generally lower than that available to urban hukou holders. The exact amount of monthly minimum income varies among cities and provinces since it is determined by local governments. For example, in Tianjian, the local government announced that rural people will receive 540 yuan/person, while urban people receive 705 yuan/person in 2015. In Zhenzhou, the standard monthly minimum income is 290 yuan/person for rural people, while 520 yuan/person for urban people in 2015.[15] One of recent aims of Chinese government is to spread DB to the national level and reduce the gap between rural and urban citizens.

Housing policy

Housing policies are also found to be different between urban and rural hukou holders.

First of all, in urban China, housing system has experienced great changes from a centralized and planned economic policy to a much more market-oriented one.

Under the 'planning period' 1949–1979, there was no private housing market in China. The State took the main responsibility for the investment in housing according to the plan and entrusted the construction, allocation, management and maintenance of housing facilities to the place of employment or working units (danwei). The property rights of these houses were owned by the State. Usually, houses were provided at a low rental price determined to cover the maintenance costs. The quality of the houses was guaranteed and determined by the State in advance (Zhang, 2000).

Between 1978 and 1998, the conflict between old housing system and market liberalization process forced China to change to a more-market oriented housing system. However, this process was very slow due to the controversy on the cession of State-owned land and working unit housing (Wu, 1996). However, from 1998 onwards, a market-oriented housing system has been the most prevalent. The distribution of social housing, such as rental dwelling provided by the municipality or working units at low price, was abolished. Social housing facilities were converted into private property (Deng et al., 2014). Nowadays, an increasing number of houses in urban areas are constructed by real estate development companies according to qualified standards. From 2008 onwards, urban housing policies put a stronger attention on housing affordability problems and move towards a more mixed ownership housing system. In addition, urban lands belong to the State, while residents only have the property rights and land-using rights, usually, up to 70 years (Yang and Chen, 2014). Finally, it is worth noting that the first mortgage in China was issued in 1986, funded mostly by retail deposits (Yang and Chen, 2014). Since the abolishment of the social housing in 1998, mortgage loans have become an important tool for urban households to purchase housing.

Due to the unique migration control established by the hukou system, internal migrants without urban hukou could not have an access to most of urban housing services and facilities. Many of them live in the outskirts of cities where the quality of both housing and living is relatively poorer than the standards usually guaranteed to urban hukou holders.

On the contrary, rural housing system has not changed much over time. There has never been any formal housing market in rural areas. According to government regulation, each household is allocated with a housing land but the ownership of this land belongs to the local collectives. Once their housing land is provided, rural households need to finance, construct and maintain their houses on their own. The residents own the property rights of their house and land-using rights. Non-commercial houses cannot be sold or leased. Rural land cannot be pledged.

Knight and Song (1999) find that living space per capita of rural households was twice as much as that of urban households between 1978 and 1995. They argue that the urban living space may be limited due to supply-constraints reflecting the problem of housing shortage in urban areas. However, we cannot just conclude that rural housing is superior to urban housing as quality is nevertheless important. Rural houses are mainly constructed by peasants. Hence, the quality of rural houses varies a lot, depending on the households' socioeconomic status and their financial capability. In contrast to the urban case, in rural areas there are not either government housing subsidies or financial intermediaries supporting housing market, such as financial institutions selling mortgages.

Pension system

The proportion of people aged 65 and above is projected to increase rapidly from around 7% in 2000 to 16.5% in 2030, eventually to reach around 23.6% in 2050 (UN, 2010). Hence, how to guarantee the social welfare of this rapidly growing aging population will be one of the most important policy concerns in China. Although the poverty rate of older individuals dropped a lot in China in recent years, the poverty rate in rural areas is still quite high. For instance, the poverty rate of people aged 60+ in urban areas is 4.6%, while rural areas have a poverty rate as high as 22.3% in 2010 (Lu, 2012). Compared with urban elderly, rural elderly are really at a serious disadvantage, accompanied with low income and incomplete social welfare system.

As discussed in the previous sections, much of the urban-rural divide in China was rooted in the introduction of the hukou system. A stark urban-rural division also exists in the pension system.

Tracing back to the beginning of the PRC (from the 1950s to 1978), a public pension system was implemented only for urban industrial and public sector workers, restricting pensions to individuals who contributed to the Social Security system during their working life. It covered most urban residents, while rural hukou holders were excluded from this pension system.

China's first formal pension scheme, the 'Basic Old-Age Insurance System for Employees' (BOISE), was introduced in 1951 and designed for urban employees. Followed by the 'Basic Old-Age Pension System for Civil Servants' (BOPSCS) in 1952, a pension scheme targeted for civil and military servants. The State-owned enterprises took main responsibility for financing the contributions of their employees. However, this system had a low coverage rate. In addition, administrative processes were inefficient. For example, workers were required to cancel their account when they changed their city of residence and had to open a new account in the new place of residence. The process of transferring individual accounts was rather complex and difficult (Lu, 2012). Besides, the replacement rate was also low and continued to decline over time (Lu, 2012).

Since 1978, due to the new era of modernization led by the paramount leader Den Xiaoping, who realized the switch from a planned to a more market-oriented economy, the State-owned enterprises observed a reduction in their market share and profits. Therefore, they had an increasingly limited financial ability in providing pensions to their urban workforce. To alleviate the financial burden on State-owned enterprises and involve private firms in the financing of the pension system, the State Council issued the 'Decision on Establishing a Unified Basic Old-Age Insurance for Enterprise Employees (BOISEE)' in 1991. BOISEE was formally introduced in 1995 and originally limited to public sector workers. It has been extended to the private sector in 1997. Under BOISEE pension funds are pooled by industry sector.

Besides, BOISEE includes urban hukou holders only and hence rural migrants without urban hukou were not eligible due to their hukou type. By 2011, around 215.7 million people contributed to BOISEE (Lu, 2012). Instead, non-employed urban residents aged 16 and over who are not eligible for BOISEE have been assigned to 'Urban Social Pension Scheme' (USPS) since 2011.

Concerning the rural hukou holders, the 'Five Guarantee Schemes' (wubao, FGS)[16] was introduced in 1956 and served as a safety net for the rural poor people. The targeting population includes individuals aged above 60, the disabled and children under 16 who have 'no income, no labor capacity, and no resources of family support' (Cai et al., 2012). Except FGS, rural older individuals were not assigned to any other statutory benefits until 1980s.

Between 1986 and 1991, China took the first step to introduce in rural areas a basic pension system called 'Basic Scheme of Rural Pensions at the County Level'. First, some pilot experiments were run at the county-level in a few provinces. They were managed by the Ministry of Civil Affairs (MoCA). Then, the system was extended to all rural areas.

This pension system was financed mainly through three ways: local governments, local collectives and individuals. However, several reasons undermined its diffusion. Local governments had the main responsibility in the design of the policies implemented at local level. This caused substantial variation in the amount of resources devoted to finance the pension system. Richer areas were better equipped, while poorer areas lagged behind. In addition, the privatization of local-level enterprises during the 1990s jeopardized the financial contribution of the employers to the system and reduced the benefit amounts paid to retirees.

Consequently, Cai et al. (2012) document that the basic scheme expanded geographically to cover 31 provinces and almost 75% of counties in 1998. Nevertheless, after this peak, its diffusion declined rapidly. For example, the number of participants dropped from 80 million in 1999 to 53.78 million in 2004 (Cai et al., 2012). Again, most of rural older individuals were not guaranteed by any rural pension schemes. Only in 2009 China launched the first nationwide rural pension system after locally piloting. This system is called 'New Rural Social Pension Scheme' (NRSPS). All the rural residents are eligible, their participation in the pension system is voluntary. Citizens who have contributed for at least 15 years will be eligible to receive pensions.

In 2014 rural and urban resident pension schemes have been integrated into one. The government aim is to reach a full coverage by 2020 (Cai et al., 2012). However, the national average replacement rate has dropped from 70.79% in 1997 to 45% in 2014,[17] which is relatively low and questions the financial well-being of retirees.

Discussion

This chapter reviewed the history of the household registration system (hukou) introduced in China in the second half of the 1950s to control internal migration from rural to urban areas. This registration system classifies Chinese citizens in urban and rural hukou holders. Having an urban or rural hukou has dramatic consequences on the degree of inclusiveness characterizing the social policies a Chinese citizen is eligible to. This chapter documented the stark differences in education, health care, income protection, housing and pensions systems available to urban and hukou holders. Social policies designed for urban hukou holders benefit of the availability of higher financial resources, while rural hukou holders receive poorer public services. Despite some recent changes in the legislation, individuals cannot easily switch their hukou type, whose change is allowed in limited cases.

These differentials in social policy architectures shape individuals' socio-economic outcomes. Previous literature suggests that rural residents achieve lower educational attainments (Liu, 2005), have poorer health outcomes (Zurlo et al., 2014), lower income (i.e. Knight and Song, 1999; Lu and Song, 2006) and experiment lower life-satisfaction (Ren and Treiman, 2015) than urban people. Lu and Song (2006) find that local urban workers earn substantially higher hourly wages than their counterparts with rural hukou. The well-being of rural hukou holders is impaired by the disadvantaged social policies they face during their whole life course.

The dual hukou system in China leads to a huge inequality between rural and urban China, which is expected to slow down economic development and integration. In response to the increasing internal migration, the Chinese government is paying much more attention to relax the strict hukou system in place for more than fifty years. For example, it has been proposed to introduce a unified hukou system to all citizens, which means dismantling the differences in hukou type paradigm in order to reduce discrimination towards rural hukou holders. These reforms can produce a breakthrough towards the socio-economic integration between rural and urban areas only if the removal of the administrative rural-urban classification imposed by hukou is accompanied by reforms that redesign the architecture of the social policies that rural residents face during their life. Indeed, simply allowing them to migrate and receive in urban areas the services that urban citizens are already eligible to might bring about dangerous consequences in terms of migration rates, depopulation of rural areas, urban areas migration inflows and long-run financial sustainability of the urban social policies as well. Instead, a policy agenda fostering sustainable economic development should improve the quality of public services and infrastructures in rural China. This goal is clearly ambitious since about 700 millions of individuals (approximately one half of the whole Chinese population) reside in rural areas. Financing welfare state services for such a wide population requires a considerable amount of resources that can be collected by resorting to a combination of strategies, including the allocation of public resources by the central and local governments, as well as the stimulation of private investments in disadvantaged areas and the support to public private partnerships.

Notes

1 There are two classifications in the Chinese household registration system. The first is the type of registration (hukou leib ie), which classified residents into the 'rural' and 'urban' hukou (or 'agriculture' and 'non-agriculture' hukou). The second is the place of registration (hukou suozaidi) based on the individuals' permanent residence. Only one of regular residences can be registered for each citizen. (Chan and Zhang, 1999). In addition, a person is not entitled to permanent urban hukou even if married with a person who has urban hukou (Whyte and Parish, 1984).
2 'Announcement on the plan of pushing 100 million of non-urban hukou holders to settle down in urban cities' ('guo wu yuan ban gong ting guan yu yin fa tui dong 1 yi fei hu ji ren kou zai cheng shi luo hu fang an de tong zhi') by the State Council, 30th of September, 2016 (www.gov.cn/zhengce/content/2016-10/11/content_5117442.htm).
3 Calculations of the authors based on China Statistical Yearbook, 2015.
4 Calculated according to the data provided by China Statistical Yearbook, 2015
5 Collectives are 'a form of publicly owned enterprise' (Naughton, 1994). In rural China, it was quite popular especially between 1958 and 1983 that multiple farmers ran their holdings as a joint enterprise and cooperated together in farming activities within and/ or between villages. Everything was shared within the collectives.
6 'Wo guo yingyou liangzhong jiaoyu zhidu, liangzhong laodong zhidu' (Our country should have two kinds of education and two kinds of labour system), 30 May 1958, in Liu SHoaqi xuanji (selected works of Liu Shaoqi), 2 vols. (Bejing: Renmin chubanshe, 1981–1985), xia:323–327.
7 NCNA-English, Peking 28 April 1959 in CB, 577 (14 May 1959), 14.
8 'Key schools' are selected to receive the priority in the assignment of teachers, equipment, fund and other resources. They are also allowed to recruit the best students for special training, of which 90% are in urban areas (Tsang, 1996).
9 NBS 2014 Statistical report on the implementation of 'China National Program for Child Development (2011–2020)'. Published by National Bureau of Statistics in 2015.
10 Tax-for-fee reform: abolished all of the previous local fees and taxes except agricultural tax and agricultural tax supplements. One-fee system: Central government set one fixed price for compulsory education for both rural and urban people.
  No charge for compulsory education: By 2009, rural schools have nationwide implemented these policies and compulsory education becomes free of charge.
11 The student-teacher ratio shows the average number of students taught by one teacher. Everything else constant, higher values of the ratio indicate lower expected quality of the education system.
12 There are three administrative units in rural areas of the People's Republic of China. During the period from 1958–1983, they were county (parallel to cities in urban areas), communes, brigades and teams. County was the largest one and supervised communes while communes controlled production brigades and production teams. Except counties, Communes were the highest administrative units and the largest collective units in rural area, which were replaced by townships later. In particular, agriculture production was decided at the commune level and then assigned to production brigades and teams. Brigades and teams were replaced by villages afterwards. Now, three administrative levels in rural area include county, townships, and villages (source: Administrative divisions of the People's Republic of China (Zhonghua Renmin Guoheguo Xingzheng Quhua), 15 June 2005, accessed 5 June 2010, from www.gov.cn).
13 See Vodopivec and Tong (2008) for more details.

14 Registered means people with urban hukou. The internal migrants with rural hukou but living in urban cities are excluded.
15 Table of the overview of dibao levels in main rural and urban areas in 2015 by Li, J.L. Chinanews.com (Zhongxinwang), 8 July 2015, www.chinanews.com/gn/2015/07-08/7390743.shtml.
16 Five Guarantees include clothes, food, residence, health care, funeral service.
17 Report on 'Strategies of rebuilding China's pension system' ('Chong Gou Wo Guo Yang Lao Jin Ti Xi De Zhan Lve Si Kao') by Professor Dong Keyong, published on China Ageing Finance Forum 50 in 2016.

References

Cai, F., Giles, J., O'Keefe, P., and Wang, D. (2012). *The Elderly and Old Age Support in Rural China*. Washington, DC: World Bank Publications.

Chan, K. W. (1994). *Cities With Invisible Walls: Reinterpreting Urbanization in Post-1949 China*. Hong Kong: Oxford University Press.

Chan, K. W. (2009). The Chinese hukou system at 50. *Eurasian Geography and Economics*, 50(2), 197–221.

Chan, K. W. (2012). Internal migration in China: Trends, geography and policies, in: *United Nations Population Division, Population Distribution, Urbanization, Internal Migration and Development: An International Perspective*, New York: United Nations, 81–102.

Chan, K. W., and Zhang, L. (1999). The Hukou system and rural-urban migration in China: Processes and changes. *The China Quarterly*, 160, 818–855.

Cheng, T., and Selden, M. (1994). The origins and social consequences of China's hukou system. *The China Quarterly*, 139, 644–668.

China Statistical Yearbook (2015). Beijing: China Statistics Press.

China Statistics Yearbook (2004). Beijing: China Statistics Press.

Chu, L., and Chi, I. (2008). Nursing homes in China. *Journal of the American Medical Directors Association*, 9(4), 237–243.

Deng, W., Hoekstra, J. S. C. M., and Elsinga, M. G. (2014). *Urban housing policy review of China: From economic growth to social inclusion*. Proceedings of New Researchers Colloquium ENHR 2014 Conference, Beyond Globalisation: Remaking Housing Policy in a Complex World, Edinburgh, 1–4 July, 2014; Authors version. ENHR.

Dong, J. (2010). Neo-Liberalism and the evolvement of China's education policies on migrant children's schooling. *Journal of Critical Education Policy Studies*, 8(1), 137–161.

Feng, Z., Zhan, H., Feng, X., Liu, C., Sun, M., and Mor, V. (2011). An industry in the making: The emergence of institutional elder care in urban China. *Journal of the American Geriatrics Society*, 59(4), 738–744.

Fu, T. M. (2005). Unequal primary education opportunities in rural and urban China. *China Perspectives*, (60).

Gao, Q. (2006). The social benefit system in urban China: Reforms and trends from 1988 to 2002. *Journal of East Asian Studies*, 31–67.

Kirkby, R. J. R. (1985). *Urbanization in China: Town and Country in a Developing Economy, 1949–2000 A.D.* London: Croom Helm, 107.

Knight, J., and Gunatilaka, R. (2010). The rural – urban divide in China: Income but not happiness? *The Journal of Development Studies*, 46(3), 506–534.

Knight, J., and Song, L. (1999). *The Urban – Rural Divide: Economic Disparities and Interactions in China*. New York: Oxford University Press.

Liang, Q. (2013). Household registration reform, labor mobility and optimization of the urban hierarchy. *Social Sciences in China*, 216(12), 61–67.

Liu, Y., Hsiao, W. C., Li, Q., Liu, X., and Ren, M. (1995). Transformation of China's rural health care financing. *Social Science & Medicine*, 41(8), 1085–1093.

Liu, Z. (2005). Institution and inequality: The Hukou system in China. *Journal of Comparative Economics*, 33(1), 133–157.

Lo, B. L. (1984). Primary education: A two-track system for dual tasks. *Contemporary Chinese Education*, 47–64.

Lu, Q. (2012). *Analysing the Coverage Gap in China*. London: HelpAge International.

Lu, Z., and Song, S. (2006). Rural – urban migration and wage determination: The case of Tianjin, China. *China Economic Review*, 17(3), 337–345.

Naughton, B. (1994). Chinese institutional innovation and privatization from below. *The American Economic Review*, 84(2), 266–270.

Pan, J., and Wei, H. (2016). *Blue Book of Cities in China: Annual Report on Urban Development of China No. 9*. Beijing: Social Sciences Academic Press (CHINA).

Ravallion, M., Chen, S., and Wang, Y. (2006). Does the Di Bao program guarantee a minimum income in China's cities? *Public Finance in China*, 317.

Ren, Q., and Treiman, D. J. (2015). Living arrangements of the elderly in China and consequences for their emotional well-being. *Chinese Sociological Review*, 47(3), 255–286.

Saunders, P., and Shang, X. (2001). Social security reform in China's transition to a market economy. *Social Policy & Administration*, 35(3), 274–289.

Seeborg, M. C., Jin, Z., and Zhu, Y. (2000). The new rural-urban labor mobility in china: Causes and implications. *Journal of Socio-Economics*, 29(1), 39–56.

Shi, L. (1993). Health care in China: A rural-urban comparison after the socioeconomic reforms. *Bulletin of the World Health Organization*, 71(6), 723.

Solinger, D. J. (1999). *Contesting Citizenship in Urban China: Peasant Migrants, the State, and the Logic of the Market*. Berkeley: University of California Press.

Sun, X. (2007). The effects of fiscal decentralisation on compulsory education in China: For better or worse? *JOAAG*, 2(1), 40–53.

Tsang, M. C. (1996). Financial reform of basic education in China. *Economics of Education Review*, 15(4), 423–444.

UN (2010). World Population Prospects: The 2010 Revision,Volume 1: Comprehensive Tables. *United Nations, Department of Economic and Social Affairs, Population Division, ST/ESA/SER.A/313*.

Vodopivec, M., and Tong, M. H. (2008). *China: Improving Unemployment Insurance*. Washington, DC: World Bank, Social Protection & Labor.

Wang, D. (2003a). China's rural compulsory education: Current situation, problems and policy alternatives. *China Agricultural Economic Review*, 1(3), 356–73.

Wang, H. (2003b). A macroscopic analysis of the formation and evolution of the Chinese present domicile system. *Journal of Chinese Communist Party History Studies*, 58(4), 22–29.

Wang, W. H. (2006). *Zhongguo huji zhidu: Lishi yu zhengzhi de fenxi* (China's Hukou System: A Historical and Political Analysis). Shanghai, China: Shanghai wenhui chubanshe.

White, L. T. (1978). *Careers in Shanghai: The Social Guidance of Personal Energies in a Developing Chinese City, 1949–1966 (No. 19)*. Berkeley: University of California Press.

Whyte, Martin K., and Parish, William (1984). *Urban Life in Contemporary China*. Chicago: University of Chicago Press.

Wu, B., Mao, Z. F., and Zhong, R. (2009). Long-term care arrangement in rural China: Review of recent development. *Journal of the American Medical Directors Association*, 10(7), 472–477.

Wu, F. (1996). Changes in the structure of public housing provision in urban China. *Urban Studies*, 33, 1601–1627.

Wu, Z., and Yao, S. (2003). Intermigration and intramigration in China: A theoretical and empirical analysis. *China Economic Review*, 14(4), 371–385.

Yan, G. (2008). Household register's character history and China's household registration reform. *Tribune of Study Journal*, 24(5), 71–75.

Yang, Z., and Chen, J. (2014). Housing reform and the housing market in urban China, in: *Housing Affordability and Housing Policy in Urban China*. Berlin Heidelberg: Springer, 15–43.

Yusuf, S., and Saich, T. (2008). *China Urbanizes: Consequences, Strategies, and Policies*. Washington, DC: World Bank Publications.

Zeng, Y., Gu, D., Purser, J., Hoenig, H., and Christakis, N. (2010). Associations of environmental factors with elderly health and mortality in China. *American Journal of Public Health*, 100(2), 298–305.

Zhang, D., Li, X., and Xue, J. (2015). Education inequality between rural and urban areas of the People's Republic of China, migrants' children education, and some implications. *Asian Development Review*, 32(1), 196–224.

Zhang, H. (2010). The Hukou system's constraints on migrant workers' job mobility in Chinese cities. *China Economic Review*, 21(1), 51–64.

Zhang, X. Q. (2000). The restructuring of the housing finance system in urban China. *Cities*, 17(5), 339–348.

Zhu, L. J. (2003). The Hukou System of the People's Republic of China: A Critical Appraisal under International Standards of Internal Movement and Residence. *Chinese Journal of International Law*, 2(2), 519–565.

Zurlo, K. A., Hu, H., and Huang, C. C. (2014). The effects of family, community, and public policy on depressive symptoms among elderly Chinese. *Journal of Sociology and Social Work*, 1–23.

5 Changing role of leadership and impact of social media

A case study of public officials in Lanzhou City, China

*Bhumika Gupta, Sajjad Haider,
Zhu Yanru and Fan Yunxin*

Introduction

The world is now moving beyond the globalization and transforming into a knowledge society, knowledge economy and of course knowledge-driven organizations. This shift from agrarian to industrial and from industrial to knowledge society has come up with both opportunities as well as challenges. Among many, one of the problems we faced in the transition from an industrial society to a global knowledge economy is the need for a new breed of leaders (Johannessen, 2013; Miller, 2005) and a rejuvenated perspective of leadership. The leaders in both the public and private sectors need to have a blend of skills (i.e.) the coventional leadership traits like a charismatic and inspirational personality, good communicator, being visionary are important of course; albeit to be successful in the modren era public leaders needs to be 'tech-savvy' and well versed with today's knowledge-driven culture.

With the explosion of the internet, print and electronic media, and the dramatic increase in the use of social media; people have unprecedented access to information. As a result, people are getting more informed and well connected with each other. Imagine, for a moment that when Christopher Columbus discovered America in 1678, if we were using smartphones and connected with the social media at the time – what would have happened? Certainly there would had been a big blast in social media. People in every nook and corner of the world would had come to know about this discovery. But in fact, in 1678 only a handful of people knew about this breakthrough discovery. Columbus would have had few people around to celebrate with at the time. On the flip-side of the coin, people's lives are now increasingly dependent on these gadgets, Apps, tools and technologies.

With the advent of new technologies, gadgets, high-tech equipment's and smart devices; human life has dramatically changed. Our daily routines are completely different from those of the past. Today we have easy access to an incredible amount of information, and all kinds of information is just a click away. In 2016, the total number of internet users in the world jumped to 3,424,971,237 which is 46% of the world's total population (Internet live stats, 2016). The People's Republic of China (PRC), having one-fifth of world's population, also has the

DOI: 10.4324/9781315102566-6

highest number of internet users in the world (McKinsey, 2015). According to Internet Live Stats, which gives the internet user statics in real time, in 2016 the total number of netizens (internet users) in PRC reached to 721,434,547 which is 52%. This number is double the internet users in the USA, which is 286,942,362, however, it's 88.5% of the total population in the US. According to McKinsey, the amount of internet users in PRC is almost equivalent to the combined populations of France, Germany, Italy, Spain, and the United Kingdom (Chiu et al., 2015).

The internet also give birth to another incredible feature of modern times (i.e. the era of social media). The number of social media users is surging with each passing day and the total number of social media users worldwide reached 2.51 million in 2017, which is predicted to climb to 2.96 billion in 2020. Whereas the number of social media users in China crossed 563.1 million in 2016, and it is estimated that it will jump to 739.7 million in 2021 (Statista, 2017). The statistics show that almost a quarter of the total population of China is connected online and using some kind of social networking platform. A Boston Consulting Group study found that Chinese Internet users are online for an average of 2.7 hours per day, considerably more than other developing countries and more on par with usage patterns in Japan and the United States (Crampton, 2015).

Nevertheless, all this technological and information booms comes with strings of challenges attached with it. One of the critical challenges faced by organizations in modern times is to effectively cope with the changing needs of the workforce and skillfully handle today's many technological challenges. In order to succeed in today's fast-paced, complex and uncertain times, a leader not only needs to be well versed in conventional administrative and management tactics, but must also have a broad understanding of the political, economic, social, legal and environmental drivers of change as well the capacity to position their organization to deal effectively with the many ensuing challenges. The challenge this study addresses is that of rapid technological innovation and its impact on organizational culture, work processes, communication patterns, and supervisory relationships.

There is dearth of academic studies to explore the relationship and influence of social media on leading and managing public sector organizations in China. There are some studies on social media and leadership in private sector context, nonetheless, specifically about the impact of social media on leadership in public sector organizations is scarce. This study seeks to explore how the executives in public sector organizations in Lanzhou city use social media for organizational and personal purposes; and how they lead and manage their human resources in the contemporary era of smart devices.

Since the research is exploratory, the specific research questions are as follows:

i   What leadership style officials in public sector organizations are adopting to manage their employees and organizations?
ii   To what extent they use the social media to connect with their teams and whether social media can be helpful or hamper their work performance?

This study explores the new leadership role in public sector organizations in the city of Lanzhou. Compared to the western world, leaders of Chinese organizations exhibit distinctly different leadership narratives and styles to achieve results-oriented success. The results of this study will be useful for understanding the subtleties of leadership in China, and guide the practicing public officials in embracing new challenges of leadership; especially related with the use of technology and social media at work. In addition, the study calls for having a comprehensive policy in organizations to deal with the emerging issues of cyber and social media.

Literature review

The study of leadership is always insightful and intriguing as it deals directly with human behavior and emotions. Albeit the primitive concept of leading and leadership had been existed in human civilizations from ancient times, nevertheless, the industrial revolution has triggered the systematic study of leadership and its various facets in organizational context. And now the study of leadership has risen to the level that it is now among the most researched concepts in behavioral sciences (Gavino and Portugal, 2013). A wealth of literature is available on almost every aspect of leadership, especially in the private sector, but also to a lesser extent in the public sector.

The theory of 'New Public Management' (Osborne and Gaebler, 1992) has strengthened the relationship between leadership in the public and private domains, and has resulted in application of termonology from the private sector being used also in the public sector. Examples include transformational, transactional, inspirational, and charistmatic leadership (Osborne and Gaebler, 1992; Vermeeren et al., 2013).

Leadership theories

In the 1840s, Scottish historian and writer Thomas Carlyle proposed the 'Great Man theory', which entailed that history can be largely explained by the impact of 'great men', or heroes – highly influential individuals who by virtue of their personal charisma, intelligence, wisdom, or political skill shaped the history of the world – like Napoléon Bonaparte, Eisenhower and Churchill etc. Nonetheless, in 1860 Herbert Spencer (1820–1903), an eminent sociologist, came up with the staunch criticism of the Carlyle's theory by asserting that the great men are great because of the situation and circumstances that enabled them to be great leaders (Changing Minds, 2015; Leadership Central, 2015; Wikipedia, 2015). Both Carlyle and Spencer's approaches to leadership remained the centre of leadership discourse throughout the nineteenth century and early twentieth century. The Great man theory also suggests that the leaders are born, not made, which opened a never ending debate on whether leaders are really born or can be made. Behavioural psychologists negate the notion asserting that the leadership skills can come through education, training, experience, surroundings and so on.

Kurt Lewin (1890–1947) identified three leadership styles which still dominate the locus of leadership style (i.e.) Autocratic, participatory or democratice and 'laissez-faire' leadership (Lewin et al., 1939). The Autocractic or Authoritarian is a leader who uses coercive force or authority to achieve the desired goals. This leadership sytle is generally considered to be undesirable in a civilized world. The second style is a participatory or democratic style of leadership. As the name suggests, the leader in this style involves his/her team, employees or folllowers in decision-making processes to build consensus. These decision-making processes, by necessity, sometimes take significant time to get everyone on board and getting everyone on the same page. The third style Lewin describes is the Laissez-faire stype of leadership. This is also called as free-reign or easy-going as these kind of leaders are generally lenient, flexible and carefree about the task, goal, or purpose at hand.

In 1960s, Blake and Mounton (1964) proposed their seminal leadership and managerial grid that measures leadership styles in two dimensions – concern for results and task, and concern for people. It includes five key managerial and leaderhsip styles: impoverished, country club, middle of the road, authoritarian, and team.

The situational leadership style proposed by Hersey and Blanchard (1969, 1977) asserts that leaders should adapt a leadership style based on the development style (or level and ability) of followers and how ready and willing the follower is to perform required tasks as well as keep in view the situation at hand. This leadership style became popular because of its practicability in real situations. Many leaders adopt this style to tackle the complexe issues and uncertain situations (Pawel, 2013).

In 1978, James MacGregor Burns first introduced the concept of transformational leadership, which later become the basis of this current leadership research. Burns (1978) suggests that transformational leadership is a process in which leaders and followers help each other to advance to a higher level of morale and motivation.

Transformational theory is an enlighted leadership theory which seeks to make tomorrow better, it endeavors to instill vision and pupose in employees. It is based on the philosophy of motivating and galvanizing employees and followers to get the desired results. As the name suggests, transactional theory largely deals with the transactional, generic, and administrative kinds of activities a leader does. Burns transformational theory was later further refined and expaned by Bass and Avolio based on the impact that it has on followers. He emphasized that transformational leaders need to gain trust, respect and followership from their followers (Bass and Avolio, 1997, 2000; Burns, 1978; Zigurs, 2002).

Social media

The importance of social networking gained popularity in the 1980s when managers who had a wide social cricle were considered to be effective managers (Pawel, 2013). The notion that people and relationship skills are critical to leadership and management extends into networking through social media. While conventional face-to-face interaction and meeting with people is still important, networking through social media is cost effective and can help connect many people at the same time (Pawel, 2013; Tredgold, 2014; Zaccaro and Bader, 2002).

The power of social media is sufficiently strong and overarching that none can escape from it (Tredgold, 2014). A leader or a manager who is not familiar with social media may considered a conventional or orthodox person. Indeed, one of the factors of success of today's leaders is their ability to effectively use social media and social networking for their personal and organizational benefits. It's convenient, cost-effective, and less time consuming because there is no need of direct interaction with other members (Pawel, 2013). Social media can also be used to connect with the employees and teams, provide them timely support, input and feedback. It's also becoming a popular tool to galvanize and motivate employees; as employees would be delighted to receive appreciation from the boss through a post on their social media page (Tredgold, 2014; Zaccaro and Bader, 2002).

Given the robust advancement in information and communication technology, the conventional leadership traits of charismatic, inspirational, authentic leaders have been transformed into a new kind of leader that can be called an 'e-leader' (Avolio and Kahai, 2003; Duarte and Snyder, 2006; Zaccaro and Bader, 2002). Now the physical presence of a leader in front of the followers, employees, and teams is not necessary; the new technology can handle it better. Sitting thousands of miles away, a leader can address his/her employees and share their future plans of action (Avolio and Kahai, 2003; Korzynski, 2013; Zigurs, 2002). Leaders and managers who can master social media skills will be able to significantly increase their influence (Tredgold, 2014) and significantly benefit their personal as well as professional life (Duarte and Snyder, 2006).

Increasingly now, executives (both public and private) are connecting with their employees and teams through virtual plateforms; saving cost, time and doing it in a convenient way. Given the fast-paced developments, challenges, and the size of tasks at hand, leaders find they can't afford to spent so much time in conventional boardroom style meetings; they find success in managing entire projects from a distance and interact with the followers or team members using information technology (Avolio and Kahai, 2003). This is a new way of doing work and it differs from the past in many ways. Hence a new barometer of leadership effectiveness has emerged which recognizes those who frequently use social media for organizational and personal networking.

Social media has provided open access for citizens and customers of a product to share their grievances, feedback, or opinion about the quality of civic services or the products instantly. Not only they can lodge complaints, but they can also share best practices and suggestions through online platforms, blogs, virtual communities etc. (Tredgold, 2014). In the US from the mid-2000s onwards there was an increase in the number of public sector organizations using one or more social media platforms to engage the public.

Duarte and Snyder emphasized that contemporary leaders need to learn new things and be able to use new technology for the benefit of the organization (2001). McKinsey and Company have identified six social media skill sets every leader needs to personify: (a) leader as producer, creating and compiling content; (b) leader as distributor, leveraging dynamics of dissemination; (c) leader as a recipient, managing communication overflow; (d) leader as adviser and orchestrator, driving strategic social-media utilization; (e) leader as architect, creating an enabling organizational infrastructure; and (f) leader as analyst, staying ahead of the curve (McKinsey and Company, 2015).

Theoretical framework

The modern era is characterized by a proliferation of gadgets, tools and technologically innovative equipment. Everyone is affected both directly and indirectly, and public leaders are no exception. This technology revolution has also affected leading and managing organizations, both public and private alike. Private sector organizations generally keep abreast of technological advancements in order to gain an edge in fierce competition. On the other hand, public organizations, having strong hierarchical control, centralized decision-making, and much red-tape inhibit adaption of new technology. Although public organizations are comparatively slow to adopt new trends, they nevertheless do accrue some benefits of new technology in their own way.

Among the host of challenges faced by organizations today, one of the most critical is to develop a new breed of leaders (Johannessen and Skålsvik, 2013) to cope up with the emerging and complex issues. Leaders need new sets of skills and competencies that were not required twenty or 25 years ago including being skillful in technology, social media, and social networking. Leaders now require not only the conventional traits and qualities of leadership such as charisma, inspirational and motivational skills, strategic vision, but also need technological expertise and the ability to use social media for carrying out the organizational tasks in an efficient and effective manner.

Among the variety of available instruments to assess leadership behaviors, we have chosen Bass and Avolio's (1994, 2000, 2004) multifactor leadership questionnaire (MLQ – also known as MLQ 5X). The questionnaire measures three aspects of leadership style: transformational, transactional, and passive/avoidant.

Keeping in view of overarching theme of social media and leadership, we employ the following conceptual model:

The model illustrates that the public leadership behavior is directly and indirectly affected by the extend to a leader use social media for carrying out day-to-day organizational tasks such as conducting meetings, project planning, execution, use of social media which all adds up to leadership effectiveness. The model shows that the leadership style of public leaders and the use of social media are independent variables. These independent variables combine together with the internal and external elements (extraneous variables and moderator) to influence leadership effectiveness.

The theoretical model tests the notion that in order to succeed in the modern era, public officials not only need to have an appropriate leadership style, but also need to be social media savvy. The underlying reason is that today's workforce is well informed and wants to stay connected with social media. The model illustrates that public leadership behavior is directly and indirectly affected by the extent to which a public official use social media for carrying out day-to-day organizational tasks such as conducting meetings, project planning, execution, and the use of social media. All this adds up to leadership effectiveness. In a nutshell, the study revolves around two important elements: (a) the leadership style of public leader, and (b) the ability of the leader to effectively use social media to carry out organizational tasks.

Hypotheses

H_{a1} Public sector officials in Lanzhou city adopt a 'transformational leadership style' to manage their employees and organizations.

H_a1_o Public officials in Lanzhou are 'passive/avoidant'.

H_a2 Public officials in Lanzhou are social media savvy and they use it for various purposes (i.e. social, organizational and personal).

H_a3 Excessive use of social media in offices during work hours impinges work performance.

Operational definition of the terms

i   Leadership; the leadership role exercised by the mid-level and upper-middle level managerial employees in public sector organization in Lanzhou city, including but not limited to, planning, directing, hiring/firing, controlling and leading employees in their respective departments. Excluded are the CEOs, GMs, director generals (DGs) of the large organizations in this sampling frame, as their role mostly of strategic nature, whereas our focus is on mid-level managers and departmental heads who play leadership roles in day-to-day affairs of their organizations.

ii Social Media; the social networking and communication websites, applications and apps widely used and legally permissible in mainland China, such as 'WeChat, QQ, Weibo, LinkedIn etc.' Since the well-known social networking sites such as Facebook, Tweeter, Instagram and Snapchat etc. are officially banned in PRC, they are therefore excluded from the study.

Data and methodology

This is an exploratory study and employs the survey method of research. The empirical data for the study has been garnered through the questionnaire of middle and upper-middle level managerial officers of the public sector organizations in Lanzhou city, and the unit of analysis is individuals.

In order to test the validity and reliability of the research instrument, the research tool has been pre-tested as a pilot study on a small sample of full time MPA and MPA Executive students who work fulltime in various government departments in Lanzhou city. Based on the pilot study, some minor modifications have been made to the questionnaire, so as to make it more succinct, clearer and objective.

The questionnaire consists of total 19 close-ended questions, excluding the demographic and personal information. The questionnaire uses a 5-point Likert scale scored from 1 as 'strongly disagree/never true' to 5 as 'strongly agree/always true'. The research tool for the leadership style portion of the questionnaire has been adopted from the widely used leadership instrument known as 'multifactor leadership questionnaire (MLQ 5X)' proposed by Bass and Avolio (1994, 2000, 2004). The MLQ model measures the leadership on three important aspects: transformational, transactional and passive/avoidant leadership styles. Since there are no existing authentic and test instruments to measure social media usage, we designed one for this study. The leadership style portion of the questionnaire consists of nine closed-ended questions, whereas there are 10 questions related with the social media usage. The questionnaire is bi-lingual (i.e. English and Chinese) to make it convenient for the respondents to better understand and respond to the questions. It has been designed to be mindful of the cultural, socio-political context, and the unique hierarchical structure of public sector organizations in China.

A stratified random sampling method has been applied to ensure a representative sample from the target population (i.e. governmental officials working in various departments in Lanzhou city). A total of 300 questionnaires were distributed, from which two 230 were returned yielding a response rate of 76.66%. Twenty-two questionnaires were incomplete, so they were rejected. There were 208 completely filled out questionnaires giving a sample size of 208. The data has been analyzed using the Statistical Package for Social Sciences (SPSS).

Results and discussion

Results

The survey data has been statistical tested using the linear regression model (for details about statistical analysis, please see Tables 5.1 and 5.2). The reliability of the research instrument has been determined by calculating Cronbach's Alpha which is an average of .623, which is satisfactory.

Results of leadership style cues

As shown in the Figure 5.1, the linear regression model gives average mean as 4.06 and average median as 4.46, as 57.2% respondents 'strongly agree', 29.8% 'agree', whereas 12.5% give neutral response. This construe that the leaders fairly often, or even frequently, go beyond self-interest for the good of the team, and

Table 5.1 Cronbach's alpha

Reliability Statistics

Cronbach's Alpha	Cronbach's Alpha Based on Standardized Items	N of Items
.623	.589	9

Table 5.2 Item statistics

Item Statistics

	Mean	*Std. Deviation*	*N*
Trnf-1	4.44	.726	208
Trnf-2	3.98	.633	208
Trnf-3	4.38	.825	208
Trnf-4	4.17	.916	208
Trnf-5	3.88	.857	208
Trnsc-6	4.35	.820	208
Trnsc-7	2.46	.735	208
PA-8	1.59	.607	208
PA-9	1.89	.628	208

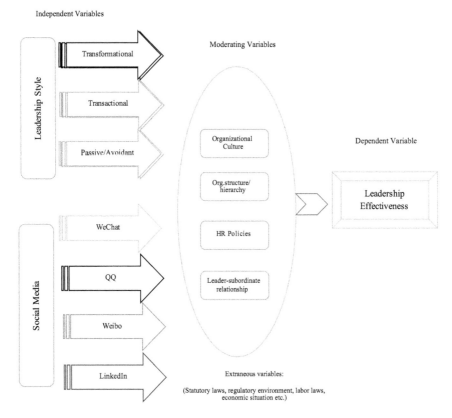

Figure 5.1 Conceptual model

(source: authors)

they adopt the transformational leadership style in managing their employees and carrying out the organizational tasks. This is one of the vital component of transformational leaders' traits. This supports the hypothesis H_a1 which entails that the public sector officials in Lanzhou city adopt a 'transformational leadership style' to manage their employees and organizations.

The responses about whether or not leaders take into consideration the moral and ethical consequences while making decisions, demonstrates positive results, as 17.30% responded 'strongly agree' and 64.42% responded 'agree', whereas 16.84 show neutral responses, as shown in the Figure 5.2. Just a small fraction of respondents (1.44%) 'disagree' to the question.

The results for the question of whether they want to help their subordinates and peers help grow and learn the necessary skills to excel in their career shows a mean of 3.87 and a median of 4.00, as shown in the Figure 5.3. This suggest that the leaders have a tendency to help others to develop their strengths and competencies.

The responses to the question of whether the leader assigns clear performance indicators and goals, indicates positive results as the mean is 4.34 and the median is 5.00, as shown in Figure 5.5. Hence, we can conclude that the leaders often clearly assign performance goals, and make sure that the team and subordinates understand the performance expectations.

The question about whether leaders keep track of their mistakes had interesting responses. The mean of 2.46, and the median of 3.00, means that the leaders are moderate in taking the record of their mistakes, as shown in Figure 5.5. In other words, leaders sometimes keep track of their mistakes. Nonetheless, the higher score on this indicates a transactional leadership trait.

The responses to the question of whether the leaders wait for the things to go wrong, gives negative responses, which indicates that the young officials and leaders are not 'Passive/ Avoidant'; rather they are active and proactive in managing

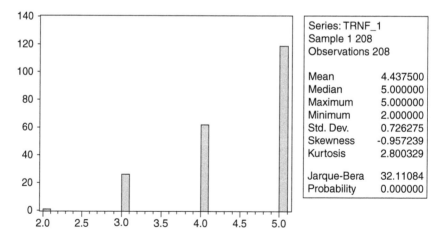

Figure 5.2 Showing the responses of the participants to the question: '*I go beyond self-interest for the good of the group*'

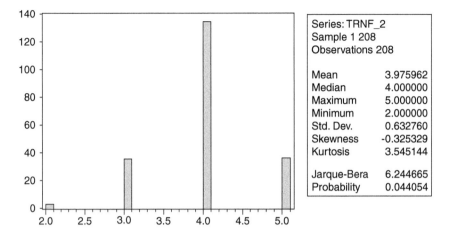

Figure 5.3 Shows the responses of the participants to the question: *'I consider the moral and ethical consequences of decisions'*

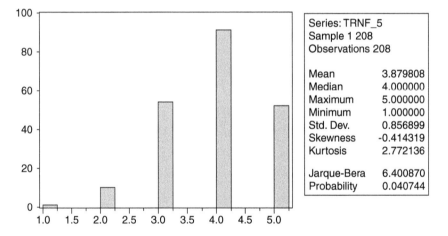

Figure 5.4 Shows the responses of the participants to the question: *'I help others to develop their strengths'*

the tasks. This rejects the Null hypothesis H_a1_o, that states that 'public officials in Lanzhou are passive/avoidant'.

Hence, we can infer that the majority of leaders in public sector organizations in Lanzhou will not wait until things go wrong, rather they take proactive or preemptive actions in order to avoid things going wrong. A high score on this question could have indicated that the leaders are passive and avoid taking proper steps and actions to prevent things going wrong. Not acting promptly could also

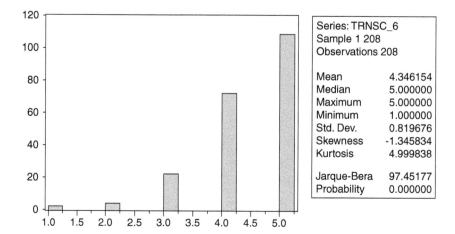

Figure 5.5 Illustrates the responses to the question: '*I make clear what one can expect to receive when performance goals are achieved*'

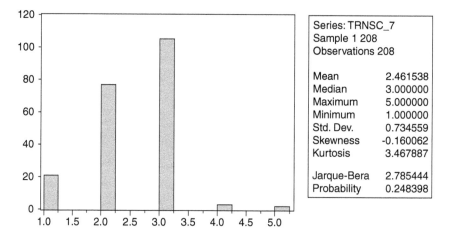

Figure 5.6 Shows the responses to the question: '*I keep track of all mistakes*'

point to a lackluster attitude that sometimes results in disastrous consequences. Nevertheless, the results are positive in this case and portray an optimistic picture about mid-level departmental heads and employees.

Results of social media usage cues

The data gleaned from the public sector officers in Lanzhou city reveals that the majority of the respondents 'agree' (68.8%) that they use indigenous social networking platforms on and off for various purposes. As shown in Figure 5.8,

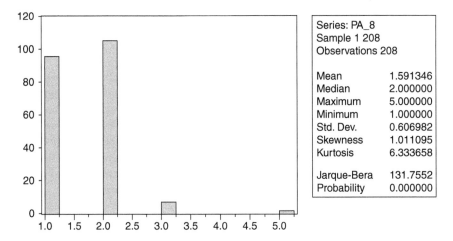

Figure 5.7 Responses to the question: *'I wait for things to go wrong before taking action'*

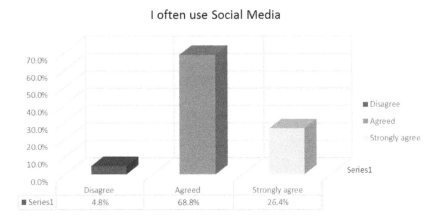

Figure 5.8 Shows the responses of the participants about whether or not they frequently connect with social media.

26.4% 'strongly agree' to connect with the social media; while a fraction of the respondents (only 4.8%) 'disagree' that they use any form of social media.

This seconds the H_a2 that hypothesize that the public officials in Lanzhou city are social media savvy and they use it for various purposes (i.e. social, organizational and personal). Moreover, this also shows the widespread popularity of the social media platforms amongst public sector officials and demonstrates that they stay connected with their teams, bosses, friends and family through social media.

The responses to the question of 'how social media has affected your life', 41% of responded believe that it made life both easy and difficult, 11% say it made life quite difficult and busy; whereas 23% responded in favor of social media and said it made life comfortable and convenient, and 25% are of the opinion that it made access to information possible, shown in Figure 5.9.

The question about whether or not 'the excessive use of Social Media in offices hampers the work performance', the responses are somehow mixed. As shown in Figure 5.10, 11% of respondents 'strongly agree', and 38% 'agree' that continuous use of social media in workplaces hampers their performance; whereas 28% are neutral and they are not sure about the disruption in work performance due to social media. However, there are some people who tend to 'disagree' (22%) with this notion. This supports H_a3 which hypothesize that 'excessive use of social media in offices during work hours impinges work performance'.

Hence, though responses are kind of mixed, majority of the respondents are of the opinion of excessive and relentless use of social media during the work hours impinges the work performance.

On question of type of social media use, the majority responded to use WeChat (69%) and QQ (63%) in Lanzhou city, as shown in Table 5.3. Weibo is another social media network people often logged-in to (21%). LinkedIn, the widely used professional networking site in western countries and elsewhere, seems less popular in a relatively smaller city of China, nonetheless; 11% responded intermittently using LinkedIn to connect with professionals of their field.

Social media is used for various purposes and broadly we categorized into three (i.e.) social, organizational and personal purposes. Accordingly, LinkedIn is primarily used for professional and personal networking (47 responses). Whereas WeChat and QQ is almost equally used for personal (189, 185) as well as social

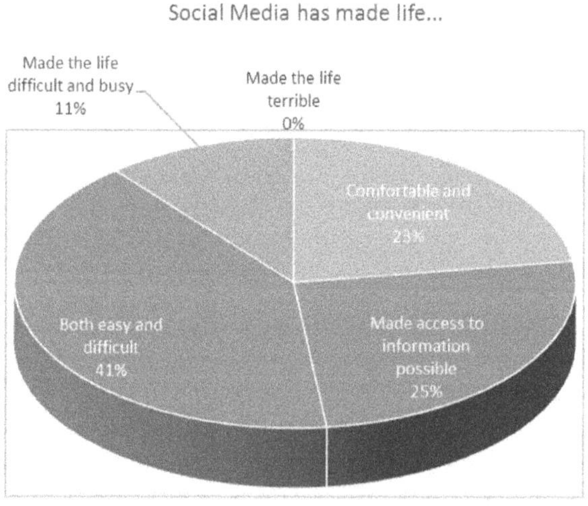

Figure 5.9 Displays how the respondents feel about the impact of social media on their lives.

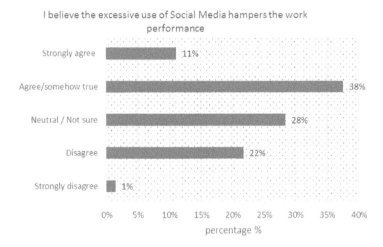

Figure 5.10 Displays the responses of participants whether or not excessive use of social media has hampered their work performance.

Table 5.3 Shows the types of social media platforms frequently used by officials

Type of Social Media	Frequency	Percentage
WeChat	144	69%
QQ	132	63%
Weibo	44	21%
LinkedIn	23	11%

networking purposes (193, 191). To lesser extent (45, 55), both networks are also used for organizational purposes such as disseminating information and news related to the services of their organizations and connecting with citizens to get their feedback. The results display that other social media, such as Weibo is mostly used for social networking purposes (103).

Figure 5.12 below shows the usage of social media for various purposes. Most responses were in favor of connecting with friends and family (87% and 85% respectively). A bunch of responses shows that social media is widely used for disseminating information and public relations (71%). Other significant usage in offices are connecting with team and employees (63%), getting feedback from clients (59%) and connecting with the top management (56%). To a relatively lesser extent, it is also used for other purposes like e-government (37%) and improving work processes and increasing efficiency (20%).

The data also unfolds that the social media is quite popular amongst the officials, especially the middle level managers, and they are well versed in using it for various purposes.

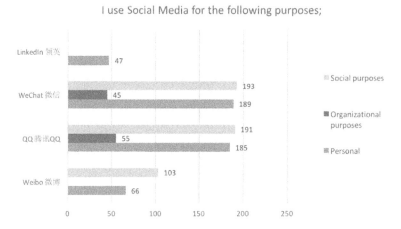

Figure 5.11 Gives a snapshot of social media usage for social, organizational and personal purposes.

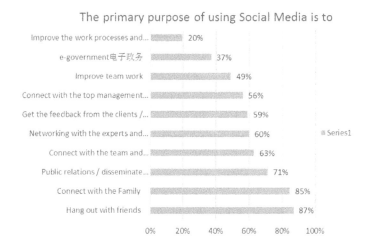

Figure 5.12 Exhibits social media usage for various purposes.

The data gathered also reflected that a staggering 4% say they have a comprehensive policy of social media covering virtually everything, nonetheless; 20% of the responses show that the organizations have a policy regarding social media but not a comprehensive one; 5% are of the opinion that the policy-making is under consideration, and 30% negate there exists any policy in their organizations. Bulk of people (40%) do not know about the existence of any policy for social media use in their organizations.

The responses regarding the 'risk associated with the social media use', 39% respondents think there is some kind of risk associated with social media use.

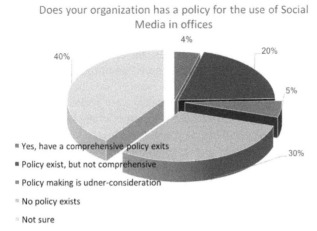

Does your organization has a policy for the use of Social Media in offices

- Yes, have a comprehensive policy exits
- Policy exist, but not comprehensive
- Policy making is udner-consideration
- No policy exists
- Not sure

Figure 5.13 Shows responses regarding whether their organizations have a policy for usage of social media in workplaces.

However, 25% believe there is 'no' risk attached with using social media, whereas 37% are not aware of any risk associated with the use of social media or have no specific opinion about this question.

Discussion

Leading and leadership being a dynamic phenomenon of human behavior, varies across cultures, geographical boundaries, socio-economic segments and much more on the contextual factors. Yet while discussing and contemplating leadership styles, an obvious question pops up: *is there one best way of leading or ideal leadership style?* While scholars responded to this question in many ways and some put weigh on transformational leadership as being forward looking, innovative and progressive way of leading. Nevertheless, majority of scholars agree to the notion that the leadership and leading need to be weigh in based on contextual and situational factors, as Burns (1978) asserts that there is no single best way of leadership and suggests that effective leaders use a combination of different styles that he calls it situational leadership style.

Morality and ethical values are engrained in the Confucian teachings and the public officials are expected to uphold them at all times. However, being a developing and emerging country, many administrative, managerial and bureaucratic functions are still evolving and have been marred by inefficiencies and news reports of corruption surfacing in the PRC. Nonetheless, the responses to the question of taking moral and ethical considerations in decision-making shows that the public officials are concerned about the moral and ethical consequences of the decisions they made. We can infer from this that their decision-making process is systematic and logical, and they account themselves for the decisions they make. They are optimistic about their future, and they have a high spirit to continue rising high. The results also imply that the leaders are frequently reflecting upon themselves and the decisions they made; they fairly and objectively evaluate their decisions and remain cautious and extra-careful about their future decisions. They learn from their mistakes, and refine and improve their decision-making. This reflects a critical trait of transformational leaders to continuously learn and improve.

Employee development, though not taken very seriously in organizations in the PRC, particularly the public sector which is often ascribed to be under the shackles of bureaucracy and having a top-down hierarchical structure. This often forestalls learning, creativity and openness to feedback and even positive criticism. However, the findings show that at least there is a feeling and desire for creating and harnessing a learning culture, though practically it is not easy to do so in public sector organizations given the rigid hierarchical structures and abundance of red tape.

While in rest of the world popular social media such Facebook, Twitter, Instagram, SnapChat are increasing their numbers and adding features to their existing portals; the indigenous social networking platforms such as WeChat, QQ, Weibo etc. are gaining a strong foothold in the PRC, and individuals, businesses, governmental agencies, and even the small shop owners and taxi drivers are offering services online. And now these networks such as WeChat and Alipay are not just confined to social networking, they are offering a wide spectrum of services, ranging from virtual wallet (online money transfer and payments), paying utility bills, buying online goods, movie tickets, calling taxi to even mutual fund investment; you name it and they have it. They incorporated virtually all the features one could desire to be on a smartphone and social media platforms. It is predicated by research and consultancy firms including McKinsey that social media usage will soar much higher in the years ahead. Hence, the world today is transformed by the power of technology and social media.

Nonetheless, there is little research on leadership behavior and online social networking in the Chinese context. However, results drawn from other countries suggest that leaders tend to connect well with diverse kinds of people to leverage both organizational and personal benefits (Pawel, 2013). Undeniably, social media has emerged as a powerful force which shapes our thinking and the way people interact with one another. Therefore, our research supports previous research being conducted in other countries and organizational settings.

While there are significant benefits for employees being social media savvy, there are also drawbacks to excessive use of social media in workplaces, especially revolving around sharing personal posts, comments, and counter-comments in a never-ending chain of communication which hampers the work performance of employees.

Undoubtedly, social media has reshaped social and organizational culure and enabled both private and public sector organziations to directly connect with citizens (Miller, 2005). However, this has posed some risk too in that some unscrupulous people may use fake identifications to deceive people and perpetrate hoaxes in the name of organizations. These cause loss of confidentiality and intrusion in personal life and privacy issues; but more importantly, social media sites are more prone to hacking. Organizations therefore need to be extra vigilant and careful about such fraudulent acts. Even so, they should not give up using the most powerful tool of the time to connect with their customers, clients, and citizens.

Public sector websites are a useful tool to provide relevant, timely and accurate information to the public, which otherwise would be provided by traditional means which require a lot time and effort. In addition, traditional websites are typically not updated in a timely fashion. Also, they are usually taken for granted and not seriously and carefully managed. Another pitfall assocated with websites of public sector organizations is that they are frequently static websites with very few being interactive to provide live information. This trend has, however, been supplemented only recently by the use of social media, which is, by definition, interactive (Dubois and Bray, 2015).

Needless to say that the success or failure of the organization is largely dependent on its leadership. The organizations fortunate enough to have wise, visionary, and forward-looking leaders have potential to soar far higher than those who do not. Successful leaders of today have a combination of transformational leadership traits as well as being social media savvy. They can use social media and technology effectively for personal as well as organizational excellence.

Summary of key finding and recommendations

i   The empirical data shows that may officials in public sector organizations in Lanzhou city prefer to use transformational leadership styles in carrying out their tasks. Some opt for a transactional style because it is hard to depart from the status quo. The young and middle-level officials, being well educated and from good institutions tend to opt for transformational leadership style. Others use a blend of both transformational and transactional style of leadership, what Hersey and Blanchard (1969, 1977, 1999) call a 'situational leadership style'; carefully switching to both ends and adopting an approach suited to the situation at hand.

ii   The study results show that the majority of public officials in Lanzhou are well versed in the use social media and they use it for various purposes including connecting with family and friends, however; its use in organizational purposes is still scant, and needs to to be improved in order to provide timely information and better services to the citizens.

iii Furthermore, the results also indicate that online social networking platforms are gaining more and more popularity in China. They are primarily conceived of as serving only social and personal networking purposes. They are, however, being used to some extent for organizational purposes (such as connecting with teams, employees and boss, and dissemination of information).

iv   Public leaders, like leaders in the private sector, play a significant role. The impact of the decisions made by public leaders are often more far reaching and have a more prominent direct and indirect impact on the lives of people than decisions made in private sector. Since the public sector is one of the largest employers in most countries, including China, and since the role of public sector organizations is inescapable from people's lives; a study to get to know the leadership dynamics in public sector organization might provide useful insight.

v   The public officials in Lanzhou city adopt the transformational leadership style in managing and leading their people and organizations.

vi   There is positive relationship between the transformational role of leadership and leadership effectiveness.

vii   Some leaders still believe in transactional role of leadership, these are mostly older people who are unwilling to change the status quo.

viii   Social media is a popular platform to connect with friends & family as well as co-workers and teams. Nevertheless, its use for organizational purposes still needs to be enhanced.

Conclusion

Public leaders in the contemporary world need to have an array of skill sets, ranging from transactional skills to transformational as well as being social media savvy. Being only inspirational and having a charismatic personality is not sufficient in today's world. Technology has revolutionized everything we do including in how we exercise leadership. E-leaders and managers are well versed in emerging technologies and use it for appropriately personal as well as organizational purposes (Avolio, 2003). Moreover, employees now feel more comfortable connecting with their bosses through social media tools, rather than through personal meetings scheduled by appointment in a bureaucratic way.

The world witnessed a surge in social media use from mid-2010 and in China from 2008 forward. Now there is no escape, but rather a need to make a strategy to use it. The good news is that officials in Lanzhou are well aware and well versed in the use the social media for personal, social, and to some extent for organizational purposes. However, its use needs to be further expanded to enable general masses to get their desired information about government activities from social media. As the result of social media's user friendliness, people can easily acquaint themselves with the work of government without any extra effort. With the information boom, a new type of relationship is emerging, more powerful, flexible and effective – the social media relationship. Hence, the social media is a powerful tool for people to stay connected and stay informed.

Despite its benefits, there are some risks associated with the use of social media if not dealt with carefully including identity theft, hacking, privacy issues, and even the potential incitement of racism and violence.

There is great potential for future research in this area because it has not been explored in a Chinese context and because social media is taking an increasing place in our professional, social, and personal lives. Finally, successful leaders in the ever changing world need to be social media savvy and conversant in the use of prevelent technologies.

Acknowledgement

The authors sincere thank **Dr. Gary Larsen**, adjunct professor of Public Administration at the Portland State University and Lanzhou University, China, for his invaluable insights and guidance in completion of this research work. We also thank **Dr. Wang Xuejun**, associate professor, School of Management Lanzhou University for his continuous guidance and input.

References

Avolio, B. J. and Bass, B. M. (2004). Multifactor Leadership Questionnaire. Manual and sampler set. (3rd ed.) Redwood City, CA: Mind Garden.

Avolio, B. J., and Kahai, S. S. (2003). Adding "E" to E-leadership: How it may impact your leadership. *Organizational Dynamics*, 31(4), 325–338.

Bass, B. M., and Avolio, B. J. (1994). Improving organizational effectiveness through transformational leadership. Thousand Oaks: SAGE Publications.

Bass, B. M., and Avolio, B. J. (1997). *Full Range Leadership Development: Manual for Multifactor Leadership Questionnaire*. Palo Alto: Mind Gorden, Inc.

Bass, B. M., and Avolio, B. J. (2000). *MLQ Multifactor Leadership Questionnaire Sample Set: Technical Report, Leaders Form, Rater Form, and Scoring Key for MLQ From 5x-Short*. Redwood City: Mind Garden, 2nd edition.

Blak, R. R., and Mounton, J. S. (1964). *The Managerial Grid*. Houston, TX: Gulf.

Burns, J. M. (1978). *Leadership*. New York: Haper and Row.

Changing Minds (2015). 4 August, http://changingminds.org/disciplines/leadership/theories/great_man_theory.htm.

Chiu, C., Ip, C., and Silverman, A. (2015). *McKinsey Quarterly*, 30 August, www.mckinsey.com/insights/marketing_sales/understanding_social_media_in_china.

Crampton, T. (2015). Social media in China: The same, but different. *China Business Review*, 24 August, www.chinabusinessreview.com/social-media-in-china-the-same-but-different/

Dillman, D. A., Smyth, J. D., and Christian, L. M. (2014). *Internet, Phone, Mail, and Mixed-Mode Surveys: The Tailored Design Method*. San Francisco: Wiley, 4th edition.

Duarte, D. L., and Snyder, N. T. (2006). *Mastering Virtual Teams: Strategies, Tools, and Techniques That Succeed*. San Francisco: Wiley, 3rd edition.

Dubois, Corina, and Bray, A. D. (2015). Improving how social media informs leadership and public initiatives. *Digital Gov*, 24 August, www.digitalgov.gov/2015/03/18/improving-how-social-media-informs-leadership-and-public-initiatives/

Gavino, J. C., and Portugal, E. J. (2013). Leadership framework: A preliminary qualitative research using the critical incident method. *World Review of Business Research*, 3(4), 40–52.

Hersey, P., and Blanchard, K. H. (1969). Management of organizational behavior: Utilizing human resources. New Jersey: Prentice Hall.

Hersey, P., and Blanchard, K. H. (1977). Management of organizational behavior: Utilizing human resources. 3rd Ed. New Jersey: Prentice Hall

Internet live stats. (2016). *Internet user*. Retrieved from http://www.internetlivestats.com/internet-users/ Accessed on May 12, 2017.

Johannessen, J. A., and Skålsvik, H. (2013). The systemic leaders: New leaders in the global economy. *Emerald Insight*, 42(1), 13–34.

Korzynski, P. (2013). Online social networks and leadership: Implications of a new online working environment for leadership. *International Journal of Manpower*, 34(8), 975–994.

Kumar, R. (2005). *Research Methodology-a Step by Step Guide*. Thousand Oaks: SAGE Publications.

Leadership Central (2015). 4 August, www.leadership-central.com/great-man-theory.html#axzz3hocL7JjG.

Lewin, K., Lippit, R., and White, R. K. (1939). Patterns of aggressive behavior in experimentally created social climates. *Journal of Social Psychology*, 271–301.

McKinsey & Company Insights and Publications (2015). 5 August, www.mckinsey.com/insights/high_tech_telecoms_internet/six_social-media_skills_every_leader_needs.

Miller, M. (2005). The digital dynamic: How communications media shape our world. *The Futurist*, 39(3), 31–36.

Pawel, K. (2013). Online social networks and leadership. *International Journal of Manpower*, 34(8), 975–994.

Statista (2017). 1 October, www.statista.com/statistics/277586/number-of-social-network-users-in-china/

Tredgold, G. P. (2014). Are you connected? Leadership in the era of social media. *Development and Learning in*, 28(6), 9–11.

Vermeeren, B., Kuipers, B., and Steijin, B. (2013). Does leadeship style make a difference? Linking HRM, job satisfaction and organizational performance. *Review of Public Personnel Administration*, 34(2), 174–195. doi:10.1177/0734371X13510853.

Wikipedia (2015). *Great man theory*, 4 August, https://en.wikipedia.org/wiki/Great_Man_theory.

Zaccaro, S. J., and Bader, P. (2002). E-leadership and the challenges of leading E-teams: Minimizing the bad and maximizing the good. *Organizational Dynamics*, 31(4), 339–351.

Zigurs, I. (2002). Leadership in virtual teams: Oxymoron or opportunity? *Organizational Dynamics*, 31(4), 339–351.

Part 2

Inward and outward FDI

6 Chinese outward foreign direct investment

Strategies for international development

*Bruno Amann, Jacques Jaussaud
and Zhang Boqi*

Introduction

Cross-border investment is considered one of the most important strategies for multinational companies (MNCs) to penetrate new markets. Foreign Direct Investment (FDI) offers companies various advantages such as overcoming trade barriers, getting access to resources at reduced cost, enhancing R&D capabilities, benefiting from low corporate tax, etc. On a macro level, FDI is an important issue as far as economic development is concerned. Most countries try to attract FDI, as it may bring technology, capital, competences in management (Cheng and Kwan, 2000), job creation, and productivity gains into the host country (Meunier, 2012).

Along with their increasing involvement in global competition, Chinese MNCs have begun to expand their presence overseas, especially since the mid-1990s (Di Minin et al., 2012), becoming key global players in many industries. Chinese globalization owes much to the 'going global' (or 'go out') strategy promoted by the Chinese government since 1999, which encourages Chinese science-and-technology-intensive companies, particularly the successful ones, to globalize for both technology upgrading and brand building (OECD, 2008). By the end of 2015, the stock of China's outward direct investment surpassed US$ 1 trillion for the first time (Mofcom, 2016).[1] At the same time, China's outward foreign direct investments (OFDI) and Chinese MNCs are attracting increasing attention among international business (IB) scholars (Child and Rodrigues, 2005; Quer et al., 2015).

The authors collected various data about the enterprises from a large number of major national and international economic news organizations: French sources (Le Monde, Le Figaro, La Tribune, Libération, Les Echos, Le Parisien), Anglo-Saxon ones (PrivCo, Deutsche Welle, the Wall Street Journal, Reuters, Financial Times, Global Atlanta), and Chinese ones (Sina financial, Phoenix Finance, Dealglobe, Baidu Baijia, CNKI database, Wanfang Data, Cqvip Data). We completed the collected information by additional data drawn from the official sites of the different companies involved. This database helped us to better identify the strategies employed by a range of emerging Chinese MNCs during the last two decades. Finally, 12 particular Chinese MNCs have been researched for this chapter, due to the sufficiency and reliability of available information in respect of the companies

DOI: 10.4324/9781315102566-8

The study analyses the 12 Chinese enterprises and their internationalization processes. We investigate whether their internationalization behaviours conform to existing theoretical frameworks, namely the Uppsala stage model (Johanson and Vahlne, 1977, 2009), the Eclectic Paradigm (Dunning, 2001, 2006), the Linkage Leverage Learning (LLL) model (Mathews, 2006), and the 'Born Global' model (McDougall et al., 1994; Cavusgil and Knight, 2015) to mention the main ones, and the study will underline some particularities revealed by this research. These case analyses are divided into two parts: the first part is devoted to a range of companies that are well known and that have been broadly addressed in the management literature; the second part will cover less well known companies that we chose to underline the diversity of international strategies adopted by Chinese enterprises.

Well known cases from the international literature

Many Chinese cases have attracted the attention of scholars in international business. As will be seen, most of the cases were to some extent representative of one or the other of the existing theories such as Porter's international theories (Porter, 1990), the Uppsala stage model (Johanson and Vahlne, 1977, 2009), the Eclectic paradigm (Dunning, 2001, 2006), and so on. However, each of these enterprises had their own particular developmental path, which we will identify in this section.

Huawei – a Chinese telecommunications giant

Huawei is a private company founded in 1988 in Shenzhen that majored in telecommunication technology, product development, research and sales. By 2013, it had 146,000 employees and had generated income of RMB 204 billion in 2011.[2] In 1988, in the context of the expansion of the switch sector in Shenzhen, Ren Zhengfei, founder and President of Huawei, was chosen as a technical engineer to build Huawei's own proprietary technology.

Since 1998, more and more international companies have arrived in China such as Ericsson, Nokia and Motorola. They were soon key players, especially in the high-end telecommunications sector. Huawei had no choice but to adopt an internationalization strategy and focused more on markets rather neglected by international giants such as those in Central and Eastern Europe, Africa, and South and East Asia where there were a lot of opportunities and low entry barriers. Generally speaking, Huawei started to enter emerging markets which are more price than quality sensitive. Then, in 1999, Huawei focused on the European market, and in 2005 Huawei became an official supplier of BT (Britain Telecom). By then, Huawei had been largely accepted by mainstream communication operators as a reliable provider of services.

Back in 1996, Huawei made its first internationalization intervention by providing services to Hutchison Telecoms in Hong Kong. Then, Huawei entered the Russian market by founding an equity joint venture (JV) with 2 local partners in 1997 (Wu and Zhao, 2007). Subsequently, Huawei entered the other East and South European countries. In 1999, Huawei founded a research centre in India, where the same approach as in some Asian countries prevails. It entered Africa in 2000 (Wu and Zhao, 2007), a region with abundant natural resources and cheap labor. The African local governments provided various incentive policies to attract foreign investors as well. Huawei entered the African market with a price advantage of 20–30% over its other competitors (Peng, 2013).

Thus, up to now, Huawei has achieved US$ 22 billion of sales overseas, has created nine regional sections, 99 representative offices and technical/sales centres, and has provided services to up to 300 telecommunication operators. It is now the second largest telecommunications equipment provider in the world. However, due to the price competition strategy adopted by Huawei, and the negative image associated with Chinese products in terms of quality, Huawei has suffered setbacks against its competitors in international markets. Indeed, in technology-intensive sectors, the development of companies depends on their technological advances. Thus, Huawei founded a research centre in Stockholm (Huawei, 2013) in 2000 and various research centres in the US, notably the Silicon Valley one in 2001 (Larçon, 2008).

In 2001, Huawei entered the European market (firstly in Germany) with their 10GSDH which is an optical network product (Xiao and Liu, 2015). Then in 2003, it signed a contract with LDCom (a French telecommunications group) to build a national network.

Looking back on their internationalization process, Huawei had to adopt at first a low price strategy, starting with low-end products and gradually entered the mainstream market. In addition, Huawei also adopted a self-brand building strategy, while upgrading their technological capabilities and complemented this by taking advantage of the brand reputation of their partners.

With the strength they had exploited and developed through internalization, Huawei expanded their presence in the domestic market and enforced their local capabilities soon afterwards. In 2002, Huawei and 3COM created a JV (H3C) in Hangzhou (Zhu, 2008) and founded another JV (49% ownership), TD Tech, with Siemens in Beijing in 2004 (Deutsche Welle, 2004). In 2006, Huawei sold 49% of H3C's shares for US$ 8.8 billion, and then created a research centre with Motorola in Shanghai (Huawei, 2006). Then Huawei founded a JV (51%) with Symantec in Chengdu (Symantec, 2008), and another one with Global Marine, Huawei Submarine Networks, in Tianjin in 2007(Huawei, 2007b). In the same year, Huawei attained a global turnover of US$ 16 billion of which 72% came from the international market (Huawei, 2007a), compared to US$ 0.55 billion in 2002.

In 2011, Huawei acquired the whole share capital of Huawei Symantec by buying the remaining 49% (US$ 530 million) of shares from Symantec (Symantec, 2011). Despite establishing research centres and entering ventures with its partners, technological purchasing is also treated as a complementary method to gain access to certain technologies (Benoit, 2012).

As a high-end technology company, Huawei needs to attain economies of scale in order to cover its high R&D costs. This has been done through the internationalization process. In addition, as China is a developing country, it provides Huawei with a precedent in how to exploit foreign markets with similar levels of development to the one of its home country (Johanson and Vahlne, 2006). In terms of entry mode, Huawei has adopted a step-by-step internationalization process that started in Hong Kong and Russia, then moved to South America, East and South Asia, the Middle-east, Africa and finally Europe and the US.

Huawei's internationalization process is in line with classical international strategy: (1) Huawei had a cost advantage in the beginning, as do other Chinese companies. In order to take advantage of this strength, and to internalize it (Dunning, 2001, 2006), Huawei's investment mode was principally a greenfield mode; (2) Huawei has internationalized step-by-step (Johanson and Vahlne, 1977, 2009), and has developed a competitive advantage in terms of services and technological capabilities (in 2009, Huawei delivered its first LTE commercial telecommunications network to Telecom Italia); (3) With its own brand, Huawei has also succeeded in operating in developed markets: by the end of 2010, 45 out of the first 50 of the world's largest telecommunications operators are customers of Huawei.

However, while Huawei was successful in developing countries it was less successful in developed countries. Huawei's business activities depend too much on emerging markets with unstable institutional environments, which impacts on the sustainable development of the company. Finally, up to now, the lack of experience in developed markets and the high cost of acquiring that experience are the main obstacles to Huawei completing their internationalization process and going up the value chain (Porter, 2001).

Huawei's internationalization process fits principally with the Uppsala stage model process (Johanson and Vahlne, 2015). According to the Uppsala stage model process, the internationalization of a firm begins from the export mode to initialize their sales network and then goes on and builds strategic alliances (Dunning, 2015) with local partners for technological acquisitions, and is completed by the accumulation of resources and assets, including advanced managerial capabilities and international brands, especially the ability to coordinate and integrate resources efficiently. Finally, the firm will engage in FDI abroad to develop independent production, research and commercial facilities. In particular, Huawei attaches great importance to the development of research capabilities and has it as one of the main purposes of internationalization (Fu and Gong, 2011).

Similar to Huawei, ZTE is another Chinese manufacturer in the field of telecommunications, whose case we will review as follows.

ZTE – another giant in telecommunications – a state- owned entity

Founded in 1985, ZTE, a 'mixed-owned' enterprise (Milhaupt and Zheng, 2014),[3] is currently one of the largest listed companies in the telecommunications devices sector. Mixed-owned firms are partially privatized former state-owned firms under the reforms launched in 2006 by the State-owned Assets Supervision and Administration Commission of the State Council (SASAC).

Like other Chinese international companies, ZTE has a competitive advantage in price, but is weak in technological endowment and brand leverage. With the support of its domestic market, ZTE can offer lower prices in foreign markets compared to other suppliers. However, in order to be able to compete with other international competitors, ZTE is oriented to improve its technical capabilities as a primary step.

In order to do so, ZTE has founded research centres around the world (New Jersey, Santiago, Silicon Valley – ZTE, 2015) which aim to: (1) collect, track and deploy the foremost technology of the sector, which are considered as sources of innovation; (2) recruit local technological talents and make full use of local universities and their infrastructure to enlarge ZTE innovative capabilities; (3) source from advanced local research information to support their headquarters; (4) acquire through these research centres knowledge about the characteristics of local consumers' needs for the improvement of ZTE products and to prepare to enter foreign markets (Liu et al., 2010)

In addition to the creation of research centres, ZTE has also established jointly broad partnerships with several global operators in different countries (France, Spain, UK, Italy, South Africa, Brazil etc.). They founded research alliances with telecommunications devices suppliers around the world (e.g. Alcatel-Lucent, Maija Pesola and Dickie, 2005) and participated in various technological federations. They also created partnerships with universities and set up research agencies in host countries (e.g. Dresden University of Technology in 2010, ZTE, 2011).

In 2005, ZTE signed an agreement with Alcatel-Lucent for an OEM (Original Equipment Manufacturer) partnership, including technology-sharing in CDMA (ZTE, 2005). At the same time, ZTE also signed an agreement with Ericsson to cooperate in TD-SCDMA for China (ZTE, 2006). Such types of partnership were also launched with Cisco in the Asia Pacific region, Intel (Intel, 2005), Microsoft (Meisner, 2013), etc.

With such rapid progress made during this period, the number of ZTE's patent applications has ranked first in the world. ZTE's sales reached RMB 86.25 billion in 2011, in which international sales dominated with RMB 46.76 billion of the total (ZTE USA, 2012).

In 2015, ZTE increased its annual revenue up to RMB 100 billion, including selling 15 million mobiles devices in the US with a market share of 7.6%, as well as being ranked 4th in the market (ZTE, 2016).

ZTE also allocates more than 10% of their sales every year to R&D. They have 26,000 employees in the field of research, being 37.5% of the total (70,000 employees), in 19 research centres located in China, America, Sweden, France, etc.[4]

Going from an OEM service provider to a manufacturer with its own brand, ZTE succeeded in taking a significant market share in the US among the other international competitors. They initiated or participated in the elaboration of many sectoral and national norms. ZTE are involved in the next generation communications technological research in which they are the main contributor.[5]

Compared to Huawei's internationalization path, ZTE has a controlling owner which is the Chinese government, so their international achievements were not as good as Huawei's. However, ZTE could still make maximum use of national resources for their technological upgrading (and also resources from foreign countries). In the same way, ZTE's entry mode into international markets is dominated by the establishment of research centres: we found little about M&A or JV projects undertaken. In this regard, ZTE's internationalization approach seems to be more dependent on others than Huawei's to some extent.

In our opinion, ZTE's internationalization process could be partially explained by the OLI paradigm and the Uppsala stage model (Gaur and Kumar, 2010), as the ownership advantages in terms of financial capacity and in price helped them to tap into the overseas markets (locational advantage) by OEM means and then to upgrade and improve their technical capabilities (internalization advantage) through the establishment of several research centres internationally. In the OLI paradigm, firms enter overseas markets to exploit their competitive advantage which is not available to their foreign competitors. Through international markets, firms start to accumulate experience and expand their international activities to reduce their transaction costs and environmental risks abroad by the internalization process (Dunning, 1981, 1988). However, in the case of ZTE, domestic market support is evidently a source of its internationalization process. At the same time, the foreign acquired strategic assets also supported the domestic market. The continuing implications of the inside-out and outside-in (Welch and Luostarinen, 1993) internationalization process may be highly relevant to ZTE's international strategy (Prange, 2012; Prange and Bruyaka, 2016).

If Huawei and ZTE do not compete effectively at an international level, they need to catch up with developed economies' companies in the telecommunications sector. The following case study of Hai'er may be an example of a company that can compete in the global economy.

Hai'er – a global player in the household appliances industry

In the late 1990s, Hai'er, a private company, entered the international market when China was in the process of becoming a member of the World Trade Organization – WTO (H. Liu and Li, 2002). A that time, many other Chinese enterprises when abroad with the support of the 'going global policy' of Chinese authorities, turned back to China when they encountered difficulties on the international markets (Lu et al., 刘再起, 2014, in Chinese). During this period, Hai'er exported their products in the Middle East and in South-Asia markets under their own brand and in 1996, the first foreign factory was built as a joint-venture in Indonesia (Larçon, 2008).

The motivation for internationalization of Hai'er is not just to generate foreign reserves but also to build a brand. With such a vision, Hai'er has located their facilities in developed economies for brand building purposes (Meunier et al., 2014; Salidjanova, 2011) with a cost competitive advantage and then in developing regions for generating some externality effects (Richet, 2013). So Haier was partially an OEM provider in the early 1990s (Yi and Ye, 2003) but then they employed their own brand all along their internationalization process. Like the CEO of Hai'er said one day: 'Difficulties at first, good times after'.

Hai'er undertook to enter in the USA with only a cost advantage in 1999 while a number of US companies entered China using their ultimate technological advances to compete with domestic firms. However, Hai'er succeeded in introducing their products in a niche market in the US and then entered mainstream markets to compete with local firms.

Since 2005, after having acquired geographical configuration on a world scale, Hai'er adopted a strategy of global brand building for the localization of the conception, production, and marketing of their products in each country or region, which was quite different from other Chinese companies which were led by the OEM mode. This strategy helped Hai'er to achieve market shares in different countries with different local customer needs according to their culture and consumption characteristics. Customer loyalty towards the Hai'er brand was also reinforced.

Eventually, Hai'er started officially to internationalize their activity in the global economy and to compete in a relatively direct way with companies from developed countries in this sector such as Siemens, Samsung, General Electric, etc. In 2012, Hai'er acquired a part of the Sanyo Electric's business in Japan and South East Asia which resulted in a successful trans-cultural integration. Then Hai'er undertook an M&A project with Fisher & Paykel, a New Zealand high-end home appliances brand. Finally, the ongoing project with GE for the integration of its home appliances business was developed. All these projects with foreign partners led Hai'er to improve their capabilities in marketing, product development and production, etc. They especially helped in building Hai'er's core competencies in R&D and innovation which could enable Hai'er to be a global player in the international market according to the chairman, ZHANG Ruimin.[6]

The Hai'er group is the fourth biggest household appliances manufacturer in the world with 50 thousand employees in 30 countries dispersed in 240 entities and with a turnover of 100 billion yuan per year. Hai'er was considered to be the most valuable brand in China in 2008.

Hai'er started to sell abroad in 1992 with the installation of sales entities in foreign countries and then set their design and production facilities for the customization processing of their products in different regions. Formalized in 1998, the internationalization process of Hai'er was accomplished by 2005 and then the process of brand globalization started in 2006. The principal idea at that time was to customize their brand according to the needs of different countries. These steps were all comprised in the previously programmed Hai'er strategy which are respectively, the 'go out' for being in international markets, 'go inside' for joining and adapting in the network of the overseas markets, and 'go up' for being a leading manufacturer on the global stage.

At the beginning of their internationalization, Hai'er chose the most developed countries and regions as their first export destinations where they had practically no competitive advantage (the USA, Europe). They penetrated into niche markets, began to construct their network with local actors and improved their brand for the preparation of entering the markets of developing countries.

Their strategy can be defined as being composed of three steps: the first step, exportation for the brand to be recognized in the markets they target; the second, setting up foreign production units when a certain sales volume is attained; the third, brand building by using innovative capabilities. The establishment of Hai'er's production facilities permitted it to construct a network of local partners which is primordial for understanding the local environment in terms of jurisdiction, of the needs of local customers and of conventional practices and adapting their behavior accordingly.

The Hai'er's case is also in line with the classical theories, (the OLI paradigm and the Uppsala stage model). More particular in Hai'er's case is that, they planned to build a world famous brand and to be able to compete with the other major international players with their ultimate advantages which relied on their global research capabilities, integrated managerial capabilities and customized product lines for every region in the world, as Bartlett and Ghoshal (2002) suggested.

Hisense – owner of multiple famous brands in China

Hisense, a state-owned enterprise based in Shandong, officially founded in 1994, is one of the biggest manufacturers in the world in the fields of flat screen TV, appliances and mobile communication devices.

Hisense started their internationalization process through export agents from its creation, until 1997, when they acquired an independent export company while the Chinese authorities placed some artificial barriers to international trade. On the other hand, Hisense did not have the capabilities for international expansion, so most of its sales were realized in mainland China. For foreign markets, they preferred to be an OEM service provider.

In 2000, Hisense signed an agreement with Hitachi for cooperation on the third generation telecommunications CDMA project.[7] The partnership was then extended to Qualcomm, Shandong University and Tsingdao University.

During 2001–2007, as China entered the WTO, Hisense initiated their first global strategy as they had broken through certain technological bottlenecks. They started to focus on foreign markets, especially in Africa and Australia. As their first overseas production base, Hisense acquired in 2001 a factory from Daewoo in South Africa for US$ 4 million after having achieved a 10% of market share in that country (Larçon, 2008). At the end of this period, Hisense were realizing more and more profits through their export facilities.

Hisense set up research centres, production facilities and representative offices in various locations in the world. Their products were increasingly displayed in East and South Asia, the Middle east, even in some developed countries and regions such as Australia (Hisense Australia in Melbourne in 2006)[8] and Europe (TV production base in Hungary in 2004[9] and TV assembly facilities in France in 2005,[10] a research centre in the Netherlands in 2007[11] and then moved into Germany[12] in 2011). Notably their sales in South Africa and the Middle East in which they have two subsidiaries (M&A in South Africa, JV in Algeria, both in 2001) are considerable (单雷, Shan, 2009, in Chinese). Hisense became involved more frequently in global competition. Their managerial capabilities were also increased through their partnerships with global actors including research institutes, through sectoral alliances and through cooperation agreements all over the world.

Since 2007, based on their existing export facility, Hisense integrated Kelon's[13] overseas sales channels. The latter was one of the largest Chinese white goods manufacturers which was acquired by Hisense through M&A in 2006. Thereafter, Hisense started to integrate global resources and focus more on international markets with their own brand and extended their sale network in America, Canada, Italy etc.

In 2008, Hisense set up a JV with local partner (Helwan) in Egypt.[14] In 2009, Hisense acquired a startup company, JAMDEO, in Canada which was transformed into a research centre (Hisense, 2013). In 2010, Hisense set up a research centre in Atlanta (Trevor, 2011) where 65% of employees are local (24 US employees of 37 in total).[15]

During 2012/2013, Hisense acquired Archcom and Multiplex respectively and transformed them into research centres in Los Angeles. Another acquisition from SJ Micro was realized in Silicon Valley in 2012 which was also a research centre (Hisense, 2013). In 2015, Hisense acquired a Mexican production base from Sharp (SmartBrief, 2015) at a cost of US$ 23.7 million and at the same time they set up an assembly factory in the Czech Republic (PMR, 2015).

During the last 20 years, Hisense continuously improved their research capabilities through international cooperation and M&A in developed regions. They continuously enlarged their production facilities. On the other hand, Hisense also improved their managerial capabilities through M&A and they adapted their managerial practices and transferred them to some of their foreign facilities. More importantly, they have established a strategic relationship with Whirlpool, the leading appliances maker, for a JV in China to deliver world class appliances in the country and share research and technology (Benton Harbor, 2008). They have also sponsored some sport clubs and competitions in Australia to reinforce their brand leverage. They also undertook the sponsorship of the European Football Championship in France in 2016.[16]

To the best of our knowledge, Hisense's internationalization process does not fit properly with the Uppsala stage model, notably in relation to the measures they undertook in developed economies (Parmentola, 2010). As aforementioned in the case of ZTE, their price and financial advantages could be regarded as the initial reasons for international activity. However, their strategic assets strengthened through international development, such as technical capabilities, contribute to building their competitive advantage in the Chinese market itself. This could be similarly explained by this 'inside-out and outside-in' (ambidextrous internationalization) strategy. According to Prange and Bruyaka (2016) however, ZTE achieved more fully an ambidextrous state than Hisense, which has been always in a state of 'outside-in'.

Compared to Hai'er, the internationalization of Hisense is still uncompleted, but the sponsorship of the European Football Championship helped them from a marketing point of view in the brand building process, to a level not attained in the Hai'er case. If we consider that the established relationships of Hisense and the global actors contributed to their technological capabilities, their ability to absorb an enterprise which is different in language and culture could be another possible advantage in the future (Deng, 2012). Possibly, the case of Lenovo would be an example of that.

Lenovo – IBM: integration of foreign assets and resources

Lenovo is a computer manufacturer with more than 60,000 employees all over the world (in 2016).[17] It was founded in 1984, by the Chinese Scientific Institute.

Reaching a 30% share of the Chinese market share in 2000, Lenovo had to choose whether they would implement diversification or internationalization as their strategy. In 2001, the choice made by the CEO was to be an international brand in the PC manufacturing sector. Around late 2003, IBM knocked on their door with an M&A proposal, thinking that a Chinese company like Lenovo needed to enlarge their international reputation and for IBM, Lenovo could help improve their position in the Chinese market which had a lot of potential. From Lenovo's point of view, they did have the ability to help IBM's PC business to be profitable by using their high efficiency platform in China. Lenovo invited three private equity investors GA (General Atlantic), TPG (Texas Pacific Group) and NC (Newbridge Capital) to invest in this project with the motive of risk reduction.

Eventually, in 2005, Lenovo entered an M&A with IBM for its personal computer division. The price of US$ 1.25 billion (Ducourtieux et al., 2014) included PCs and laptops business, a related research centre, production equipment, global sales networks, a service centre, and the right to use the IBM PC brand for five years. That also helped Lenovo maintain an enduring relationship with IBM, which also kept a share of this merged PC division. Lenovo have established their head office in New York and two operational centres in South Carolina and Beijing. This acquisition has enabled Lenovo to jump to third place in the PC manufacturers of the world. After two years, Lenovo founded more than 60 facilities all over the world and participated in the sales network across 160 countries.

Initially, opposition from the US government was strong, as they thought that it might lead to some risks to their national security in terms of information protection if a Chinese company becomes their supplier. Due to the intervention of TPG Private Equity, this acquisition was realized. Thereafter, the three private equity firms also helped Lenovo with some operational issues in terms of cultural conflict, brand building, custom loyalty, supply chain etc. (Jolly, 2013).

After Lenovo's IBM purchase, they adopted a dual brand strategy as they had not themselves a marketable reputation. In this M&A case, Lenovo quickly acquired a 'ready to take' mechanism through which they have reduced their degree of foreignness, thereby enabling them to access foreign markets and acquired a highly recognized international brand which permitted them to get access to a significant part of the market. However, their ability to absorb the dysfunctions generated by the culture gap of the two enterprises and even the two countries was a crucial issue.

Lenovo spent four years (2004–2008) observing and learning western managerial practices by appointing two foreign CEOs (Steve Ward and then Bill Amelio) and have made great efforts in stabilizing the IBM team and improving cost control. Lenovo moved their head office from New York to Raleigh in North Carolina, integrated the PC production unit in China, and moved the European, Central and Eastern Europe and African customer support centres from Scotland to Slovakia. But they also had some disputes in personnel appointments, which led to them having a bad financial year during 2006. However, from 2006 to 2008, Lenovo made greater profits, with their net profit rate rising to 3% from 0.17% in 2006. When everyone thought that the integration of these two companies was nearly coming to completion, the global financial crisis broke out, leading Lenovo to register deficits of up to US$ 226 million. The previous progress made on integrating IBM into Lenovo was now being questioned.

The period from 2008–2012 was one of re-integration. The founder of Lenovo returned as chairman. With the experience that had been cumulated, they started to establish a Lenovo Executive Committee to consolidate the relationship between the Lenovo and IBM teams. Thereafter, they put forward an executive plan that prepared on the one hand a consolidation of the Chinese market presence for greater profit generation and on the other hand an international expansion for sustaining international development. This four-year plan made Lenovo the leader in the Chinese market with a profit of US$ 1.8 billion in 2012 and then they also signed an agreement with NEC (first Japanese computer brand) to establish a joint venture that integrates the PC research, production and components purchase segments of both sides (Bembaron, 2011). The same year, Lenovo acquired 80% shareholding of Median (German PC manufacturer) in order to penetrate the European market and their sales channel in shopping centres (Lenovo, 2011). Simultaneously, Lenovo also entered emerging markets such as Russia, India, etc. All these strategic moves have resulted in Lenovo becoming the second largest PC producer in the world, only seven years after they purchased IBM's PC division.

As previously explained, the decision to internationalize Lenovo was made before the IBM acquisition, which was very different to the other cases. Through all the development of Lenovo's history, it is hard not to notice that the difficulties generated by psychic distance (Johanson and Vahlne, 1990) in Lenovo only occurred when the IBM PC division was inside the Lenovo group. Lenovo's internationalization through the IBM acquisition is a significant case of absorption of international resources.

Shanghai electric – government-backed giant in the electric industry

Shanghai Electric (SEC), a state-owned enterprise (which is in ongoing reform to a mixed- owned enterprise), is one of the largest energy equipment manufacturers in China. They have started their internationalization trajectory by forming more than 125 local joint ventures abroad with companies like Westinghouse,

Schneider, Mitsubishi, etc. (Prange, 2012). Working with foreign partners at home helped them to prepare for this challenge.

In 1995, Shanghai Electric founded a JV with Siemens for manufacturing power station equipment in China which is a mixture of the advanced techniques of turbine generator manufacturing of Shanghai Electric and the technologies and managerial experiences of Siemens. During this cooperation, the Chinese company absorbed the technologies that were provided by its foreign partner and in the next step exported to Pakistan, Iran, India, etc.

In 1997, Shanghai Electric created a JV with the Japanese firm Fanuc in Shanghai in the development of industrial robots. During a 15-year development period, they produced up to 4,000 robots and rank first in China in this field. In 2000, Shanghai Electric created a JV with IHI (a Japanese company listed in the World 500), in Shanghai, in environmental protection engineering of power stations. At the end of 2001, Shanghai Electric founded a JV with Westinghouse Electric in Shanghai to improve their technologies in steam turbine fabrication.

In 2001, Shanghai Electric (160,000 workers in China at that time), together with the Hong Kong-based investment firm, Morning Side, bought Akiyama Printing Machine, which ranked sixth worldwide in its sector, but had become bankrupt. Akiyama Printing Machine was founded in 1948 (Drifte and Jaussaud, 2010). Its turnover had reached 15 billion yen when it was well managed. Due to mismanagement in 2001, Akiyama had to find investors. Shanghai Electric bought it for US$ 9 million, and worked hard to improve its operations, notably in terms of cost and supplier management. Three Chinese employees were sent to this Japanese company which employed 170 workers in total. However, because of some foreign exchange control measures in China, the fund for the acquisition of Akiyama was hardly in place which led to tremendous difficulties (Wang Yu et al., (王玉 et al., 2007, in Chinese).

In 2002, Westinghouse Electric transferred its share of the JV to Siemens which consolidated the cooperation between Siemens and Shanghai Electric.

In 2004, Shanghai Electric acquired total ownership of Ikegai, a famous Japanese machine tool manufacturing company, for US$ 1.5 million (Zhang Qingsong, 张青松, 2014, in Chinese). By utilizing its existing sales network, Shanghai Electric introduced the quality control system of Ikegai to China (Xiang Bing, 项兵, 2012, in Chinese). In 2004 also, Shanghai Electric acquired in Germany a 53.5% stake of Wohlenberg GmbH, a machine tool manufacturer based in Hanover.

The same year, they acquired a 75% stake in Ikea Corp, a machine tool manufacturer, for US$ 4.5 million (Larçon, 2008). In 2005, Ikea founded a subsidiary in Shanghai, which increased its sales to RMB 5 billion that year, six times more than before the acquisition (Xiang Bing, 项兵, 2012, in Chinese).

In 2007, in Vietnam, Shanghai Electric started building a Vietnam-financed thermoelectricity power plant with a capacity of 600 MW in the Northern Quang Ninh province. The investor was Quang Ninh Thermoelectricity joint stock company (Larçon, 2008). During 2010 and 2011, Shanghai Electric successively created in Vietnam and India subsidiaries for the development of local markets, trade services and to collect and integrate market information.

During 2011, Shanghai Electric created several JVs in China, for energy control by contract and by eco-building with Schneider Electric, Mitsubishi Electric and Carrier respectively. In 2012, Shanghai Electric created a JV with SPX Corporation in Shanghai, for air cooling systems in the Chinese market. That helped them to take a 20% market share in this field, ranked second in China.[18]

During the reform of mixed ownership of SOEs, Shanghai Electric acquired a 40% stake in Ansaldo Energia, a large Italian polyvalent industrial company. Shanghai Electric can share its markets with Ansaldo, keeping its own employees and brand, but its motivation for the investment was related to accessing Ansaldo's technological resources.[19]

Shanghai Electric has followed the Uppsala stage model of internationalization, relying first on the potential of the Chinese market to exchange with foreign partners for access to higher-ended technological information, and other strategic assets (Dunning, 2000). However, its financial power which supported its acquisitions may be reduced by the ongoing reform of SOEs, i.e. the mixed ownership reform, and whether Shanghai Electric will sustain its internationalization process remains questionable.

In order to summarize Section 1, Table 6.1 synthetizes the internationalization processes of these well known Chinese firms.

Table 6.1 Well known cases and the internationalization process

AMANN TABLES

Company	Ownership	Products	Internationalization process
Huawei	Private	Networking and Telecom	Uppsala stage model process (Johanson and Vahlne, 2015)
ZTE	Mixed-owned enterprise	Telecom	OLI paradigm and Uppsala model (Gaur and Kumar, 2010)
Hai'er	State-owned enterprise	Consumer electronics and home appliances	OLI paradigm and Uppsala model (Gaur and Kumar, 2010)
Hisense	State-owned enterprise	White goods and electronics manufacturer	'inside-out and outside-in' (ambidextrous internationalization), Prange and Bruyaka (2016)
Lenovo	Mixed-owned enterprise, listed in Hong Kong, 31% of capital in the hands of the Chinese State	Personal Computers (PCs)	Specific case of absorption of resources from abroad through M&A (IBM PC division)
Shanghai Electric	State-owned enterprise	Electronics industry	Uppsala stage model process (Johanson and Vahlne, 2015)

Emerging cases with some particular characteristics

In this section, we will try to identify and analyze a range of other Chinese firms which are less known than the ones in Section 1. These firms have great diversity in terms of their international strategies. They are more difficult to be categorized by the traditional theoretical frameworks due to the changing global economic background.

COMAC – a young player in Chinese aviation

Commercial Aircraft Corporation of China (COMAC) was founded in 2008. It is a state-owned enterprise in large aircraft development. Initially, with almost no experience in the field, COMAC learned from the development of civil aircraft through international cooperation. COMAC needed to identify and acquire the best engines, the best components and parts from the best suppliers to produce aircraft. In order to do that, COMAC established a network initially with many other related institutes, factories and agencies as a development alliance including Aviation Industry Corporation of China (AVIC – COMAC, 2016) and then constructed a supply chain with various international enterprises such as General Electric in 2009 (GE Aviation, 2010), Safran in 2009 (Safran (2009), and Honeywell in 2010 (Honeywell, 2010). All of these relationships and the study of the organization of Boeing and Airbus enabled COMAC to set up a modularized managerial system to adapt their research and production projects.

   COMAC signed a cooperation agreement with Bombardier[20] in 2012 and with Fokker, an old Dutch aircraft producer, in 2015, for the development of the C919, a large civil aircraft with an additional program (GCAT)[21] with GE. In the future, the C919 model will be commercialized and more and more dynamic aeronautical suppliers will be involved in the Chinese aircraft market. COMAC has then just taken the first step of their internationalization process.

   From the viewpoint of the Uppsala stage model, COMAC may not have an internationalization strategy if they do not export, but the fact that they tried to build their network on an international scale could be framed in the Linkage, Leverage, Learning model (Mathews, 2002). This LLL model 3 stages (Linkage, Leverage, Learning), notably applies in the development of its activities by such a latecomer who did not have any competitive advantage (Peng, 2012).

   According to the LLL framework, the motivation for the internationalization of MNCs in emerging economies is their concern to access externally available resources. With this ambition, these firms in emerging economies strive to build relationships through strategic alliances by establishing joint ventures and other kinds of cooperation relationships with foreign firms. The next step for them after the establishment of linkages is to leverage the resources. For this reason, the focus of its internationalization will be on the resource itself and the resource availability. The third element of the LLL model is learning, which refers to the application of the linkage and leverage effects. By this mechanism, link, leveraging and learning then form a cycle to accelerate internalization (Mathews, 2006).

Dongfeng – PSA in the car industry

Dongfeng was founded in 1969 and was initially known as Second Auto Works. They produced mainly trucks, including for military purposes. They changed the name to Dongfeng in 1992 (Sit and Liu, 2000). Currently it is the second largest automobile manufacturer in China, under a state-owned holding company, employing 142,000 workers.

PSA founded a joint venture in Wuhan (China) with Dongfeng in 1992 after terminating an unsatisfactory relationship with Guangdong Automobile (GAC) in Guangzhou, South China (CCIFC, 2011). The JV with Dongfeng produces and sells Citroën and Peugeot cars in China. However, the JV did not achieve high market shares in China compared to other worldwide leading automobile manufacturers, including other latecomers in the country. So, PSA cooperated with Chang'an Motors in 2010, for the release of the DS series in China, which did not perform well until 2014 (Mathieu, 2013).

PSA still had not found an ideal way to exploit the Chinese market. Furthermore, its continuing failure in the European market resulted in financial problems in 2013. Regarded as a potential large investor in PSA, General Motors held a 7% stake in PSA (Franceinfo and AFP, 2013), but eventually, PSA turned from GM to Dongfeng by asking for financial help and tried to re-establish its presence in the Chinese market with the help of Dongfeng. Dongfeng agreed to take a 14.1% stake in PSA in 2014 even if there are potential risks, as they plan to become more international oriented. Although the cooperation is currently concentrated on the Chinese market, PSA will help Dongfeng to expand their production and sales in Asia and other emerging markets in the future under the deal. For PSA, China became its largest market with sales of 736,000 vehicles in 2015.[22]

In the case of Dongfeng, the cooperation with PSA before the shareholding acquisition was solely for the development of the Chinese market. Dongfeng currently has limited sales in the international markets. If we analyze the process of internationalization of Dongfeng from this perspective, then the acquisition of the PSA stake by Dongfeng is difficult to be reconciled with the Uppsala stage model. However, it may be considered to be in accordance with the three main points of the Eclectic paradigm theory (Ownership, Localisation, Internalisation), as Dongfeng internalizes through its financial ownership advantages (Sun et al., 2012). What is similar to this case is the case of Xinjiang Chalkis, which started with an M&A project, as illustrated as follows.

Xinjiang Chalkis – Le Cabanon in the food industry

Xinjiang Chalkis, a state-owned enterprise, was founded in 1994. They started tomato production in 2000. Relying on the special incentive policies of the Chinese regional authority in Xinjiang Uyghur Autonomous region, their tomato production increased to 5,500 tons by 2001, which was almost totally sold in European markets. By 2003, Xinjiang Chalkis' production reached 360,000 tons, and the company became the dominant tomato producer in China (Zhou et al., 周清杰 et al., 2013, in Chinese).

In 2004, in order to obtain a brand and marketing network, Xinjiang Chalkis acquired 55% of 'Conserve de Provence' which was a major shareholder (98%) of 'Le Cabanon'. The investment amounted to € 7 million. 'Le Cabanon', a 50-year-old food-processing company, held 40% of the market share in France (Haski, 2004).

In 2005, Xinjiang Chalkis acquired the remaining 45% of 'Conserve de Provence' through a subsidiary in Tianjin (Molga, 2005). The M&A deal helped Xinjiang Chalkis to increase their production and build their competitiveness at an international market level. At the same time, they expanded their range of products.

Early in 2008, the partnership between Chalkis and Conserve de Provence encountered industrial unrest.[23] This may have been caused by Xinjian Chalkis' lack of knowledge of the macroeconomic, social, legal environment in France. Then the Chinese managerial practices in reaction to the social unrest discredited the shareholders (Guilhot et al., 2013).

With the production expansion of Xinjiang Chalkis, their debt ratio increased to 98.39% from 2008 to 2011. Since 2009, the profitability of Xinjiang Chalkis has continuously decreased due to their production overcapacity. In addition, as a company focused on exports, they have been affected by the exchange rate appreciation of the RMB. Xinjiang Chalkis' profits were being increasingly pressurized and operational risks subsequently increased (Zhou et al., 周清杰 et al., 2013, in Chinese). In 2014, Conserve de Provence was sold by Chalkis to Unitom, the number one Portuguese tomato processor.[24]

YTO – McCormick: technical upgrading of tractors

China First Tractor Group Corporation (YTO) is part of China National Machinery Industry Corporation (Sinamach) since 2008. It was founded in 1955, was a state-owned enterprise (SOE), and was the largest tractor manufacturer in China, specializing in agriculture and construction machinery.

From its foundation, YTO has benefited from technologies obtained from the USSR, Italy and the UK. By the 1990s, YTO had already entered Mali and Côte d'Ivoire in Africa, and then Serbia, South Africa, Poland and Kyrgyzstan in which YTO had progressively set up assembly plants for expansion in international markets (Guo and Cao, 郭振华 and 曹熙, 2015, in Chinese). Since 2004, they have jointly undertaken and implemented research activities with the other advanced manufacturers into technological upgrading. In 2005, YTO discussed with Agco, the world's third largest manufacturer of farm equipment, a proposed joint-venture which was never realized (Grant, 2005) but cooperation with Agco continues through Valtra, a 100% subsidiary of Agco.

In 2011, YTO acquired ARGO's (an Italian tractor manufacturer) McCormick factory located in France and changed its name to YTO France (Gonzalez, 2015). It was the first international M&A for a Chinese agricultural machinery manufacturer (Han and Guo, 韩文 and 郭振华, 2016, in Chinese). YTO France was then treated as an important innovative hub for the integration of transmission technologies in tractor production in China, and also as a base for exploiting models suitable for the European market. Particularly, YTO France exports almost 100% of its production to China; however, these products would have been reintegrated into European markets since 2016 (Lecocq, 2015).

After the M&A project, in 2015, YTO launched an online tractor shop in the Chinese market that permitted their customers to personalize the configuration of each tractor purchase (Guo and Cao, 郭振华 and 曹煦, 2015, in Chinese). The same year, YTO established an East European research centre with Minsk Tractor Works in Belarus. YTO has also concluded an order for 587 tractor units from Cuba, which is part of their sales in more than 100 countries in 2015. Foreign sales amount to 10% of total sales according to the chairman of YTO, which would be ideally increased to 30% for foreign markets in the future (Guo and Cao, 郭振华 and 曹煦, 2015, in Chinese).

The case of YTO is compatible with the Uppsala stage model to some extent, at least from the exports and the establishment of production units in some geographically- and culturally-close countries. The fact that it undertook an M&A project in Europe, however, is quite similar to the case of Dongfeng. They acquired a foreign company mainly for their domestic market or to support their domestic production. Such type of event is more in accordance with the LLL model previously mentioned. It created a linkage with McComick through acquisition, then the acquired entity acted as a source for generating resources and capabilities which could be gained by establishing knowledge-sharing across the network (Mathews, 2006). Whether or not the YTO case may have reached the learning process stage is an open question. However, this will eventually happen as YTO will have accumulated enough resources and capabilities from McCormick.

Lisa airline – Heima mining: exploiting the Chinese civil aviation market

Heima Mining is a small private company specialized in phosphate rock production, created by Tiri-Maha, an ethnic minority orphan born in Sichuan province in China. After studying in the UK (UWC Atlantic College) and the USA (Middlebury College), Tiri-Maha was recruited by a world top 500 Korean company, Kolon industries, in New York in 2008. He rapidly quit his job and then founded in May 2008 his own company, Heima Mining in his hometown. The company had RMB 530,000 as capital. It set up a JV (RMB 210,000) with Khanvis International in Hong Kong in July, the same year.

Zhang Yao, another young Chinese entrepreneur who had studied in France, saw in a newspaper that a French small airplane company, Lisa Airline, was in liquidation in 2012 (Dyan and Testard, 2014). He realized that civil aviation for Chinese investors would be an important and profitable sector in the future. He contacted Erick Herzberger, the founder of this small company. Zhang introduced Tiri-Maha to Herzberger and the two young Chinese were interested in the company and planned to invest € 15 million on an M&A project for 70% of the shares and core assets of the company. Finally, with the help of the existing directors of Lisa Airplane, Zhang and Tiri-Maha's proposal has been approved by a local court in Chambéry. There are seven other investors in the project, mostly Chinese. 'He has a vision for 30 years in the future', explained Benoît Senellart, the general director of Lisa Airplane.[25]

The project was initially more about helping Lisa Airline to continue their ongoing production of their Agoya model, for which they had received an order for 20 units from the USA. The differences in language and culture between the French managers and their Chinese directors obliged them to employ a Chinese executive assistant.[26] For Zhang and Tiri-Maha, this acquisition would help them to enter in the general aviation market in China that had been strictly reserved for the Chinese government and military use before but which is now more and more open for private actors.

Three years after the acquisition, Lisa Airplanes changed their principal shareholder, as Zhang and Tiri-Maha were not able to continue their engagement due to financial problems. However, due to the network created in China, they found another Chinese partner, General Aviation Inner Mongolia (GAIM),[27] an SOE with three shareholders, Inner Mongolia Communication Investment, China Aviation Industry General Aircraft and the municipality of Hulunbuir in Inner Mongolia.

The case of Lisa Airlines is more or less consistent with the Born Global theory, which was put forward by McDougall et al. (1994). This theory underlines a new and faster way of internationalization that a company often takes, from its foundation. Born Global firms take advantage through the use of resources from multiple countries and sell their products or services in various markets and actively seek competitive advantages. This type of business usually has specific characteristics such as that they are small businesses, technology-oriented and are able to earn a larger income in the international market from the very beginning of their establishment (Cavusgil and Knight, 2015).

The following example of Upsolar may illustrate the Born Global theory in a clearer way, from the Chinese point of view.

Upsolar – EPC Solstyce: the international photovoltaic solar market

Upsolar was founded in 2006 by a Chinese Masters graduate of NEOMA Business School. It is a private solar photovoltaic solution supplier based in China.[28] After having identified the potential of the European market, Upsolar established a subsidiary in Paris in 2008.

In 2009, a Greek and an American subsidiary were founded. The same year, Upsolar employed an American executive director, Troy Dalbey, for the US market, and another operations director who is Chinese with a background in International studies, Eric Liu.[29]

With the help of Liu, Upsolar established from 2010 to 2011 four subsidiaries, in Germany, Italy, Japan and the UK, respectively, which are now up and running. In 2012, Upsolar had already finished 10 roof solar photovoltaic projects in

France (three solar photovoltaic centres around Paris and seven others for educational institutions in Charente) under a JV (Novengo) created with EPC Solstyce.[30] The same year, another project, a solar power station was also completed in Bologna under another JV (EVI3 = Energia Verde Investimenti 3) created with Protesa SPA.[31]

In 2013 after the success realized in France and Italy, Upsolar founded two representative offices in Australia and Turkey respectively for local projects. Two solar photovoltaic power station projects[32] with Tigo Energy (US photovoltaic technology manufacturer) were completed in Japan, three years after the Japanese subsidiary had been established. They have also transferred their competences acquired from foreign markets to China through the distributed solar photovoltaic power generation project in Jiaxing initiated by the local government.[33]

In 2014, a representative office was founded in Singapore. Their Sino-French joint venture, Novengo, has completed a project which consists of a photovoltaic shade structure for the parking facility at Angoulême-Cognac airport.[34]

Upsolar has completed two important roof solar photovoltaic projects with China North Industries (Norinco), a military-owned SOE in Beijing,[35] and a building-integrated photovoltaics (BIPV) project in Shanghai Pudong Airport.[36]

At present, Upsolar's international managerial team includes Eric Liu, Troy Dalbey, but also Stephane Dufrenne, a French chief technology officer, and Enrico Carniato, an Italian European sales director.[37]

As suggested previously, the Born Global theory may be more suitable in framing the international activities of Upsolar. It has a global leader who had an international vision through his international educational and work background. Upsolar is involved in a niche market, and its entrepreneurship is also based on innovations.

Table 6.2 summarizes the internationalization process of Chinese companies considered in Section 2, i.e. less known companies than those in Section 1, as they are emerging cases in internationalization. The diversity of internationalization processes undertaken should be noted.

Table 6.2 Emerging firms and the internationalization process

Company	Ownership	Products	Internationalization process
COMAC	State-owned enterprise	aerospace manufacturer	LLL model (Mathews, 2002)
Dongfeng	State-owned enterprise	automobile manufacturer	OLI paradigm (Dunning, 1981)
Xinjiang Chalkis	State-owned enterprise	agri-food sector	Failure of internationalisation
YTO	State-owned enterprise	farm machinery manufacturer	Uppsala stage model process (Johanson and Vahlne, 2015)
Heima Mining	Private company	mining company	Born globals (McDougall et al., 1994)
Upsolar	Private company	solar photovoltaic solution supplier	Born globals (McDougall et al., 1994)

Conclusion

As discussed in these cases, we have identified a range of firms which conform to existing international theories to different extents. However, their development paths varied according to their own characteristics in terms of related sector, market, financial capability, degree of development, ownership, etc.

Based on these cases, we find out that most of the Chinese enterprises often benefited from some country-specific advantages (CSA) such as a cost advantage or capital advantage, to promote their firm-specific advantages (FSA) in the process of internationalization (Rugman et al., 2007). However, these advantages become smaller and smaller over time (Ceglowski et al., 2012; Yang et al., 2010). As a result, those Chinese enterprises will use the internationalization processes, transforming themselves from owning those initial inherent advantages into possessing intangible advantages (technology, management, brand, product, innovation, etc.). This does not meet the definition of internalization advantages of Dunning's Eclectic paradigm because often in the internationalization process, Chinese enterprises are eager to get the advantages from outside when they internationalize. Accordingly, the LLL theory (Cuervo-Cazurra and Ramamurti, 2014) can better explain the development strategy of Chinese enterprises in developed countries, although it cannot fully explain the development of these enterprises in other developing countries and less developed countries.

In addition, the Chinese government has played an important role in the process of internationalization of Chinese enterprises, in promoting some incentive policies such as the 'going out' policy since 1999 and 'one belt one road' policy since 2013, guiding enterprises to develop abroad and providing various financial supports, all of which have made the internationalization of Chinese companies extremely active (MOFCOM, 2014). Naturally, it is also accompanied by some less successful cases, such as the failure of internationalization of the Xinjiang Chalkis and Heima Mining show.

Based on Ghoshal and Bartlett (1990), only the internationalization of Haier in the sample may be defined as a transnational corporation, a network of units geographically dispersed but highly-integrated, including headquarters and subsidiaries in different countries. This entity can be regarded as an internal and heterogeneous inter-organizational network rooted in an external network. From the perspective of network organization, the relationship of parent companies and subsidiaries differs depending on the characteristics of the subsidiary company. The interdependencies and synergies of the bilateral network relationships between the various subsidiaries are greatly enhanced. China has only a few such cases like this, which may be due to the accelerated globalization based on information and communication technologies (de Matías Batalla, 2014). As a consequence, the global market is becoming more and more homogeneous, for instance, Apple mobile phones are sold globally.

Similarly, due to Information and Communication Technologies (ICT) and more and more developed infrastructure and transportation, the internationalization of Chinese enterprises has been characterized by significant speed and breadth. But Chinese firms are still in the early phase of internationalization (Pang et al., 庞

明川 et al., 2012, in Chinese). This open environment may also lead to the enterprises getting less and less competitive advantages derived from market imperfections, advantages which are also more difficult to keep within the enterprises.

Finally but not least, an increasingly open international environment nurtures more and more international talent who are inherently multi-lingual and cross-cultural. They have the insights and entrepreneurial capabilities for the internationalization of small and medium-sized enterprises (SMEs) in niche markets. It is thus unnecessary for such SMEs to rely on the advantages of strong economies of scale (Gassmann et al., 2007; Van De Vrande et al., 2010) or to internationalize by linking to a network of existing relationships in foreign markets (Karra et al., 2008).

In conclusion, this chapter describes the internationalization path of 12 Chinese enterprises in different industries of different scales, different equity structures and backgrounds with an examination of the match of mainstream internationalization theory and the actual situation of these Chinese enterprises. Then the authors highlighted that the Chinese government strongly supported the internationalization of Chinese firms, particularly, but not only, state-owned enterprises (SOEs). In addition the international environment is much different in terms of communication and transportation development from when the internationalization of Western companies occurred. These characteristics lead to the exposure of some inadequacies in the existing theories in describing the ongoing internationalization of some Chinese enterprises.

Notes

1 http://english.mofcom.gov.cn/article/newsrelease/policyreleasing/201602/20160 201251488.shtml
2 www.privco.com/inside-huawei-of-chinas-private-financials-privco-reveals-that-the-privately-held-telecom-giant-just-declared-by-congress-a-national-security-threat-to-the-us-is-minting-billions-annually-twitter-acquires-vine
3 As described in this article: '*The shares of ZTE Holdings, in turn, are held by Xi'an Microelectronics (34%), Aerospace Guangyu (17%), and Zhongxing WXT (49%). Xi'an Micro Electronics and Aerospace Guangyu are both SOEs. State-owned entities, therefore, control 51% of ZTE Holdings . . .*'
4 http://tongxinxiaoxikuaidi.baijia.baidu.com/article/396195
5 http://xuyong.baijia.baidu.com/article/384485
6 Haier official website: www.haier.net/cn/about_haier/strategy/internationalization_strategy/
7 Hisense – About Us. Retrieved 10 October 2016, from www.hisense.cn/en/about/hsht/cpht/200810/t20081021_12840.html
8 Hisense Milestones of 2006. Retrieved 10 October 2016, from http://global.hisense.com/about/copr/mile/2006/
9 Hisense Milestones 2000–2004. Retrieved 10 October 2016, from http://global.hisense.com/about/copr/mile/2006_1_1/
10 Hisense Milestones 2005. Retrieved 10 October 2016, from http://global.hisense.com/about/copr/mile/2006_1/
11 Hisense – About Us – Innovation System. Retrieved 10 October 2016, from www.hisense.cn/en/about/hstc/insy/
12 Hisense Germany GmbH introduction. Retrieved 10 October 2016, from www.hisense.cn/hxjt/gl/germany/

13   Hisense – About Us – Hisense Kelon. Retrieved 10 October 2016, from www.hisense.cn/en/about/ivrt/kelo/
14   Hisense – About Us – Company History 2008. Retrieved 10 October 2016, from www.hisense.cn/en/about/hsht/cpht/200811/t20081111_12842.html
15   www.hisense.cn/kx/HiTimes/index/201502/t20150203_92408.shtml
16   Hisense signs as UEFA EURO 2016 global sponsor – UEFA.com
17   http://appserver.lenovo.com.cn/About/Introduction.html
18   http://finance.sina.com.cn/leadership/mroll/20130331/155915008381.shtml
19   http://cn.dealglobe.com/上海电气如何进行混合所有制改革：海外并购打造/
20   www.latribune.fr/entreprises-finance/industrie/aeronautique-defense/20121114trib000730865/l-alliance-entre-bombardier-et-le-chinois-comac-monte-en-puissance-sera-ce-suffisant-face-a-airbus-et-boeing.html
21   www.geaviation.com/press/other/other_20130605.html
22   Marché automobile Chine et Asie : PSA Dongfeng. Retrieved 15 October 2016, from www.groupe-psa.com/fr/groupe-automobile/presence-internationale/chine-asie-sud-est/
23   www.fldhebdo.fr/fin-de-greve-au-cabanon-apres-5-jours-de-negociations-art7376-5.html
24   http://friaapaca.com/index.php?option=com_content&view=article&id=620:le-cabanon-repris-par-unitom-&catid=34:actualites
25   www.leparisien.fr/magazine/grand-angle/economie-mon-patron-est-chinois-11-02-2015-4524841.php
26   www.aeroweb-fr.net/actualites/2015/04/ou-en-est-lakoya-lisa-airplanes-nous-ouvre-ses-portes-en-savoie
27   www.brefeco.com/actualite/lisa-airplanes-change-dactionnaires-chinois
28   www.china-upsolar.com/uploads/UploadFile/20101205124026.pdf
29   经营团队 – Upsolar
30   www.ne21.com/news/show-28414.html; www.businesswire.com/news/home/20120627005372/fr/
31   www.ne21.com/news/show-26811.html
32   http://solar.ofweek.com/2013-07/ART-260009-8460-28706979.html; www.businesswire.com/news/home/20130723006716/en/Upsolar-Expands-Presence-Japan-Completion-Projects
33   www.cpnn.com.cn/zdyw/201408/t20140820_707786.html
34   www.solstyce.fr/2014/11/25/inauguration-de-laeroport-international-angouleme-cognac/
35   www.ne21.com/news/show-51907.html
36   www.ne21.com/news/show-61325.html
37   www.china-upsolar.com/about/index.aspx

Bibliography

Baidu Baijia. (2016, April 6). Mobile giant earnings in 2015, ZTE even more international - Baidu Baijia Retrieved 16 January 2018, from https://baijia.baidu.com/s?old_id=396195
Barrie, D. (2015, April 21). Où en est l'Akoya? Lisa Airplanes nous ouvre ses portes en Savoie. Retrieved from http://www.aeroweb-fr.net/actualites/2015/04/ou-en-est-lakoya-lisa-airplanes-nous-ouvre-ses-portes-en-savoie
Bartlett, C. A., and Ghoshal, S. (2002). *Managing Across Borders*. Cambridge, MA: Harvard Business Press, http://doi.org/10.1080/10803920.1999.10392010.
Bembaron, E. (2011). *Lenovo et Nec se marient dans le PC*, 27 January, www.lefigaro.fr/societes/2011/01/27/04015-20110127ARTFIG00477-lenovo-et-nec-se-marient-dans-le-pc.php.

Benoit, D. (2012). *Huawei already can't get deals done*, 8 October, http://blogs.wsj.com/deals/2012/10/08/huawei-already-cant-get-deals-done/

Benton Harbor, M. (2008). *Whirlpool Corporation and Hisense-Kelon Electrical Holdings Co. Ltd. announce joint venture in China (NYSE:WHR)*, 28 April, http://investors.whirlpoolcorp.com/releasedetail.cfm?releaseid=531706.

BrefEco. (2016, Mars 8). Lisa Airplanes change d'actionnaires chinois | Bref Eco. Retrieved from http://www.brefeco.com/actualite/lisa-airplanes-change-dactionnaires-chinois

Cavusgil, S. T., and Knight, G. (2015). The born global firm: An entrepreneurial and capabilities perspective on early and rapid internationalization. *Journal of International Business Studies*, 46(1), 3–16, http://doi.org/10.1057/jibs.2014.62.

CCIFC, L. B. (2011). *Le défi des investissements français en Chine*. Disponible sur, www.ambafrance-cn.org/IMG/pdf/livre-blanc.pdf.

Ceglowski, J., and Golub, S. S. (2012). Does China still have a labor cost advantage? *Global Economy Journal*, http://doi.org/10.1515/1524-5861.1874.

Cheng, L. K., and Kwan, Y. K. (2000). What are the determinants of the location of foreign direct investment? The Chinese experience. *Journal of International Economics*, http://doi.org/10.1016/S0022-1996(99)00032-X.

COMAC (2016). 中国商用飞机有限责任公司-中国航空报：中航飞机与中国商飞上飞院在京签署合作协议 (COMAC and Avic sign operation agreement in Beijing). *China Aviation Journal*, 19 May. www.comac.cc/xwzx/mtjj/201605/19/t20160519_3842930.shtml.

CPNN. (2014, August 14). Jiaxing Distributed Photovoltaic Survival from Export to Domestic Sales. Retrieved from http://www.cpnn.com.cn/zdyw/201408/t20140820_707786.html

Cuervo-Cazurra, A., and Ramamurti, R. (2014). *Understanding Multinationals From Emerging Markets*.

de Matías Batalla, D. (2014). ICT impact on internationalization: A critical review of the eclectic paradigm. *Journal of Socioeconomic Engineering*, (2), 16–24.

Deng, P. (2012). Effects of absorptive capacity on international acquisitions of Chinese firms, in: Alon, I., Fetscherin, M., and Gugler, P. (eds.), *Chinese International Investments*. London: Palgrave Macmillan UK, 137–153, doi.org/10.1057/9780230361577_8.

Deutsche Welle (2004). *Siemens, China's Huawei in joint-venture | business*, 1 December, www.dw.com/en/siemens-chinas-huawei-in-joint-venture/a-1414990, accessed 22 December 2016.

Di Minin, A., Zhang, J., and Gammeltoft, P. (2012). Chinese foreign direct investment in R&D in Europe: A new model of R&D internationalization? *European Management Journal*, http://doi.org/10.1016/j.emj.2012.03.004.

Drifte, R., and Jaussaud, J. (2010). Chinese businesses in Japan: An emerging phenomenon, in: Andreosso O'Callaghan, B., and Zolin, B. (eds.), *Issues in Economic Integration: Can Asia Inspire the West?* Farnham: Ashgate Publishing Group, 137–146.

Ducourtieux, C., Julien, D-C., and Fournier, A. (2014). *Le Chinois Lenovo rachète les ordinateurs d'IBM*, 23 January, www.lemonde.fr/economie/article/2014/01/23/le-chinois-lenovo-rachete-les-ordinateurs-d-ibm_4353000_3234.html.

Dunning, J. H. (1981). *International Production and the Multinational Enterprise*. London: George Allen & Unwin.

Dunning, J. H. (1988). The eclectic paradigm of international production: A restatement and some possible extensions. *Journal of International Business Studies*, 19(1), 1–31, http://doi.org/10.1057/palgrave.jibs.8490372.

Dunning, J. H. (2000). The eclectic paradigm as an envelope for economic and business theories of MNE activity. *International Business Review*, 9(2), 163–190.

Dunning, J. H. (2001). The Eclectic (OLI) paradigm of international production: Past, present and future. *International Journal of the Economics of Business*, 8(2), 173–190, http://doi.org/10.1080/13571510110051441.

Dunning, J. H. (2006). Towards a new paradigm of development: Implications for the determinants of international business. *Transnational Corporations,* 15(1), 173–227.

Dunning, J. H. (2015). Reappraising the eclectic paradigm in an age of alliance capitalism. *The Eclectic Paradigm*, http://doi.org/10.4324/9780203016527.ch3.

Dyan, B., and Testard, H. (2014). *Quand la Chine investit en France* (When China Invests in France). Paris: Agence Francaise pour les Investissements Internationaux.

FLD. (2008, Mars 18). Fin de grève au Cabanon après 5 jours de négociations. Retrieved from www.fldhebdo.fr/fin-de-greve-au-cabanon-apres-5-jours-de-negociations-art7376-5.html

Franceinfo, and AFP (2013). *Pourquoi General Motors sort du capital de PSA-Peugeot Citroën*, 12 December, www.francetvinfo.fr/economie/entreprises/l-americain-general-motors-annonce-sa-sortie-du-capital-de-psa-peugeot-citroen_481312.html.

FRIAA. (n.d.). Le Cabanon repris par Unitom. Retrieved from http://friaapaca.com/index.php?option=com_content&view=article&id=620:le-cabanon-repris-par-unitom-&catid=34:actualites

Fu, X., and Gong, Y. (2011). Indigenous and foreign innovation efforts and drivers of technological upgrading: Evidence from China. *World Development*, 39(7), 1213–1225, http://doi.org/10.1016/j.worlddev.2010.05.010.

Gassmann, O., and Keupp, M. M. (2007). The competitive advantage of early and rapidly internationalising SMEs in the biotechnology industry: A knowledge-based view. *Journal of World Business*, http://doi.org/10.1016/j.jwb.2007.04.006.

Gaur, A., and Kumar, V. (2010). Internationalization of emerging market firms: A case for theoretical extension. . . . in: *International Management: The Past.*

GE Aviation (2010). *GE and AVIC Providing Systems for China's First Large Commercial Aircraft COMAC's C919 aircraft will have leading open-architecture avionics.* Press Release | GE Aviation, 12 July, www.geaviation.com/press/systems/systems_20100712.html.

Ghoshal, S., and Bartlett, C. A. (1990). The multinational corporation as an interorganizational network. *Academy of Management Review*, 15(4), 603, http://doi.org/10.2307/258684.

Gliszczynski, F. (2012, November 14). L'alliance entre Bombardier et le chinois Comac monte en puissance : sera-ce suffisant face à Airbus et Boeing? Retrieved from https://www.latribune.fr/entreprises-finance/industrie/aeronautique-defense/20121114trib000730865/l-alliance-entre-bombardier-et-le-chinois-comac-monte-en-puissance-sera-ce-suffisant-face-a-airbus-et-boeing.html

Gonzalez, L. (2015). *Yto France, repreneur de McCormick au salon du machinisme agricole de Villepinte – France 3 Champagne-Ardenne*, 2 March, http://france3-regions.francetvinfo.fr/champagne-ardenne/haute-marne/yto-france-repreneur-de-mccormick-au-salon-du-machinisme-agricole-de-villepinte-666157.html.

Grant, J. (2005). First tractor in talks with Agco on China venture. *FT.com*, 2 June, www.ft.com/cms/s/0/9f80968e-d3a2-11d9-ad4b-00000e2511c8.html?ft_site=falcon&desktop=true#axzz4TaAVNITO.

Guilhot, L., Mercier-Suissa, C., and Ruffier, J. (2013). *Face aux nouvelles stratégies déployées par les investisseurs chinois en Europe et en France: quelle(s) réponse(s) adopter?* Université Jean Moulin Lyon 3. Retrieved from https://hal.archives-ouvertes.fr/hal-00926720.

Guo and Cao (2015) – 郭振华, 曹煦. (2015). 东方红拖拉机 "变形记" 赵剡水详述 60 岁老国企 '一拖' 的创新基因与国际化路径. 中国经济周刊 (which translates in: Guo Zhenhua, and Cao Xi (2015). Dongfanghong tractor "transformation" Zhao Yanshui details of the 60-year-old state-owned enterprises 'YTO' innovation and internationalization of the path of *China Economic Weekly*).

Han and Guo (2016) – 韩文, 郭振华. (2016). 全国人大代表, 中国一拖集团董事长赵剡水: 一拖将打造海外战略 "升级版. 中国经济周刊 (which translates in: Han Wen, and Guo Zhenghua (2016). National People's Congress, China YTO Group Chairman Zhao Yanshui: YTO will create an overseas strategy "upgrade version". *China Economic Weekly*).

Haski, P. (2004). Les Chinois croquent la tomate transformée française. *Libération*, 12 April, www.liberation.fr/futurs/2004/04/12/les-chinois-croquent-la-tomate-transformee-francaise_475823.

Hisense (2013). Hisense to recruit in Silicon Valley and other cities across North America for over 100 high end positions. *Hisense*, 19 July, http://global.hisense.com/news/cone/201307/t20130719_76916.html.

Honeywell (2010). *Honeywell helps drive Chinese aerospace growth with four major systems for new passenger aircraft*, 19 November, http://www51.honeywell.com/honeywell/news-events/press-releases-details/11.19.10C919.html.

Huawei (2006). Motorola and Huawei create new UMTS venture for customers worldwide. *About Huawei*, July, www.huawei.com/ilink/en/about-huawei/newsroom/press-release/HW_089102?KeyTemps=News.

Huawei (2007a). *Annual report 2007 – enriching life through communication.*

Huawei (2007b). Global marine systems and Huawei to establish joint venture addressing submarine telecommunications market. *About Huawei*, 14 May, www.huawei.com/ilink/en/about-huawei/newsroom/press-release/HW_089374?KeyTemps=News.

Huawei (2013). *Huawei reaffirms commitment to Europe and European R&D investment*. Huawei Press Center, 11 November, http://pr.huawei.com/en/news/hw-308442-european.htm#.WFvbVh1rgTs.

Intel (2005). Intel and ZTE collaborate to deliver global wireless broadband networks. *Intel Newsroom*, 12 January, www.intel.com/pressroom/archive/releases/2005/20050112corp_a.htm.

Johanson, J., and Vahlne, J.-E. (1977). The internationalization process of the firm – a model of knowledge development and increasing foreign market commitments. *Journal of International Business Studies*, 8(1), 23–32, http://doi.org/10.1057/palgrave.jibs.8490676.

Johanson, J., and Vahlne, J.-E. (1990). The mechanism of internationalisation. *International Marketing Review*, 7(4), 02651339010137414, http://doi.org/10.1108/0265133 9010137414.

Johanson, J., and Vahlne, J.-E. (2006). Commitment and opportunity development in the internationalization process: A note on the Uppsala internationalization process model. *Management International Review*, 46(2), 165–178, http://doi.org/10.1007/s11575-006-0043-4.

Johanson, J., and Vahlne, J.-E. (2009). The Uppsala internationalization process model revisited: From liability of foreignness to liability of outsidership. *Journal of International Business Studies*, 40(9), 1411–1431, http://doi.org/10.1057/jibs.2009.24.

Johanson, J., and Vahlne, J.-E. (2015). The Uppsala internationalization process model revisited: From liability of foreignness to liability of outsidership, in: *Knowledge, Networks and Power*. London: Palgrave Macmillan UK, 153–186, http://doi.org/10.1057/9781137508829_7.

Jolly, D. (2013). Les firmes chinoises à la conquête de l'Ouest. *L'Expansion Management Review*, 151(4), 106–115, http://doi.org/10.3917/emr.151.0106.

Karra, N., Phillips, N., and Tracey, P. (2008). Building the born global firm: Developing entrepreneurial capabilities for international new venture success. *Long Range Planning*, http://doi.org/10.1016/j.lrp.2008.05.002.

Larçon, J. P. (2008). *Chinese Multinationals*. World Scientific Publishing Company. Retrieved from https://hal-hec.archives-ouvertes.fr/hal-00808761

Le Parisien. (2015, February 11). Économie : mon patron est chinois – Le Parisien. Retrieved from http://www.leparisien.fr/magazine/grand-angle/economie-mon-patron-est-chinois-11-02-2015-4524841.php

Lecocq, R. (2015). Yto France à la conquête de l'Europe, Machinisme. *Pleinchamp*, 13 March, www.pleinchamp.com/machinisme/actualites-machinisme/yto-france-a-la-conquete-de-l-europe.

Lenovo (2011). Lenovo acquires Median AG to expand its business in Western Europe. *Lenovo Newsroom*, 1 June, http://news.lenovo.com/news-releases/lenovo-acquires-medion-ag-to-expand-its-business-in-western-europe.htm.

Liu, H., and Li, K. (2002). Strategic implications of emerging Chinese multinationals: The Haier case study. *European Management Journal*, 20(6), 699–706, http://doi.org/10.1016/S0263-2373(02)00119-6.

Liu, J., Wang, Y., and Zheng, G. (2010). Driving forces and organisational configurations of international R&D: The case of technology-intensive Chinese multinationals. *International Journal of Technology Management*, 51(2/3/4), 409, http://doi.org/10.1504/IJTM.2010.033812.

Mathews, J. A. (2002). *Dragon Multinational*. Oxford: Oxford University Press.

Mathews, J. A. (2006). Dragon multinationals: New players in 21st century globalization. *Asia Pacific Journal of Management*, 23(1), 5–27, http://doi.org/10.1007/s10490-006-6113-0.

Mathieu, D. (2013). *Citroën DS 5LS, taillée pour la Chine*, 19 December, http://news.autoplus.fr/Citroen/Chine-Berline-Tricorps-Citroen-DS-5LS-1478356.html.

McDougall, P. P., Shane, S., and Oviatt, B. M. (1994). Explaining the formation of international new ventures: The limits of theories from international business research. *Journal of Business Venturing*, 9(6), 469–487, http://doi.org/10.1016/0883-9026(94)90017-5.

Meisner, J. (2013, April 23). With ZTE, most major android makers choose licensing. *Microsoft on the Issues*, https://blogs.technet.microsoft.com/microsoft_on_the_issues/2013/04/23/with-zte-most-major-android-makers-choose-licensing/

Meunier, S. (2012). *Political impact of Chinese foreign direct investment in the European Union on transatlantic relations*. European Parliament Briefing Paper, Princeton.

Meunier, S., Burgoon, B., and Jacoby, W. (2014). The politics of hosting Chinese investment in Europe – an introduction. *Asia Europe Journal*, 12(1–2), 109–126, http://doi.org/10.1007/s10308-014-0381-y.

Milhaupt, C. J., and Zheng, W. (2014). Beyond ownership: State capitalism and the Chinese firm. *Georgetown Law Journal*. p.674–675

MOFCOM (2014). *2013 Statistic Bulletin of Chinese Outward Foreign Direct Investment*. Beijing: Ministry of Commerce.

MOFCOM. (2016, January 18). Official of the Department of Outward Investment and Economic Cooperation of the Ministry of Commerce Comments on China's Outward

Investment and Economic Cooperation in 2015. Retrieved 16 January 2018, from http://english.mofcom.gov.cn/article/newsrelease/policyreleasing/201602/20160201251488.shtml

Molga, P. (2005). *Xinjiang Chalkis Tomato acquiert 100 % de Conserves de Provence*, 22 September, www.lesechos.fr/22/09/2005/LesEchos/19504-084-ECH_xinjiang-chalkis-tomato-acquiert-100 − -de-conserves-de-provence.htm.

NewEnergy21. (2014, February 17). Upsolar's 1.3MW rooftop photovoltaic project and network in Beijing. Retrieved from http://www.ne21.com/news/show-51907.html

NewEnergy21. (2014, February 17). Upsolar's 1.3MW rooftop photovoltaic project and network in Beijing. Retrieved from http://www.ne21.com/news/show-51907.html

OECD (2008). *China − Encouraging Responsible Business Conduct, OECD Investment Policy Review, Organization for Economic Cooperation and Development: Paris*. Paris: Organization for Economic Cooperation and Development.

OFweek. (2013, July 26). Upsolar seize the Japanese PV market, announced the completion of two photovoltaic power plants. Retrieved from http://solar.ofweek.com/2013-07/ART-260009-8460-28706979.html;

Parmentola, A. (2010). The internationalization of Chinese companies: Are the traditional resource based theories valid yet. *Review of International Comparative Management*.

Peng, M. W. (2010). *Global Business*. Cincinnati, OH: Cengage Learning.

Peng, M. W. (2012). The global strategy of emerging multinationals from China. *Global Strategy Journal*, 2(2), 97–107, http://doi.org/10.1002/gsj.1030.

Peng, M. W. (2013). *Global Business*. Cincinnati, OH: Cengage Learning.

Pesola, M., and Dickie, M. (2005). *ZTE seals deal with Alcatel*, 15 February, www.ft.com/content/d426d3dc-7f72-11d9-8ceb-00000e2511c8.

PMR (2015). Hisense invests in Czech Republic − ICT market. *CEE & CIS − PMR*, 29 September, www.ceeitandtelecom.com/news/249772/hisense-invests-in-czech-republic.

Porter, M. E. (1990). The competitive advantage of nations. *Harvard Business Review*, 68(2), 73–93.

Porter, M. E. (2001). The value chain and competitive advantage, in: *Understanding Business: Processes*, (p. 50–66). Routledge.

Prange, C. (2012). Ambidextrous internationalization strategies: The case of Chinese firms entering the world market. *Organizational Dynamics*. 41(3), 245–253.

Prange, C., and Bruyaka, O. (2016). Better at home, abroad, or both? How Chinese firms use ambidextrous internationalization strategies to drive innovation. *Cross Cultural & Strategic Management*. 23(2), 306–339.

PrivCo. (2012). Inside HUAWEI Of China's private financials: PrivCo reveals that the privately-held telecom giant just declared by congress a 'National Security Threat' to the U.S. Retrieved from www.privco.com/inside-huawei-of-chinas-private-financials-privco-reveals-that-the-privately-held-telecom-giant-just-declared-by-congress-a-national-security-threat-to-the-us-is-minting-billions-annually-twitter-acquires-vine

Quer, D., Claver, E., and Rienda, L. (2015). Chinese outward foreign direct investment: A review of empirical research. *Frontiers of Business Research in China*, 9(3), 326–370.

Richet, X. (2013). *L'internationalisation des firmes chinoises: croissance, motivations, stratégies*.

Rugman, A. M., and Li, J. (2007). Will China's multinationals succeed globally or regionally? *European Management Journal*, http://doi.org/10.1016/j.emj.2007.07.005.

Safran (2009). Safran partenaire de COMAC sur l'avion de 150 places C919. *Safran*, 21 December, www.safran-group.com/fr/media/20091221_safran-partenaire-de-comac-sur-lavion-de-150-places-c919.

Salidjanova, N. (2011). *Going Out: An Overview of China's Outward Foreign Direct Investment.*

Shan Lei (2009 – 单雷. (2009). 海信集团跨国投资模式研究. 商場现代化, 12(2009年6), 44–45 (which translates in: Shan Lei (2009). Study on transnational investment mode of Hisense Group. *Market Modernization*, 12 (6), 44–45).

Sina Financial. (2013, Mars 31). Shanghai Electric formed New Industry. Retrieved from http://finance.sina.com.cn/leadership/mroll/20130331/155915008381.shtml

Sit, V., and Liu, W. (2000). Restructuring and spatial change of China's auto industry under institutional reform and globalization. . . . *Annals of the Association of American Geographers.*

SmartBrief (2015). Hisense buys Sharp's Mexico TV plant; Sharp exits the Americas. *SmartBrief*, 8 March, www.smartbrief.com/s/2015/08/hisense-buys-sharps-mexico-tv-plant-sharp-exits-americas.

Solstyce. (2014, November 25). Inauguration de l'aéroport international Angoulême-Cognac « Energie solaire. Retrieved from http://www.solstyce.fr/2014/11/25/inauguration-de-laeroport-international-angouleme-cognac/

Song, R. (2012, May 14). Upsolar and EVI3 cooperate in Italy for 1MW photovoltaic power plant project. Retrieved from http://www.ne21.com/news/show-26811.html

Sun, S. L., Peng, M. W., Ren, B., and Yan, D. (2012). A comparative ownership advantage framework for cross-border M&As: The rise of Chinese and Indian MNEs. *Journal of World Business*, 47(1), 4–16, http://doi.org/10.1016/j.jwb.2010.10.015.

Symantec (2008). Huawei and Symantec commence joint venture. *Symantec*, 5 February, www.symantec.com/about/newsroom/press-releases/2008/symantec_0205_01.

Symantec (2011). Huawei acquires Symantec stake in Huawei Symantec joint venture. *Symantec*, 14 November, www.symantec.com/about/newsroom/press-releases/2011/symantec_1114_03.

Trevor, W. (2011). China's Hisense posts strong growth from Georgia base. *Global Atlanta*, 7 January, www.globalatlanta.com/chinas-hisense-posts-strong-growth-from-georgia-base/

Upsolar. (2010). Energie photovoltaîque - Upsolar, un acteur international basé en France. Retrieved from www.china-upsolar.com/uploads/UploadFile/20101205124026.pdf

Van De Vrande, V., and Vanhaverbeke, W. (2010). Broadening the scope of open innovation: Past research, current state and future directions. *International Journal*, http://doi.org/10.1504/IJTM.2010.035974;wgroup:string:metapress:journal:journal:ijtm;page:string:Article/Chapter.

Welch, L. S., and Luostarinen, R. K. (1993). Inward-outward connections in internationalization. *Journal of International Marketing*, http://doi.org/10.2307/25048483.

Wu, D., and Zhao, F. (2007). Entry modes for international markets: Case study of Huawei, a Chinese technology enterprise. *International Review of Business Research Papers.*

Xiao, W., and Liu, L. (2015). *Internationalization of China's Privately Owned Enterprises: Determinants and Pattern Selection.*

Yang, D. T., Chen, V. W., and Monarch, R. (2010). Rising wages: Has China lost its global labor advantage? *Pacific Economic Review*. 15(4), 482–504.

Yi, J. J., and Ye, S. X. (2003). *The Haier Way: The Making of a Chinese Business Leader and a Global Brand.*

Zhu, B. (2008). *Internationalization of Chinese MNEs and dunning's eclectic (OLI) paradigm: A case study of Huawei Technologies Corporation's internationalization strategy.*

ZTE (2005). ZTE and Alcatel sign OEM agreement for CDMA radio access solutions. *ZTE Corporation*, 4 April, http://wwwen.zte.com.cn/endata/magazine/ztetechnologies/2005year/no3/articles/200504/t20050404_161461.html.

ZTE (2006). Partnership breakthroughs in 2005. *ZTE Corporation*, 7 February, http://wwwen.zte.com.cn/endata/magazine/ztetechnologies/2006year/no1/articles/200602/t20060207_161558.html.

ZTE (2011). ZTE establishes R&D centre in Germany at Technical University Dresden. *ZTE Corporation*, 8 July, http://wwwen.zte.com.cn/en/press_center/news/201107/t20110708_351146.html.

ZTE (2015). *ZTE joins the Center for Global Enterprise to develop management insights for the* – ZTE Corporation, 24 April, http://wwwen.zte.com.cn/en/press_center/news/201504/t20150424_433377.html.

ZTE (2016). *ZTE reports over RMB100.1 billion in revenues for 2015*, 6 April, www.zte.com.cn/global/about/press-center/news/201604/2016040702.

ZTE USA (2012). ZTE revenue grows 23% to RMB 86 billion. *ZTE USA Blog*, 28 March, http://blog.zteusa.com/zte-revenue-grows-23-to-rmb-86-billion/

Completed with Chinese research documents (CNKI, Wanfang, CQVIP data)

倪乃顺, 庞. 刘. (2012). *欧债危机背景下中国对欧盟直接投资问题研究. 财贸经济.*

(Pang Mingchuan, Liu Dianhe, and Ni Naishun (2012). The research of the Chinese outward foreign direct investment in EU under the context of European debt crisis. *Trade and Economy*, (7), 79–87.)

刘再起, 王阳. (2014). 中国对欧盟直接投资的区位选择动因. 学习与实践, 0(8), 28–34.

(Liu Zaiqi, and Wang Yang (2014). The location determinants of Chinese Outward Direct Investment in EU. *Learning and Practice*, 8, 004.)

单雷. (2009). 海信集团跨国投资模式研究. 商场现代化, 12(2009年6), 44–45.

(Shan Lei (2009). Study on transnational investment mode of Hisense Group. *Market Modernization*, 12 (6), 44–45.)

周清杰, 王雪坤, 尹俊伟. (2013). 我国番茄酱加工业的发展与演进. 食品科学技术学报, 31(3), 64–68.

(Zhou Qing-jie, Wang Xue-kun, and Yin Jun-wei (2013). Developement and evolution of tomato ketchup manufacture industry in China. *Journal of Food Science and Technology*, 31(2), 64–68.)

郭振华, 曹煦. (2015). 东方红拖拉机 "变形记" 赵剡水详述 60 岁老国企 '一拖' 的创新基因与国际化路径. 中国经济周刊.

(Guo Zhenhua, and Cao Xi (2015). Dongfanghong tractor "transformation" Zhao Yanshui details of the 60-year-old state-owned enterprises 'YTO' innovation and internationalization of the path of *China Economic Weekly*.)

王玉, 翟青, 王丽霞, 王丹(2007). *自主创新路径及技术并购后价值链整合* – *上海电气集团收购日本秋山印刷机械公司案例分析.* 管理现代化, 3(1), 38–41.

(Wang Yu, Zhai Qing, Wang Lixia, and Wang Dan (2007). The path of independent innovation and the integration of value chain after M & A – a case study of Shanghai Electric

Group acquiring Japanese Akiyama Printing Machinery Company. *Modernization of Management*, 3(1), 38–41.)

韩文, 郭振华. (2016). 全国人大代表, *中国一拖集团董事长赵剡水：一拖将打造海外战略 "升级版*. 中国经济周刊.

(Han Wen, and Guo Zhenghua (2016). National People's Congress, China YTO Group Chairman Zhao Yanshui: YTO will create an overseas strategy "upgrade version". *China Economic Weekly*.)

张青松 (2014). 中国企业的对日投资之路 – 以上海电气集团收购秋山机械为例 。中日友好交流三十年 (1978~2008) 经济卷。

(Zhang Qingsong (2014). Chinese enterprises invest path in Japan, Shanghai Electric Group acquisition of Akiyama Machinery as an example. 30 Years of Sino – Japanese Friendship and Exchanges (1978 ~ 2008).)

项兵, 李梦军（2012）. 上海电气:日本技术 中国市场。长江商学院2012年2月。

(Xiang Bing, and Li Mengjun (2012). Shanghai electric: Japan technology in Chinese market. *Cheung Kong Graduate School of Business*, February.)

7 Chinese companies Go Global

The case of Chinese investments in France

Ni Gao and Jan Schaaper

Introduction

China is the world's third largest source of outward foreign direct investment (FDI). Its total overseas FDI now exceeds its total incoming FDI. In Europe, the absolute value of its outward FDI remains small (Clegg and Voss, 2011), yet its size has increased rapidly, establishing the continent as the most rapidly growing destination for Chinese FDI (Zhang et al., 2013). These trends show no sign of stopping, especially as European companies continue to struggle with the lingering financial challenges of the economic slowdown in many European markets. France is the second largest recipient of Chinese FDI, attracting 165 of Chinese projects in Europe (AFII, 2015).

During the last decade, academic research has contributed to a better understanding of Chinese FDI motivation in general (Child and Rodrigues, 2005; Buckley et al., 2007; Rui and Yip, 2008; Kolstad and Wiig, 2012; Peng, 2012; Deng, 2013; Si, 2013) and regions such as Australia (Drysdale and Findlay, 2009), Africa (Kaplinsky and Morris, 2009) or Europe (Minin and Zhang, 2010; Clegg and Voss, 2011; Zhang et al., 2013; Dreger et al., 2015). However, no studies have been undertaken researching Chinese FDI motivation in France. To fill this gap, the authors interviewed Chinese expatriate and French local managers of 17 Chinese subsidiaries in France with the objective of deepening understanding of the motivation of Chinese companies that invest in France. In the past decade, quantitative research has offered some macroeconomic conclusions about the reasons for outward Chinese FDI, but a lack of qualitative empirical research exists explaining the underlying motives of Chinese firms investing in advanced economies such as France. With this study, we first look to see if the motivation of Chinese FDI in France fits in with the priorities of the Chinese Go Global policy. Second, we look to see if the FDI motivation of the Chinese companies in France fits in with reverse FDI theories.

The findings reveal that Chinese companies pursue two complementary goals when investing in France. First, market-seeking Chinese companies want to increase their sales in French, European and French-speaking African markets or compete back in the Chinese market. Second, asset-seeking Chinese companies want to improve their global competitiveness by acquiring strategic assets

DOI: 10.4324/9781315102566-9

including industry-related technology, advanced production methods, R&D, innovation capabilities, internationally recognized brands and international managerial skills. Our interviews reveal that the Chinese firms investing in France benefited, directly or indirectly, from Chinese government support. Chinese investment in France serves two goals of the Chinese Go Global policy: first, the upgrading of Chinese production capacity to meet the long-term needs of the Chinese domestic markets and, second, the transformation of Chinese multinationals to become competitive in global markets. From a theoretical perspective, the FDI motivation of the Chinese companies in France fits in with the 'linkage, leverage, and learning' theory (Mathews, 2002, 2006) and the 'springboard theory' (Luo and Tung, 2007).

In the next section, we first review classic FDI theory and note why it cannot explain the rapidly growing Chinese outward FDI in developed countries such as France, and then we consider reverse FDI theories. Second, we review the Chinese outward FDI policy, including the prerequisite structural reforms of the 1980s and 1990s, its WTO membership and the Go Global policy. We then present our qualitative research methodology and describe our sample of Chinese subsidiaries which we interviewed. In answering our research questions, we first detail the Chinese companies' motivation for investing in France and finish with a discussion comparing our findings with the main goals of the Chinese Go Global policy and we look to see if Chinese direct investments in France can be explained by classic or reverse FDI theory.

Background of Chinese outward foreign direct investments

To highlight our research objective, in the background section we first review classic and reverse FDI theory, followed by an overview of the Chinese outward FDI policy since 1978, including the prerequisite structural reforms the Chinese government carried out in the 1980s and 1990s, its WTO membership in 2001 as well as the Go Global policy.

Foreign direct investment theory

Initial FDI theories, which were developed between 1960 and 1980, empirically studied investment flows undertaken by firms from developed economies to other developed economies or to developing economies. However, nowadays we observe that FDI from emerging countries flowing to industrialized countries is increasing. Traditional FDI theories cannot adequately explain such 'reverse' FDI, because emerging countries' multinationals exhibit essential differences from MNCs from developed countries. For example, Chinese companies sometimes tend to expand quickly internationally, even without technological advantages, brands or international experience. Therefore, since the 1980s, academic management research has developed some alternative theories explaining emerging countries' multinationals' FDI in developed countries. The most representative of those reverse FDI theories are the small-scale theory, the linkage, leverage, learning framework theory and the springboard theory.

Classic FDI theory

FDI has been the subject of academic research since the early sixties. One of the first FDI theories is the monopolistic advantage theory (Hymer, 1960), stating that multinational firms from developed countries have financial, technological and organizational advantages over local firms especially in imperfect, less developed markets. A second early FDI theory is Vernon's (1966) product life cycle theory, which states that a product is developed in industrialized countries where it is produced and sold in the first stage. Then, in the second stage, it spreads to international markets, where production plants move from developed to developing countries, searching for lower production costs. As such, the pace of FDI flows matches the product life cycle. Following the transaction cost theory (Williamson, 1975; Buckley and Casson, 1976; Teece, 1977; Rugman, 1981), the costs of doing international business could be lower within, rather than outside a multinational's organization. An MNC is more efficient using its own internal markets for international transfers, especially in situations where foreign markets are imperfect or failing, which is the case for most developing economies. With the concomitant aim of reducing risks and raising profitability, MNCs set up their own production and distribution subsidiaries abroad. Dunning (1979) generalized this so-called 'internalization theory' with the comprehensive ownership-localization-internalization (OLI) framework, stating that multinational companies set up subsidiaries abroad when they simultaneously have an ownership advantage, a localization advantage and an internalization advantage. A final classic FDI theory is the Uppsala model of FDI (Johanson and Vahlne, 1977; Johanson and Wiedersheim-Paul, 1975) which states that firms internationalize gradually. In the first stage, they export directly overseas and then they export indirectly through foreign agents. In the third stage, firms establish sales offices abroad and in the final stage they establish manufacturing plants overseas. Rugman et al. (2011) added to this gradual internationalization model, stating that firms initially tend to expand to nearby countries with similar country-specific conditions before expanding into more distant countries with unfamiliar cultural, economic, or political environments.

The small-scale technology and localized
technological innovation theory

According to Wells (1981, 1983), small-sized firms from developing countries possess specific features such as labour-intensive production, low costs and a rather high degree of flexibility. Their small scale and low costs production technology can meet demand for low priced commodities of consumers even in developed countries. Their flexibility and low prices allow emerging countries firms to capture such demand faster than multinationals, which often need more time to respond to such opportunities or even sometimes choose to ignore them. Lall's localized technological innovation theory complements the small-scale technology theory by showing empirically that FDI from developing countries' firms is not necessarily confined to low-technology, small-scale and labour-intensive production. Through learning and technology accumulation, the competitive advantages of emerging countries' multinationals can evolve from low-cost production to more innovative and value-added production. Developing countries multinationals may have the ability to absorb foreign technological knowledge. After an imitation stage, these companies may improve the absorbed foreign knowledge and technology and become innovative themselves, to meet local demand in foreign markets beyond purely low-priced and low value-added commodities.

The linkage-leverage-learning framework of FDI

Twenty years after Lall's localized technological innovation theory, Mathews (2002, 2006) shows that the latecomer disadvantages which obviously emerging countries' multinationals suffer from in global markets, can be transformed into a source of competitive advantage through a deliberate 'linkage, leverage and learning' strategy. During the initial stage, latecomer firms from emerging countries link with firms from industrialized countries, with specific competitive advantages such as a leading technology, through strategic alliances, mergers or acquisitions. During the second stage, after FDI in an industrialized country, the emerging country's multinational absorbs the acquired resources, including technology, international brands, organizational and managerial skills, and thus upgrades its production methods and diversifies its product portfolio. The emerging country's multinational transforms its new resources into opportunities while benefitting from a leverage effect. Entering into a learning stage, emerging countries' multinationals access new opportunities through repeated linkage and leverage, evolving in this way towards high value-added international market segments. This theory gives a rationale for the asset-seeking FDI behaviour of some emerging countries' firms in industrialized countries. When these firms have accumulated a certain level of technological knowledge, they look for supplementary advanced knowledge and technology in industrialized countries. This behaviour can rather frequently be observed with Chinese firms when they undertake mergers and acquisitions in Europe.

The springboard theory of reverse FDI

Luo and Tung (2007) suggest that emerging countries' multinationals, despite their competitive disadvantages, plan their international expansion strategically in accordance with the springboard perspective, with the final aim of acquiring critical resources which they need to compete against their global rivals both in their own domestic and in global markets. To improve their global level of competitiveness, emerging countries' multinationals use international expansion as a springboard to overcome their latecomer disadvantage through FDI in mature

Western economies. Springboarding FDI searches both for strategic assets, such as global brands, key technologies, global human resources or international distribution channels, and markets for selling their low-cost production or reaching mid-end markets in developed countries. Unlike Western MNCs, which usually globally exploit the specific capabilities they developed and possess, springboarding emerging countries' firms intentionally globalize to acquire strategic resources which they do not have yet but which they need for improving their global competitiveness. Emerging countries' firms sometimes use their foreign partners and networks, such as international joint venture partners, in their home markets, to acquire initial experience and deepen their understanding of international markets before undertaking outward FDI. Also, in some cases, springboarding firms receive home government support for going global, which is clearly the case for Chinese multinationals investing in Europe.

MNCs with deliberate springboard strategies exhibit some typical behaviour. First, unlike the incremental internationalization processes as described, for instance, by the Uppsala model, they often internationalize rapidly. Second, large springboarding firms may directly undertake high-risk acquisitions and partake in greenfield investments. Third, ignoring institutional and cultural distances, springboarding companies do not hesitate to undertake FDI in advanced markets. Finally, unlike many Western or Japanese MNCs, springboarding MNCs tend to retain local senior management teams after acquisitions rather than staffing foreign subsidiaries with expatriated parent countries' nationals.

Prerequisites of the Chinese outward FDI policy

In 1978 the Communist Party and Chinese Government started to implement a policy of economic reform and opening up to the world, known as the 'Open Door Policy'. The third plenum of the 11th Central Committee of the Communist Party marked the beginning of a slow liberalization of the Chinese economy. At the launch of the congress, Deng Xiaoping, China's paramount leader, announced the 'four modernizations', related to agriculture, industry, national defence, as well as science and technology, which were intended to make China a great economic power at the dawn of the twenty-first century. The resulting economic reforms consisted of three major elements: land reform, the creation of special economic zones and the privatization of state-owned enterprises (SOEs).

Land reform

The earliest market mechanisms were introduced in agriculture. Farmers, who previously had to hand over part of their production to the Chinese Government, obtained the right to individually exploit part of their land and freely sell their crops in the market (Huang and Rozelle, 1998). The system of collective land ownership was replaced by family-based contracts, called the household responsibility system. As a result of the farmers freedom on land-use and decision-making, as well as the link between individual reward and economic performance, China's agricultural sector was revitalized. After the previous 30 years of stagnation, the growth in agricultural output in the 1980s accelerated significantly.

Special economic zones

In 1980, four special economic zones were approved in the provinces of Guangdong and Fujian, close to Hong Kong and Macau. In these special zones, foreign companies were allowed to set up subsidiaries and collaborate locally with Chinese companies. In exchange, foreign firms benefitted from preferential policies in the fields of taxation, finance, land and wages. Also, in addition to Chinese legislation, inside the special zones the Chinese Government introduced specific FDI regulations. Foreign companies were allowed to set up factories for re-exporting processed goods to foreign markets. As such, foreign multinational companies brought in production methods and technologies, which were not oriented towards the Chinese domestic market, but towards developed Western markets. Although inward FDI and international trade expanded quickly, in the initial stages the opening up of China remained cautious and was strictly controlled by the Chinese government. The opening up progressed step by step. After 1990, the number of special economic zones multiplied and generalized and foreign multinational firms extensively installed their factories in these zones. As a result, China was labelled the 'workshop of the world'. Inward FDI has played a key role in transforming the Chinese economy, while foreign companies have brought new technologies into many sectors, new management methods for Chinese enterprises and new business sectors.

Reform of the SOEs

The privatization of SOEs probably constituted the core of China's economic reforms. When the Chinese government decided to gradually open up the Chinese economy, all Chinese firms were state-owned, on the Soviet model, and not at all adapted for international competition. At that time, SOEs were administrative organizations with economic, political and social functions. Decisions on production output, purchases, sales and even wage rates were all decided by the Chinese government. Moreover, SOEs had multiple functions, including the housing of their employees, managing schools, canteens and sometimes even hospitals etc. SOEs had simultaneously to reach production targets and to act as policy executors, provide jobs and undertake social welfare functions for their employees. With these sometimes conflicting tasks, the economic performance of the companies was often poor. The profit and loss of the SOEs was not oriented towards efficiency, while integrated in the Chinese State budget. As a result, many SOEs were in deficit. At the start of the reforms, the Chinese government separated the ownership and management of SOEs. While the state retained ownership and majority control, it gave increasingly more autonomy to SOEs' managers to run the firms. SOEs integrated new economic functions such as procurement, marketing, financial and personnel management and were relieved of social responsibilities in the areas of housing, education, health insurance etc. Henceforth, SOEs had to operate according to market logic, face competition and ensure their profitability. The Chinese state also began to open up the capital of SOEs and privatize some of them. During the 1990s and 2000s, many mid and small-sized SOEs were privatized and progressively transformed into limited liability and shareholding companies. Twenty years after the start of these reforms, most SOEs had obtained a new legal status. According to the National Bureau of Statistics in China, approximately one-third of the SOEs were transformed into limited liability companies, one-third were converted into companies with shares and one-third were still majority state-owned. Thus, the reform of SOEs has profoundly changed the structure of Chinese enterprises.

WTO membership

In addition to structural economic reforms, the second prerequisite condition for developing Chinese outward FDI was China's membership of the WTO in 2001. In order to join the WTO, China had to accelerate the modernization of its economy. China reformed its monetary regime, developed a legal system, reduced its tariffs and abolished most quantitative restrictions on international trade flows. After 20 years of special economic zones, where foreign multinationals were only allowed to produce for re-exporting, China opened up its huge domestic consumption market to foreign firms. WTO membership was a huge step forward for China to integrate into the world economy. After joining the WTO, China signed free trade agreements with most countries in the world. Ten years after accessing the WTO, Chinese imports and exports had increased sharply and China had effectively integrated into the world economy.

The de-collectivization of agriculture, the opening up of the country to foreign investments within the special economic zones, the privatization of SOEs as well as the right of entrepreneurs to start businesses were necessary prerequisite conditions for Chinese enterprises to evolve and invest abroad.

Chinese outward FDI policy

Thanks to the combined effects of the privatization of SOEs and the opening up of the Chinese economy to foreign multinational companies, the internationalization of Chinese enterprises accelerated gradually. However, the quick internationalization of Chinese firms cannot be understood, without underlining the role played by the Chinese government. This role has evolved over the last four decades. The Chinese government's policy of promoting Chinese outward FDI can roughly be divided into several overlapping periods.

During the first period, which started in the late 1970s, the Chinese government played a key role in Chinese outward FDI. Although regulations and approval processes theoretically allowed Chinese SOEs to invest abroad, companies had to undergo stringent administrative approval processes, including the evaluation of the financial and managerial capacities of the investing firms and their foreign partners. The number of Chinese companies allowed to invest abroad was pur-posely limited, which explains the slow growth of Chinese foreign investment during that period, despite the overvalued Chinese Yuan (Voss et al., 2008). Dur-ing the second period in the 1990s, the Chinese government progressively intro-duced several new outward FDI regulations, while still maintaining control over large-scale investments.

Go global policy

The third period started in 1999 when the Chinese government initiated the 'Develop International Economic Cooperation and Trade' policy, aimed at stimu-lating Chinese overseas investment. Outward FDI approval procedures were com-pletely changed. The 10th Five Year Plan in 2001, adopted the famous Go Global policy. Aimed at increasing the competitiveness of Chinese firms and accelerating the restructuring and development of the Chinese economy, the Go Global policy encouraged and supported Chinese firms' efforts to internationalize. The Chinese government shifted from a policy of controlled restrictive outward FDI to a policy of encouragement, reflecting the Chinese perception that China had become suf-ficiently developed to participate fully in the global economy. One of the main reasons for this shift towards an intentional Go Global policy was that, due to China's accession to the WTO, Chinese enterprises faced increasing competition from foreign enterprises in their own domestic markets. In order to face this inter-national competition, Chinese firms needed new technology and production meth-ods. In this context of the Go Global strategy, the Chinese government launched a series of measures to support Chinese companies to internationalize, including the decentralization and simplification of outward FDI approval procedures, the abro-gation of preliminary feasibility studies, reform of foreign exchange management, the creation of special financial funds to support overseas investments, import-export credit support, tax reduction for overseas investments, and information services to help companies to invest abroad.

The goals the Chinese government pursues with outward FDI support

With its support for Chinese enterprises to internationalize, the Chinese govern-ment pursues three main objectives. First, despite the strong economic growth of the last decades, a deep transformation of the Chinese economy remains nec-essary to ensure long-term balanced economic development. China is shifting from an external demand-driven to a domestic demand-driven economy. Cur-rently, domestic consumption has become the most important driver of Chinese economic development. Chinese production has to be upgraded from low-cost to high-quality goods, meeting the evolving needs of the growing Chinese mid-income class. Through their foreign investments, Chinese enterprises must bring in the knowledge and technology to transform the Chinese industrial structure from low to high value-added production.

Second, the strong economic growth of China of the last three decades requires increasing resources. Moreover, despite 30 years of its one-child policy, due to the aging of its huge population, the overall number of Chinese people is still growing and will continue to grow until 2050. At the same time, the country has few natural resources per capita. In order to cope with its long-term economic development, China has to import all kinds of raw materials and energy resources. The Chinese investments abroad are intended to provide these natural resources. The second objective which the Chinese government pursues with its policy of encouraging outward FDI is securing natural resources.

The third major goal which the Chinese government pursues with its outward FDI policy is raising the level of competitiveness of Chinese enterprises. Due to China's adhesion to the WTO, in 2001, and the resulting opening up of its enormous consumption market, Chinese companies have to increasingly face international competition in their own domestic markets. To cope with this competition, Chinese firms must increase their competitiveness and acquire strategic assets, resources and competencies abroad. At the same time, improving their competitiveness allows these firms also to compete in international markets, which will stimulate long-term economic growth in China.

Qualitative research methodology

The main purpose of this study is to understand the main motivation of Chinese firms investing in France and to see if these motivations fit in with, on the one hand, the priorities of the Chinese Go Global policy and, on the other hand, with the main reverse FDI theories.

Although several recent academic studies contribute to a better understanding of the main motives for Chinese outward FDI, both globally (Rui and Yip, 2008; Deng, 2013; Kolstad and Wiig, 2012; Si, 2013) and specifically, in Europe (Clegg and Voss, 2011; Zhang et al., 2013; Dreger et al., 2015), no study has explicitly considered Chinese direct investment in France. Also, most of the research on Chinese FDI motivation is still executed on the basis of macro-economic statistics. There is a dearth of empirical contributions on the detailed motivation of Chinese companies investing in France. For these complementary reasons, we opted for qualitative interviews with, mostly Chinese, managers of Chinese subsidiaries established in France, to clarify the deeper motivation of Chinese firms investing in France

The empirical field is France

France is a developed, industrialized country and an attractive destination for Chinese outward FDI. In 2014, France and China celebrated the 50th anniversary of the establishment of diplomatic relations between the countries. This event intensified the development and cooperation between China and France. According to Business France (2015) data, Chinese firms were the seventh largest investors in

France, after firms from the USA, Japan and four neighbouring countries (Germany, Italy, UK and Belgium), with 51 new investment projects, involving 1,370 jobs. According to a 2016 survey by the European Union Chamber of Commerce in China, 67% of the Chinese firms have investment projects in Germany, which confirms it as the premier European destination for Chinese investment, 41% have FDI projects in France and 37% in Italy. The European Union Chamber of Commerce in China also underlines that the UK is only the fifth most important destination with 33% of the Chinese firms having projects there after Brexit. In total, around 600 companies from China and Hong Kong now operate in France, employing around 45,000 people. The total Chinese direct investment stock in France is € 2.8 billion.

In 2016, France's GDP of € 33,400 per capita is the ninth highest in Europe. With 66 million inhabitants, its total GDP of € 2.5 billion (IMF, 2016) is the third largest in Europe, after Germany (€ 3.5 billion) and the UK (2.6 billion), and sixth largest worldwide. Although not growing quickly since the 2007 recession, the French consumer market is the third largest in Europe, and offers good opportunities for Chinese firms. Furthermore, France is located in the Western part of the European Union. It is bordered by the North and Mediterranean Seas and the Atlantic Ocean. The air, road, maritime and rail transport systems are highly developed. Its neighbouring countries, Belgium, Luxembourg, Germany, Switzerland, Spain and Italy, and the UK (connected by tunnel), also offer very attractive consumer markets. So, France is clearly a gateway to European markets.

French firms have competitive advantages in many sectors, including aviation, nuclear power, chemical industries, medicine, and agriculture. France's strong mathematics, physics, and engineering cultures lead to the creation of excellent research output and innovation centres, both public and private. According to the statistics of the World Intellectual Property Organization (WIPO, 2015), France ranks sixth worldwide in terms of international patents ownership. This has attracted the attention of Chinese companies, especially those looking for strategic assets. Despite the attractive characteristics of France for Chinese outward FDI, there is no academic research empirically investigating Chinese subsidiaries in France. This study fills in this gap.

Sample of Chinese subsidiaries in France

We initially contacted nearly 200 managers of Chinese subsidiaries located in France. However, the hierarchical nature of Chinese corporate culture often leads Chinese expatriates to avoid interviews. Furthermore, expatriates who agreed to cooperate did not always fulfil our sample requirements. In total, we conducted face-to-face interviews with managers of 17 Chinese subsidiaries in France, including 11 Chinese expatriates and six local French managers. At the request of most of these interviewees, we do not provide the names of the companies, nor the interviewees' personal identities. With this guaranteed anonymity, the respondents spoke more freely and did not feel the need to ask for permission from supervisors in the powerful Chinese corporate hierarchy. Consequently, we only indicate industries in broad terms. We underline that the 17 interviews led to information saturation so that the last interviews which we conducted did not supply any new or significant information related to our research questions (Symon and Cassel, 1998). Table 7.1 contains an overview of the sample.

The sample is diversified and interesting to analyze. Our sample contains both SOEs (eight cases) and private companies (nine cases), which invested in various industrial and service activities, including manufacturing (steel, diesel engines, tractors, consumer goods, medical equipment), transport, and services (real estate, telecommunication, broadcasting). This confirms Rui and Yip's classification (2008: 213) when they ranked Chinese acquisition firms in three categories: large SOEs which are impelled by the Go Global policy; large or small public share-issuing companies and private companies. Concerning the preferred entry mode, most of the investing Chinese companies use wholly owned subsidiaries to settle in France (15 out of 18 cases), of which eight are through greenfield investments and seven are through M&As. Three Chinese companies opted for an M&A through an international joint-venture with a local French partner. However, in case of IJVs, the Chinese partner holds a strong majority part of the IJV shares (70%, 75% and 80% respectively). Our sample characteristics fit in largely with the observations of Zhang et al. (2013: vii) that, based on MOFCOM and Eurostat data, 'Chinese investors largely opt for wholly owned subsidiaries and majority owned joint venture to establish in Europe'.

Data analysis

The interviews were held in 2015. They lasted between 45 minutes and 2.5 hours, sometimes including a visit to the company. Intentionally, we did not record the interviews, because doing so with the Chinese subordinate expatriates would have required permission from corporate hierarchies, which is difficult to obtain within Chinese corporate culture. Instead, during the interviews we took carefully handwritten notes and immediately after the meeting we fully wrote out the content of the interview. We sent back the written transcriptions to the interviewees and asked for their feedback and validation.

The data analysis followed the qualitative methodology of Silverman (2005) and Miles and Huberman (1994), who recommend a full transcription of the interviews, the development of a coding frame which fits in with the theoretical background, a pilot test and coding. More precisely, after the full transcription of the interviews, we distributed the text of the full transcription of the 17 interviews into a thematic content analysis grid, with one column per interview and one row per question or sub-question on the interview questionnaire. Then, on the basis of our research questions and expectations as well as empirical results published in academic journals, we drew up an initial list of pre-specified codes (numbers, keywords, short phrases) related to the main motivation of Chinese firms investing in France. We reduced the fully transcribed interview grid, question by question and interview by interview (i.e. cell by cell) according to these pre-specified codes. During the coding of the interviews, we added some spontaneously evoked codes,

Table 7.1 Sample characteristics

Case	Founded	Ownership	Age years	Employees worldwide	Industry sector	Manufacture trade service	Entry year France	Entry mode	Subsidiary capital structure	Employees in France
CE 1	2006	SOE	9	1,000	Consumer goods	Service	2012	M&A	IJV 70%/30%	15
CE 2	1997	SOE	18	30,000	Maritime transport	Service	1999	Greenfield	100% China WOS	23
CE 3	1995	SOE	20	19,000	Real estate industry	Service	2012	Greenfield	100% China WOS	6
CE 4	1996	Private	19	1,400	Nuclear industry	Manufacturing	2013	M&A	100% China WOS	10
CE 5	2001	Private	14	4,000	Wig manufacturing	Manufacturing	2012	Greenfield	100% China WOS	20
CE 6	1988	Private	27	150,000	Telecommunications	Service	2003	Greenfield	100% China WOS	650
CE 7	1955	SOE	60	16,000	Engine manufacturing	Manufacturing	2011	M&A	100% China WOS	100
CE 8	1996	Private	19	2,500	Broadcasting & cable TV	Service	2009	Greenfield	100% China WOS	5
CE 9	1996	Private	19	1,200	Wolfberry processing	Manufacturing	2012	M&A	100% China WOS	20
CE 10[1]	2004	SOE	11	110,000	Chemical industry	Manufacturing	2006 / 2007	M&A / M&A	100% China WOS / IJV 80%/ 20%	3,100
CE 11	1903	Private	112	28,000	Beer production	Manufacturing	1995	Greenfield	100% China WOS	5
CE 12	1991	Private	24	10,000	Medical equipment	Manufacturing	2008	M&A	100% China WOS	47
CE 13	1946	SOE	69	55,000	Diesel manufacturing	Manufacturing	2009	M&A	100% China WOS	190
CE 14	1978	SOE	37	130,000	Steel manufacturing	Manufacturing	1995	M&A	100% China WOS	25
CE 15	1980	SOE	35	16,000	Service sector	Service	1992	Greenfield	100% China WOS	20
CE 16	1961	SOE	54	130,000	Maritime transport	Service	1991	Greenfield	100% China WOS	30
CE 17	2008	Private	7	100	Mining industry	Mining	2013	M&A	IJV 75%/25%	20

Notes: SOE = state-owned enterprise, M&A = merger and acquisitions, WOS = wholly owned subsidiary, IJV = international joint venture. For the IJVs, the first percentage listed refers to the amount held by the Chinese partner, and the second percentage is the amount held by the French partner

[1]Chinese enterprise (CE) 10 conducted two acquisitions in 2006 and 2007.

which Miles and Huberman (1994) call 'emerging codes'. Thus we obtained a reduced content analysis grid. To check the reliability of the coding, each member of the research team performed individual coding. Any differences were resolved through discussion. We also added some supplementary variables drawn from external secondary data sources, such as websites, trade directories and Chinese government investment agencies, which enabled us to understand the FDI choices made by the interviewed companies. In relation to our research question, we looked specifically, row by row, for similarities and contrasts between the interviewed Chinese companies. We finished the analysis with repeated readings of the interviews.

Main motivation of Chinese direct investment in France

Our central research question is to understand the main motivation of Chinese firms investing in France. We base our analysis on Dunning's classification of FDI motivation into four categories, of which Meyer (2015) gives a useful overview. First, market-seeking FDI tries to protect existing foreign markets, for instance, by circumventing trade barriers, or to promote new ones, typically in the host country of the subsidiary. Second, efficiency-seeking FDI looks for lower production costs by means of global economies of scale or scope and lower costs of input, including labour costs and costs of intermediate production goods. Third, resource-seeking FDI secures natural resources such as minerals, oil, gas or agricultural products. Fourth and last, strategic asset-seeking FDI enhances the capabilities of the acquisition firm with a view to long-term competitiveness in home and global markets. These latter capabilities include the upgrading of technology, organizational knowledge and successful brands (Meyer, 2015).

Our interviews reveal a diversity of reasons for Chinese firms to invest in France, which, according to Dunning's classification, can essentially be ranked as 'market-seeking' motivation and 'strategic asset-seeking' motivation. Table 7.2 gives an overview of the main motivation of Chinese firms investing in France.

Chinese direct investment in France searching for
French, European and African markets

Table 7.2 shows clearly that the most important reason for Chinese investment in France is market-seeking (16 of 17 cases), in line with the findings of both Kolstad and Wiig (2012) that Chinese outward FDI is attracted to large markets and of Dreger et al. (2015) that market size is the primary factor driving Chinese direct investment in the European Union. For four Chinese firms, operating in maritime transport (CE 2), the chemical sector (CE 10), medical equipment (CE 12), and in diesel manufacturing (CE 13), accessing the French market is their main goal, sometimes in combination with a search for strategic assets (CE 10, CE 13). France is a vast consumer market, with a high degree of openness and large export opportunities for Chinese products.

Table 7.2 Main FDI motivation of Chinese subsidiaries in France, ranked as market-seeking and asset-seeking motivation

Motivation	Market-seeking motivations				Strategic asset-seeking motivations				
	French market	European market	African market	Chinese market	Knowledge	Brand	Technology	Diversification portfolio	Improve industrial structure
Chinese firm (CE)	CE 2	CE 2	CE 5	CE 1	CE 1	CE 1	CE 4	CE 2	CE 2
	CE 3	CE 5	CE 13	CE 9	CE 9	CE 13	CE 7	CE 13	CE 6
	CE 5	CE 6		CE 10			CE 10	CE 14	CE 10
	CE 6	CE 7		CE 17			CE 14	CE 17	
	CE 7	CE 8					CE 17		
	CE 8	CE 9							
	CE 9	CE 10							
	CE 10	CE 11							
	CE 11	CE 12							
	CE 12	CE 13							
	CE 13	CE 14							
	CE 14	CE 15							
	CE 15	CE 16							
	CE 16								
Total number of firms	14	13	2	4	2	2	5	4	3

With its location in the western part of the European Union and its well-developed transport system (railways, tunnel to the United Kingdom, roads, harbours at both Mediterranean and Atlantic coasts), France offers a perfect hub, connecting Chinese investors to the other large European Union consumer markets, such as Germany, the United Kingdom, Italy, Spain, and the Benelux. Many respondents note that France possesses localization advantages that no other European country has, and three-quarters of our sample (13 cases) acknowledge that their French FDI represents a gateway to the broader European market. The companies are active in different sectors of activity, such as real estate (CE 3), consumer goods (CE 5, 11), services (CE 6, 8, 15), engine manufacturing (CE 7), chemicals (CE 10), medical equipment (CE 12), steel (CE 14), and transport (CE 16).

Two firms in our sample also invest in France while having an eye on African markets. Many West African (Ivory Coast, Senegal, Mali, Cameroon, Gabon etc.) and North African (Tunisia, Algeria, Morocco) countries are former French colonies, with continuing cultural, political, and economic links to France. In total, around 20 countries in Africa have French as a common language, spanning a total population of around 400 million people. Furthermore, for many of these countries, France is a primary trading partner and the principal access to the European markets. As the CE 5 and 13 managers explained, their French subsidiaries help them build bridges to French-speaking African markets, by setting up sales and transport networks to Africa. For CE 5, a wig manufacturer, Africa is a critical market; it also represents a very appealing market for the diesel engines produced in France by CE 13.

Rui and Yip (2008) also note that some domestically oriented Chinese firms acquire firms abroad with the strategic intent of competing with foreign MNCs in the Chinese market, while benefitting from acquired strategic assets. For many Chinese firms (CEs 1, 9, 10, and 17 in our sample), winning the domestic market remains very important. For CEs 1 and 9, which operate in consumer goods industries, meeting the needs of the immense Chinese consumer market remains a primary strategic goal. They acquired French companies to integrate these companies' brands (CE 1) and production knowledge (CE 1 and 9). In the mining sector, the representative of CE 17 explained that the firm is less interested in developing its French or European market. It entered into a joint venture with a French company to diversify its product portfolio and upgrade its technology, which in turn should help expand its sales in China.

Two Chinese companies further explained that they set up subsidiaries in France in order to bypass the regulatory barriers in French and European markets (CE 6, CE 10). The example of CE 6 is very demonstrative. The Chinese firm, CE 6, is a big player in the Chinese telecommunication market and seeks new markets in Europe. However, the telecommunication sector generally is considered as quite sensitive in Europe, so most European countries impose complex regulations on foreign companies. For this reason, so as to circumvent political and other non-tariff barriers to enter the French and European telecommunication markets, CE 6 set up a wholly owned subsidiary, through a greenfield investment in France. Moreover, this Chinese company had already failed in its attempt to merge, through an international joint venture, with a US partner. To avoid the same mistake, it therefore established a 100% greenfield French subsidiary, without any local partner.

Chinese outward FDI in France is also strategic asset-seeking

For 11 Chinese firms, the search for strategic resources and assets constitutes their main motivation to invest in France. This strategic asset-seeking behaviour in some cases complements the market-seeking motivation. Three Chinese companies, CE 5 (wigs), CE 6 (telecommunication), and CE 10 (chemicals), underlined that their manufactured products are situated at the low end of their respective value chains, so their investments in France serve their goal of upgrading their production methods in China. Four Chinese companies, CE 4 (nuclear energy), CE 7 (tractors), CE 14 (steel), and CE 17 (mining), acquired technological knowledge in France, according with their goals of evolving toward higher value-added products that they can offer in both Chinese and international markets. In addition, the Chinese companies CE 1 (consumer goods) and CE 9 (wolfberries) talk about acquiring knowledge more generally, while the Chinese companies CE 2 (maritime transport), CE 13 (diesel engines), CE 14 (steel), and CE 17 (mining) have invested in France with the idea of diversifying their portfolios of products and services.

For a long time, Chinese manufacturing companies relied on China's demographic-led low labour cost advantages to export Chinese products worldwide. However, production costs are presently rising in China and the traditional cost advantages are gradually weakening, so fostering new competitive advantages has become imperative for most firms in our sample. Our Chinese interviewees explain that FDI in industrialized countries is a suitable means to quickly enhance their level of global competitiveness. They also confirm that, in Chinese eyes, France is a creative, innovative country, with high-skilled engineers and managers. As many small and medium-sized technology firms in France suffer financially from the enduring economic crisis in Europe, they need new capital to survive. An M&A with a Chinese firm offers a reasonable solution to avoid bankruptcy or new bank borrowing.

The interviewees also made the point that a 'Made in China' label tends not to inspire much trust among consumers. China is still considered the world's factory, producing low cost products. Thus CE 13, which produces diesel engines, sought to enhance its sales in France and Europe by acquiring a well-known French brand. In addition, recent scandals involving Chinese brands, especially in the food industry, have prompted greater scepticism among Chinese consumers, who increasingly seek foreign brands with better reputations. Chinese consumers believe that foreign brands offer better quality and service and regard them as safer, particularly in the food sector and more durable. Thus, CE 1 acquired a well-reputed French brand to develop its sales in the Chinese market.

To meet China's massive energy needs, while also addressing increasing concerns about air quality, climate change, and fossil fuel shortages, the Chinese government is actively expanding its nuclear power industry. In turn, CE 4, China's first producer of forged and cast parts for the nuclear industry, has entered into international cooperative agreements to access advanced technology and nuclear safety information. Through its successful M&A of a French company that produces nuclear power – related parts, CE 4 extended its industrial chain to Europe, thereby contributing to the mission of ensuring China's ability to meet its future energy needs.

The chemical industry faces a strong development of the huge Chinese consumer market. Many foreign MNCs have created subsidiaries in China in the past decade, raising the level of competition and challenging local Chinese firms, which are often not sufficiently competitive. To improve its competitiveness but avoid immediate and direct conflict with foreign MNCs in China, the Chinese chemical firm CE 10 undertook two acquisitions in France, in 2006 and 2007, with the clear goal of strengthening its technological and innovative capacity to sell products in the Chinese market. This FDI behaviour corresponds with the springboard theory (Luo and Tung, 2007). For CE 10, the home country market remains its primary operations territory. Therefore, its international expansion serves as a springboard to acquire critical resources and assets with the aim of competing more effectively against global rivals, abroad and in its home market.

Discussion and contributions

Our central research question is to understand first the main motivation of Chinese firms investing in France. We look to see if these motivations fit in with, on the one hand, the main goals of the official Chinese Go Global policy. On the other hand, we analyze if Chinese outward FDI needs specific theoretical development or if it fits in with the main reverse FDI theories.

Our interviews reveal very clearly that Chinese companies investing in France pursue two main goals. The primary motivation (16 of 17 cases) is market-seeking. The Chinese interviewees acknowledge that their Chinese mother-companies want to increase their sales in French and European markets. Two Chinese firms also target the French-speaking West African markets, with which France has historical connections. Another Chinese firm hopes to enter the highly protected European telecommunication market through a wholly owned French subsidiary because direct access for a Chinese company is complicated. These conclusions fit in with Kolstad and Wiig's (2012) econometric results, which show that 'the only variable to be significantly associated with Chinese outward FDI is host country GDP; in other words, Chinese outward FDI is attracted to countries with large markets' (Kolstad and Wiig, 2012: 31). Our conclusions are also supported by several other studies showing that Chinese FDI is attracted to host countries with large GDPs (Buckley et al., 2007; Cheung and Qian, 2008; Cheng and Ma, 2008). More specifically, in Europe, Dreger et al. (2015) underline that market size is one of the primary factors driving Chinese direct investment in the European Union. They underline that, by entering any European Union member state, Chinese firms can access the entire European market. This is what we also observed through our interviews.

The second goal the Chinese firms in our sample pursue with their direct investment in France is asset-seeking. By acquiring strategic assets, the Chinese firms seek to enhance their global level of competitiveness in both international markets and their domestic market. The Chinese companies in our sample are looking for a set of different and complementary categories of strategic resources and assets, including industry-related technology, advanced production methods to upgrade their industrial capacity, R&D, innovation capabilities to develop higher value-added products and services, internationally recognized brands, as well as managerial skills to help address the lack of international experience of Chinese managers and engineers. These conclusions are in line with Deng's (2013: 517) observation that empirical research largely supports rationale predicting the likelihood of Chinese overseas M&As to be asset-seeking and with Luo and Tung's (2007: 481) conclusion that 'Chinese MNCs aim to overcome latecomer disadvantages via acquisition of critical assets from mature MNCs to compensate for their competitive weakness'.

By encouraging Chinese enterprises to internationalize, the Chinese government pursues three main objectives. First, Chinese production capacity has to be upgraded to meet the evolving needs of Chinese consumers and ensure long-term balanced economic growth in China. Second, Chinese outward direct investment has to secure natural resources and, third, Chinese firms must increase their global competitiveness. The two main motivations for Chinese direct investments in France, market and strategic asset-seeking, fit in with both the first and third goals of Chinese outward FDI policy. With their acquisitions of technology, production methods, international brands, and international managerial experience in France, Chinese firms at the same time develop their capacity to meet rapidly changing domestic consumer demand and become more competitive in global markets. We thus confirm the observation of Child and Rodrigues (2005: 387) that leading Chinese firms 'have begun to internationalize with a view to becoming global players in international markets' (third goal). Our conclusions also accord with Rui and Yip's (2008) findings that Chinese firms use foreign acquisitions, including product technology, globally recognized brands and international managerial experience, with the ultimate strategic goal of transforming themselves from domestic market players to global players (first and third goals). On the contrary, Chinese investment in France does not serve the second goal which is to secure long-term natural resources. This finding underlines Minin and Zhang's (2010: 439) statement that 'Chinese outward FDI is now undergoing a shift from nature-resource seeking to strategic asset and market-seeking to build competitive advantages'.

Our research contributes to FDI theory, in general, and in particular, to 'reverse FDI' theory. Our empirical observations fit in with Lall's (1984) localized technological innovation theory. Chinese investment in France is no longer confined to low-technology, small-scale and labour-intensive production. Through learning and technology accumulation, the competitive advantages of Chinese firms are evolving from typical 'Made in China' low-cost products to more innovative and value-added products. Many Chinese firms in our sample especially, implement a 'linkage-leverage-learning' strategy. These firms intentionally transform their 'latecomer disadvantages', which they suffer from in global markets, into a source of competitive advantage. The Chinese firms in our sample link with small and medium-sized innovative French firms, with specific competitive advantages such as technology, production methods, brands and international experience. The Chinese acquisition firms absorb these newly acquired French resources and assets and transform them into new opportunities, for instance, in the Chinese domestic market, benefitting from a leverage effect. Entering a repeated learning stage, we can predict that Chinese firms will continue to acquire strategic assets in France and Europe, with the final aim of evolving towards high value-added segments in their domestic and global markets.

Also, the Chinese cases in our sample fit in partially with the springboard theory of Luo and Tung (2007). Typically, springboarding firms are searching in mature Western markets for strategic assets and market opportunities to sell their products. Most Chinese firms in our sample exhibit several elements of typical springboard behaviour, including quick internationalization, high-risk acquisitions, greenfield investments in advanced markets and, last but not least, the maintenance of existing local senior management teams after acquisitions, rather than staffing their French subsidiaries with Chinese expatriates.

Our research offers a new theoretical lens to look at Chinese FDI in Europe, which we call the 'bridging theory'. Some Chinese companies acquired French firms with the aim of building bridges to West African markets, which have strong historical ties with France. Thanks to the distribution networks and knowledge of their French subsidiaries about African markets, Chinese multinationals seek to enhance their sales in those French-speaking African markets.

Finally, our research underlines the involvement of the Chinese government in Chinese outward FDI. Chinese acquisition firms benefited significantly from government support at critical stages in their international efforts and asset acquisitions, offsetting their competitive weakness in global competition. China's huge foreign exchange reserves facilitate such government support. Also, Deng (2013: 519) finds that the sharp growth of Chinese overseas investments is the outcome of the Chinese government's Go Global strategy, with a priority to serve its national development priorities. We confirm that the Chinese firms in our sample, both private and state-owned, receive direct (subsidies) or indirect (low interest rates, loans, tax advantages) support from Chinese authorities, confirming the involvement of the Chinese government in Chinese outward FDI. The Chinese investments in France serve two priorities of the Chinese Go Global policy, i.e. the upgrade of Chinese production capacity to meet the long-term needs of Chinese domestic markets and the transformation of Chinese multinationals to become globally competitive.

Conclusion

The central research purpose of this chapter was to understand the motivation of Chinese firms investing in France and to find out if this motivation fits in with the priorities of the Chinese Go Global policy. We also analyzed if Chinese direct investment in France fits in with FDI theories. To answer these questions, we interviewed Chinese expatriate and French local managers of 17 Chinese subsidiaries in France in 2015.

Our interviews reveal that Chinese companies investing in France pursue two complementary goals. First, market-seeking Chinese companies want to increase their sales in French, European and French-speaking African markets as well as competing back In the Chinese market. Second, asset-seeking Chinese companies want to improve their global competitiveness by acquiring strategic assets including industry-related technology, advanced production methods, R&D, innovation capabilities, internationally recognized brands and international managerial skills.

Our research reveals that the Chinese companies in our sample benefitted from the Go Global policy, receiving direct and indirect government support. The FDI motivation of the Chinese firms in our sample fits in with two priorities of the Chinese Go Global Policy, which are the improvement of Chinese production capacity in order to meet the domestic needs of Chinese consumers and to ensure long-term balanced economic growth in China, and also the increase in the level of competitiveness of Chinese enterprises in global markets.

Classic FDI theory, empirically based on Western FDI, cannot adequately explain the sharp increase in Chinese investment in Europe. On the contrary, the FDI motivation of the Chinese firms in our sample fits in with the more recently developed reverse FDI theories, especially the 'linkage, leverage, learning' framework (Mathews, 2002, 2006) and the springboard theory (Luo and Tung, 2007). Our research also suggests a new 'bridging theory', which suggests that Chinese FDI in France also aims at building bridges to African markets.

Academic literature on Chinese outward FDI to industrialized countries is still scarce and lagging behind the speed of development of Chinese investment in Europe. Therefore, we intentionally adopted an inductive posture and undertook qualitative research for this study. With semi-structured interviews, we obtained in-depth insights into the underlying reasons that lead Chinese companies to invest in France. However, the shortcomings of qualitative interviews are well known. Generalizing the conclusions from our research findings require caution. To address this limitation quantitative survey could be conducted, using the findings of this study, on a larger panel of Chinese subsidiaries in Europe.

In relation to future research, our conclusions suggest two directions. First, reverse FDI theory until recently, tries to explain why emerging countries' multinationals invest in developed countries. To the best of our knowledge, very few studies investigate what management style and practices Chinese firms adopt when investing in advanced European economies such as the UK, France or Germany. Do Chinese companies adopt ethnocentric or polycentric management attitudes in their subsidiaries abroad? Are Chinese management practices different when their FDI is resource-seeking, in Africa or Australia, for instance, or takes place in geographically and culturally close countries in South-East Asia? Further research could also deepen understanding of the bridging perspective of Chinese FDI in Europe. Specifically, does Chinese FDI in the UK look for bridges to former countries of the British Empire?

References

AFII (2015). *The International Development of the French Economy, AFII Annual Report.* Paris: Foreign Investment in France, Invest in France Agency.

Buckley, P. J., and Casson, M. C. (1976). *The Future of the Multinational Enterprise.* London: Macmillan (25th Anniversary Edition, 2001).

Buckley, P. J., Clegg, L. J., Cross, A. R., Lin, X., Voss, H., and Zheng, P. (2007). The determinants of Chinese outward FDI. *Journal of International Business Studies*, 38(4), 499–518.

Business France (2015). *Rapport sur l'internationalisation de l'économie française.* Bilan 2015 des investissements étrangers en France.

Cheng, L. K., and Ma, Z. (2008). *China's outward foreign direct investment.* Paper presented at the Indian Statistical Institute, 12 December, www.isid.ac.in/pu/seminar/12_12_2008_Paper.doc.

Cheung, Y. W., and Qian, X. W. (2008). *The Empirics of China's Outward Direct Investment.* Munich: Cesifo GmbH.

Child, J., and Rodrigues, S. B. (2005). The internationalization of Chinese firms: A case for theoretical extension? *Management and Organization Review*, 1(3), 381–410.

Clegg, J., and Voss, H. (2011). Inside the China – EU FDI bond. *China & World Economy*, 19(4), 92–108.

Deng, P. (2013). Chinese outward direct investment research: Theoretical integration and recommendations. *Management and Organization Review*, 9(3), 513–539.

Dreger, C., Schüler-Zhou, Y., and Schüller, M. (2015). *Determinants of Chinese direct investments in the European Union.* Discussion Paper, no. 1480, Deutsches Institut für Wirtschaftsforschung.

Drysdale, P., and Findlay, C. (2009). Chinese foreign direct investment in Australia: Policy issues for the resource sector. *China Economic Journal*, 2(2), 133–158.

Dunning, J. H. (1979). Explaining changing patterns of international production: A search for the eclectic theory. *Oxford Bulletin of Economics and Statistics*, 161, 269–295.

European Union Chamber of Commerce in China (2013). *Chinese outbound investment in the European Union*, January, www.europeanchamber.com.cn.

Huang, J., and Rozelle, S. (1998). Market development and food consumption in rural China. *Economic Review*, 9, 25–45.

Hymer, S. H. (1976). *The international operations of national firms: A study of direct foreign investment.* Ph.D. Thesis 1960, published in 1976, MIT Press, Cambridge, MA.

Johanson, J., and Vahlne, J. E. (1977). The internationalization process of the firm: A model of knowledge development and increasing foreign market commitments. *Journal of International Business Studies*, 8(1), 23–31.

Johanson, J., and Wiedersheim-Paul, F. (1975). The internationalization of the firm: Four Swedish cases. *Journal of International Business Studies*, 10, 305–322.

Kaplinsky, R., and Morris, M. (2009). Chinese FDI in sub-Saharan Africa: Engaging with large dragons. *European Journal of Development Research*, 21(4), 551–569.

Kolstad, I., and Wiig, A. (2012). What determines Chinese outward FDI? *Journal of World Business*, 47(1), 26–34.

Lall, S. (1984). *The New Multinationals: The Spread of Third World Enterprises*, IRM Series on Multinationals. New York: Wiley.

Luo, Y., and Tung, R. L. (2007). International expansion of emerging market enterprises: A springboard perspective, *Journal of International Business Studies*, 38(4), 481–498.

Mathews, J. (2002). *Dragon Multinational: Towards a New Model of Global Growth.* New York: Oxford University Press.

Mathews, J. (2006). Dragon multinationals: New players in 21st century globalization. *Asia-Pacific Journal of Management*, 23(1), 5–27.

Meyer, K. E. (2015). What is "strategic asset seeking foreign direct investment"? *The Multinational Business Review*, 23(1), 57–66.

Miles, M., and Huberman, A. (1994). *Qualitative Data Analysis*. London: SAGE Publications.

Minin, A. D., and Zhang, J. (2010). An exploratory study on international R&D strategies of Chinese companies in Europe. *Review of Policy Research*, 27(4), 433–455.

Peng, M. W. (2012). The global strategy of emerging multinationals from China. *Global Strategy Journal*, 2, 97–107.

Rugman, A. M. (1981). *Inside the Multinationals: The Economics of Internal Markets*. New York: Columbia Press. (Reissued 25th Anniversary Edition, Basingstoke, Palgrave Macmillan, 2006).

Rugman, A. M., Verbeke, A., and Nguyen Quyen, T. K. (2011). Fifty years of international business theory and beyond. *Management International Review*, 51(6), 755–786.

Rui, H., and Yip, G. (2008). Foreign acquisitions by Chinese firms: A strategic intent perspective. *Journal of World Business*, 43(2), 13–26.

Si, Y. (2013). *Outward FDI from China; historical development, geographical distribution and the obstacles to subsidiary business success*. Dissertation zur Erlangung des akademischen Grades, Doctor rerum naturalium (Dr.rer.nat.), Justus-Liebig-Universität Gießen.

Silverman, D. (2005). *Doing Qualitative Research: A Practical Handbook*. London: SAGE Publications.

Symon, G., and Cassel, C. (1998). *Qualitative Methods and Analysis in Organizational Research*. Newbury Park: SAGE Publications.

Teece, D. J. (1977). Technology transfer by multinational firms: The resource cost of transferring technological know-how. *Economic Journal*, 87(346), 42–261.

Vernon, R. (1966). International investment and international trade in the product cycle. *Quarterly Journal of Economics*, 80(2), 190–207.

Voss, H., Buckley, P. J., and Cross, A. R. (2008). *Thirty years of Chinese outward foreign direct investment*. 19th Annual Conference of the China Economic Association, University of Cambridge.

Wells, L. (1981). Foreign investors from third world, in Kumar, K., and McLeod, M. G. (eds.), *Multinationals From Developing Countries*. Lexington, MA: Lexington Books.

Wells, L. (1983). *Third World Multinationals: The Rise of Foreign Investment from Developing Countries*. London: MIT Press.

Williamson, O. E. (1975). *Markets and Hierarchies*. New York: The Free Press.

WIPO (2015). World intellectual property indicators. *Economics & Statistics Series*. World Intellectual Property Organization, yearly report 2015.

Zhang, H., Yang, Z., and Van Den Bulcke, D. (2013). *Euro-China Investment Report 2013– 2014. Chinese Owned Enterprises in Europe: A Study of Corporate and Entrepreneurial Firms and the Role of Sister City Relationships*. Antwerp: Euro-China Centre at the Antwerp Management School.

8 Chinese firms in France

Investment motives and related top manager staffing practices

Cuiling Jiang and Romain Belz

Introduction

Recent decades have witnessed a significant rise in cross-border operations. Such internationalization requires companies to balance the process of integrating their sites locally yet retaining company-wide standardization (Eriksson et al., 1997; Bartlett and Ghoshal, 1989). Most of the existing research on foreign direct investment (FDI) focuses on companies from well-developed countries and their operations in developing and emerging countries. These companies seek to replicate their successful business models in foreign host countries (Dunning, 1981). However, internationalization strategies are not only the privilege of companies from developed countries. Numerous companies from emerging markets (CEMs) also have expanded their business abroad. For instance, according to Ministry of Commerce in the People's Republic of China (MOFCOM, 2016), China has become the second largest overseas investor in the world in 2015.

The aim of this chapter is to investigate the motives behind Chinese outward foreign direct investment (OFDI) and explain how Chinese companies achieve their organizational goals through related overseas top manager staffing practices. Based on previous research, we identify that differences exist in the motives attached to companies' internationalization strategies. For example, the motives for CEMs like China to do business in developed countries are to seek strategic assets to address latecomer disadvantages and competitive weakness (Zheng et al., 2016; Cui et al., 2014). Additionally, CEMs have grown rapidly in recent years. These companies are generally young and lack international experience, which may hinder their efficiency in international management (Cooke, 2011; Thite et al., 2012). Companies from well-developed countries have a rich experience in international business. Their motives to invest overseas are more likely to exploit their existing ownership advantage and to benefit from the lower cost in certain host countries (e.g., less-developed countries) and larger scale of market share (Rui and Yip, 2008). These differences in internationalization motives need to be fully understood because they may have important consequences for the appropriate top manager staffing practices companies should adopt to facilitate the overseas operations.

DOI: 10.4324/9781315102566-10

Despite the increased interest in understanding FDI from CEMs (Buckley et al., 2007; Child and Rodrigues, 2005), little research has been conducted regarding the relationship between the motives behind the OFDI of CEMs and their respective top manager staffing practices. Knowledge of how internationalization motives may shape the staffing practices in CEM subsidiaries remains limited (Cooke, 2014; Jackson, 2014). Therefore, we seek to answer two research questions: (1) What are the motives for CEMs to expand business to well-developed countries?; and (2) what top manager staffing practices can CEMs adopt to best implement their internationalization strategies in the well-developed countries?

We chose to study Chinese FDI in France. Compared to CEMs from other home countries, China's OFDI has its own characteristics and receives a lot of attention from scholars. First, China is the world's second largest economy as well as second largest cross-border investor. The majority of Chinese overseas investors are state-owned enterprises (SOEs). These companies are backed up by the Chinese government, which plays a crucial role in designing formal and informal institutional frameworks to push up the Chinese OFDI (Ren et al., 2010) and even assigns the CEOs for the largest Chinese state-owned multinational companies (Andreff, 2015). Second, since 1999, the Chinese government has launched the 'go-global' strategy (in Chinese: 走出去战略), which has significantly boosted the numbers of Chinese OFDI. More and more Chinese non-SOEs have joined the international business world even though they may receive a lower level of government support in the forms of credit lines and low-interest loans from state-owned banks (Andreff, 2015). Therefore, the strong involvement and control of Chinese government toward companies' expansion in different countries is a reality. Third, we wonder whether the nature of Chinese companies (e.g., SOEs or privately owned companies) may have effects on human resource management (HRM). Given that few studies have examined the top manager staffing practices in relation to Chinese OFDI (Cooke, 2011), we are interested in investigating this phenomenon.

We chose to study France as the focal host country for two reasons. On the one hand, prior studies on Chinese FDI focused on Chinese companies' management practices in Vietnam (Cooke, 2011), localized learning capabilities in Australia (Fan et al., 2016), Chinese OFDI in Africa (Jackson, 2014), and overseas investment motives (Wang et al., 2012; Rui and Yip, 2008). As far as we know, there is no research on the Chinese OFDI in France and the related top manager staffing practices except for Nicolas's work (2010). It is important to note that France is one of the top fifteen destinations to receive Chinese FDI in the world. In Europe, France is the second largest receiver of Chinese FDI in 2016 (Business France, 2016). But little research has investigated FDI from CEMs to France. Therefore, this study fills some of the research gaps by examining the internationalization strategies and related HRM practices in two distinct categories of Chinese firms – SOEs and privately owned companies, greenfield investments and brownfield investments.

This chapter aims to provide several contributions. First, it offers a framework to better understand the internationalization strategies of Chinese state-owned and privately owned companies. We explain why Chinese companies invest in business overseas, how they realize internationalization, and how they staff members to lead their foreign subsidiaries. Second, we enrich the research related to French business context, which national culture, institutional environment, and language are very different from those in Europe and other countries on other continents. Third, our recommendations to Chinese and French companies may facilitate their understanding of each other and boost their cooperation synergy.

The next section provides a literature review on motives behind Chinese companies' international expansion and their respective top manager staffing practices. Thereafter, we explain our methodology through adopting qualitative data – interviews with top managers in Chinese subsidiaries in France. The empirical results are then presented. Recommendations to companies and future research are discussed at the end.

Literature review

A number of theoretical perspectives have been developed to analyze the motives behind the internationalization strategies of companies from well-developed countries. However, the research on CEMs' internationalization starts to attract more attention. Given that CEMs face significant internationalization challenges in terms of regulative, normative and cognitive differences between home and host countries (Palthe, 2014), this section begins with a review of the development of Chinese overseas investments.

The development of Chinese OFDI

In China, several governmental departments participate in making, implementing, and supervising FDI policies and practices (Andreff, 2015). First, China State Council makes the overall FDI blueprints. Then, the National Development and Reform Commission (NDRC) formulates OFDI by examining and approving the key projects in the areas of research & development (R&D), natural resource seeking, development of advanced technologies and managerial practices, talent acquisition and development, and so forth. Next, the Ministry of Commerce (MOFCOM) is responsible for conducting multilateral negotiations on international trade and investment, drafting the operational aspects of FDI measures and regulations (Andreff, 2015). Then, the Ministry of Finance administers macroeconomic policies and the annual budget for OFDI projects. The State-owned Assets Supervision and Administration Commission (SASAC) guides and implements the reform and restructuring of Chinese SOEs, advancing the establishment of modern enterprise systems in the SOEs. Meanwhile, the State Administration of Foreign Exchange (SAFE) works with the China Development Bank, the Export-Import Bank of China, and the China Export & Credit Insurance Corporation on development and supervision of the foreign exchange account and international investment. In total, there are at least six layers of supervision and regulation needed to put Chinese companies' internationalization into motion (see Table 8.1).

Table 8.1 Key layers in managing Chinese OFDI

Governmental Department	Functions
China State Council	Makes overall FDI blueprints
National Development and Reform Commission (NDRC)	Examines and approves key projects in natural resource seeking, R&D, development of advanced technologies and managerial practices, talent acquisition and development
Ministry of Commerce (MOFCOM)	Negotiates the conditions of international trade and investment, drafts the operational aspects of FDI measures and regulations
Ministry of Finance	Administers macroeconomic policies and the annual budget for OFDI projects
State-owned Assets Supervision and Administration Commission (SASAC)	Reforms and restructures Chinese SOEs if necessary, advances the establishment of modern enterprise systems in the state-owned companies
State Administration of Foreign Exchange (SAFE)	Supervises the international payment, foreign exchange accounts, works with China Development Bank, Export-Import Bank of China, and China Export & Credit Insurance Corporation

Source: Andreff (2015) and authors' data.

Regarding the development of China's OFDI, there are three basic stages. The first stage (between 1979 and 1991) can be named as 'cross the river by feeling the stones'. Thanks to the 'open door' policy, OFDI has become possible in China since 1979. However, only a very limited number of companies can have OFDI at that moment and, in particular, only few SOEs can get access to international trade. In 1992, during Deng Xiaoping's journey to Shenzhen in China, further liberalization on domestic economic and international trade was put in place. From the state level to the sub-national level, authorities actively promote international business activities of companies, but under supervision (Buckley et al., 2007). Therefore, we can name the second stage (between 1992 and 1999) as the 'further rise of OFDI' with a positive regulatory environment. Subsequently, China launched the 'go-global' initiatives in 1999 and became a WTO member in 2001. In addition, Xi Jinping proposed 'the Silk Road Economic Belt' and 'the 21st-century Maritime Silk Road' (in Chinese: 丝绸之路经济带和21世纪海上丝绸之路) in 2013. Since then, administrative controls by the Chinese government have been reduced to a lower level, and more and more state-owned plus privately owned Chinese companies have expanded their business abroad. More measures on OFDI have been introduced, for instance, the list of specific industries that the Chinese government encourages domestic companies to invest in overseas, export tax reduction, foreign currency exchange assistance, financial support, and so forth. The measures related to OFDI become more and more formalized and operation-based (Blomkvist and Drogendijk, 2013; Buckley et al., 2007). There is

Table 8.2 Key stages in development of Chinese OFDI

Stage I (between 1979 and 1991)	'Cross the river by feeling the stones'
Stage II (between 1992 and 1999)	'Further rise of OFDI'
Stage III (from 1999 until now)	'Strong state promotion of OFDI'

Source: authors' data.

a very positive regulatory environment to promote the international expansion of Chinese companies, which leads to naming the third stage (from 1999 until now) as 'strong state promotion of OFDI'. Table 8.2 describes the three different stages of Chinese outward FDI (see Table 8.2).

Motives behind the internationalization strategies

Investment motives are important components of an internationalization strategy framework. According to Yip et al. (1988), there are four groups of FDI motives – market, cost, government, and competitiveness:

(1) Market motives. Companies can expect a convergence of needs and tastes as well as an emergence of global customers. It is through this that companies can transfer marketing and product strategies across borders.
(2) Cost drivers. Thanks to the economies of scale and lower costs of resources (e.g., labor, raw material, transportation, electricity, and so forth), companies can be more efficient in profit-making.
(3) Government driver. According to Blomkvist and Drogendijk (2013), institutions can promote or impede the internationalization strategy of companies. For example, if the host country government hopes to protect the local market, it may impose high tariffs and regulatory barriers to the foreign investors, vice-versa.
(4) Competitiveness driver. Companies' internationalization strategies are also affected by competitors' global strategies. The capability to react faster than competitors is one of major sources of sustainable competitive advantage for companies (Ichijo and Kohlbacher, 2008).

Chinese international expansion in Africa follows these motives. For instance, the China National Petroleum Corporation (CNPC) signed a petroleum exploration contract with the Sudanese government in 1999. Other companies such as Sinopec also established oil drilling sites in Algeria, Angola, Côte d'Ivoire, and Gabon. These internationalization strategies show that Chinese OFDIs are in search of natural resources, increased market share, competitiveness, and cost-effectiveness. Furthermore, the 'go-global' initiative in 1999 and 'One Belt One Road' initiative in 2013 continually have encouraged Chinese companies to invest overseas and make Chinese companies competitive on a global level.

It is important to note that motives for Chinese OFDIs in Africa can vary from those in developed countries, such as France. Nicolas (2010) and Battat (2006) argue that Chinese investment in Europe seeks market access and strategic assets. Encouraged and supported by the Chinese government, Chinese companies expand business abroad to upgrade their technology know-how and compete in more profitable areas, such as distribution, design, and branding (Nicolas, 2010). As an example, Huawei's growth in foreign-developed countries confirms these motives. Huawei is a leader in the information and communication technology sector, founded in 1987 in Shenzhen, China. In 1999, it set up the first foreign R&D centre in Bangalore, India. Thereafter, Huawei established R&D centres in Sweden, the United States, Canada, the United Kingdom, Pakistan, Finland, France, Belgium, Germany, Colombia, Ireland, Russia, Israel, and Turkey. Meanwhile, Huawei has several joint ventures with companies such as 3Com, Siemens, Symantec, and Global Marine.

From Huawei's international expansion, we can identify its key FDI motives. First, Huawei pays very close attention to cost-effectiveness, which is why Huawei keeps its production in China. Second, Huawei has set up several R&D centres in specific countries. Some of them are located in the emerging markets (e.g., India, Turkey, Russia) and some of them are in the well-developed countries (e.g., Canada, France, Finland). Through the establishment of R&D centres, Huawei can best offer customized products and services to meet the expectation of the local consumers. In search of bigger market shares, Huawei is a pioneer in doing business in emerging markets. To behave more actively in the developed countries, Huawei has been keen to learn advanced technologies and management practices, which are in line with the motive of strategic asset seeking. Last but not the least, thanks to the 'go-global' strategy, Huawei as well as Haier and Lenovo have been selected as the key Chinese multinational companies, which the Chinese government has supported by showing a strong commitment to building them into 'global champions' (Yang and Stoltenberg, 2008).

Chinese OFDIs in France

An increasing number of Chinese companies are doing business in France across sectors such as mining, finance, manufacturing, electronic and IT equipment, food and wine, hotels, and so forth. According to the Business France report (2016), China is the second largest Asian investor in France, after Japan. More than 700 companies from Mainland China and Hong Kong are operating businesses in France, which offer more than 45,000 jobs in the French market. Chinese companies in France include Huawei, ZTE, China National Blue Star Enterprise, Bank of China, Alibaba, and so forth. From Table 8.3, one can see that in 2016 China was among the top seven investors in France (see Table 8.3).

Among the Chinese companies in France, Jin Jiang International (holdings) Co., Ltd is the largest Chinese employer in France and has between 10,000 and 15,000 employees in the French hotel sector. CK Hutchison Holdings Ltd has offered between 3,500 and 4,000 jobs, which is the second largest Chinese

Table 8.3 Top seven FDIs in France in 2016

Country of origin	Project Nb	Employee Nb
Germany	191	4,737
United States	182	6,802
Italy	141	3,228
United Kingdom	85	3,713
Japan	67	1,490
Belgium	53	734
China (including Hong Kong)	51	1,370

Source: Business France (2016).

Table 8.4 Examples of Chinese companies that entered the French market in 2016

Company	FDI Type	Motives
Bank of Communication	Greenfield	Market, government, competitor, strategic asset seeking
Tongling Nonferrous Metal	Brownfield	Market, government, competitor, technology, strategic asset seeking
Horizons Ventures	Brownfield	Government, technology
Dalian Wanda	Brownfield	Market, government, competitor, strategic asset seeking

Source: Business France (2016) and authors' data.

employer in France for the distribution sector. The third largest Chinese employer in France is China Nation Chemical Corporation, which employs between 2,000 and 2,500 employees in France. The fourth biggest Chinese employer in France is Yantai Taihai Company, which specializes in the metal industry and has offered between 1,500 and 2,000 jobs. The fifth largest Chinese employer in France is Fosun International Ltd, which has acquired the Club Mediterranean, and offers between 1,000 and 1,500 jobs in France. Table 8.4 shows that four new Chinese FDIs came to France in 2016. Three in four companies acquired French companies to expand the business to the French market. The common motives for these Chinese OFDIs include market and strategic asset seeking, competitor impact, and responding to the Chinese government's 'go-global' initiative (see Table 8.4).

Staffing top managers for Chinese foreign subsidiaries

The success of companies' international expansion depends on various conditions. One of the key conditions is to have a well-performing top management team. Rich research has been done on manager staffing decisions for foreign subsidiaries (Kang and Shen, 2014; Mahajan and Toh, 2013; Tarique et al., 2006; Belderbos and Heijltjes, 2005; Delios and Bjorkman, 2000; Perlmutter, 1969). According to Zhu et al. (2007), cultures and regulations are crucial factors that lead companies to adopt certain HRM dimensions. Zhu et al. (2008) point out that the nature of ownership may affect the HRM practices adopted by the company. In a similar vein, Cooke and Lin (2012) suggest that patterns of HRM are positively influenced by industrial relations. Delios and Bjorkman (2000) highlight that strategic objectives have significant influence on manager staffing decisions and subsidiary performance. The previous research on manager staffing practices for foreign subsidiaries confirms that HRM practices are affected by home country and host country institutional factors (Cooke, 2014; Child and Tsai, 2005). However, despite these contributions, there are few studies that systematically examine how CEMs staff their foreign subsidiaries' top management team to meet their internationalization motives.

Gill et al. (2008) identify China's motives for investing in Africa as three-fold: resource seeking (fuel), market seeking (sustain the domestic economy), and political seeking (to have more global influence). The adoption of an internationalization strategy should target not only 'economic' benefits but also take legitimacy into consideration, such as responding to the Chinese government's 'go-global' initiative (Li and Ding, 2013). According to Bräutigam (2011), Chinese companies send a large portion of their Chinese workforce to work construction projects in the oil-rich countries. Importantly, Chinese companies that expand business to Africa are mainly SOEs, which treat Chinese employees and African ones according to collectivism principles (Hofstede, 1980) of in-group and out-group members (Jackson, 2014). As a result, top manager positions in Chinese subsidiaries in Africa are privileged for Chinese for the consideration of coordination, control, and efficient communication. However, we have limited knowledge about the top manager staffing practices of Chinese companies in France. This study is among the pioneers exploring this phenomenon. In a general sense, what we know is that the ways to lead the French teams and to comply with French regulative, normative and cognitive factors cannot remain the same as those in Africa. There are some similarities but internationalization motives matter in how companies staff top management teams and manage host country employees (Cooke and Lin, 2012).

Methodology

According to Miles and Huberman (1994), the qualitative approach is efficient in answering questions that are rare and/or underdeveloped and that describe the group norms through individual experience. Given that few studies have systematically investigated the motives of Chinese companies to do business in France and how they staff top managers to support internationalization strategies, we consider the qualitative approach to be appropriate for our research. Two main qualitative methods are used in our study: in-depth interviews and documentary data searching. In-depth interviews enabled us to collect data from informants' perspectives and their real experiences of the specific subjects. Documentary data are suitable for verifying the information collected and providing further understanding of companies' international management practices.

To collect information, we targeted interviewing professionals who are managers in Chinese subsidiaries in France. We did not have any preference about the nationalities of the informants. They could be French, Chinese, or any other nationality. The most important aspect was that the informants were familiar with the international management practices of headquarters in China. Hence, managers in Chinese subsidiaries in France are considered to be ideal profiles who have information on our research topic.

A question list was used as our interview guide, which was prepared in English, Chinese, and French. The three versions were pilot-tested with two professors who do research in the area of international management and who can speak the three languages. These preparations ensured that informants would have no misunderstandings about the questions. With the help of interview guide, we sought to understand: (1) the motives behind Chinese OFDI in France; (2) who hold the top positions in the Chinese subsidiaries in France and why they were selected.

Based on the Nicolas's work (2010), we prepared a list of main Chinese investors in France. We contacted the managers via phone call, e-mail, and LinkedIn. Frankly, we faced a lot of difficulties in getting managers, especially Chinese ones, to participate in our research. Some managers refused our interview request because they did not trust the good intention of the study. Other managers either did not have time or some of them had to get the approval from headquarters in China, which was time-consuming and complex. From the company A informant, we learned that the hesitation by Chinese companies was related to their unfamiliarity with cooperating with academic institutions on research projects. To encourage free discussion during the interview, it was agreed that the informants would remain anonymous and their answers would stay confidential. Thus, no one or their companies would be individually identified in our study.

Because of the difficulties in getting Chinese companies to participate in our research, plus some data that were missing in certain companies, we finally chose to focus our study on four detailed case studies. We chose these four companies for three reasons. First, we got rich information from the interviews, and we were able to get access to the companies' documents in both Chinese and French versions. Second, among the four companies, two were SOEs and two were privately owned companies. Third, the four companies have adopted an entry mode as either a greenfield or brownfield investment. With companies' different characteristics, we wanted to show the big picture of Chinese OFDI in France in the areas of internationalization motives and the related top manager staffing practices.

Our analysis is based on a case study of four Chinese companies in France. Two of them have purchased French companies and the other two have adopted greenfield investments. The two types of internationalization are equally presented in the study, which enables us to have a diverse, comparative, and complete source of data. The four companies come from different sectors. The first case describes a Chinese chemical SOE (company code: A), which purchased a French indus-trial manufacturer in 2007. The second case describes a Chinese real estate group (privately owned) (company code: B), which purchased a vineyard in Dordogne, France, in 2013. The third case describes a Chinese consulting company (pri-vately owned) (company code: C), which opened its office in France in 2015. The fourth case describes a transportation-based Chinese SOE (company code: D), which opened a representative office in France in 2012 (see Table 8.5).

Findings

Case A describes a French chemical company that was purchased by a Chinese SOE in 2007. The French company was a manufacturer of chemical components for clients in sectors such as pharmaceutic, construction, cosmetic, electronics, and so forth. The informant is French. Before the acquisition, the informant had the position of production director and had been working in the company for eight years. Starting in 2006, he was promoted to the position of chief operating officer at headquarter in Shanghai. He speaks French, English, and Chinese.

According to our informant, the main motives for this acquisition were seek-ing technology and production lines, distribution, market share, branding, and legitimacy. In addition, the Chinese SOE had been selected by the Chinese gov-ernment to be a potential enterprise to become a Chinese 'global champion'. Note that the French and Chinese companies were not in competition before the acquisition, but they used the same raw materials for production. Given that the French company had a good reputation in the industry and offered rich expe-rience in production and expansion in Europe, the acquisition has allowed the Chinese company to: (1) expand business into new areas; (2) learn updated tech-nology and management practices; and (3) respond to the Chinese government's 'go-global' initiative.

Regarding the top manager staffing practices in the French company in the post-acquisition stage, the informant indicated that the Chinese investor had no inten-tion of changing the organizational structure in France. Furthermore, no Chinese expatriates have been sent to work in France either. The Chinese investor prefers

Table 8.5 Company presentation

Company	Sector	Entry year	Informant position	Informant's working experience in China	Informant's language skills
A	Chemistry	2007	COO (M)	10 Y	Fr, En, Ch
B	Vineyard	2013	Manager (F)	0	Fr, En
C	Consulting	2015	Manager (M)	5 Y	Fr, En, Ch
D	Transport	2012	Manager (M)	17 Y	Fr, En, Ch

Note: The informants are French. 'M' means male, 'F' means female, 'Fr' means French, 'En' means English, and 'Ch' means Chinese, 'COO' means chief operating officer, 'Y' means years.

to use local management and keep the same top management team. By contrast, the French top managers were invited to work at headquarters in China, and one of the French top managers has been selected to be a board member. Additionally, some French managers have been offered leading positions in the important business units at headquarters. The strategies of Company A are twofold: respect the French expertise and keep management localization while encouraging the transfer of advanced technology and management practices from French sites to China. All staffing decisions are made in France (see Table 8.6).

Case B describes a French vineyard in Dordogne, which was acquired by a Chinese investment group in 2013. Before the acquisition, the French vineyard had fifteen permanent employees for production, commercialization, and administration. The French manager of the vineyard participated in our interview and has been working in the vineyard for ten years.

According to the informant, the Chinese investor is interested in French wine-making technology but also in the value of the vineyard itself. The Chinese investor is not specialized in wine-making but in the real estate sector. The motives behind the international acquisition are profit and technology seeking. All staff members kept their positions in the vineyard after the acquisition. The Chinese investor trusted the French employees' know-how in wine production and quality control. Furthermore, it looked highly on the reputation of the vineyard. However, a Chinese specialist in wine industry has been assigned to work as a representative of Chinese company B in the French vineyard. This Chinese representative speaks French and has working experience in France in the wine sector. He is in charge of the operation of the vineyard and observing the wine-making techniques, and he implements the control and coordination for the Chinese company B in the French vineyard.

In general, the decisions are made by the French managers in the vineyard. However, the business activities of the vineyard have changed since the arrival of the Chinese representative. The first change in the vineyard was to add the dimension of tourism to the business strategies. In the post-acquisition stage, tourists can visit the vineyard, and tea is now available for sale in the vineyard. The major considerations for this strategy change are twofold: first, the Chinese investor hopes that the vineyard can multiply the channels to earn money. Second, the

Table 8.6 The internationalization strategies of Chinese company A

Item	Chinese Company A
Sector	Chemistry
Type of company	SOE
Entry mode	Brownfield investment
Motives behind investment in France	'Go-global' initiative, market, technology, management practices, reputation and global influence seeking, competitor
Top manager staffing in France	Management localization, laissez-faire

Source: Authors' data.

Chinese investor has a personal interest in and knowledge of both the wine and tea businesses (see Table 8.7).

Case C describes a Chinese consulting company that set up office in France in 2015. Company C offers consulting services to European companies that have interests in expanding business to China and/or to other Asian countries. Meanwhile, company C also offers consulting services to Chinese companies that plan to have FDI in Europe. The major clients for company C come from the pharmaceutic, IT, telecommunications, and automotive sectors. Our informant is a French manager who has working experience at headquarters in China and who can speak Chinese. When the Chinese company decided to expand the business to Europe, our informant was selected to join the French office.

According to the informant, there are three reasons that led company C to expand the business to the French market. First, Chinese clients consider that consulting firms like company C are more reliable when they have offices in Europe. Second, the consulting company C hopes to actively compete with local companies in France and to reach more European clients. Third, company C has noticed that the Chinese government promotes the internationalization of Chinese companies. Hence, the Chinese company hopes to gather more information for the existing and future Chinese clients about the European market.

Regarding the top manager staffing practices for the French office, the manager is French but he previously worked as a manager in an international group in China for five years. He speaks Chinese and has rich knowledge of Chinese business cultures. The two other employees are consultants. One of the consultants is French, and he had working experience at the headquarters of company C. The second consultant is a Chinese who has a master diploma from a French business school and can speak fluent French. Note that all the staffing decisions for the French office were made in China. Furthermore, before joining the French office, the informant received a three-month intensive training at headquarters in China (see Table 8.8).

Case D describes a Chinese multinational company from the transport and logistic industry. This Chinese group expanded its operations all over the world, including in France. Their business activities cover ocean, air, and land transportation; freight forwarding; storing; and warehousing. It is a Chinese SOE that has more than 60,000 employees in China. Our informant is a French manager. He

Table 8.7 The internationalization strategies of Chinese company B

Item	Chinese company B
Sector	Real estate
Type of company	Privately owned company
Entry mode	Brownfield investment
Motives behind investment in France	Profit, technology, reputation and distribution seeking, competitor
Top manager staffing in France	Management localization but supervision by a Chinese representative

Source: Authors' data.

Table 8.8 The internationalization strategies of Chinese company C

Item	Chinese C
Sector	Consulting
Type of company	Privately owned company
Entry mode	Greenfield investment
Motives behind investment in France	'Go-global' initiative, competitor, Chinese clients' perceived legitimacy, market seeking
Top manager staffing in France	High involvement of headquarters in the operations of the French office

Source: Authors' data.

started his career in the logistic industry in France. Then, he moved to China to work for company D's competitors. Interestingly, he joined company D in China afterward and occupied several positions. He was selected to take charge of the French office in 2016. In total, he worked in China for 17 years.

According to our informant, the motives behind the Chinese investment in France are twofold: first, to respond to Chinese government's 'go-global' initiatives and then, to have the representative office deal with customer relationships and promote the activities of company D in France. Such a representative office of company D in France plays a bridging role between headquarters and all European clients, which in return can facilitate the trust-building and business expansion.

Regarding the staffing practices for the French office, two Chinese expatriates were sent to work in France at the beginning. They had both worked at headquarters in China for several years. It was their first expatriation. Both are fluent in English, and one can speak French, too. Recently, one Chinese expatriate went back to work at headquarters, and our informant has been selected to replace him. According to our informant, he was chosen because he is French and has occupied managerial positions at headquarters for many years. As a result, the Chinese top managers trust our informant's loyalty. The most important thing is that French clients value the legitimacy of having a French manager in the French office of company D, which can facilitate communication and business cooperation between the home and French offices.

The management practices and systems in the French office stayed the same as those at headquarters. In terms of governance, headquarters play an important role in decision-making in the French office. For example, strategic decisions have to be validated by the headquarters in China, and there is a rigid reporting system set up by headquarters for the French office. All the top managers are sent from China to work in France. High involvement of headquarters at the French office is therefore strongly ensured (see Table 8.9).

Discussion

In Figure 8.1, we combine our findings about the top manager staffing practices and investment type. We can see that the nature of the company may not directly affect the decision-making on top manager staffing for Chinese companies in

Table 8.9 The internationalization strategies of Chinese company D

Item	Chinese company D
Sector	Transportation and logistic
Type of company	SOE
Entry mode	Greenfield investment
Motives behind investment in France	'Go-global' initiative, competitor, market seeking, French clients' perceived legitimacy
Top manager staffing in France	High involvement of headquarters in the operation of the French office

Source: Authors' data.

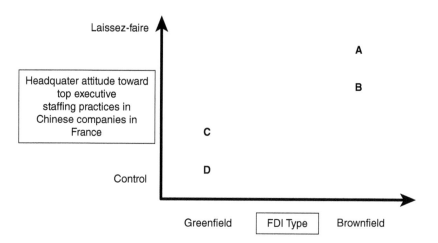

Figure 8.1 Positioning the archetypes of top manager staffing practices

France. In Figure 8.1, Companies A and D are SOEs, but they have different levels of involvement in staffing foreign subsidiaries in France. However, companies with greenfield investments in France tend to control the top manager staffing practices whereas companies with brownfield investments prefer to adopt a more laissez-faire attitude and have local management in France (see Figure 8.1).

Among the four cases, we can identify some common staffing criteria for top managers of overseas Chinese companies.

- First, the managers should have knowledge of the Chinese culture as well as the host country's (see cases A, C, and D). Such a criterion can better facilitate the coordination between headquarters and their foreign subsidiaries, achieving better understanding toward home and host country institutional contexts. Furthermore, speaking Chinese and the host country language is appreciated.
- Second, internal recruitment is widely adopted in the Chinese business companies (see cases A, B, C, and D), which look highly on the employees'

loyalty records and their respective expertise achieved in the area of management and technology. Candidates' past experience at headquarters is highly valued by the Chinese companies, which has been used as an indicator for international and/or internal recruitment and promotion.

- Third, when the motives are related to seeking technology, management practices, and legitimacy, Chinese companies prefer to adopt local management (see cases A and B) and they are keen to observe the host country's know-how. When Chinese companies have deep industry knowledge and expert perspectives on clients' needs, they tend to take more control on the staffing practices of foreign subsidiaries (see cases C and D). Concerning the seeking of legitimacy, Chinese companies value harmony, and they know that host country employees have the best knowledge of local norms, cultures, and regulations. Hence, Chinese investors will not interfere in the local business if it is not necessary, and they give a certain level of autonomy to the top management teams in the host country.

Based on the findings, we propose some managerial implications to Chinese OFDI in France:

(1) In order to get better access to the host country clients, top managers should be carefully selected. Companies should pay attention to candidates' past experience, language skills, and understanding of the Chinese as well as host country business contexts.

(2) Chinese investors must figure out how to balance the control and coordination of the foreign subsidiaries while realizing internationalization motives. If autonomy is given to the managers to lead the foreign subsidiaries, control should be carefully put in place while respecting the legitimacy which is impacted by factors such as regulation changes. Given that more qualified French professionals exist who can speak Chinese and who have working experience in China, Chinese companies can send Chinese expatriates to establish the management framework and systems in France at the beginning. Implementing a standardized framework in all foreign subsidiaries can facilitate the control driver. Then, companies can replace expatriates with qualified host country nationals.

(3) Regarding the managerial implications for French companies acquired by Chinese investors, we suggest that French companies should perceive the acquisition as an opportunity instead of a threat. Indeed, Chinese OFDI in France can receive support from the Chinese government. Moreover, most of them are large multinational companies which have rich experience and a good understanding of Chinese markets. The managers of the French subsidiaries should appreciate the experience of working with the Chinese investors as well as employees, find best-fit practices in managing multicultural teams, and realize the development of a personal career path. For example, in case A, the managers of the acquired French company were invited to lead the business units at headquarters in China. Furthermore, French managers can

also learn from Chinese partners' business ideas. For instance, Company B has proposed vineyard visiting and tea selling in addition to wine-making and -selling to make the winery more dynamic in generating revenues.

Conclusion

The aim of this chapter was to provide an understanding of the motives behind Chinese OFDI in France and the related top manager staffing practices. Our results highlight that at a micro-economic level, the entry mode (e.g., brownfield or greenfield investments) and the specific motives of internationalization can make a difference in terms of staffing top managers abroad. There is a positive relationship between internationalization motives and top manager staffing practices.

Although we are able to obtain significant results from this study, there are still some limitations to keep in mind. The first limitation is related to the size of the samples, which occurred because of the difficulties in getting accessing to Chinese companies. Chinese managers, for reasons of language inefficiency, confidentiality consideration, or a lack of 'guanxi' between the Chinese companies and us, refused to participate in our research. This work is also limited by its focus on interviews with only French managers. We assume that managers have the knowledge and experience to provide us with expert information. However, discussions with Chinese managers at the same companies could enrich the findings. Based on the research limits, an in-depth study on the same topic with a larger sample size is necessary. Then, given that different CEMs may have different strategic asset seeking in different industries (Zheng et al., 2016), further research could therefore expand the current study to other countries and include more greenfield and/or brownfield investments across different industries.

References

Andreff, W. (2015). Outward foreign direct investment from BRIC countries: Comparing strategies of Brazilian, Russian, Indian and Chinese multinational companies. *The European Journal of Comparative Economics*, 12(2), 79–131.
Bartlett, C., and Ghoshal, S. (1989). *Managing Across Borders and the Transnational Solution*. Boston: Harvard Business School Press.
Battat, J. (2006). *China's Outward Foreign Direct Investment: FIAS/MIGA Firm Survey. Foreign Investment Advisory Service*. Washington, DC: World Bank.
Belderbos, R. A., and Heijltjes, M. G. (2005). The determinants of expatriate staffing by Japanese multinationals in Asia: Control, learning and vertical business groups. *Journal of International Business Studies*, 36(3), 341–354.
Blomkvist, K., and Drogendijk, R. (2013). The impact of psychic distance on Chinese outward of foreign direct investments. *Management International Review*, 53(5), 659–686.
Bräutigam, D. (2011). *The Dragon's Gift: The Real Story of China in Africa*. Oxford: Oxford University Press.
Buckley, P. J., Clegg, L. J., Cross, A. R., Liu, X., Voss, H., and Zheng, P. (2007). The determinants of Chinese outward foreign direct investment. *Journal of Investment Business Studies*, 38(4), 499–518.

Business France (2016). *Rapport sur l'internationalisation de l'économie Française: Bilan 2016 des investissements étrangers en France*, www.businessfrance.fr/Media/Default/BlogPost/2017_RA_BF_FR_Complet_BD.pdf, accessed 4 September 2017.

Child, J., and Rodrigues, S. (2005). The internationalization of Chinese firms: A case for theoretical revision? *Management and Organization Review*, 1(3), 381–410.

Child, J., and Tsai, T. (2005). The Dynamic between firms' environmental strategies and institutional constraints in emerging economies: Evidence from China and Taiwan. *Journal of Management Studies*, 42(1), 95–125.

Cooke, F. L. (2011). The globalization of Chinese telecom corporations: Strategy, challenges, and HR implications for host countries. *International Journal of Human Resource Management*, 23(9), 1832–1852.

Cooke, F. L. (2014). Chinese multinational firms in Asia and Africa: Relationships with institutional actors and patterns of HRM practices. *Human Resource Management*, 53(6), 877–896.

Cooke, F. L., and Lin, Z. H. (2012). Chinese firms in Vietnam: Investment motives, institutional environment and human resource challenges. *Asia Pacific Journal of Human Resources*, 50(2), 205–226.

Cui, L., Meyer, K. E., and Hu, H. W. (2014). What drives firms' intent to seek strategic assets by foreign direct investment? A study of emerging economy firms. *Journal of World Business*, 49(4), 488–501.

Delios, A., and Bjorkman, I. (2000). Expatriate staffing in foreign subsidiaries of Japanese multinational corporations in PRC and the United States. *International Journal of Human Resource Management*, 11(2), 278–293.

Dunning, J. H. (1981). *International Production and the Multinational Enterprise*. London: George Allen & Unwin.

Eriksson, K., Johanson, J., Majkgard, A., and Sharma, D. D. (1997). Experiential knowledge and cost in the internationalization process. *Journal of International Business Studies*, 28(2), 337–360.

Fan, D., Cui, L., Li, Y. and Zhu, C. J. (2016). Localized learning by emerging multinational enterprises in developed host countries: A fuzzy-set analysis of Chinese foreign direct investment in Australia. *International Business Review*, 25(1), 187–203.

Gill, B., Morrison, J. S., and Huang, C. (2008). China – Africa relations: An early, uncertain debate in the United States, in: Alden, C., Large, D., and Oliveira, R. S. (eds.), *China Returns to Africa: A Rising Power and a Continent Embrace*. London: Hurst Publishers.

Hofstede, G. (1980). Motivation, leadership and organization: Do American theories apply abroad? *Organizational Dynamics*, 9(1), 42–63.

Ichijo, K., and Kohlbacher, F. (2008). Tapping tacit local knowledge in emerging markets – the Toyota way. *Knowledge Management Research & Practice*, 6(3), 173–186.

Jackson, T. (2014). Employment in Chinese MNEs: Appraising the dragon's gift to Sub-Saharan Africa. *Human Resource Management*, 53(6), 897–919.

Kang, H., and Shen, J. (2014). International human resource policies and practices of South Korean MNEs: A review of the literature. *Asia Pacific Business Review*, 20(1), 42–58.

Li, F., and Ding, D. Z. (2013). The effect of institutional isomorphic pressure on the internationalization of firms in an emerging economy: Evidence from China. *Asia Pacific Business Review*, 19(4), 506–525.

Mahajan, A., and Toh, S. M. (2013). Facilitating expatriate adjustment: The role of advice-seeking from host country nationals. *Journal of World Business*, 49(4), 476–487.

Miles, M. B., and Huberman, A. M. (1994). *Qualitative Data Analysis*. Thousand Oaks: SAGE Publications.

Ministry of Commerce in the People's Republic of China (MOFCOM) (2016). *China's foreign direct investment flow ranks second largest in the world*, www.mofcom.gov.cn/article/i/dxfw/nbgz/201609/20160901399593.shtml, accessed 4 September 2017.

Nicolas, F. (2010). *Chinese Direct Investments in France: No French Exception, No Chinese Challenge*. London: Chatham House.

Palthe, J. (2014). Regulative, normative, and cognitive elements of organizations: Implications for managing change. *Management and Organizational Studies*, 1(2), 60–66.

Perlmutter, H. (1969). The tortuous evolution of the multinational corporation. *Columbia Journal of World Business*, 4(1), 9–18.

Ren, B., Liang, H., and Zheng, Y. (2010). *Chinese Multinationals' Outward Foreign Direct Investment: An Institutional Perspective and the Role of the State*. Tianjin: Nankai University.

Rui, H., and Yip, G. S. (2008). Foreign acquisitions by Chinese firms: A strategic intent perspective. *Journal of World Business*, 43(2), 213–226.

Tarique, I., Schuler, R., and Gong, Y. (2006). A model of multinational enterprise subsidiary staffing composition. *International Journal of Human Resource Management*, 17(2), 207–224.

Thite, M., Wilkinson, A., and Shah, D. (2012). Internationalization and HRM strategies across subsidiaries in multinational corporations from emerging economies: A conceptual framework. *Journal of World Business*, 47(2), 251–258.

Wang, C., Hong, J., Kafouros, M., and Boateng, A. (2012). What drives outward FDI of Chinese firms? Testing the explanatory power of three theoretical framework. *International Business Review*, 21(3), 425–438.

Yang, X., and Stoltenberg, C. (2008). Growth of made-in China multinationals: An institutional and historical perspective, in: Alon, I., and McIntyre, J. (eds.), *Globalization of Chinese Enterprises*. Basingstoke: Palgrave Macmillan.

Yip, G. S., Loewe, P. M., and Yoshino, M. Y. (1988). How to take your company to the global market. *Columbia Journal of World Business*, 23(4), 37–48.

Zheng, N., Wei, Y., Zhang, Y., and Yang, J. (2016). In search of strategic assets through cross-border merger and acquisitions: Evidence from Chinese multinational enterprises in developed economies. *International Business Review*, 25(1), 177–186.

Zhu, Y., Collins, N., Webber, M., and Benson, J. (2008). New forms of ownership and human resource practices in Vietnam. *Human Resource Management*, 47(1), 157–175.

Zhu, Y., Warner, M., and Rowley, C. (2007). Human resource management with "Asian" characteristics: A hybrid people-management system in East Asia. *International Journal of Human Resource Management*, 18(5), 745–768.

Interview guideline

1   Please introduce your company.

- Mission, values, corporate culture, core business, entry year in France, etc.

2   Why did your company enter French market?

- What were the motivations behind the investment in France?

- What difficulties/challenges did you have when you set up the business in France?

3 What are the management practices adopted in the current company (e.g., organization, coordination, control, etc.)?

- Regarding the management practices, who set the process? By headquarters? Etc.
- For the case of brownfield investment, has any management practice been transferred from headquarters to French sites? If the answer is yes, what are they and how to realize the transfer? If the answer is no, for what reasons? And what practices have been put in place?
- For the case of greenfield investment, did Chinese headquarters transfer the home-based management practices to France? If the answer is yes, what were the reasons for such a transfer? If the answer is no, for what reasons? And what practices have been put in place?

4 What kinds of human resource management (HRM) policies and practices have been put in place in the Chinese firms in France?

- What are the staffing criteria for top manager position? (Studied abroad? Language skills? Work experience in France? Working experience at headquarters? Age? Female? Male? Etc.)
- What kinds of responsibilities do top managers have in the Chinese firms in France? To which extent, they have autonomy in decision-making?
- Regarding the HRM practices, who set the policies and practices in the Chinese firms in France? By headquarters?

9 The Chinese way to the development of corporate social responsibility

Gildas Lusteau, Isabelle Barth and Jacques Jaussaud

Corporate Social Responsibility (CSR), and more broadly Organisation Social Responsibility (OSR) have been widely addressed issues in Western circles following the contributions by Bowen (1953), Carroll (1979) and subsequently many others. In China, the concept seems to have entered through foreign firms' activities, as they were in need of satisfying their stakeholders at home and elsewhere regarding their business practices worldwide, including China, where MNCs have dramatically increased their activities since the 1980s.

Hu Jintao, who was President of the People's Republic of China from March 2003 to March 2013, promoted the development of a 'harmonious society'. While the economic achievements were noticeable, increased inequality, social tensions and environmental issues remained major concerns. Xi Jinping, who was elected in March 2013, emphasised the need to lessen inequality, to avoid food safety scandals that were too frequent in previous years, to address environmental problems and in addition, to fight corruption.

In the 2000s, the United States and the European Union threatened to ban imports from firms that were not certified to be compliant with Social Accountability 8000 standards (Xi and Fleming, 2008). Although regarded in China as a disguised protectionist move, the threat led Chinese authorities to strongly support the development of CSR in China. Chinese firms themselves had to follow in order to secure access to markets worldwide, particularly in developed countries.

This chapter is devoted to the specific development of CSR in China, trying to identify its main determinants and characteristics. Section 1 investigates the emergence of CSR in China, and why Chinese authorities eventually strongly supported the move. Section 2 identifies the main characteristics of the process of the emergence of CSR in China, in contrast to what happened in other countries.

Emergence of the CSR concept in China

Although Xi and Fleming (2008) underline that in 1824, Cadbury Schweppes 'already had a clear understanding of its obligations to shareholders as they realised that good ethics and business go together naturally', it is widely accepted that the concept of CSR is rooted in the book by Bowen in 1953, *The Social Responsibility of the Businessman*. Carroll (1979) identifies at least four levels of CSR:

DOI: 10.4324/9781315102566-11

economic responsibility (to be profitable); legal responsibility (to comply with the laws); ethical responsibility (to behave as society expects the company to behave) and voluntary or philanthropic responsibility.

Basu and Palazzo (2008) identify three different types of CSR: *stakeholder driven*, in response to specific demands by various stakeholders such as governments, NGOs, consumer associations etc.; *performance driven*, in order that the products and activities of the firm are better accepted in the marketplace, thereby increasing profitability; or *motivation driven*, being willing to promote socially responsible actions (either because it is in line with its own promoted corporate values or in order to avoid any damage to the image of the corporation). Freeman (1984) had already emphasised how taking into account stakeholders' interests was a way to support profitability of firms in the long run.

Following the *Triple Bottom Line* model Profit, People and Planet by Elkington (1994), it is widely accepted that CSR should articulate three dimensions: social, environmental and economic. Firms should make profitability compatible with sustainability, which requires both respecting workers and other people's social needs and protecting the environment from an ecological point of view. Following the United Nations report by Bruntland in 1987, the Jonas principle of responsibility, according to which, satisfying the needs of present generations should not be done at the expenses of future generations (Jonas, 1984), has been widely accepted and provides a bridge between the social and environmental dimensions of CSR.

Under pressure from NGOs, and following the success of quality standards such as the ISO 9000 in promoting quality management worldwide, a number of standards have been set up in the field of CSR. The SA8000 standard for instance has been provided by Social Accountability International (SAI) since 1997. The SAI is an NGO aiming to improve workplaces and communities through the implementation of socially responsible standards. The SA8000 standard has been designed on the basis of the basic principles of the International Labour Organization (ILO) and of various United Nations conventions (including on children rights and on the eradication of any form of discrimination against women), not to mention the *Universal Declaration of Human Rights*. OHSAS 18001 and 18002 refer to risk management systems in the fields of health and security at work. ISO 14000 standards refer to environmental protection, in order to help firms to limit as much as possible the negative impact of their activities on natural resources (water consumption, CO_2 and other pollutants emissions etc.), from the perspective of sustainability. The ISO 26000 standard, however, provides general principles and guidelines for CSR, without any certifying process; it has been adopted in 2010 by almost all members of the International Standards Organization (ISO), including China.

The idea and the principles of CSR do not appear to be in contradiction with the most deeply rooted values in Chinese culture, such as Confucianist values which are nowadays widely promoted, even from a political point of view, although they were rejected under Chairman Mao's leadership (1949–1976) and particularly during the *Cultural Revolution* (1966–1976). The concept of benevolence (*ren* in Chinese), which refers to such words as love, goodness, human-heartedness, humanity etc., would fit perfectly with CSR principles. Wisdom (*zhi* in Chinese) and righteousness (*yi* in Chinese), two other of the five virtues in Confucianism, would also fit (Redfern and Crawford, 1994; Lu, 1997; Chan, 2008; Ip, 2009).

Under the leadership of Mao, all kinds of social responsibilities were regarded as pertaining to the state itself. Working and private lives were under the control of the work unit (the *danwei* in Chinese) which had to provide jobs, food, health care and free education, and under the control of the Popular Communes in the countryside. Private firms appeared only following the reforms by Deng Xiaoping, in 1978 and 1979. Thus, only from the end of the last century did the question of CSR emerge in China (Darrigan and Post, 2009), particularly in reaction to huge environmental and social damage caused by high growth levels fueled mainly by foreign inward investment and to a lesser extent by local investors, supported by the Chinese authorities, and the dismantling of many uncompetitive state-owned firms. Although trade unions were authorised by Den Xiaoping in 1978 (Child and Warner, 2003), labour law was inconsistent at that time and labour rights widely unspecified and it was the same as far as environmental protection regulation was concerned. The country was developing at a rapid pace, but the social and environmental costs were huge.

Since the 1980s however, political leaders in China have been aware of the threat that economic activity imposed on the environment and of the threat that environmental issues would consequently impose in the near future on economic development. In 1983, on the occasion of the second *National Environmental Protection Work Conference*, it was clearly stated that 'economic development, urban and rural construction and environmental protection should be planned, implemented and developed simultaneously'. The following year, the Environmental Protection Commission was established in order to coordinate all ministerial and governmental agencies activities where they might impact on the environment (Wu and Flynn, 1995). In the 1980s however, development was the first priority in China, not to mention political issues; environmental issues remained of secondary importance.

In China, the concern with CSR seems to have grown through foreign firms' activities, as they needed to satisfy their stakeholders at home and elsewhere regarding their business practices worldwide, including in China where they have dramatically developed their activities since the 1980s. Nike suffered a lot of pressure in the 1990s, including boycott of their products, as some of their subcontracting units were employing children in Asia. From 2001, they relied on Price Waterhouse Coopers to audit their subcontractors on such issues. Levi Strauss was accused of imposing very harsh working conditions in China, which led the firm in 1992 to adopt the first charter in the textile industry in China on better working conditions. The cases of Nike, Levi Strauss and several others led most MNCs to realise that they would be caught out if not having proper working conditions in place, whatever the country, in a world of rapidly exchanged information and strong NGOs. This also clearly applied to China.

The pressure on foreign MNCs in China came also from local media and authorities. Hägen-Dazs has been criticised for unsatisfactory production conditions from a sanitary point of view; Kentucky Fried Chicken (KFC) for using a forbidden red food coloring and Nestlé for inappropriate use of a given preparation (Li-Wen, 2010). A number of MNCs have been criticised by the Chinese Ministry of Commerce for fiscal fraud, corruption, insufficient protection of labour, pollution and insufficient product safety (Li-Wen, 2010). Following the huge earthquake in Sichuan, in 2008, MNCs such as McDonalds, Nokia and Samsung were targeted by the media for not having provided large enough donations to support the victims; the Minister of Commerce himself had to intervene in order to deny the accusations.

Facing such pressures both in their worldwide markets and in China, MNCs have often reacted by revising their social and environmental practices, and by trying to show their compliance with CSR through certification. For instance, in 2006, 38 foreign MNCs in the pharmaceutical industry in China, including such major MNCs as Pfizer, Novartis and Roche, started to work together in order to stop corruption and enhance transparency in this market (Darrigan and Post, 2009). Auditing by independent organisations has been a growing practice, although firms should transparently select their auditors in order to avoid bribery suspicions. MNCs have also developed cooperation with NGOs such as WWF China (Lafarge, Ikea, BP, HSBC and many others) on environmental issues. MNCs have also adopted worldwide CSR guidelines that they, however, may have difficulty implementing in some specific countries, including China, as they sometimes do not fit with local values and habits (Hanson and Rothlin, 2010).

According to Xi and Fleming (2008), since the mid-1990s, Chinese authorities have acknowledged the poor image the label *Made in China* has had among foreign customers. In order to enhance this image, they decided that at both national and local levels, governments should encourage producers to be socially responsible, including through subsidies or reduced tax payments. They also emphasized, as the 2006 report by the NGO Business for Social Responsibility does, that 'Multinational enterprises need to work with their Chinese suppliers to jointly shoulder the burden of implementing CSR standards, as opposed to simply requiring small Chinese enterprises to improve labour conditions while coming to them with a voracious appetite to continually drive down prices' (BSR, 2006). Another reason for the Chinese authorities to support CSR practices development is the *Go out Policy* they have implemented since 1999, which strongly encourages Chinese firms to invest and develop abroad, in order to better use China's inflated exchange reserves and to reduce dependency on foreign MNCs exports. Chinese authorities identified compliance by Chinese firms to worldwide accepted CSR standards as a prerequisite to be allowed to enter the largest foreign markets in North America, Europe and Japan. Thus, it is not surprising that the revised Company law in 2005 explicitly refers to CSR in its article 5.

A loose legal framework in the field of labour and of environmental protection makes it more difficult to implement satisfactory CSR practices in a given country. A firm may find it difficult to behave according to accepted CSR practices while competitors aggressively benefit from legal permissiveness. Fortunately, both social and environmental regulations have been strengthened during this period, almost up to some Western standards as far as environmental regulation is concerned in some highly developed urban areas such as Beijing and Shanghai that still suffer huge pollution levels. Regarding labour regulation, the *labour law* of 1994 specified fundamental principles such as work duration (8 hours a day, 44 hours a week), minimum age at work (16 years old), compensation principles etc. Subsequently, several other laws have been adopted, including the *law on trade unions* in 2001, the *law on prevention and treatment of professional diseases* in 2001, the *law on safety at work* in 2002 etc. The *labour law* of 1994 was widely revised in 2008 regarding labour contracts and labour disputes (Jaussaud and Liu, 2011). However, workers still face tremendous difficulties for their rights to be upheld, as trade unions are under the control of the authorities through the *All China Federation of Trade Unions*, the only one which is allowed by articles 10 and 11 of the *law on trade unions* of 2001.

As far as corruption is concerned, another crucial issue in the field of CSR, the *law against unfair practices* of 1993 provided a framework to fight it, and a *Central Anti-Business Bribery Leading Group* was set up to focus on the most corrupt industries. Acknowledging poor results however, President Xi Jinping made the fight against corruption one of his highest priorities when elected in March 2013, and his anti-corruption campaign has been pursued aggressively.

The main characteristics of the Chinese way to develop CSR

As already mentioned, imported standards in the field of CSR have been quite often regarded as disguised protectionist moves excluding a number of Chinese firms that did not succeed in implementing them. This has been particularly the case for the SA8000 standard regarding social accountability. Thus, Chinese leaders have called for the development of specific Chinese standards in the field.

In the textile industry, Chinese firms in the framework of the China National Textile and Apparel Council (CNTAC) developed and adopted in 2005 the *China Social Compliance 9000 for Textile and Apparel Industry* (CSC 9000T).[1] As underlined by Li-Wen (2010), the CSC 9000T has been designed as a social management system with the ISO 14000 standard in mind, which is the worldwide, well-known standard in the field of environmental management. The CSC 9000T defines objectives in the fields of labour contracts, number of work hours, wages and welfare, occupational health and safety, trade unions and collective bargaining, discrimination, harassment and abuse, child workers, forced or compulsory labour etc.

Although no specific certificate is attached to this standard, auditing on the basis of the CSC 9000T by an independent auditor helps Chinese suppliers to acknowledge their social management situation and identify the fields they might try to improve through specific policies, under the supervision of the *Responsible Supply Chain Association* (RSCA). One of the main advantages from the supplier's point of view is that it appears to be more flexible than most international standards, which call for immediate action when not at the level required by the standard in a given field. The CSC 9000T, according to its Chinese defenders, promotes cooperation and self-discipline in order to improve the situation rather than strict and immediate control, and potential conflict.

Following the adoption of the CSC 9000T, other initiatives have been developed in order to promote CSR in China with a 'Chinese' approach (Li-Wen, 2010). For instance, a *Social Responsibility Guide of the China Industrial Companies and Industrial Associations* was released by a group of eleven industrial associations in 2008, covering, among others, coal mining, steel, petrol, chemicals, light industries, textiles, building materials, electricity and mechanical industries. It is stated in this reference document that 'the behavior principles, the goals and the indicators set forth in the Industrial Guide are compatible with the current reality of China's socioeconomic and industrial development'. The objectives of the group of associations are to draw 'a set of corporate-level and industrial-level guidelines that connect with the international trend, match China's reality, and possess Chinese characteristics, thereby promoting and advancing the implementation of social responsibility by the Chinese industrial companies and industrial associations'. Although it is not a CSR standard, the guide aims at helping Chinese firms to become familiar with CSR issues, to improve their CSR practices and eventually to apply for certification.

The same year, 2008, the State-Owned Assets Supervision and Administration Commission (SASAC) released a *Guide Opinion on the Social Responsibility Implementation for the State-Owned Enterprises Controlled by the Central Government*. Some 150 large public state-owned enterprises (SOEs) are directly concerned by the guide, which develops into the official Chinese position on CSR. Four dimensions are emphasized (Li-Wen, 2010): 'First, CSR is a concrete measure of promoting social harmony. Second, these SOEs are the backbone of China's economy and security, affecting every aspect of Chinese people's living. Therefore, implementation of CSR is important to meet public expectations. Third, CSR is the unavoidable option for sustainable development. Fourth, CSR is a necessity for the SOEs to participate in the international market and society'. Thus, one can say that Chinese authorities strongly and officially support CSR initiatives. The guide identifies the main fields to be addressed from a CSR perspective: (1) abiding by the law and being honest in business; (2) increasing profitability; (3) increasing product quality; (4) increasing efficiency in resources use and protecting the environment; (5) developing innovation and technology; (6) increasing production process safety; (7) respecting workers' rights; and (8) supporting the community through charity. Corporate governance, CSR education of managers and other staff members, publication of CSR reports etc., are other issues that are addressed by the guide, in line with other worldwide-known CSR initiatives (e.g. the UN Global Compact, ISO 26000), although the human-rights issue is not specifically addressed.

The more specific question of information disclosure was addressed significantly during the same period. For instance, in 2006, the Shenzhen Stock Exchange published its *Guide on Listed Social Responsibility*, the State Environmental Protection Administration (SEPA) released in 2007 a *Regulation on Environmental Information Disclosure*, and the Shanghai Stock Exchange in

2008 published the *Guide on Environmental Information Disclosure for Companies listed on the Shanghai Stock Exchange*. Listed companies were strongly encouraged to produce CSR reports in addition to financial reports, and since 2008, some 300 have done so in Shanghai. Furthermore, in 2008 the China Top 100 CSR Development Index was released by the China Academy for Social Sciences, based on both a stakeholder approach and the triple-bottom line principles (while most CSR indices, such as the Dow Jones Sustainability Index, the FTSE4Good Index or the JSE-RSI Index are based only on a triple-bottom line approach – Hou et al. (2010)).

Currently, thousands of listed firms release CSR reports which have become more and more standardized in line with the *Global Reporting Initiative* (GRI). Thus, researchers have studied CSR reports by Chinese firms, underlining the effects on performance, both in terms of profitability and growth, on production of CSR reports (Cheng et al., 2015), and the positive relationship between CSR performance and financial performance (Li and Foo, 2016). Wang and Li (2015) found a positive relationship between CSR performance and stock valuation, which also reveals an awareness of investors of CSR practices in China. Marquis and Qian (2014) found that state-owned enterprises perform worse than private Chinese firms in terms of disclosure, as they produce less detailed information, which may result from the fact that they are not dependent on private investors. Investigating the CSR reports of the firms in the China Top 100 CSR Development Index, Sun et al. (2011) found that the larger the company, the higher the CSR score.

It should be underlined in addition that Chinese standards such as the CSC 9000T did not prevent Chinese firms applying for international standards such as the SA8000. Chinese standards appear to have been an alternative initially for firms who would not have been able to achieve international standards certification. Subsequently, many Chinese firms decided to apply for SA8000 certification in order to secure markets abroad. As displayed on the website of the Social Accountability Accreditation Services, almost 20% of firms that are accredited with SA8000 certification are in China, both foreign affiliates and Chinese firms, i.e. almost 700 firms out of almost 3,500 firms worldwide.

As emphasized by Rothlin (2010), a huge difference with the development of CSR in emerging countries in comparison with developed ones, is the low pressure from so-called 'civil society', i.e. all kinds of movements and organizations (trade unions, NGOs and other kinds of associations and institutions, including churches). Such organizations are, for well-known political reasons, under strict control in the People's Republic of China. As stipulated in the trade union law of 2001, trade unions across the country must be affiliated to the All China Federation of Trade Unions (ACFTU – articles 10 and 11 of the Act), which remains under the control of the Communist Party. NGOs, although varied in nature, developed rapidly in China from the beginning of the century. They, however, must be registered under one or other of a limited number of statuses, such as 'social organizations', or 'higher education affiliated' etc., which helps the supervising authorities to control them (Yang, 2005). As underlined by Li-Wen (2010)

NGOs active in the field of environmental issues benefit from greater autonomy than those acting on social issues, and particularly those acting in the field of human rights. The ones acting on environmental issues seem to be regarded as helping to solve a crucial concern in the country, whereas the latter are regarded as potentially subversive.

Conclusion

The way CSR developed in China is rather specific compared to other countries. CSR initially developed in that country because of consumers' concerns in developed markets, and thus has been introduced by MNCs working in China since the 1980s. Subsequently, China launched its *Go out Policy* in 1999, as the country was due to enter the World Trade Organization in 2001, and it appeared clear that CSR would be a crucial issue to get access to and to secure foreign markets. Thus, the development process of CSR in China was widely government driven. The weaknesses of so-called 'civil society', because of strong political control both of workers and other groups, including NGOs, is also a contrasting feature of the development process of CSR compared to other countries, particularly developed ones.

Different features and contexts lead, at least to some extent, to different results. CSR in China emphasizes environmental issues more than social ones and pays little attention to human rights. A lot of further research, however, still needs to be undertaken in comparing CSR performance in China with that in other countries, although it has already been established that higher CSR performance also supports higher financial performance in China.

Note

1 http:/www.csc9000.org.cn/

References

Basu, K., and Palazzo, G. (2008). Corporate social responsibility: A process model of sensemaking. *The Academy of Management Review*, 33(1), 122–136.

Bowen, H. R. (1953). *Social Responsibilities of the Businessman*. New York: Harper and Row.

Bruntland, G. H. (1987). *United Nations Report of the World Commission on Environment and Development: Our Common Future*. Oxford: Oxford University Press.

BSR, 2006 - Business for Social Responsibility (BSR) (2006). *In* perspective – CSR in the People's Republic of China. *Leading Perspectives*, Summer.

Carroll, A. (1979). A three-dimensional conceptual model of corporate performance. *Academy of Management Review*, 497–505.

Chan, G. K. Y. (2008). The relevance and value of Confucianism in contemporary business ethics. *Journal of Business Ethics*, 77(3), 347–360.

Cheng, S., Lin, K. Z., and Wong, W. (2015). Corporate social responsibility reporting and firm performance: Evidence from China. *Journal of Management and Governance*, 1–21.

Child, J., and Warner, M. (2003). Culture and management in China, in: *Culture and Management in Asia*. London: Routledge Curzon, Chapter 2.

Darrigan, K. H., and Post, J. E. (2009). Corporate citizenship in China – CSR challenges in the "Harmonious Society". *The Journal of Corporate Citizenship*, (35), Autumn, 39–53.

Elkington, J. (1994). Towards the sustainable corporation: Win-win-win business strategies for sustainable development. *California Management Review*, 90–100.

Freeman, R. E. (1984). *Strategic Management: A Stakeholder Approach*. Boston: Pitamn.

Hanson, K. O., and Rothlin, S. (2010). Taking your code to China. *Journal of International Business Ethics*, 3(1), 41–55.

Hou, S., Fu, W., and Li, X. (2010). Achieving sustainability with a stakeholder-based CSR assessment model for FIEs in China. *Journal of International Business Ethics*, 3(1), 41–55.

Ip, P. K. (2009). Is Confucianism good for business ethics in China? *Journal of Business Ethics*, 88(3), 463–476.

Jaussaud, J., and Liu, X. (2011). When in China. . . . The HRM practices of Chinese and foreign-owned enterprises during a global crisis. *Asia Pacific Business Review*, 17(4), October, 473–491.

Jonas, H. (1984). *The Imperative of Responsibility: In Search of an Ethics in the Technological Age*. Chicago: University of Chicago Press.

Li, Y., and Foo, C. T. (2016). Managing CSR in China, in: Foo, C. T., *Diversity of Managerial Perspectives From Inside China*. Series: Managing the Asian Century. Singapore: Springer, 19–33.

Li-Wen, L. (2010). Corporate social responsibility in China: Window dressing or structural change? *Berkeley Journal of International Law*, 28(1), March, 64–100.

Lu, X. (1997). Business ethics in China. *Journal of Business Ethics*, 16(14), 1509–1518.

Marquis, C., and Qian, C. (2014). Corporate social responsibility reporting in China: Symbol or substance? *Organization Science*, 25(1), January–February, 127–148.

Redfern, K., and Crawford, J. (1994). An empirical investigation of the ethics position questionnaire in the People's Republic of China. *Journal of Business Ethics*, 50, 199–210.

Rothlin, S. (2010). Towards a socially responsible China: A preliminary investigation of the implementation of the Global Compact. *Journal of International Business Ethics*, 3(1), 3–13.

Sun, M., Nagata, K., and Onoda, H. (2011). *The current status and promotion of Chinese Corporate Social Responsibility*, International Conference on Biology, Environment and Chemistry, *IPCBEE*, Vol. 1, IACSIT Press, Singapore.

Wang, K. T., and Li, D. (2015). Market reaction to the first-time disclosure of corporate social responsibility reports: Evidence from China. *Journal of Business Ethics*, 138(4), 661–682.

Wu, B., and Flynn, A. (1995). Sustainable development in China: Seeking a balance between economic growth and environmental protection. *Sustainable Development*, 36, 1–8.

Xi, S., and Fleming, C. (2008). *"Made in China", and the drive to include CSR*. Center for Global Finance Working Paper, The University of Nottingham, Ningbo, China, April.

Yang, G., (2005), Environmental NGOs and Institutional Dynamics in China, *The China Quarterly*, Vol. 181, p. 46–66

10 The corporate social responsibility strategy of a French multinational

A global and local approach in China

Claire Etienne

Acronyms

BSR:	Business for Social Responsibility
CCP:	Chinese Communist Party
CEO:	Chief Executive Officer
CSR:	Corporate Social Responsibility
CSRP:	Corporate Social Responsibility Plan
DJSI:	Dow Jones Sustainability Index
HRD:	Human Resource Department
ILO:	International Labour Organization
MNC, MNE:	Multinational Corporation, Multinational Enterprise
NGO:	Non-governmental Organization
RDF:	Registration Document Fiscal
SDR:	Sustainable Development Report
WWF:	World Wildlife Fund

Introduction

In 2006, according to Mohan (2006: 6), the debate concerning the international dimensions of CSR was still at its beginning. Egri and Ralston (2008) also highlight a lack of CSR salience among articles linked to corporate responsibility and published in international management reviews of the 1998–2007 period. This gap in theoretical or empirical research particularly relates to CSR management by multinationals (Hah and Freeman, 2014: 130), motivation for CSR (Rodriguez et al., 2006: 739), and aspects of localization and standardization in the strategies of local subsidiaries (Jamali, 2010: 197).

However, more and more studies analyze, guide or explain the adoption and implementation of CSR strategies by multinationals through the conception of theoretical frameworks (Arthaud-Day, 2005; Yang and Rivers, 2009; Tan and Wang, 2011 – for a more ethically-oriented approach; Hah and Freeman, 2014), or through empirical research (Gifford et al., 2010; Campbell et al., 2012; Bondy et al., 2012; Bondy and Starkey, 2014; Park et al., 2014). This is especially the case in developing countries (Reimann et al., 2012): in India (Mohan, 2006), in Mexico (Husted and Allen, 2006; Muller, 2006), in Lebanon (Jamali, 2007, 2010), in China

DOI: 10.4324/9781315102566-12

(Kolk et al., 2010), in Brazil (Barin Cruz and Boehe, 2010), in Malawi (Mzembe and Meaton, 2014) and in Kazakhstan (Mahmood and Humphrey, 2013).

Nevertheless, studies dealing specifically with determinants of multinationals CSR internationalization strategies remain scarce (Husted and Allen, 2006; Huemer, 2010; Jamali, 2010; Hah and Freeman, 2014; Bondy and Starkey, 2014) while some studies do not clearly specify the factors that justify the selection of a local or global CSR strategy (Muller, 2006; Mohan, 2006; Barin Cruz and Boehe, 2010; Kolk et al., 2010). This paper aims to study such factors. A review of the literature will now be conducted on this topic.

Literature review

It follows from previous papers that the choice of a CSR internationalization strategy by a multinational may be determined by pressure for CSR global integration or local responsiveness (Bondy and Starkey, 2014; Arthaud-Day, 2005; Husted and Allen, 2006), organizational identity (Huemer, 2010) and in particular by the influence of institutional process given the internal pressure for institutional isomorphism (Husted and Allen, 2006) or the search for external or internal legitimacy (Jamali, 2010; Hah and Freeman, 2014). This former driver will now be specifically analyzed.

The management of international CSR according to an institutional or a strategic approach (Husted and Allen, 2006)

According to Husted and Allen (2006: 840), the management of international CSR by multinationals first requires the identification of CSR issues as being global or local. The concept of local CSR relies on firms' obligations resulting from the local community norms whereas the notion of global CSR refers to firms' obligations arising from norms to which any society can be bound.

Firms must then determine which CSR issues are of strategic importance depending on two alternative processes (Husted and Allen, 2006: 840).

Under a strategic approach to the analysis of the importance of CSR issues, a firm addresses CSR issues in accordance with 'demands for responsiveness and integration by local and global NGOs, host and home country governments, and local market structure', whatever the organizational strategy of the firm in the product market (Husted and Allen, 2006: 841).

Under an institutional approach, a relationship between organizational strategy based on the product market and CSR strategy can be found as a result of organizational inertia and imitation (Husted and Allen, 2006: 839). The results from Husted and Allen (2006: 845–846) are in line with the institutional approach. They are only to be applied to multinationals operating in developing countries (e.g. Mexico) and to the specific CSR issues analyzed (i.e. job creation, community projects, the environment and social causes).

It should be noted that Husted and Allen (2006: 839) adapt the organizational strategy typology of the MNE developed by Bartlett and Ghoshal (1989), by Prahalad and Doz (1987), and extended by Yip (1992) to CSR, but they only consider two kinds of CSR internationalization strategy by multinationals: global and local CSR strategy. Based on a similar theoretical framework, Bondy and Starkey (2014: 8) suggest by contrast that companies could select one of three CSR internationalization strategies:

> 'A global CSR internationalisation strategy would see the company creating standards to be used across all operating units, requiring commitments that are "universal" in nature and relevant in virtually any business in any context. Local (multi-domestic) internationalisation strategies would see the company focusing on regional or national solutions that deal with culturally specific issues. Integrated (transnational) internationalisation strategies have two variations: (1) efficiency response, which would see companies working on culturally tailored solutions where universal commitments are tailored to local cultures, typically at the national level; and (2) interpenetration, where companies focus on solutions that blend global and local (typically national) cultures'.

Other studies use both institutional theory and stakeholder theory to shed light on the adoption and implementation process of CSR strategies by multinationals and underline the role that CSR plays in the construct of legitimacy within such organizations.

The search for legitimacy as a driver of international CSR within multinationals (Hah & Freeman, 2014; Jamali, 2010)

Some studies suggest that to be considered as a legitimate entity in a host country, foreign companies must give the appropriate ethical response to institutional pressure arising from local stakeholders (Yang and Rivers, 2009; Gifford et al., 2010; Reimann et al., 2012; Park et al., 2014; Mzembe and Meaton, 2014).

Furthermore, to survive, firms need to gain local legitimacy which signifies a willingness to abide by the rules and belief systems of the local stakeholder environment (Reimann et al., 2012: 2–3). Institutional pressure and stakeholder demands are then tightly linked (Park et al., 2014: 968).

Besides, legitimacy is also at stake for multinationals from the perspective of consistent CSR management across institutionally different countries, responding to the expectations of different stakeholders in the home country and in the host countries (Hah and Freeman, 2014; Yang and Rivers, 2009). Multinationals subsidiaries have to face the '*institutional duality*' challenge in their CSR practices and strategies across the world: they have to address both host country pressure to gain external legitimacy by adopting local practices and parent company pressure to obtain internal legitimacy (Yang and Rivers, 2009: 158).

To solve this internal-external paradox, it is likely that a pragmatic legitimacy will be acquired by multinationals subsidiaries thanks to exchange and influence relationships with diverse stakeholders (Suchman, 1995: 578–579). According to

Kostova et al. (2008: 1,001), as multinationals are confronted with various and contradictory institutional expectations, they would not be able to get legitimacy through isomorphism but through the negotiation of this status with every important legitimating actor. This political process of exchange and communication would create a perception about the organization without certain models and practices being necessarily implemented.

However, only a few articles systematically study the localization and standardization issues in the CSR activities of multinationals.

Hah and Freeman (2014: 131–134) develop a multi-level conceptual framework aimed at describing the adoption and implementation process of CSR strategies by multinationals subsidiaries in emerging countries.

According to the authors, those subsidiaries respond to local stakeholder demands by means of CSR strategies (cf. Yang and Rivers, 2009). But from the subsidiaries perspective, pressure to either adopt global or local CSR strategies stems from conflicting expectations between home country and host country stakeholders and from institutional isomorphic pressure in the host country to meet local societal issues (cf. DiMaggio and Powell, 1983; Kostova and Zaheer, 1999; Tan and Wang, 2011). Indeed, through a local CSR strategy developed to address local needs, subsidiaries will acquire an external legitimacy, while through a global CSR strategy these subsidiaries will keep a consistent strategy within the organization and will construct internal legitimacy (Hah and Freeman, 2014: 131–134). This pressure to either adopt global or local CSR can be found at different levels: at level of CSR motivation, CSR decision-making and explicit CSR manifestations (Jamali, 2010). It does not imply a dichotomy but constitutes a continuum (Hah and Freeman, 2014: 131, 133). Finally, facing diverging institutional logic in home and host countries, multinationals subsidiaries could opt for four different ethical approaches (Tan and Wang, 2011) or CSR strategies (Hah & Freeman, 2014: 132) depending on the degree of CSR ingrainedness of multinationals and on the level of local ethical pressure in the host country: defiance, camouflage, negotiation and compliance (Tan and Wang, 2011: 377–384).

Moreover, Jamali (2010: 187–188, 194, 196–197) explores localization and standardization features in the CSR strategies of ten multinationals subsidiaries in Lebanon. In her study, the business and society literature through institutional theory and stakeholder theory has contributed in highlighting that CSR motivation is primarily anchored at a local level in legitimization, adaptation, reputation and public relations. Other findings have emerged from the use of the international business political behaviour stream. Subsidiaries and their local stakeholders are marginalized in CSR decision-making and the involvement of subsidiaries in CSR decision-making depends upon subsidiary size, competence, strength in the multinationals network and market context aspects. Both streams have turned out to be helpful to describe philanthropic-type CSR activities developed by most of the subsidiaries as only three of the ten subsidiaries tend to systematically practice strategic CSR. These CSR activities also appear to be aligned with central directives and limited as a response to local issues.

The present study also contributes to analyzing determinants of multinationals CSR internationalization strategies, particularly in order to assess to what extent institutional and strategic factors influence such strategies.

Methodology and data

A single case study

This paper studies the CSR strategy of a French multinational operating in China (the Group), at the group level (the Group level) and at the level of its Chinese subsidiary (the Subsidiary level) (cf. Results below).

The Group can justify being a single case study (Yin, 2014). Indeed, it was named global leader in its sector by the Dow Jones Sustainability Index (DJSI) for the 12th consecutive year in September 2016 (Fiscal 2016 Corporate Responsibility Report: 29). It has operated in China since 1995 and has published a yearly sustainable development or CSR report since 2005 – as the terms 'CSR' and 'sustainable development' are used interchangeably in the Group's public documentation, the same interchangeability applies here.[1] The approach of this study is exploratory, considering that few studies have been conducted to date on the chosen subject.

Case studies are particularly appropriate when investigating complex CSR issues in transitional markets (Zhao et al., 2014: 660).

China defines itself as a socialist market economy. It has experienced exceptional economic growth since the opening up of the country in 1978, in spite of a slowdown over recent years. However, the sustainability of its economic model is highly questionable given the negative externalities that arise from it, such as environmental pollution, income disparities in spite of an indisputable reduction in extreme poverty since 1978, the bad working conditions of Chinese employees and the absence of political freedom.

Interviews

This article relies in particular on the qualitative content analysis of eight interviews of leaders at a Group and Subsidiary level, conducted in 2013 and completed with 4 other interviews conducted in 2014 (cf. Table 10.1 below). Each interview was recorded and entirely transcribed.

To construct the validity of the analysis (Yin, 2014: 198), the draft paper was sent for potential comments in May 2015 to all the interviewees and after modifications, in January 2016, to the Group chief marketing and strategic planning officer and to the chief executive officer (CEO) of the Subsidiary in place at the time of the interviews who is the only one to have answered solely by e-mail – 17 and 20 July 2015, 14 and 21 March 2016 and 19 May 2016.

The interviews were conducted following a semi-directive interview guide containing the questions resumed in Box 10.1 below.

Table 10.1 List of the interviewed leaders and characteristics of the interviews

Interviewed leaders	Number of interviews	Date and Duration of the interviews	Acronym of the function used in the study to indicate which interviewed leader is answering
Group level	8		
Group Chief Marketing and Strategic Planning Officer; One in two members of the Group Executive Committee in charge of driving continuous improvement in the Group Corporate Responsibility performance	3	7 May 2013: **1 h 15**; 23 July 2013: **1 h 45**; 20 August 2014: **2 h**	GCM
Group Vice President Sustainable Development and Director Sustainability Metrics and Performance Measures	1 double interview	9 July 2013: **1 h 10**	GVSD DSM
Director Sustainability Metrics and Performance Measures	2	12 September 2014: **38 min**; 19 September 2014: **54 min**	DSM
Group Vice President Ethics, HR Research and Progress, Group Human Resources and Project Manager Workplace Rights, Group Human Resources	1 double interview	14 May 2013: **1 h 30**	GVE PMWR
Group Chief Legal Officer	1	30 April 2013: **49 min**	GCLO
Subsidiary level	4		
CEO, China	3	24 May 2013: **1 h 10**; 4 July 2013: **1 h**; 20 November 2014: **1 h 10**	CEOC
Legal and Governmental Affairs Director, China	1	5 July 2013: **1 h 15**	LDC

Box 10.1 Guide of interview

(1) How does your company conceive sustainable development or CSR?;
(2) How are sustainable development or CSR activities developed by your company chosen?;
(3) How does your company translate its sustainable development or CSR strategy at world level?;
(4) How does your company implement its sustainable development or CSR policy in general and in particular in the context of China? What are the legal tools used in this perspective?
(5) How does your company segment the stakeholders at the Group level and in China? How do you take into account the difference in the stakeholders weighting from one country to another? How does your company manage its relationship with its stakeholders?

To proceed to a triangulation of the data (Yin, 2014), the interviews were completed by public documents issued by the Group and its subsidiaries, in particular on their website, as well as by internal documents given in the course of, or following the interviews. The interviews were prepared by studying the aforesaid public documents, press articles concerning the Group and some of its subsidiaries, as well as the above-mentioned internal documents concerning the second series of interviews.

The interviews were coded by using NVIVO software to identify, retrieve and gather the data (Miles and Huberman, 2003: 112, 128). The created codes are descriptive (Miles and Huberman, 2003: 113). They were linked to sentences or to entire paragraphs and distinguished between the two organizational levels of analysis (Group, Subsidiary) and the guide themes evoked in the interviews or identified following the interviews.

The present analysis is focused on the one hand, on two stages of the model describing the process of adoption and implementation of CSR strategies of companies proposed by Maon et al. (2009: 76–77) dealing with the development of the strategy (the unfreeze stage) and its implementation (the move stage) and on the other hand on the stakeholder dialogue that is continuous during this process (Maon et al., 2009: 83–85).

Results

The Group is a world leader in quality of life services. Its business covers three sectors: on-site services, benefits and rewards services, personal and home services.

At the top of its organizational structure is a holding company in the form of a public limited company listed on the CAC 40, which assumes all reporting obligations. The holding company represents the Group level. The Group has subsidiaries in all the countries in which it operates, that is, in 80 countries. They assume an operational role by acting on customer sites (GCLO, 30 April 2013). The Group is organized on a country by country basis (the Countries) and by divisions, which bring together several legal entities.

The process of adopting and implementing CSR activities and dialogue and interaction with stakeholders shall now be described at a Group and Subsidiary level.

The adoption of CSR activities and their implementation

In 2003, the Group formalized its sustainable development strategy for the first time and became a member of *Global Compact*. In 2005, it integrated sustainable development into the company's strategy and published its first sustainable development report. In 2009, it launched a new strategic roadmap (referred to in the paper as 'the CSR Plan' or 'CSRP') in order to reinforce the Group sustainable development performance (SDR, 9 March 2010: 8).

Prior to the establishment of the CSRP, the Group adopted a number of worldwide CSR topics according to an unstructured process and with very different determinants from one topic to the next. Starting with the establishment of the CSRP, these CSR topics are included in the Group CSR strategy and others are added in accordance with a process that was then specifically defined. The CSR subjects defined at a Group level are then applied in countries, particularly in China.

The CSR subjects adopted prior to the establishment of the CSRP, reiterated by the CSRP in detail

Before 2005, as the company expanded, various actions, in terms of CSR were undertaken in the Countries in a decentralized manner, with a poorly structured approach and initiated at the request of clients or employees, and in line with the company's culture. However, there are several exceptions in terms of the coordination and centralization of CSR programmes (GCM, 23 July 2013).

Indeed, the ethical principles and values that have been put forward since the Group was founded in 1966 and upon which the Group CSR commitment is based (SDR 2007–2008: 6; 'Registration Document Fiscal' (RDF) 2014: 89) are already formalized in order to ensure a coherent deployment across the 80 countries where the Group is located (GVE, 14 May 2013): in 2003, the Group's executives signed a charter on ethics and sustainable development (SDR, 2007–2008: 10) and in 2007, the Group executive committee adopted a code of conduct based on principles of integrity (SDR, 1 March 2011: 20). The identity section of the CSRP reiterates, in 2009, the main values and principles of the Group in terms of business ethics included in this code.

Ethical policies are defined at a Group level and must then be deployed in each country, where appropriate, depending on the institutional context of the country. The objective is to create a culture of ethics within the Group (PMWR, GVE, 14 May 2013).

However, the problems of transposing a global model of ethical principles in 80 different countries can arise and highlight the tension between the establishment of a global model and the necessary local adaptation, depending on the culture of the country, without calling into question the global nature of the model (GVE, 14 May 2013).

Moreover, as the company is further organized around human resource management, the Group is particularly focused on the involvement of its employees in the implementation of its CSR activities (GVSD, 9 July 2013). Prior to the launch of the CSRP, the social, and responsible employer components were already coordinated and centralized (GCM, 23 July 2013). In particular, the policy on social rights at work and the diversity policy were developed prior to 2009.

With respect to the fundamental rights at work policy, the Group adhered to the United Nations Global Compact in 2003 and in 2010 (SDR, 1 March 2011: 21), it decides to supplement its pre-existing human rights policy to meet the requirements of stakeholders, and in particular customers, rating agencies and social partners. In September 2011, the executive committee of the Group adopted and published a charter of fundamental rights at work based on the four fundamental principles defined by the ILO (PMWR, 14 May 2013). The guide to fundamental rights at work was subsequently created to help HRDs in each country update their internal policies and procedures, which both comply with the Group's commitments and local laws (PMWR, 14 May 2013).

In some countries, including China, the challenge is to respect the law, which is the first requirement of the Group, but also the ILO principles (PMWR, 14 May 2013).

On the other hand, the diversity and inclusion policy resulted directly from the signature in 2005 of a transaction to settle a class action within the Group's US subsidiary, initiated by Afro-American managers who considered themselves to be victims of racial discrimination within the company's internal promotion mechanisms. The class action was perceived as a shock by the executives insofar as it contradicted the Group's values (GCM, 20 August 2014; see the 2003 charter of the Group on ethics and sustainable development: 6).

The Group CEO has therefore decided at Group level to transform this litigation into an opportunity to challenge human resources management processes by instituting a Group diversity and inclusion policy as of 2004 (GCM, 20 August 2014).

A global, organised and coherent CSR commitment for local communities also existed prior to 2009. This related to an initiative to combat hunger, launched by the employees of the American subsidiary of the Group in Chicago in order to provide free meals to the poorest schoolchildren in the city. The CEO of the US subsidiary, the current CEO of the Group, then had the idea to transform this local initiative into a major, global undertaking binding all stakeholders (GCM, 23 July 2013), extended since 2003 to countries where the Group is established (SDR, 2005: 56), that is 44 in 2016 (SDR, 2015–1016: 98).

Finally, upon taking office in 2005, the current CEO initiated the development of a more coherent and coordinated approach to sustainable development by the Group (GVSD, 9 July 2013). Sustainable development was then integrated into the company's strategy. As a large global company, the company felt the need for a global roadmap.

The CSRP was intended to consolidate the organization's efforts, to leverage its global strengths, and create coherence, which was demanded by clients. This made it possible to put an end to distractions that were taking place, that is to say, initiatives that were not related to the company's business or that were not requested by customers, consumers or employees in order to focus on what was important for stakeholders (GVSD, 9 July 2013).

Before 2007–2008, CSR activities outside of those subjects that were previously studied, were developed in order to be communicated, without guaranteeing that such CSR topics would be integrated into the offer proposed by all the sites, throughout the world. At this time, the Group CSR policy was managed by the communications department. Consequently, the CSRP was developed to ensure that the CSR strategy infiltrated all of the Group's businesses and to ensure that it does not just reflect reputational concerns (GCM, 20 August 2014). This new road map reflects the Group's CSR vision: making decisions responsibly means that the Group 'makes decisions that are not entirely 100% based on profitability [and] that these [CSR] commitments, also on the contrary, shall one day help to increase profitability, that is to say that CSR works in both directions' (GCM, 23 July 2013).

The adoption and implementation of the CSR components within the framework of the CSRP

The Group's new CSR strategic roadmap, the CSRP, is the result of an 18-month materiality analysis initiated by the Group in 2007–2008. Different stakeholders (NGOs, customers, suppliers and consumer groups) were consulted (GVSD, 9 July 2013; SDR, 9 March 2010: 8) to identify and prioritize the most important sustainability issues (SDR 2007–2008: 11) that the organization should focus on (GVSD, 9 July 2013) and in order to achieve the strategic objectives set out in the Group strategic plan (SDR 2007–2008: 11).

The firm Utopies participated in the organization of stakeholder consultation and, for example, conducted interviews with about 15 NGOs and forums with clients were organized (GCM 23 July 2013; SDR, 9 March 2010: 8). The roadmaps of major groups such as Unilever and iconic companies at the time (Marks & Spencer, Body Shop, Nature et Découvertes) were analyzed. Interviews on the theme of sustainable development were conducted with the most committed companies such as Unilever or Danone (GCM, 23 July 2013).

The consultation with stakeholders, with executives of subsidiaries of major Countries, with certain members of the executive committee and key members of the operational teams (DSM, 19 September 2014, 9 July 2013), enabled the selection of 14 major commitments sorted into 4 pillars under the action section of the CSRP, namely, [The Group] employer, nutrition-health-well being, local communities and the environment, the employer section with 4 additional commitments not being reworked (GCM, 7 May 2013, 23 July 2013).

The fourteen selected initiatives correspond to 'important topics for our business, our customers, our consumers, our stakeholders and for us' (GCM, 7 May 2013). These are global issues such as nutritional problems related to excess salt or fat, which make sense on a local stakeholder level and which can be translated into action plans, through which progress can be measured (GCM, 23 July 2013).

In preparing the CSRP, stakeholders as well as Countries were selected on the basis of criteria relating to the representative nature of the company's main business activities. The selected NGOs were those that could work with the Group around the world, not just within a single country or in relation to a single issue (DSM, 19 September 2014). They are mainly French, British or American NGOs (GCM, 23 July 2013; SDR, 9 March 2010: 8). Similarly, the clients or suppliers that were interviewed (Danone, Unilever, Johnson & Johnson, Coca Cola, etc.) were involved in several geographical areas and are global in nature. A client has been chosen in different business sectors (education, hospital, company), in the United States, in France etc. (DSM, 19 September 2014). Clients were also selected for their interest in sustainable development (DSM, 9 July 2013). Western countries were more represented in this process given their presence on the committee which created the CSRP, their greater representativeness at the time in terms of their share of the Group's business and their greater capacity to respond to the issues in question (DSM, 19 September 2014).

The CSRP was the subject of an approval process prior to publication, in the form of a consultation with different stakeholders, including clients, NGOs such as WWF (World Wildlife Fund) or BSR (Business for Social Responsibility) (DSM, 12 September 2014).

Furthermore, the CSRP is evolving.

A new materiality analysis took place in 2014–2015 within the company (RDF 2014–2015: 78; GCM, 20 August 2014). This resulted in a new roadmap entitled the CSRP 2025 presented during autumn of 2016 (RDF 2015–2016: 73).

Within the context of this new analysis, the Group's two most significant extra-financial analysis agencies (DJSI; Oekom) were consulted in addition to the main NGOs, WWF and BSR, which were already consulted in 2009 (DSM, 19 September 2014).

On the other hand, Countries also play a special role in the preparation (see above) and implementation of the CSRP. In this respect, it should be recalled that the Group's growth and strengths were based on people who could develop business activities in different countries and that the Group's development would be carried out, on a country by country basis, within the framework defined by the Group. Similarly, the CSRP is designed as a framework at a Group level (GVSD, 9 July 2013). To fulfil the commitments included in the plan, Countries are allowed to set their own objectives and priorities (DSM, 9 July 2013), which reflect what is important for customers or consumers in the country (GVSD, 9 July 2013).

In conclusion, the CSRP is a roadmap that 'satisfies the needs of clients and consumers to all stakeholders'; the CSRP's strength lies in its ability to bind 80 countries to the same strategy and to measure progress (GCM, 23 July 2013).

The adoption and implementation of CSR activities phase shall now be studied at a Subsidiary level.

CSR activities developed in China

Interviews conducted with executives of the Group and the Subsidiary revealed many difficulties in developing business activities in China, impacting on how to develop the Group CSR strategy in the country.

The specific nature of the Chinese context is taken into account by the Group, which gives autonomy to countries in implementing the CSRP (CEOC, 24 May 2013; GCM, 23 July 2013). This involves being selective and setting priorities for CSR issues (GCM, 23 July 2013).

To the extent that CSR can make sense internally to employees, detecting themes which resonate for those employees and which the firm is able to respond to would also allow them to further increase their commitments (CEOC, 20 November 2014).

In order to discuss CSR activities that the Subsidiary could develop, a meeting was organized in July 2014 with employees expressing an interest in the subject of CSR and a person attached to the team responsible for implementing CSPR at a Group level (CEOC, 20 November 2014).

Two local issues emerged from this discussion: providing care to migrant workers coming from the country ('*mingong*'), beyond what is already being done (see below), and the care of the elderly (CEOC, 20 November 2014), as families in China are only responsible for looking after their ancestors even though the one-child policy reduced the number of offspring. Actions implementing these two subjects are to be determined subsequently, if applicable (CEOC, 20 November 2014).

Certain CSR activities associated with the CSRP are developed in China as in the rest of the Group, irrespective of the wishes of the clients and their interest in CSR.

In this way, the company's values are disseminated to the Subsidiary's employees. This is illustrated notably by the granting of financial or non-financial bonuses, including with respect to migrants (CEOC, 4 July 2013). Respect for this category of people is promoted in the company in contrast to what is observed in Chinese society and no distinction is made in the distribution of bonuses (CEOC, 24 May 2013).

In terms of human resources, the Subsidiary develops the same principles and pursues the same objectives as the other Countries with respect to priority for internal promotion, development of the employees, reduction of turnover and employee retention. The human rights policy is applied in China as in the rest of the Group (see above). However, certain institutional specificities must be taken into account (GCM, 7 May 2013).

Indeed, trade union freedom does not exist in China and the Chinese collective bargaining system does not correspond to the fundamental principles and rights at work defined by the ILO. To remedy this institutional weakness, collective meetings of employees on site where all employees can express themselves collectively are organised every quarter (PMWR, 14 May 2013). Operational managers must put these meetings in place but not all of them do so as some do not feel comfortable with it. The percentage of sites where these meetings are held is not measured. On a quarterly basis, the central human resources department in Beijing provides operational managers with 'content' to support these meetings. This includes information that the company wishes to communicate to employees on site, how to improve the quality of service on the site and the working conditions for employees (CEOC, 20 November 2014).

The diversity policy relates to the status of migrants in order to take into account their difficult living conditions. For example, migrants and their families, as non-residents, do not benefit from the city's public services where they work. Allowances are granted to them to return home during holidays and additional paid holidays are also granted to them beyond what is provided by law (CEOC, 24 May 2013). The company makes sure to directly finance or to have clients finance accommodation, in this case dormitories that are clean, maintained, and having a minimum level of comfort so that the employees in question are not crammed in together (CEOC, 20 November 2014).

The project to combat hunger deployed globally is only just being applied in China (CEOC, 17 July 2015). Indeed, it is not well received, especially among employees, and does not correspond to the Subsidiary's priorities or respond to a customers' request. It does not meet a local need as China is proud to have achieved good results in terms of fighting extreme poverty. Moreover, the status of an undemocratic state, controlled by the Chinese Communist Party (CCP) makes any interference in social affairs more difficult (CEOC, 24 May 2013, 19 May 2016).

On the other hand, the choice of CSR activities set out in the CSRP developed by the Subsidiary, is also determined by customer priorities that focus on regulatory compliance, food safety and the effectiveness of supply chains (CEOC, 20 November 2014).

Dialogue and collaboration with stakeholders shall now be analyzed, at a Group level and within China.

Dialogue and collaboration with stakeholders

Dialogue and collaboration with stakeholders at a Group level

The stakeholder engagement section of the CSRP organizes a dialogue and collaboration with stakeholders (RDF 2014–2015: 79, 80, 98) which comprises two types of action: on the one hand, awareness and information and on the other hand, the 'real' stakeholder engagement, namely a collaborative work with working groups created by including different stakeholders (DSM, 19 September 2014).

The stakeholder engagement plan focuses on two issues: a project combating malnutrition (see above) and the coalition fighting against general waste, of food in particular (see below) (DSM, 19 September 2014). These actions are carried out by the Group with a contribution from the Countries, but the Countries no longer implement their own approach (DSM, 19 September 2014).

The coalition's project to combat food waste was launched by the Group in 2012–2013 in view of the role that the company could play on this issue in association with its core business and the high cost of waste (GCM, 23 July 2013). This commitment echoes a societal demand that was recently taken up by the European and French public authorities (Sénat, 2014; Assemblée Nationale, 2015; Ministère de l'Agriculture, de l'Agroalimentaire et de la Forêt, 2013).

Stakeholder engagement also takes place within the framework of processes that are already in place within the organization, which may be adapted and supplemented by specific tools. For example, supplier engagement in building sustainable supply chains relies on an existing supplier dialogue, on the training of suppliers and the signing of a Group Supplier Code of Conduct.

Moreover, in the absence of a specific formal approach to collecting information relating to stakeholders that initially were thought to be involved (DSM, 12 September 2014), studies (for example of consumers) and the structured processes already in place within the organization are used to the maximum extent to feed back information relating to stakeholders' requests. For instance, information about suppliers' expectations result from regular interviews with buyers. Considering stakeholders' needs that go beyond those set out in the materiality analysis strictly speaking thus makes it possible to develop the Group CSR strategy (DSM, 12 and 19 September 2014).

As an illustration, the issue of animal welfare has become a priority issue since 2012–2013 following the involvement of several stakeholders (media, customers, student campaigns, in particular in the United States, socially responsible investors) (DSM, 12 September 2014).

Dialogue and interaction with stakeholders in China

Public authorities and employees are central to the Subsidiary's concerns, being even more important than suppliers. Moreover, the Subsidiary does not have any dealings with NGOs (CEOC, 20 November 2014).

A policy of permanent institutional relations is thus carried out in particular by the CEO and the Legal Director of the Subsidiary with a wide range of authorities, local or central (CEOC, 4 July 2013).

The first aspect of this communication work is aimed at limiting the difficulties encountered by the Subsidiary in its operations in China and to serve its development (LDC, 5 July 2013) in a State which can often be characterized by vague or incomplete regulations, and a different application of the law depending on whether the firms in question are foreign or Chinese (CEOC, 4 July 2013), large or small (LDC, 5 July 2013). The objective is then to make themselves known and to know the competent authorities, and possibly to influence them.

The Subsidiary's contribution to social development and the improvement of daily life for all businesses and the general population, as well as the absence of environmental damage resulting from the extension of its business activity have then been highlighted. These are important issues for both local and central authorities (LDC, 5 July 2013).

The second aspect of the relationship building work developed with the authorities is to educate the authorities, at their request, in certain areas including with respect to food security, so that the authorities themselves can educate the commercial restaurant market. The development of food safety benefits both the

Subsidiary and the authorities, who have every interest in ensuring that quality in the Group's different business areas is standardized and improved (CEOC, 24 May 2013).

This public relations work has sometimes resulted in a change in the regulation or organization of the authorities (CEOC, 24 May 2013). It can thus make up for a lack of regulation adapted to the company's scope of activity or the misinterpretation of the applicable texts (CEOC, 4 July 2013).

A dialogue with employees of the Subsidiary is organized, notably within the framework of training. Training employees in relation to the CSRP commitments is carried out for employees working directly on these commitments. Integration programs for on-site staff do not cover the CSRP but are related to the company's values (CEOC, 20 November 2014). In this respect, the CEO of the Subsidiary has emphasized that Chinese employees [in the procurement department] are generally uncomfortable with ethical principles that are perceived as obstacles to business development and are not well accommodated given a certain 'pragmatism' (CEOC, 20 November 2014). Furthermore, this divergent perception of ethics and the behaviours that result from it, explains the renewal of purchasing teams every three years on average (CEOC, 20 November 2014).

In addition, a social dialogue takes place within the context of on-site meetings organized with employees, when they take place. These meetings are used to discuss working conditions (CEOC, 20 November 2014). The social dialogue organized by the Subsidiary also aims to improve employees' commitments to meet a major challenge in China for many companies: attracting and retaining talent (CEOC, 4 July 2013, 20 November 2014). The employee engagement survey carried out in 2014 by the Group in the Countries revealed a very good rate of engagement in China and significant progress, particularly as a result of the communication actions that were implemented. The leaders and senior managers met with employees on the ground and set up exchange and discussion forums to disseminate more information about the company, its activities and the progress it has made (CEOC, 20 November 2014). Finally, the dialogue with employees at the July 2014 meeting revealed two CSR themes that the Subsidiary could develop in the future (see above).

Discussion

The purpose of this study is to analyze to what extent the CSR internationalization strategy of a multinational is determined by institutional or strategic factors. Several findings emerge from the case study.

The Group CSR internationalization strategy is determined both by institutional and strategic factors highlighted by Husted and Allen (2006)

The way the Group CSR internationalization strategy was adopted does not mirror the process described by Husted and Allen (2006) (cf. Figure 10.1 below). Indeed,

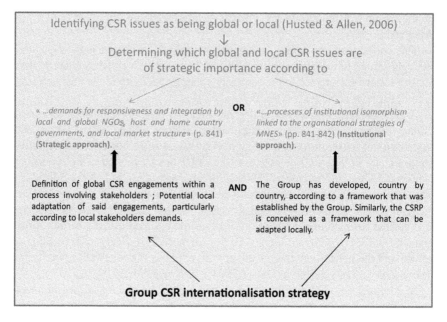

Figure 10.1 Application to the Group of the analysis concerning the management of international CSR by a multinational proposed by Husted and Allen (2006)

the process implemented by the Group, especially from the launch of its CSRP in 2009 combines both the strategic and institutional approaches established by Husted and Allen (2006).

The Group used a collaborative approach with stakeholders to identify CSR issues and priorities of the Group CSR policies. This process is quite original in comparison to the results from Bondy and Starkey's study (2014: 12–14). Indeed, in their study only four of the 37 British MNCs used a similar collaborative approach.

This process led to the definition of commitments required to be fulfilled in respect of all Countries. These commitments deal with two kinds of global CSR issues: universal ones concern 'firm's obligations based on those standards to which all societies can be held' (Husted and Allen, 2006: 840) such as protection of human rights or environmental preservation (Husted and Allen, 2006: 840; Bondy and Starkey, 2014: 16); additional global CSR issues concern meaningful issues in all the Countries (for instance, the reduction of salt, sugar and fat proportions in meals sold by the company). However, issues such as animal welfare may appear less relevant in developing countries in comparison to development imperatives (cf. Bondy and Starkey, 2014: 11–14; Jamali, 2010: 196).

At the development level, the CSR internationalization strategy of the Group based on global commitments and standardized policies at world level can then be qualified as global (Bondy and Starkey, 2014: 8). The adoption of such a strategy corresponds to a tendency reported in two different studies by Bondy and Starkey (2014: 10) and Jamali (2010: 192).

At the implementation level, the Group used an integrated CSR strategy (Bondy and Starkey, 2014: 8, 10) similar to most of the MNCs studied by Bondy and Starkey (2014: 14–17), where 30 out of the 37 MNCs used an integrated CSR strategy. Husted and Allen (2006) do not take this kind of strategy into account.

Global CSR issues can thus be adapted at local level. Local adaptation seems inevitable resulting from pressure from national institutions and from isomorphic institutional pressure arising from local stakeholders in host countries: in this study, China.

This sort of strategy can be criticized as it would lead to local issues being largely ignored and to reflecting more the MNC home country culture (Bondy and Starkey, 2014: 16–17).

In this case study, for instance, the programme fighting against hunger and malnutrition, one of the main CSR programmes of the Group, does not seem to respond to local demand in China. However, an effort was made by the Subsidiary to detect meaningful local issues in the course of a meeting organized with Chinese employees in July 2014 (CEOC, 20 November 2014). The issues that arose dealt with migrants and elderly people. The issue of migrants is already dealt with through the Group's diversity policy or the diffusion of the Group's values.

Furthermore, organizational inertia and the mimetism mechanism have led to an alignment between the Group internationalization strategy for products and service activities and CSR internationalization strategy (Husted and Allen, 2006, cf. Figure 10.1 above). For instance, as the Group has developed country by country according to a framework designed at the Group level, CSRP is conceived as a framework at the Group level and is likely to be adaptable locally depending on the economic, social and cultural context of host countries.

The institutional analysis also highlights that CSR contributes to the construct of legitimacy within multinationals (Jamali, 2010; Hah and Freeman, 2014).

The Group builds an internal and a local legitimacy through its CSR internationalization strategy

The results of the study show that the development of a global CSR strategy by the Group allows it to maintain a consistent strategy within the organization and to build an internal legitimacy (Hah and Freeman, 2014: 131–133) which is preserved thanks to the management of the logic dilemma by the Group (Tan and Wang, 2011: 377).

Given the high degree of ingrainedness of CSR in its strategy and its organization and given different levels of local ethical pressure in the host countries depending upon the issues concerned, the Group is likely to adopt two kinds of CSR strategy in China: camouflage and defiance strategy (Tan and Wang, 2011: 377–384; Hah and Freeman, 2014: 132; cf. Figure 10.2 below).

The camouflage CSR strategy of the Subsidiary deals with issues that are subject in China to high local ethical pressure, such as the non-compliance with

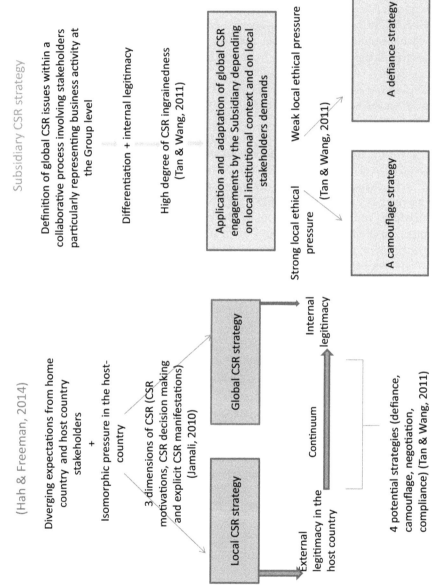

Figure 10.2 Application of the conceptual framework developed by Hah and Freeman (2014) to the Subsidiary CSR strategy

fundamental rights at work governed by ILO Conventions related to freedom of association and collective bargaining. This strategy seeks a compromise between adaptation to the host country ethical pressure and preservation of the fundamental values of the organization rooted in the home country (Tan and Wang, 2011: 381). It can be illustrated here by the organization of collective meetings of onsite employees.

The defiance CSR strategy of the Subsidiary deals with issues that are subject in China to weak local ethical pressure. For instance, some Chinese employees don't comply with the Group ethical principles in business conduct, which reflects a certain pragmatic conception of doing business in China but little pressure is placed on the Group to abide by such practices. This strategy defies local ethical pressure but allows the maintenance of organization consistency (Tan and Wang, 2011: 379–380). It can be illustrated here by the termination of contracts of employees who did not comply with the Group ethical principles.

Moreover, the Subsidiary has developed a special dialogue with two local stakeholders, i.e. its employees and authorities, who are frequently connected to firms' local legitimacy (Reimann et al., 2012: 3).

Because of this dialogue, in particular focused on its involvement in sustainable development, the Subsidiary was accepted by these local stakeholders, gaining social licence and local legitimacy (Gifford et al., 2010: 306).

It is easy to underscore that the lack of such support, especially from authorities, would have seriously hampered the activities of the Subsidiary as a firm from a foreign group (Reimann et al., 2012: 3).

In contrast to the suggestion by Reimann et al. (2012: 3), the results reveal that the concept of local legitimacy does not necessarily imply a compliance with the norms and beliefs of local stakeholders as they may conflict with the CSR strategy of the Subsidiary.

The Subsidiary does not gain local legitimacy through isomorphism but through the negotiation of this status with every important legitimating actor, which confirms the analysis of Kostova et al. (2008: 1,001) on this topic.

These results introduce a different perspective on the link between local legitimacy and CSR strategies of multinational firms that emerges from articles studying both CSR implementation and building of legitimacy within multinationals (Yang and Rivers, 2009; Gifford et al., 2010; Jamali, 2010; Reimann et al., 2012; Hah and Freeman, 2014: 130–131; Park et al., 2014; Mzembe and Meaton, 2014: 194–196).

The CSR strategy of the Group was conceived as a source of differentiation used to construct a competitive advantage in order to be chosen by clients or employees on this criterion. The Subsidiary applies the CSR strategy of the Group, however, in a different way, and also adopts this strategic approach to CSR. In contrast to the results from Jamali (2010: 196), acquiring legitimacy in the host country was thus not the central reason for the Subsidiary to engage in CSR practices. However, the Subsidiary takes advantage of this CSR strategy within its relationship with local stakeholders in order to construct local legitimacy.

Moreover, results show that other factors beyond strategic or institutional factors which were analysed previously (Husted and Allen, 2006; Jamali, 2010; Hah and Freeman, 2014) influenced the development of the Group CSR internationalisation strategy.

Other factors influence the development of the Group CSR internationalization strategy

The selection of a CSR internationalization strategy, especially concerning the diversity policy and the policy for business integrity, was also determined by the Group organizational identity (Huemer, 2010). The CSR commitment of the Group relies on core values and principles promoted since the Group was created in 1966 (SDR, 2007–2008: 6). These values and principles are incidentally included in the identity section of the CSRP (cf. Huemer, 2010: 267) which aims at establishing a global model of ethical principles in 80 countries, likely to be adapted to local contexts without undermining the global nature of the model.

Another factor which was crucial to the development of the Group CSR internationalization strategy was organization agency.

Managerial discretion or agency constitutes the core of the concept of explicit CSR (Blindheim, 2015: 57–58; Carroll, 1979: 500; Matten and Moon, 2008). In accordance with this principle of agency, 'each entity, individual or group [is allowed] some relative freedom to act according to its awareness, capabilities and best understanding of its situation' (van Marrewijk, 2003: 98) given a specific political, economic and cultural context (Blindheim, 2015: 58).

Prior to 2009, CSR programmes such as the business integrity policy and employer policy resulted partly from the Group agency and since 2009 the Group has decided to adopt a strategic, global and locally adaptable CSR policy.

Organization agency was never mentioned to date in articles studying the determinants of CSR internationalization strategies of multinationals (Husted and Allen, 2006; Jamali, 2010; Huemer, 2010; Hah and Freeman, 2014; Bondy and Starkey, 2014).

Finally, the findings of this paper seem to confirm that studies concerning the implementation of CSR strategies by multinationals in a single country may be biased if their strategies are not taken into account at a global level (Husted and Allen, 2009).

Indeed, Jamali (2007, 2010) studied the kind of CSR, strategic or philanthropic, implemented by companies operating in Lebanon and in particular subsidiaries of multinationals. She concludes that CSR in developing countries tends to be limited to the field of philanthropy or public relations (Jamali, 2010: 197). However, Jamali (2007, 2010) does not analyze the CSR strategies of Lebanese subsidiaries of multinationals in comparison to the CSR strategies of their respective groups. Similarly, Husted and Allen (2009: 794) investigate to what extent the CSR programmes of multinationals in Mexico coincide with their mission without examining if CSR is integrated into the group strategy.

The Group and Subsidiary CSR strategy is adopted according to a strategic approach (Porter and Kramer, 2006) aimed at differentiation and constructing a competitive advantage. The concerns of Group subsidiaries related to the development of CSR activities, especially in emerging countries such as China, do not only deal with the gaining of external legitimacy or with the management of the logic dilemma (cf. Hah and Freeman, 2014; Jamali, 2010).

Besides, the response to local stakeholders is provided within the CSRP framework. This can entail that specific local expectations are not taken into account in the process of CSR strategy development or implementation (cf. Jamali, 2010: 196; Bondy and Starkey, 2014: 11–14).

Figure 10.3 below summarizes the determinants of CSR internationalization strategy of the Group according to the results.

Conclusion

This case study reveals an association of factors, in particular strategic and institutional, influencing the CSR internationalization strategy of the Group.

It brings new insights that were not shown before in previous studies concerning the determinants of CSR internationalization strategies of multinationals (Husted and Allen, 2006; Huemer, 2010; Jamali, 2010; Hah and Freeman, 2014; Bondy and Starkey, 2014).

• Using an exploratory study has facilitated highlighting organization agency (van Marrewijk, 2003: 98) as a major determinant of the CSR internationalization strategy of the Group.

The Group agency was translated into the adoption of a CSR that is strategic, global and locally adaptable at the implementation level. This factor combined with the involvement of stakeholders in the development of the CSR strategy emphasizes the importance of the influence of strategic factors on the CSR internationalization of the Group.

However, the results also show that the influence of national institutions and of institutional isomorphic pressure arising from local stakeholders in host countries leads to an inevitable local adaptation concerning the implementation of the CSR strategy of a multinational, while the search for internal legitimacy implies that this local adaptation should not conflict with the development of a global CSR model.

• This exploratory study through the analysis of the influence of institutional factors and also of rival factors (Yin, 2014) such as strategic factors, enabled a better assessment of the weight of institutional factors on the CSR internationalization strategy of the firm. It also highlights the way institutional and strategic factors are articulated in the process of adoption and implementation of CSR internationalization strategy of the Group. These results support an

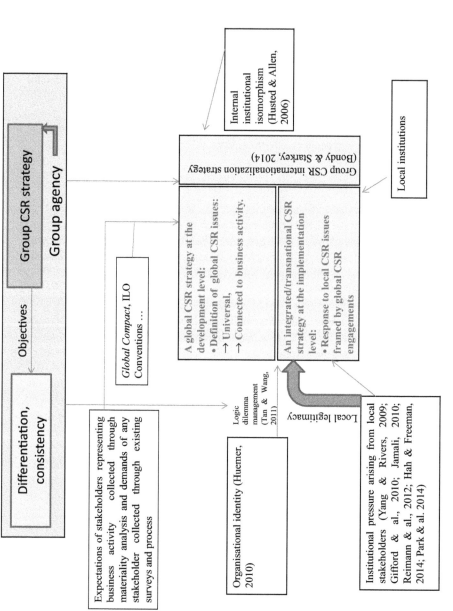

Figure 10.3 Summary of factors influencing the CSR internationalization of the Group

institution-based view of international business strategy proposed by Peng et al. (2008) and adapted to CSR.
• The results of this study also underscore the link between the CSR strategy of the Group, its internationalization and its implementation in host countries.

The objectives (legitimacy or differentiation) pursued by the subsidiaries of multinationals in the implementation of their CSR strategies can only be fully understood in view of the CSR strategy developed by their group at world level.

Arising from the Group study, a hypothesis can be formed and could be tested on a broader sample of companies in future studies: the choice of a strategic CSR focused on a small number of activities tied to firms' business and 'whose social and business benefits are large and distinctive' (Porter and Kramer, 2006: 88) would by definition tend to enable the adoption of global strategies.

Moreover, the scope of the study and especially the possibility to generalize conclusions from it are limited as it is based on a single multinational whose corporate purpose, oriented towards quality of life services, certainly favours the adoption of a CSR strategy. Therefore, other case studies concerning multinationals operating in different sectors and in different countries should be conducted.

In this regard, undertaking studies about multinationals from developing countries would facilitate the abandonment of an ethnocentric vision of the world and to correct a western, especially Anglo-Saxon, cultural bias that, according to some authors, characterizes CSR developed and implemented by multinationals, in particular Anglo-Saxon ones (Bondy and Starkey, 2014: 18) and in general, western ones.

Another limitation of the study is related to the vastness of the topic which does not facilitate a comprehensive accounting of the CSR strategy of the Group. The objective of the study was to point out the salient features of this strategy.

Finally, while Lindgreen et al. (2009: 252) suggested that practitioners should be guided on different CSR implementation issues such as design, management, communication or performance measures, this study offers avenues of reflection to practitioners wishing to initiate a CSR strategy or renew their existing one at world level.

Note

1 All reports associated with the Group social responsibility will be referred to in the rest of the chapter under the acronym SDR (Sustainable Development Report), regardless of the initial name (e.g. sustainable development, CSR or corporate citizenship).

Bibliography

Arthaud-Day, M. L. (2005). Transnational corporate social responsibility: A tri-dimensional approach to international CSR research. *Business Ethics Quaterly*, 15(1), 1–22.
Assemblée Nationale (AN) (2015). *Rapport n° 2530 sur la proposition de loi visant à lutter contre le gaspillage alimentaire (n° 2492)*, www.assemblee-nationale.fr/14/rapports/r2530.asp, accessed 8 May 2015.

Barin Cruz, L., and Boehe, D. M. (2010). How do leading retail MNCs leverage CSR globally? Insights from Brazil. *Journal of Business Ethics*, 91(2), 243–263.

Bartlett, C., and Ghoshal, S. (1989). *Managing Across Borders: The Transnational Solution*. Boston: Harvard Business School Press.

Blindheim, B-T. (2015). Institutional models of corporate social responsibility: A proposed refinement of the explicit-implicit framework. *Business & Society*, 54(1), 52–88.

Bondy, K., Moon, J., and Matten, D. (2012). An institution of Corporate Social Responsibility (CSR) in Multi-National Corporations (MNCs): Form and implications. *Journal of Business Ethics*, 111, 281–299.

Bondy, K., and Starkey, K. (2014). The dilemmas of internationalization: Corporate Social Responsibility in the multinational corporation. *British Journal of Management*, 25, 4–22.

Campbell, J. T., Eden, L., and Miller, S. R. (2012). Multinationals and corporate social responsibility in host countries: Does distance matter. *Journal of International Business Studies*, 43(1), 84–106.

Carroll, A. B. (1979). A three-dimensional conceptual model of corporate social performance. *Academy of Management Review*, 4, 497–505.

DiMaggio, P. J., and Powell, W. W. (1983). The Iron cage revisited: Institutional isomorphism and collective rationality in organizational fields. *American Sociological Review*, 48(2), 147–160.

Egri, C. P., and Ralston, D. A. (2008). Corporate Social Responsibility: A review of international management research from 1998 to 2007. *Journal of International Management*, 14, 319–339.

Gifford, B., Kestler, A., and Anand, S. (2010). Building local legitimacy into corporate social responsibility: Gold mining firms in developing nations. *Journal of World Business*, 45, 304–311.

Hah, K., and Freeman, S. (2014). Multinational enterprise subsidiaries and their CSR: A conceptual framework of the management of CSR in smaller emerging countries. *Journal of Business Ethics*, 122, 125–136.

Huemer, L. (2010). Corporate social responsibility and multinational corporation identity: Norwegian strategies in the Chilean aquaculture industry. *Journal of Business Ethics*, 91, 265–277.

Husted, B. W., and Allen, D. B. (2006). Corporate Social Responsibility in the multinational enterprise: Strategic and institutional approaches. *Journal of International Business Studies*, 37(6), 838–849.

Husted, B. W., and Allen, D. B. (2009). Corporate Social Responsibility and value creation: A study of multinational enterprises in Mexico. *Management International Review*, 49(6), 781–799.

Jamali, D. (2007). The case for strategic Corporate Social Responsibility in developing countries. *Business and Society Review*, 112(1), 1–27.

Jamali, D. (2010). The CSR of MNC subsidiaries in developing countries: Global, local, substantive or diluted? *Journal of Business Ethics*, 93, 181–200.

Kolk, A., Hong, P., and Van Dolen, W. (2010). Corporate social responsibility in China: An analysis of domestic and foreign retailers' sustainability dimensions. *Business Strategy and the Environment*, 19, 289–303.

Kostova, T., Roth, K., and Dacin, M. T. (2008). Institutional theory in the study of multinational corporations: A critique and new directions. *Academy of Management Review*, 33(4), 994–1006.

Kostova, T., and Zaheer, S. (1999). Organizational legitimacy under conditions of complexity: The case of the multinational enterprise. *Academy of Management Review*, 24(1), 64–81.

Lindgreen, A., Swaen, V., and Maon, F. (2009). Introduction: Corporate social responsibility implementation. *Journal of Business Ethics*, 85(Suppl. 2), 251–256.

Mahmood, M., and Humphrey, J. (2013). Stakeholder expectation of corporate social responsibility practices: A study on local and multinational corporations in Kazakhstan. *Corporate Social Responsibility and Environmental Management*, 20, 168–181.

Maon, F., Lindgreen, A., and Swaen, V. (2009). Designing and implementing corporate social responsibility: An integrative framework grounded in theory and practice. *Journal of Business Ethics*, 87, 71–89.

Matten, D., and Moon, J. (2008). Implicit and explicit CSR: A conceptual framework for a comparative understanding of corporate social responsibility. *Academy of Management Review*, 33(2), 404–424.

Miles, M. B., and Huberman, A. M. (2003). *Analyse des données qualitatives*. Bruxelles, De Boeck Supérieur, 2ème édition, 5ème tirage, 2013.

Ministère de l'Agriculture, de l'Agroalimentaire et de la Forêt (2013). *Pacte national de lutte contre le gaspillage alimentaire.*

Mohan, A. (2006). Global Corporate Social Responsibilities management in MNCs. *Journal of Business Strategies*, 23(1), 2–26.

Muller, A. (2006). Global versus local CSR strategies. *European Management Journal*, 24(2–3), 189–198.

Mzembe, A. N., and Meaton, J. (2014). Driving corporate social responsibility in the Malawian mining industry: A stakeholder perspective. *Corporate Social Responsibility and Environmental Management*, 21, 189–201.

Park, B. I., Childlow, A., and Choi, J. (2014). Corporate social responsibility: Stakeholders influence on MNEs' activities. *International Business Review*, 23, 966–980.

Peng, M. W., Wang, D. Y. L., and Jiang, Y. (2008). An institution-based view of international business strategy: A focus on emerging economies. *Journal of International Business Studies*, 39(5), 920–936.

Porter, M. E., and Kramer, M. R. (2006). Strategy and society: The link between competitive advantage and Corporate Social Responsibility. *Harvard Business Review*, 84(12), 78–92.

Prahalad, C. K., and Doz, Y. L. (1987). *The Multinational Mission: Balancing Local Demands and Global Vision*. New York: Free Press.

Reimann, F., Ehrgott, M., Kaufmann, L., and Carter, C. R. (2012). Local stakeholders and local legitimacy: MNEs' social strategies in emerging economies. *Journal of International Management*, 18, 1–17.

Rodriguez, P., Siegel, D. S., Hillman, A., and Eden, L. (2006). Three lenses on the multinational enterprise: Politics, corruption, and corporate social responsibility. *Journal of International Business Studies*, 37(6), 733–746.

Sénat (2014). *Amendement au projet de loi sur la nouvelle organisation territoriale de la République*, www.senat.fr/amendements/2014-2015/175/Amdt_744.html, accessed 8 May 2015.

Suchman, M. C. (1995). Managing legitimacy: Strategic and institutional approaches. *Academy of Management Review*, 20(3), 571–610.

Tan, J., and Wang, L. (2011). MNC strategic responses to ethical pressure: An institutional logic perspective. *Journal of Business Ethics*, 98(3), 373–390.

van Marrewijk, M. (2003). Concepts and definitions of CSR and corporate sustainability: Between agency and communion. *Journal of Business Ethics*, 44, 95–105.

Yang, X., and Rivers, C. (2009). Antecedents of CSR practices in MNCs' subsidiaries: A stakeholder and institutional perspective. *Journal of Business Ethics*, 86(Suppl. 2), 155–169.

Yin, R. K. (2014). *Case study research: Design and methods*. Thousand Oaks: SAGE Publications, 5th edition.

Yip, G. (1992). *Total Global Strategy: Managing for Worldwide Competitive Advantage*. Englewood Cliffs: Prentice Hall.

Zhao, M., Tan, J., and Park, S. H. (2014). From voids to sophistication: Institutional environment and MNC CSR Crisis in emerging markets. *Journal of Business Ethics*, 122, 655–674.

Part 3

Services and consumption

11 The PER and PBR in China

Where do we stand?

Sophie Nivoix and Yugang Guo

The impressive development of equity markets in China since the beginning of the century has attracted many investors, who supported the industrial and financial development of the country. Following the encouragement of the Chinese authorities to invest in stocks, the stock market experienced a record high in June 2015. Before that excessive outbreak, the government has decided to ban margin trading (which allows small shareholders to invest by borrowing money to their brokerage), which has resulted in a fall of the Shanghai Stock Exchange by 30% during the next three weeks. Despite the liquidity support from the Chinese central bank to the China Securities Finance Corp, a public company that finances margin trading, international investors were not reassured after this shock. It is interesting to investigate whether the Chinese markets show the same characteristics as the other major stock markets in terms of profitability, and if abnormalities can be detected. This is a major challenge for both shareholders, as they aim to optimize their risk-return equilibrium, and companies, as they frequently look for financing, whether they are listed or not. That is why we decided to analyze the situation of the Chinese market by relying on two essential international indicators, namely the PER (price-earnings ratio) and PBR (price-to-book ratio). If their contribution, in terms of forecasting the returns of equity as well as in detection of market abnormalities, is well established for Western markets, their most recent use in the Chinese market needs further investigation. As a consequence, our approach is based on the viewpoint of investors and securities portfolio managers, i.e. we try to determine how these indicators can help to take advantage of market inefficiencies to generate abnormal returns.

Our study aims to show to what extend the PER and PBR are leading indicators in the markets of Shanghai and Shenzhen with a view to optimizing the profitability of stock investments. Thus, it is important to determine if these two indicators can help to optimize the stock picking, for an investment horizon of one year or more.

The remainder of this chapter is organized as follows. The first section presents the theoretical context of the research. The second section details the data and methodology used. The third section is dedicated to the results and discussion, before we conclude.

DOI: 10.4324/9781315102566-14

Literature review

The presence of the PER and PBR effects

Both PER (defined as Price/Earnings per share) and PBR (defined as Price/Book value of equity) have been widely analyzed on Western stock exchanges in the recent decades. The main contribution of these ratios is that in many markets they are significantly associated with future stock returns, and thus allow investors to take advantage of market inefficiencies, considering the semi-strong efficiency market hypothesis.

Initial work has focused on the US market, considering the PER with the studies of Basu (1977) and Schwert (2003), and the PBR with those of Jaffe et al. (1989) and Kothari or Shanken (1997), among others. The PBR and PER effects mean that the stocks with low ratios exhibit higher returns. Such observations are inconsistent with the efficient market theory, seeing that markets are supposed to integrate all public information while pricing stocks. Indeed, in principle the use of an indicator based on stock market information (prices) and accounting (equity value or net earnings) should not afford to implement an investment strategy that exceeds the market return. Analyses made in Asia show the existence of a PER effect in Japan on fairly old data (Chan et al., 1991, or Bae and Kim, 1998) and on more recent ones (Nivoix, 2007). In the French market some works has been done on this point long ago, including Girerd-Potin (1992) and Hamon and Jacquillat (1992).

In a perspective of market efficiency, as part of a model such as the Capital Asset Pricing Model (CAPM), abnormal profitability can only be explained by a higher risk taking by the company or the investor. If not, the profitability exists only during a short time and shareholders do not have the time to take advantage of it. On the contrary, if we consider that markets are imperfect, price disequilibrium may last longer before the market moves back to equilibrium. In this case, an adjustment process occurs because there is a momentum effect or a mean reverting effect.

According to Fama and French (1992), PER or PBR effects could be explained by the structural inability of a single factor model such as the CAPM to explain equity returns. That is why they built the well-known three-factor model incorporating the PER, the PBR and the size of the company (Fama and French, 1993, 1995, 1996). The last two factors are supposed to explain characteristics that are weakly correlated with the PER and not directly removable via a diversified equity portfolio. Although the PER and the PBR cannot be totally uncorrelated, it is interesting to check the relevance of each of these return leading indicators, on recent stock markets like those of China. The latest work of Fama and French (2015, 2016) are moving towards a five-factor model, including return on equity and firm investment, in the same theoretical and empirical perspective as their previous works. In another variation of this multifactor and linear approach of returns, Stambaugh and Yuan (2015) selected a model with four factors: market, firm size, and two indicators of valuation bias (differences between profitability of undervalued and overvalued firms of two stock groups, built according to several kind of accounting or financial factors).

As emphasized by Berdot et al. (2007), the methodology of Fama and French has some potential weaknesses. Indeed, there may be some biases in the sample selection, the hazard can have some influence, there may exist a data mining effect (Black (1993), MacKinley (1995)), a survivorship bias (Davis et al. (2000), Bernard (2003), Chou et al. (2004)), or a confusion between specific factors and systematic factors (Cochrane (2001)). As our study is almost comprehensive, it is unaffected by the drawbacks related to with sample selection, to the impact of hazard or to the data collection. The high number of listed companies strongly reduces the survivorship bias, but the distinction between systematic and specific parameters remains potentially tricky, as in any study of that kind.

Our study therefore focuses only on two sources of abnormal returns of stocks, knowing that Hou et al. (2015) reported no less than 73 anomalies, divided into six categories: (1) momentum effect; (2) discrimination between growth and value stocks; (3) investment effect; (4) profitability effect; (5) intangible items influence; and (6) transaction frictions.

The meaning of the PER and PBR effects considering the market disequilibrium

Considering that the abnormal returns associated with PER and PBR effects are not associated with a different risk level of the market, they may be related to difficulty in assessing the assets of the firms that are analyzed. This is the case of companies whose business forecasts are difficult to do, because they belong to an emerging sector, to a new market, or simply because they are fairly small or too recent. As a consequence, the growth potential of high PER or high PBR stocks could be overvalued, while the market would be less confident in those with low ratios. We can see here the idea of a higher specific risk among stocks with high PER or PBR; this risk is then diversifiable in a portfolio of various securities, and should therefore not be associated with a higher return for shareholders.

These reasons may have a larger impact in a newly industrialized country like China than in mature economies. Thus, this is another important reason to analyze the possible existence of PER or PBR effects on this stock market.

Considering the accounting viewpoint, Lev and Sougiannis (1988) indicated that the PBR effect could be explained by the importance of intangible assets in the balance sheet of firms. According to Davis (2001) growing share of intangibles such as patents, trademarks and Research & Development in the balance sheet of some companies makes them difficult to evaluate on an accounting basis, which contributes to increase their PBR ratio (Cazavan-Jeny, 2004). In this situation, the profitability expectations related to intangible assets are not only difficult to assess but they are sometimes overvalued due to the rapid growth of an industry. The performances observed in the market then may be disappointing for overvalued securities. For Chinese companies, this setting is potentially lower than for companies in mature markets, as we will discuss in the next section.

Another explanation for the effect PER or PBR is the under or overshooting of markets to some financial information (Daniel and Titman (1997), Wouter and Plantinga (2004)), which is linked with the notion of inefficiency. Assuming an overreaction in the market, firms with high PER or PBR present rather low basic indicators (such as revenues, earnings or book value). In this situation good news tend to be interpreted too positively by the market and bad news are perceived in a too pessimistic way (de Bondt and Thaler (1985, 1987), Lakonishok et al. (1994), Barberis et al. (1988)). In order to limit their expectation errors, investors tend to rely on past trends (momentum effect or conservatism bias) regarding earnings growth (Lakonishok et al., 1994), both for high potential companies and for those who experience hard times. As a consequence, firms with good past returns are overvalued and those with bad past returns are undervalued. Thus, any information that does not confirm the past trend (which obviously cannot continue forever) leads to a price correction: downward for high PER or PBR firms, upward for those with low ratios. In this context of market overreaction, the PER or PBR effects come from a mechanical and inevitable correction over a more or less long timespan. This explanation is often associated with a negative autocorrelation of stock returns during a period of mean reverting prices back to an equilibrium. When this mean reversion occurs over a short period it is particularly difficult to detect.

The behavior of investors on the markets can also be biased by overconfidence in the way they analyze information. According to Daniel et al. (1988), investors underestimate their potential forecast errors and gradually correct their expectations while new information are issued. Meanwhile, the way back to the 'fundamental' equilibrium value of a stock can be challenged at any time by new expectations about the future of the firm business. Such a pattern may be somewhat similar to the extrapolation effect or momentum effect, or appear as opposite to the mean reverting effect of returns. In both cases, profitable investment strategies are achievable and measurable over a period of several months, as we will test in the empirical part of this study.

Alongside this overconfidence there can be a self-attribution bias. According to the attribution theory of Bem (1967), individuals tend to attribute to themselves, at least partly, the cause of the events that confirm the validity of their opinions or actions, and to reject what invalidate them. A possible cognitive dissonance between opinions and facts can be eliminated by a convergence between attitude and acts. Thus, an investor who holds shares of a company can justify this ownership afterwards by his confidence in the future development of this firm, even if at first his strategy was mainly a short term trading. This bias then causes the investor to ignore or underweight public or private information that may invalidate his choices, and overweight those that strengthen his decisions. Overconfidence in high PER or high PBR stocks can incent to keep the same strategy, even if it is questioned by low returns. This may explain the persistence of PER or PBR effect, or momentum effect, despite disappointing returns.

Last but not least, the PER or PBR effects may be related to slow adjustment of prices following the arrival of accounting information. For example, if the price of a stock drops more slowly than earnings per share during the disclosure of the annual accounts, the PER effect will tend to persist. But the disappointment about results will eventually have an effect on the share prices, which will fall. Similarly, in case of unexpected high earnings per share the adjustment may not be immediate, because of a momentum effect or a self-attribution bias. The same reasoning applies to the disclosure of book value of equity and the PBR effect.

More recently, on the US market Penman and Reggiani (2013) reported on the 1963–2006 period that the PER and PBR effects were higher when mixed. Very recently, Anderson and Zastawniak (2016) also confirmed the existence of a PER effect on the US market since 1983.

The first studies in China

Since the end of the last century several insightful studies have been made on the situation of the Chinese stock market. The oldest is, to our knowledge, that of Lu Yufeng (1999) who built portfolios according the PER and PBR values of stocks, and calculated their returns on a one-year horizon. He pointed out that low PER or PBR portfolios have higher than average returns, indicating a potential under- or overreaction to the publicly available financial information. However, as this research has been one of the very first, it was based on a limited number of listed companies, and is not very representative of the current situation of Chinese markets.

Another pioneering study was that of Lu Jing and Liu Gang (2002), over the 1999–2001 period, and it showed that the PBR is a better indicator of the expected profitability of the Chinese market than the PER. Shu Yi (2003) also compared the PBR and PER effects in China, and also noticed that the PBR is a better leading indicator of expected profitability. Over the period 2000–2002, Huang Yan (2005) found a PER effect on the Chinese market.

Using a small sample of 30 firms over the period 1994–2005 Wang Weijun (2006) found an over-performance of low PBR portfolio, which confirms the existence of a PBR effect. As for Li Jing and Liao Hong (2007), they did not identify any PER effect while analyzing the returns of the 20 highest PER stocks and the 20 lowest PER stocks during 2001–2005 period. As for Chen et al. (2007), during the 1998–2001 period they found a size effect and a PBR effect. Considering the predictability of returns, Chen et al. (2010) conclude that the Chinese market is less efficient than the US market due to a higher homogeneity of the characteristics of firms, a lower informative power of financial indicators, and a larger noise in price changes. Finally, over the period 1994–2011 Çakicin et al. (2011) point out both size and PBR effect, but few PER effect, according to quintiles of value of the tested indicators.

Data and methodology

Brief presentation of the Chinese stock markets

Considering the almost parallel history of the development of markets in Shanghai and Shenzhen, and their rather strong relationship since they (re)-opened at the end of the last century (Wu Mingli, 2001), we analyzed these two stock markets. As the Hong Kong market has had another evolution and hosts a different class of shares, we have not included it in this study for consistency.

The various shares issued in China are classified into 4 categories according to their place of issuance and possible buyers.

The A shares are issued by local companies on the local market, in Shanghai or Shenzhen. These securities are valued in local currency, i.e. in Renminbi (CNY), and may be held by local or foreign investors.

The B shares are also issued by local companies on the local market, in Shanghai or Shenzhen, but unlike A shares they are listed and traded in foreign currencies, US dollars in Shanghai and Hong Kong dollars in Shenzhen. Originally these titles were reserved for foreign investors, but they are available since 19 February 2001 to the Chinese investors who hold foreign currencies.

The H shares are issued in the Hong Kong market by Chinese companies listed in Hong Kong dollar and accessible to all investors (including those from Chinese mainland since November 2014). Since then there is indeed a connection between the Shanghai and Hong Kong markets ('HK SH-connect'), which also allows international investors to buy A shares directly through the Hong Kong market. This opening has allowed an increase in companies' equity, while their debt was multiplied by six since 2005. At the end of 2016 the long-awaited trading link between Shenzhen stocks and Hong Kong's market was ready. This so-called 'Connect' will enable international investors to trade stocks listed in Hong Kong market, which includes many tech and start-up firms.

Finally, the N shares are listed on the New York stock exchange or the NASDAQ and are accessible to all investors.

Our research focuses on A shares, i.e. shares issued by Chinese companies in the Shanghai and Shenzhen markets, which are far more numerous than B shares.

The Shanghai and Shenzhen markets have (re)-opened officially respectively in November (re-opening for Shanghai) and December 1990 (opening for Shenzhen). In 2016, there were 2808 companies listed on these two markets: 1,071 in Shanghai and 1,729 in Shenzhen, with a market capitalization close to US$ 7,000 billion (more than CNY 45,000 billion), among which nearly 4,000 for Shanghai and 3,000 for Shenzhen (see Figure 11.1). Another major indicator of the growing importance of equity markets in the Chinese economy is the ratio of market capitalization to GDP: it increased from 4% in 1992 to nearly 50% in 2015, but with wide variations. This ratio reached 48% in 2000 and 123% in 2007, but its value was only 18% in 2005. Globally, the capitalization of these two markets is the second in the world since 2013, behind the US market but ahead of Japan. It should be mentioned that according to this criterion Hong Kong is in the top six, just after France, with close to US$ 3.2 trillion.

Shanghai and Shenzhen stock markets

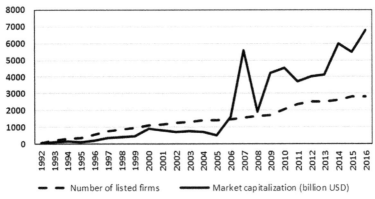

Figure 11.1 Evolution of Shanghai and Shenzhen stock markets
Source: National Bureau of Statistics of China (2015).

Accounting relevance

Considering the financial accounts, it is important to check whether the calculation of the net income is the same in China and in other countries, to be sure that the definition and meaning of the PER is relevant for international comparisons.

China introduced the accounting rules related to fair value with the IFRS (International Financial Reporting Standards) in 2006. In this context, the listed companies have to choose between fair value and historical value, and apply one of these methods to evaluate their fixed assets. According to Ding (2012) 43% of listed companies in China have assets linked to real estate investments, and most of them have opted for the historical cost while only 3% chose the fair value method. This generally implies an undervaluation of the fixed assets of Chinese firms, especially with the surge in prices in the housing market. Therefore there is a potential mechanical over-valuation of PER and PBR ratios compared to their levels in other industrialized countries.

Regarding the goodwills in the intangible assets, they are on average much lower than in the balance sheets of Western firms, mainly because of less seniority in Chinese companies, which did not have time to accumulate much acquisitions over the past decades. This Chinese specificity is therefore bound to fade gradually in the future. In general, we can say that the Chinese accounting standards since 2006 are very similar to IFRS.[1] As our study starts in 2007, there are no comparability problem with studies on Western financial markets.

As for the determination of the net income, Zhou and Habib (2013) studied the reform of China's regulation on asset impairment on earnings determination. Chinese Accounting Standard 8 (CAS 8) prohibits the reversal of long-lived asset impairments, in order to limit any opportunistic behaviour of managers possibly incented to make some window dressing. With a sample of Chinese listed companies during the 2001–2008 period, Zhou and Habib concluded that firms used few current asset write-downs but more frequently reversal short term asset impairments after adoption of CAS 8.

Data description

Our sample comes from the XunHan Technology database, which originally included all the listed companies in Shanghai and Shenzhen. Over the 2007–2016 period the potential sample of companies increased from 1430 in 2007 to 2808 in 2016. The final sample size was however lower each year for two reasons. First, for consistency of data, we have selected only the firms that end their fiscal year in December (which is the case of over 90% of the companies), in order to measure their returns after the disclosure of their annual results, usually three months after their fiscal year end. Second, we have removed the firms for which the PER or PBR was negative, because it was not significant for that year (only 5% of the observations were removed.) Our sample therefore covers the vast majority of the listed Chinese firms (Table 11.1).

In order to make comparisons, we adopted the traditional approach of incorporation of equally weighted portfolios, according to the PER and PBR of the firms. In order to have a wide variety of securities in each portfolio we have built quintiles, which avoids a large rebalancing of portfolios each year in late March. Stock returns were computed annually, without transaction costs or tax effects.

Our benchmark index was the SHSZ300 (Shanghai Shenzhen 300), based on 300 shares listed on both markets and weighted by the market capitalization. It is large and relevant enough to represent precisely the indexes of the two markets.

Regarding the characteristics of the PER over the 10 years (Table 11.2), we can see a particularly high average due to some extreme values, which create a huge standard deviation. The median, which is more relevant here, also shows high levels (always higher than 30) compared to what is usually found in Western markets.

Table 11.1 Number of listed firms in both Chinese markets

	Shanghai	Shenzhen	Total	Sample analyzed
2007	850	657	1507	1134
2008	854	727	1581	1285
2009	860	818	1678	1300
2010	884	1157	2041	1407
2011	921	1399*	2320	1866
2012	944	1528*	2472	2122
2013	944	1524*	2468	2138
2014	986	1606*	2592	2218
2015	1073	1735*	2808	2337

* including the Growth Enterprise Board of Shenzhen market, or Chinext, which gathers firms that do not meet the main market requirements (like the NASDAQ in the United States).
Source: XunHan Technology database

Considering the PBR, the statistics show that the average values consistently represent twice or even three times what is observed on Western stock exchanges. The average standard deviations are also very high due to some extreme values, and the median (more representative) is usually greater than four times (Table 11.3).

For both PER and PBR we can notice that the increasing number of observations, in relation to the number of listed companies, does not cause any change to the overall level values. Moreover, they are not sensitive to China's economic and financial conditions or global market capitalization, like the stock market falls in 2008 because of the subprime crisis or the slowdown of the Chinese growth (less than 10% in 2011).

Results

Analysis of the PER effect

In order to check if there is a PER effect in China, we initially calculated the average PER of our portfolios, from the lowest PER quintile (PER 1) to the highest one (PER 5). As shown in Table 11.4, the highest PER portfolios exhibit very much higher values than others, as well as significant standard deviations, because of the extreme values.

As we anticipated with the accounting elements above mentioned, our results show that PER values are on average higher than those of Western countries, including the low PER quintile.

Secondly, we calculated the returns of each portfolio on a fiscal year basis when all the annual results were disclosed to the market, i.e. three months after the fiscal year end (Figure 11.2). Portfolios were then rebalanced as much as required for the next year.

The differences in returns between portfolios vary from one year to another, but cumulated returns over 10 years show clear results. Unexpectedly, the low PER portfolio does not exhibit higher returns. The high PER portfolio shows very uneven results from one year to another, which indicates neither a PER effect (this portfolio would then have the lowest return) nor a complete lack of influence of PER among portfolios. The intermediate PER portfolios do not always exhibit intermediate returns, as evidenced by the high returns of portfolio 4 at the end of the studied period. Meanwhile, there is a persisting result in the long run: our five portfolios show substantially higher returns than the index.

The low returns of SHSZ300 index relative to our portfolios could be explained by a size effect, to the extent that the firms in our sample include the vast majority of listed companies while the index contains only 300 company, most of them very large. Without performing an extensive analysis of company sizes, we see immediately that the proportion of mid-cap firms of Shanghai and Shenzhen markets is significantly higher than this proportion in the SHSZ300 index (Figure 11.3). Such a result has been found in many markets: the mid-size firms show higher stock return than large groups.

Table 11.2 Descriptive statistics of the PER of our sample

PER	2007	2008	2009	2010	2011	2012	2013	2014	2015	2016
Mean	121.2	125.3	92.1	121.9	116	65	80.4	156.2	180.6	170.4
Standard deviation	226.1	703.4	338.7	288.26	696.4	259	302	3097.2	874.6	966.8
Median	56.5	45.4	37.4	58.7	49.6	30	33.6	40.6	68.9	64.8
Minimum	12.72	10.53	6.15	9.35	6.78	5.16	4.65	1.7	2.55	5.28
Maximum	3188	17152	7434	4909	26866	7299	10067	145540	36094	44152
Number of observations	1137	1165	1300	1405	1863	2122	2138	2218	2337	2402

Table 11.3 Descriptive statistics of the PBR of our sample

PBR	2007	2008	2009	2010	2011	2012	2013	2014	2015	2016
Mean	5.19	5.43	3.95	6.89	5.93	3.31	3.94	5.89	14.92	9.95
Standard deviation	7.42	4.43	3.68	10.3	6.6	3.66	16.7	49.1	212.7	65.1
Median	4.05	4.29	3.18	5.07	4.48	2.58	2.41	2.76	4.89	4.43
Minimum	1.07	1.06	0.84	1.12	0.91	0.58	0.57	0.48	0.96	0.63
Maximum	235	71.7	63,3	344	215	123	538	2199	9763	2049
Number of observations	1291	1382	1438	1622	1959	2215	2368	2462	2604	2774

Table 11.4 Mean and standard deviations of PER (PER 1 is the 20% lowest PER and PER 5 is the 20% highest)

Shanghai and Shenzhen	2007	2008	2009	2010	2011	2012	2013	2014	2015	2016
PER 1	25.2	21.5	16.7	24.6	20.1	13.3	14	12.8	24.3	20
PER 2	40.7	34.1	27.7	41.2	36.6	22.4	23.8	25.9	46	40.9
PER 3	57.4	45.7	38.1	58.6	49.9	30	33.6	41.1	69.7	66.1
PER 4	93.6	68.3	59.4	86.1	68.5	41.9	51	68.8	121.9	112
PER 5	388	456	321.4	400	406	217.8	279.2	632	640	646
PER 1 Std deviation	5.4	4.65	4.2	5.6	5.4	3.2	3.7	4.2	7.8	6.9
PER 2 Std deviation	4.5	3.13	2.8	4.7	4.1	2.2	2.5	3.6	6	6
PER 3 Std deviation	5.8	3.8	3.83	6	3.8	2.2	3.3	5.3	8.6	9
PER 4 Std deviation	18.4	10.8	9.53	11.7	8	5.8	8	12.2	25.7	22.3
PER 5 Std deviation	403	1530	716	564	1527	553.9	637	6908	1885	2234

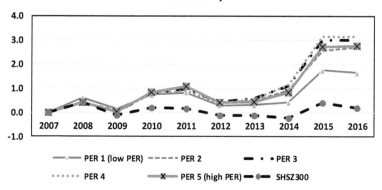

Figure 11.2 Cumulated returns of PER portfolios (Shanghai and Shenzhen)

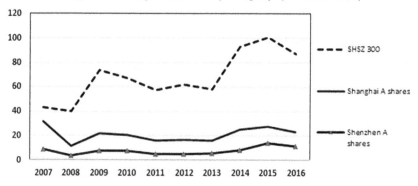

Figure 11.3 Compared average market capitalizations

These results confirm those of Li and Liao (2007) and those of Cakici et al. (2011), but not the conclusions of Lu (1999) and Huang (2005). We can then assume that the composition of the Chinese stock market, related to both the number of listed companies and the kind of investors, led to an attenuation of the PER effect that seemed to exist in the first decade of the (re)-opening of Chinese stock markets. This could indicate a higher efficiency level over the years, evolving from a very low efficiency to a semi-strong efficiency.

Let's see now if these first results are confirmed by the PBR analysis.

Analysis of the PBR effect

To detect a possible PBR effect in the Chinese market, we calculated the average PBR of our portfolios, from the lowest PBR quintile (PBR 1) to the highest one (PBR 5). As illustrated in Table 11.5, the high PBR portfolios exhibit values far higher than the others. It is the same for their standard deviations, which are moderate portfolio for 1 to 4, but very large for high PBR due to extreme values.

Cumulated annual returns, calculated as previously for PER portfolios, show low returns for the high PBR portfolio. As for low PBR portfolios 1 and 2, they exhibit the best returns. This not only indicates a marked PBR effect, but also a strong effect size. Again, the index contains on average larger companies than those of the whole market and shows a significantly lower profitability over the entire period (Figure 11.4).

Our results about PBR confirm those of Lu (1999), Lu and Liu (2002), Shu (2003), Huang (2005), Chen et al. (2007) and Çakicin et al. (2011). This indicates that the PBR ratio is useful and better than the PER to forecast returns on the Chinese market. As a consequence, we cannot say that the efficiency level of the Chinese stock market has increased during the last decade, but that investors can implement some profitable investment strategies to outperform the market. Indeed, investing in low PBR stocks enables to create abnormal positive returns.

Now let us examine if the values of PER and PBR are associated with specific characteristics of the firms.

Table 11.5 Mean and standard deviations of PBR (PBR 1 is the 20% lowest PBR and PBR 5 is the 20% highest)

Shanghai and Shenzhen	2007	2008	2009	2010	2011	2012	2013	2014	2015	2016
PBR 1	2.16	2.3	1.71	2.58	2.26	1.4	1.28	1.23	2.22	1.75
PBR 2	3.11	3.31	2.52	3.92	3.48	2.02	1.87	2	3.58	3.03
PBR 3	4.02	4.31	3.19	5.08	4.49	2.59	2.42	2.78	4.97	4.47
PBR 4	5.3	5.67	4.17	6.89	6.14	3.46	3.32	4.04	7.25	6.6
PBR 5	11.1	11.5	8.17	16.2	13.3	7.06	10.7	19.5	57.1	32
PBR 1 Std deviation	0.36	0.42	0.31	0.48	0.5	0.26	0.23	0.3	0.49	0.45
PBR 2 Std deviation	0.25	0.27	0.19	0.33	0.28	0.15	0.15	0.2	0.36	0.34
PBR 3 Std deviation	0.28	0.31	0.21	0.36	0.34	0.18	0.19	0.27	0.48	0.47
PBR 4 Std deviation	0.51	0.6	0.38	0.74	0.72	0.34	0.36	0.47	0.89	0.8
PBR 5 Std deviation	14.7	6.63	6.52	20.6	11.9	6.8	36.4	109	476	143

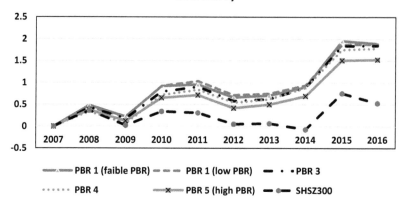

Figure 11.4 Cumulated returns of PBR portfolios (Shanghai and Shenzhen)

Sorting according to both PER and PBR

In order to check the relationship between PER and PBR, not according to their correlation in the whole the sample but with an investment logic in a stock portfolio, we analyzed the returns of the portfolios of 25% lowest or highest PER and PBR.

If there is no relationship between these two criteria, the probability of belonging to two quartiles in particular (e.g. the 25% lowest PER and 25% lowest PBR) is statistically 0.25^2, which means 0.0625. Our results indicate (Table 11.6) that the proportion is almost double (11.2% of all firms) when we consider both a low PER and a low PBR, and also higher (8.7% of all firms) when we consider both a high PER and a high PBR. We can conclude that there is an association between these two criteria, as evidenced by the low number of shares with divergent indicators (39 and 74 on average per year for the entire sample). This association is clearly related to the stock price, which is a common parameter of these ratios, while a lack of association can be explained by the return on equity (ROE) value. Indeed, we have by definition:

ROE = Net earnings/Equity
But we can also write: ROE = (Price/Equity)/(Price/Net earnings)
which means: ROE = PBR/PER.

Table 11.6 shows that firms with high PBR and low PER actually have a huge ROE on average (42.59%), whereas those with a low PBR and high PER exhibit

Table 11.6 Cross-sectional analysis of PER and PBR ratio over the 2007–2015 period

Average number of firms	25% lowest PER	25% highest PER
25% highest PBR	39	159
25% lowest PBR	205	74
Average proportion of firms		
25% highest PBR	0.024	0.087
25% lowest PBR	0.112	0.045
Average ROE		
25% highest PBR	42.59%	8.37%
25% lowest PBR	13.00%	1.70%

a low ROE on average (1. 70%). The other cases are associated with more usual values of ROE. The question is whether the firms with these specific characteristics in terms of PER and PBR belong to particular industries, and if in a portfolio investment logic some stocks have to be selected according to the risk and return strategy that is implemented.

The analysis of the most frequent industries according to the PER end PBR levels is interesting (Table 11.7). Indeed, the sectors including the most promising firms considering growth (high-tech and media) are more frequently in the high PER and high PBR category. The moderate level of ROE of these companies (8.37%) suggests some disappointments considering their expectations of large stock price increases.

In contrast, the sectors with low PER and low PBR are related to bank, utilities and transportation. Markets generally expect few growth of the companies in such industries, as these firms are seen as value stocks in mostly mature sectors.

Regarding activities in high PBR but low PER, the market value of these stocks is high compared to their book value whereas the expectations of earnings growth if low. These companies can have a good ROE, and there main sectors are electrical and mechanical equipment.

Finally, considering the activities with low PBR and high PER, the market value of these stocks is low compared to their fairly high book value, but the expectation of earnings growth is high. These companies appear to be able to reach only a low ROE, and they are mostly located in the coal, mining, chemical and steel industries.

Table 11.7 Industries according to PER and PBR levels

Major industries	Low PER	High PER
High PBR	Electric equipment, Mechanic equipment	High-tech, Medias
Low PBR	Bank, Utilities, Transportation	Steel, Coal, Chemical industry, Mining

Conclusion

Our analysis of equity markets in Shanghai and Shenzhen gave useful results compared to earlier studies in a fast growing country. We have shown that there is no PER effect over the period analyzed (2007–2016), which is in line with the latest studies. It is possible that the composition of the Chinese stock markets, considering both the number of listed companies and the nature of its investors, led to an attenuation of the PER effect that seemed to exist in the first decade after the (re)-opening of these stocks markets. Meanwhile, there is a significant PBR effect because high PBR portfolios exhibit the lowest stock returns. The PBR ratio seems to be far more relevant than the PER as part of an investment strategy in the Chinese market.

Theoretically, the absence of PER effect indicates a higher level of efficiency of Chinese markets over the years, evolving from no or a weak efficiency to a semi-strong efficiency. At the same time, the existence of a PBR effect signals that it is worth building a multifactor model that could lead to abnormal positive returns. In a similar viewpoint of a potential multifactor model, we detected a significant size effect that could be more detailed in future studies.

Note

1 www.china-briefing.com/news/2013/02/05/china-gaap-vs-u-s-gaap-and-ifrs.html;   and in Chinese at www.casplus.com/home.asp

References

Anderson, K., and Zastawniak, T. (2016). Glamour, value and anchoring on the changing P/E. *The European Journal of Finance*, 22–1, 1–32.
Bae, K. H., and Kim, J. B. (1998). The usefulness of earnings versus book value for predicting stock returns and cross corporate ownership in Japan. *Japan and the World Economy*, 10, 467–485.
Barberis, N., Shleifer, A., and Vishny, R. (1998). A model of investor sentiment. *Journal of Financial Economics*, 49, 307–343.
Basu, S. (1977). Investment performance of common stocks in relation to their price-earnings ratios: A test of the efficient market hypothesis. *Journal of Finance*, 32–3, June, 663–682.
Bem, D. (1967). Self-perception: An alternative interpretation of cognitive dissonance phenomena. *Psychological Review*, 74, 183–200.
Berdot, J-P., Leonard, J., and Nivoix, S. (2007). Le book-to-market: quelles capacités prédictives? *La revue du Financier*, (158), 19–35.
Bernard, P. (2003). *Notes sur le modèle de Fama-French*. Working Paper, EURISCO, Université Paris IX.
Black, F. (1993). Beta and return. *Journal of Portfolio Management*, 20, 8–18.
Cakici, N., Chan, K., and Topyan, K. (2011). *Cross-sectional stock return predictability in China*. SSRN Research Paper, N° 2038497.
Cazavan-Jeny, A. (2004). Le ratio Market-to-Book et la reconnaissance des immatériels – Une étude du marché français. *Comptabilité, Contrôle, Audit*, 20(2).

Chan, L. K. C., Hamao, Y., and Lakonishok, J. (1991). Fondamentals and stock returns in Japan. *Journal of Finance*, 46–5, 1739–1764.

Chen, J., Kan, K. L., and Anderson, H. (2007). Size, book/market ratio and risk factor returns: Evidence from China A-share market. *Managerial Finance*, 33–8, 574–594.

Chen, X., Kim, K. A., Yao, T., and Yu, T. (2010). On the predictability of Chinese stock returns. *Pacific-Basin Finance Journal*, 8–4, 403–425.

Chou, P-H., Chou, R. K., and Wang, J. S. (2004). On the cross-section of expected stock returns: Fama-French ten years later. *Finance Letters*, 2(1), 18–22.

Cochrane, J. H. (2001). *Asset Pricing*. Princeton: Princeton University Press.

Daniel, K., Hirshleifer, D., and Subrahmanyam, A. (1998). Investor psychology and security market under- and overReactions. *Journal of Finance*, 53–6, 1839–1886.

Daniel, K., and Titman, S. (1997). Evidence on the characteristics of cross sectional variation in stock returns. *Journal of Finance*, LII(1), March, 1–33.

Davis, J. L. (2001). Is there still value in the book-to-market ratio? *Dimensional Fund Advisors*, January.

Davis, J. L., Fama, E. F., and French, K. R. (2000). Characteristics, covariances, and average returns: 1929 to 1997. *Journal of Finance*, 55(1), February, 389–406.

de Bondt, W., and Thaler, R. (1985). Does the stock market overreact? *Journal of Finance*, 40.

de Bondt, W., and Thaler, R. (1987). Further evidence on investor overreaction and stock market seasonality. *Journal of Finance*, 42, 557–581.

Ding Lu, 丁露. (2012). 投资性房地产公允价值计量对我国上市公司的影响 [J]. *湖南行政学院学报*, 3.

Fama, E. F., and French, K. R. (1992). The cross-section of expected returns. *Journal of Finance*, 47–3, 427–465.

Fama, E. F., and French, K. R. (1993). Common risk factors in the returns on stocks and bonds. *Journal of Financial Economics*, 33, 3–56.

Fama, E. F., and French, K. R. (1995). Size and book to market factors in earnings and returns. *Journal of Finance*, 50(1), 131–155.

Fama, E. F., and French, K. R. (1996). Multifactor explanations of asset pricing anomalies. *Journal of Finance*, 51(1), 55–84.

Fama, E. F., and French, K. R. (2015). A five-factor asset pricing model. *Journal of Financial Economics*, 116–1, 1–22.

Fama, E. F., and French, K. R. (2016). Dissecting anomalies with a five-factor model. *Review of Financial Studies*, 29–1, 69–103.

Girerd-Potin, I. (1992). La dominance en France des portefeuilles d'actions à faible capitalisation boursière ou à bas PER. *Finance*, 13–1, 23–51.

Hamon, J., and Jacquillat, B. (1992). *Le marché français des actions, études empiriques 1977–1991*. PUF.

Hou, K., Xue, C., and Zhang, L. (2015). Digesting anomalies: An investment approach. *Review of Financial Studies*, 28, 650–705.

Huang Yan, 黄艳. (2005). *PER指标在中国股票市场应用的实证研究[D]*, 华中科技大学.

Jaffe, J., Keim, D. B., and Westerfield, R. (1989). Earnings yields, market values, and stock returns. *Journal of Finance*, 44, March, 135–148.

Kothari, S. P., and Shanken, J. S. (1997). Book to market, dividend yield, and expected market returns: A time-series analysis. *Journal of Financial Economics*, 44, 169–203.

Lakonishok, J., Shleifer, A., and Vishny, R. W. (1994). Contrarian investment, extrapolation, and risk. *Journal of Finance*, 49–5, 1541–1578.

Lev, B., and Sougiannis, T. (1998). Penetrating the book-to-market black box: The R&D effect. *Journal of Business Finance & Accounting*, 26(3 & 4), 419–449.

Li Jing, and Liao Hong, 李敬,廖洪. (2007). 市盈率投资策略:评价与检验[J]. *经济管理*, (6).

Lu Jing, and Liu Gang, 陆静和廖刚. (2002). PER、PBR和自由现金流乘数与证券组合收益率的比较"[J], *经济管理（新管理）*, 14, 57–62.

Lu Yufeng, 陆宇峰. (1999). 净资产倍率和PER的投资决策有用性:[博士学位论文].上海:上海财经大学.

Mackinley, A. C. (1995). Multifactor models do not explain deviations from the CAPM. *Journal of Financial Economics*, 38, 3–28.

Nivoix, S. (2007). Does the PER effect exist in the Japanese market? in: Andreosso-O'Callaghan, B., Bassino, J-P., Dzever, S., and Jaussaud, J. (eds.), *The Economic Relations Between Asia and Europe: Organization, Control, Trade and Investment*. Oxford: Chandos Publishing Ltd., 65–80.

Penman, Z., and Reggiani, F. (2013). Return to buying earnings and book value: Accounting for growth and risk. *Review of Accounting Studies*, 18, 1021–1049.

Schwert, G. W. (2003). Anomalies and market efficiency, in: Constantinides, G. M. (ed.), *Handbook of the Economics of Finance*.Amsterdam: Elsevier Science B.V., 937–972.

Shu Yi, 易姝. (2003). 小议市盈率与市净率指标 [J]. *市场周刊（财经论坛）*, (04)

Stambaugh, R. F., and Yuan, Yu (2015). *Mispricing factors*. NBER working paper 21533.

Wang Weijun, 王伟俊. (2006). 证券投资的相对估价法研究 [D]. 上海社会科学院.

Wouters, T., and Plantinga A. (2004). *Dynamic behaviour of value and growth stocks*. Working Paper, SOM Research Report, 0413 August, Groningen, Theme E, Financial Markets and Institutions.

Wu Mingli, 吴明礼. (2001). 我国股市的市盈率结构分布和分析[J]. *数量经济与技术经济研究*, 5.

Zhou, D., and Habib, A. (2013). Accounting standards and earnings management: Evidence from China. *Accounting Perspectives*, 12, 213–236.

12 Emerging opportunities, challenges and constraints in the Chinese food industry

M. Bruna Zolin and Matilde Cassin

Introduction

Given the phenomenon of growing urbanization, the pressure on food demand for an increasing population as well as changing diet, China has had to resort to imports, becoming a net importer of food. In the absence of external flows, this scenario is set to continue and could result in a future Malthusian scenario.

Starting from these premises, the Chapter, based on three core areas (production, consumption and trade), aims to analyze the current situation, identifying opportunities, challenges and constraints that could prevent the development of the Chinese food industry. Firstly, the study provides an analysis of the context in which Chinese food companies evolve, analyzing supply (with a focus on the main food and beverages companies), consumption, and trade trends. Then, an identification of the main policies involving the food sector is outlined. Moreover, the Chapter focuses on the obstacles that could affect the sustainable development of the Chinese food industry, such as increased urbanization, climate change threats and conflicts for limited natural resources (particularly land and water). A summary of the findings of this study and some recommendations for the Chinese food industry conclude the Chapter.

The sources used are mainly sources referred to at an international level: the World Bank and WTO in order to define socio-economic profiles and trends; the FAOSTAT datasources to describe the agricultural context and production as well as some environmental issues.[1] At the national level, data have been extracted from the Chinese National Bureau of Statistics and from the China Statistical Yearbook (2014).

The context

The role of China in the global economy has been increasing and becoming more and more important in recent years, thanks to a gradual transition to a market-based economy and consequent rapid economic development and strong social changes.

However, as shown in Figure 12.1, after years of constant economic growth, recently China seems to be facing a new phase, characterized by deceleration (Lee

DOI: 10.4324/9781315102566-15

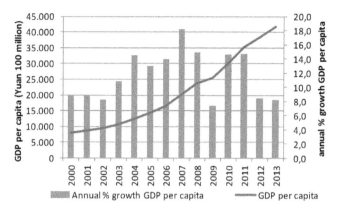

Figure 12.1 China's GDP per capita and GDP annual growth per capita

Source: Authors' elaboration on China Statistical Yearbook data, 2014

et al., 2016): GDP in 2012 and 2013 have grown at the lowest rate since 2000. Moreover, 2015 was the year of the Chinese stock market crash. China seems to have entered a new era, as it seeks to transition from an investment-and export-led economy to consumption-led growth. Despite the inevitable bumps and back-tracking along this path, this transformation is expected to result in economic growth that could be more sustainable in the long term (USDA, 2015).

Besides the growth of GDP per capita (which has quintupled in value between 2000 and 2013, with an annual growth rate that reaches 10% on average, Figure 12.1), important socio-demographic changes have occurred. The Chinese population, while continuing to grow (going from 500 million in 1959 to 1.37 billion in 2014, equal to 19.48% of the world's population), has slowed its growth rate since the 1970s (from an average of six children to 1.4 children per woman in 2013 and the birth rate from an average of 44 births per 1,000 inhabitants to 12 births) due to the one-child policy (一 胎 制, yītāizhì) (Figure 12.2).[2] The progressive aging of the population is one of the dark side effects of the one-child policy, as well as the imbalance of the country's overall gender ratio towards males (roughly between 3% and 4% more males than females). A third consequence of the policy were instances where the births of subsequent children after the first went unreported or were hidden from authorities. Those children, most of whom were undocumented, faced difficulties in obtaining education and employment.

In 2015, the Chinese news agency Xinhua (www.xinhuanet.com) announced the intention of the government to abolish the one-child policy and Chinese families could have two children without incurring the payment of penalties.

Furthermore, there has been a progressive population shift from rural to urban areas (Figure 12.3); in particular, the population living in urban areas, which has steadily continued to increase, exceeds those living in rural areas (in marked decline from the mid-1990s).

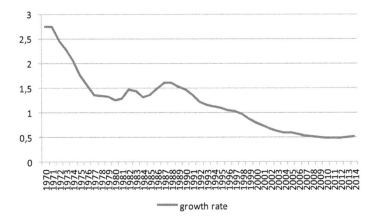

Figure 12.2 China's population growth rate (1979–2014)

Source: Authors' elaboration on World Bank data, 2014

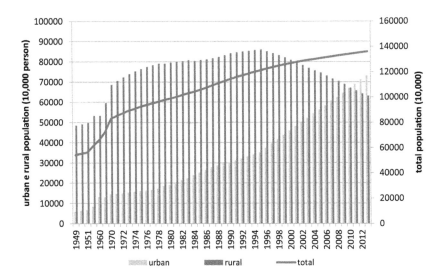

Figure 12.3 China's population trend (1949–2013): total population (right) and urban/
rural population (left)

Source: Authors' elaboration on China Statistical Yearbook data, 2014

In 2014 the Chinese authorities adopted the National New-type Urbanization Plan (2014–2020) aimed at moving 250 million rural residents to newly built cities by 2020 to set off a new wave of growth, the effects of which could weigh on generations to come. The ultimate goal of the government's modernization plan is to have 70% of the Chinese population in cities by 2025 and, as a consequence,

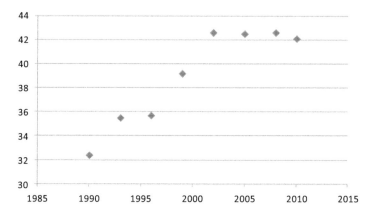

Figure 12.4 China's inequality trend: GINI index

Source: Authors' elaboration on World Bank – Poverty and Equity databank, 2014

land disputes with farmers who do not wish to relocate could exponentially increase (Li, 2014).

Urbanization is only one of the challenges that Chinese rapid economic ascendancy has brought abought, along with the exploitation of natural resources and consequent environmental issues, social inequality and external imbalances.

Despite fast economic growth, China still remains a developing country, with a per capita income that is still a fraction of those in advanced countries and with a high and increasingly unequal income distribution among the population. Although the number of poor is steadily declining – but still high (Figure 12.5) – social disparities are rising, as shown by the GINI index trend (Figure 12.4) and by the distribution of income among the population: in 2010, the wealthiest had 47% of the total income compared to 40.7% in 1990.[3]

Food supply

China is the world's fourth largest country by total land area behind Russia, Canada and the USA with a land area equal to 9.4 million km², but has just 10% of the world's agricultural land and 7% of the world's fresh water (ANZ, 2013). Severe pollution issues exacerbate this scarcity, particularly in North China.

According to the literature (Lam et al., 2013), only about 40% of the available Chinese arable land can be considered most suitable for crop production, with much of the remaining area subject to environmental stresses such as drought and high salinity content.

Chinese arable land data vary according to differing sources. FAOSTAT statistics highlight a lower land area compared to that reported by the Chinese government, (equal to 121.7 million hectares in late 2012), and under the so-called 'red

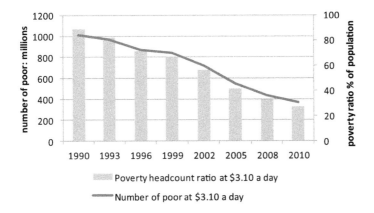

Figure 12.5 People living on less than $3.10 a day in China

Source: Authors' elaboration on World Bank – Poverty and Equity databank, 2014

line'[4] (耕地 红线, *gēngdìhóngxiàn*) of 120 million hectares (OECD, FAO, 2013), required for food self-sufficiency.

The size (1990–2010) of available arable land in China (Figure 12.6) is steadily decreasing, while the overall agricultural area is stable. In 2010 arable land represented 10% of the total land area and is less than 0.1 ha per capita (less than 40% of the world average). This negative trend can be largely traced to a variety of climatic, environmental and human factors which caused land use conflicts and soil degradation (Asia has the highest proportion of soil degradation of the global regions, (FAO, 2015)), land diversion for bio-fuel production and unequal land distribution (Zhao, 1986).

As a reaction to the decreasing farmland, the Government approved in 1994 the 'Basic Farmland Protection Regulations' which prohibited basic farmland conversion to non-agricultural activities and mandated counties and townships to designate basic farmland protection districts in accordance with provincial farmland protection plans[5] (Ding, 2003). According to the several times modified and integrated Land Administration Law (LAL), land acquisition can be carried out only when the purpose of the acquisition is to serve public interests, even if commercial projects accounted for 22% of all acquisitions in 2000–2001 (Ding, 2007).

The Chinese Constitution states that land is collectively owned by farmers but contracted by individual households (Xiwen, 2006). As a consequence, the Chinese agricultural sector is characterized by extreme fragmentation. According to the agricultural census in China, in 2007 there were almost 200 million farms (FAO, 2013), representing 35% of all the farms in the world, most of them (93%) less than 1 ha, 5% between 1 and 2 ha, 2% between 5 and 10 ha and only 0.4% of the farms were larger than 10 ha. Farming in China has always been very labor intensive.

Despite the shortage of usable natural resources, agriculture has played a very important role in China's economic growth since the ends of the 1970s. In the

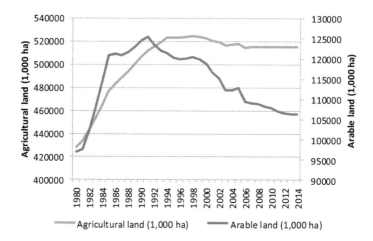

Figure 12.6 Agricultural land*and arable land** in China, trend

  * Agricultural land refers to the share of the land area that is arable, under permanent crops, and under permanent pastures. Land under permanent crops is land cultivated with crops that occupy the land for long periods and need not be replanted after each harvest, such as cocoa, coffee, and rubber. This category includes land under flowering shrubs, fruit trees, nut trees, and vines, but excludes land under trees grown for wood or timber. Permanent pasture is land used for five or more years for forage, including natural and cultivated crops.

** Arable land includes land defined by the FAO as land under temporary crops (double-cropped areas are counted once), temporary meadows for mowing or for pasture, land under market or kitchen gardens, and land which is temporarily fallow. Land abandoned because of shifting cultivation is excluded.

Source: Authors' elaboration on FAOSTAT data, 2015

first reform period (1978–1984) agricultural GDP grew very quickly and also its yields: agricultural labor productivity grew by 5–10% per year (Park, 2009), so China became one of the world's largest food producers. Despite the decline in surface area, total cereal production is steadily growing – in particular corn production is recording the highest growth (Figure 12.7) – and China is still self-sufficient in a number of basic strategic crops and food sources, providing food security and ensuring social stability.

However, over time, the percentages of the agricultural work force and GDP of the total decreased (Liu et al., 2012): from 70% of employment and 30% of GDP in 1980 to little more than 30% of employment and less than 10% of total GDP in 2014. Pollution (of water and soil) has contributed to this trend. Also, China has been (and is) facing criticism about the quality and safety of its domestic and export food products.

During the past decade, the food industry in China has rapidly developed and expanded. In 2013, China is the world's largest consumer market for food and beverage products (Figure 12.8) surpassing the United States since 2011 and the second-fastest growing Asian F&B market with an average annual growth rate of

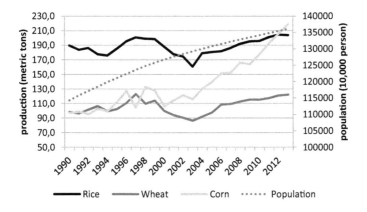

Figure 12.7 Main cereals production in China (10,000 tons)
Source: Authors' elaboration on FAOSTAT data

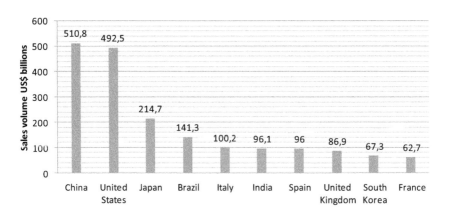

Figure 12.8 Foodservice Markets Worldwide in 2013 (sales volume, US$ Billions)
Source: Authors' elaboration on Euromonitor International, 2014

30% between 2009 and 2014. Modern retail formats are profiting from this development (Euromonitor, 2014).

A substantial proportion of processed food is produced and consumed in coastal areas. This is due to strong urbanization and higher total consumer purchasing power in these regions. In inland areas, due to lower urbanization and income, high-value processed foods are consumed mainly in big cities. A rule of thumb is that the majority of food is produced in the North (above Shanghai) and consumed in the South.

The food industry structure is dualistic: a large number of small businesses are matched by large companies with predominantly Chinese capital and whose

market is dominated by domestic demand. The top 10 food and beverage companies are listed in the Appendix.

Expanding food service expenditure is the result of greater disposable income
and of new and modern ways of life. According to Euromonitor (2014), the Chinese food service sector is the largest worldwide with 7.3 million outlets and sales
valued at US$ 510 billion in 2013. In the food services sector two international
companies are at the top of the list (Figure 12.9): McDonald's and Yum! The first
is the largest chain of hamburger fast food restaurants in the world, founded in the
United States in 1940. The American company is adopting a new business model
in Asian countries using larger franchising models. Yum! Brands, Inc. (previously
Tricon Global Restaurants, Inc.) is a US fast food company. It includes very well
known brands such as KFC, Pizza Hut and in May 2011, Yum! agreed to purchase
the mainland Chinese hot-pot chain, Little Sheep. This company, even though its
sales on the international market are about half those of McDonald's, holds first
place in the Chinese market with a turnover more than twice that of McDonald's.

In relation to food retailing, there are a number of different types of marketing
strategies used in China (Table 12.1).[6] Euromonitor (2014) and official statistics
show supermarkets/hypermarkets are now dominating the retail landscape, with a
market share of around 50%.

Even if modern forms of retailing are growing, Chinese agricultural produce is
predominantly purchased directly from farmers (Ren, 2008), often just after harvest
and on the roadside, by hundreds of thousands of private traders who cruise villages

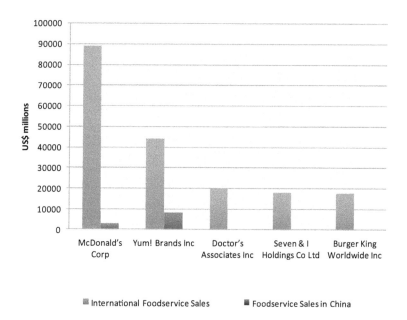

Figure 12.9 Top 5 Foodservice Companies Worldwide, US$ Millions (2013)

Source: Authors' elaboration on Euromonitor International, 2014

Table 12.1 The structure of China's food distribution network

	2003	2004	2005	2006	2007	2008	2009	2010	2011	% of growth 2003– 2011
Restaurants/fast food/eat-out stores	5000	6500	9000	11000	12000	12000	13000	14000	15000	200.0
Supermarkets/ hypermarkets	16000	16500	22000	24000	35000	33000	38000	40000	42000	162.5
Convenience stores	4500	8000	9500	13000	13500	18000	13000	14000	14000	211.1
Total	**25500**	**31000**	**40500**	**48000**	**60500**	**63000**	**64000**	**68000**	**71000**	**178.4**

Source: Authors' elaboration on data from EUSME, The Food & Beverage Market in China, 2015

Table 12.2 Ownership structure of food and beverage wholesale industry in China in 2011

	Number of enterprises	Annual sales (100 mn RMB)
Privately owned	26000	22500
Collective/JV owned	8700	13300
Foreing owned	4900	14600
State-owned enterprises	1500	4600

Source: Authors' elaboration on data from ANZ, Chinese National Bureau of Statistics

and the surrounding countryside in small trucks. State-owned enterprises no longer monopolize the wholesale (processing/marketing/distribution) part of the supply chain (Table 12.2). This has resulted in a diversified ownership structure of the industry and increased competition. Private enterprises in 2011 now constitute 63% of wholesale companies, but only 41% of annual sales. The popularity of private small-sized wholesalers in the industry is likely to constrain further development.

Consumption

In 1990 food expenditure (total consumption expenditure index=100) was 54.2% of the total per capita consumption expenditure in urban areas and 58.8% in rural areas (China Statistical Yearbook, 2014). The indices have been decreasing over time and disposable income spent on food in 2013 averaged around 35% for urban households and 38% for rural households (Figure 12.10).

As Engel's law suggests, there is a wide range of different types of consumers, depending on income levels. The wealthiest 20% of urban households (10% of all Chinese households) spend less than 22% of their disposable income on food. On the other hand, the poorest 10% of urban households (accounting for 5% of all Chinese households) spend more than 40% of their disposable income on food, and 66% in the case of their rural counterparts (ANZ, 2013).

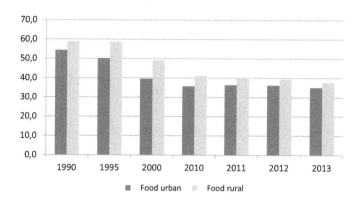

Figure 12.10 Food Consumption Expenditure per capita (index=100): Urban and rural households in China

Source: Authors' elaboration on China Statistical Yearbook, 2014

Some changes have been occurring in consumption habits: in urban areas expenditure on clothing, the second most important item after food in the 1990s (equal to 13%), has been surpassed by 'transport and communications' (15.2% in 2013) and 'education, culture and recreation' (12.7% in 2013). In rural areas, instead, housing expenditure is confirmed in 2013 as the second highest expenditure after food (15% and 19%), followed by 'transport and communications' (12% in 2013) and 'health care' (7% in 2013). People's consumption habits are mainly connected to rising disposable incomes: per capita income in urban areas went from 1,500 yuan in 1990 to 30,000 yuan in 2013 and in rural areas from 700 yuan in 1990 to 9,000 yuan in 2013 (Figures 12.13 and 12.14). It is worth noting that in 2012 the ratio between per capita income in rural areas and that in urban areas decreased, passing from about a half to one third. Analyzing data (China Statistical Yearbook, 2014) concerning consumption expenditure on goods and services,[7] a different trend in rural and urban households is detected.[8]

Differences in consumption habits can be observed when comparing urban and rural areas; rich and poor consumers; and the population of different regions. In rural areas meat consumption per head is lower and lags behind that of urban residents by about 30 years (the consumption by rural residents in 2010 was equal to that of urban residents in 1982). High income residents consumed more of all food types compared with poorer people, with two exceptions: food grains and Chinese liquor (Cao et al., 2013).

In addition to income levels, urbanization, brand exposure and consumer affluence, food safety concerns, health consciousness, demand for convenience, improved infrastructure and the development of the retail industry, which are other aspects that affect consumption patterns, changed significantly with improved standards of living. More consumers are exposed to a greater diversity of consumer products, both locally and when travelling abroad. Chinese consumers are increasingly discerning, and many now seek the following qualities when making purchases: confidence in food safety and the integrity of ingredients; high quality; excellent nutritional value; a better lifestyle through the variety of food and beverages; modern packaging; freshness and convenience.

If the rate of food expenditure tends to decrease as income rises, food expenditure in absolute terms has risen sharply: for urban households from nearly 694 in 1990 to 6,311 yuan in 2013, and for rural households from 156 in 1990 to 2,054 yuan in 2013 (Figures 12.11 and 12.12).

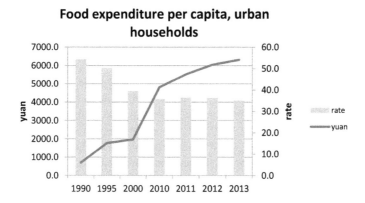

Figure 12.11 Food expenditure per capita (yuan and rate of total consumption) in urban households in China

Source: Authors' elaboration on China Statistical Yearbook, 2014

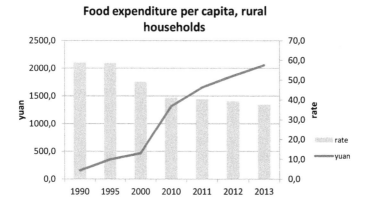

Figure 12.12 Food expenditure per capita (yuan and rate of total consumption) in rural households in China

Source: Authors' elaboration on China Statistical Yearbook, 2014

In the evolution of consumer patterns, three periods can be identified. In the first period (1990–2000), food expenses in absolute values (increasing) and as a percentage of total consumption expenditure (decreasing) move in the opposite direction, with equal magnitude and is more pronounced in urban areas. The index, which in 1990 amounted to 54.2%, decreases to 39.4% in 2000 for urban households and, in rural areas, from 59% to 49%.

The decade 2000–2010 represents a period of great growth in food expenditure. For urban households it increased from 1,971 yuan in 2000 to 4,804 yuan and for rural from 464 to 1,313 yuan with, however, decreasing index movements.[9] In the period (2010–2013), the indices show a relative stability in urban areas, while decreasing most significantly in rural households against an increase in absolute values.

2.3 Trade

The importance of agricultural trade to China's total trade, has been declining since 1980 and particularly since the early 1990s due to the decreasing trend of agriculture in China's economy (Huang et al., 2007). Since China joined the World Trade Organization in late 2001, agricultural exports to the country have grown exponentially (WTO, 2015). Until the middle of the first decade of the 2000s, the balance of Chinese food trade was positive and China was a net food exporter country (Table 12.3).

In 2008 China's food trade deficit began and it gradually widened and reached US$ 41.8 million in 2014. China imports food from 192 countries and regions.

At a global level, among the top ten importers of agri-food and seafood, China ranks second, after the United States. It can be observed (Table 12.4) that the exchange between European countries is carried out mainly between EU countries (as a consequence of a well-established feature of the Common Agricultural Policy), while trade in other countries appears more diversified.

Currently, achieving Market Economy Status (MES) at the WTO is one of China's core strategic goals. As expected, the recognition of China as a market economy is hampered by the EU (southern European countries especially) and the US, worried about having to face competition based on lower costs of production. Moreover, according to the WTO, China still applies price controls on commodities and services with a direct impact on the domestic economy and people's livelihoods. As a consequence, China has launched a legal challenge against the EU and US.

Furthermore, there are concerns in the food trade regarding trade between China and the EU, arising from the legal protection of geographical indication (GI) products (European Commission, 2013) being continuously a source of conflicts. To better protect these products, the EU signed various multilateral and bilateral agreements. Among these initiatives, it is worthwhile mentioning the '10 plus 10' project (European Commission, 2012) started in July 2007 when both the EU and China formally lodged' applications for the protection of 10 agriculture

Table 12.3 China's food trade 1980–2014 (US$ millions)

	China's food trade		
	Imports	*Exports*	*Trade balance (exports-imports)*
1980	3,206.3	3,128.9	−77.4
1985	1,755.6	4,274.7	2,519.1
1990	4,618.7	7,867.5	3,248.8
1995	9,236.4	12,299.1	3,062.7
2000	9,042.6	13,559.3	4,516.8
2001	9,366.2	14,222.1	4,855.9
2002	9,891.2	16,163.5	6,272.4
2003	14,970.5	19,241.8	4,271.3
2004	21,121.1	20,815.2	−306.0
2005	21,540.7	24,635.4	3,094.6
2006	22,917.3	27,862.6	4,945.4
2007	32,422.3	33,160.8	738.5
2008	49,521.7	35,887.5	−13,634.2
2009	45,248.4	35,318.6	−9,929.8
2010	59,556.2	44,152.5	−15,403.7
2011	75,455.2	54,167.8	−21,287.4
2012	90,650.4	56,311.9	−34,338.5
2013	98,646.3	59,977.6	−38,668.7
2014	105,263.6	63,490.9	−41,772.7

Source: Authors' elaboration on WTO data, 2014

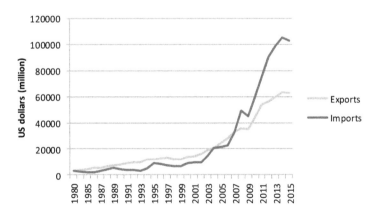

Figure 12.13 China's food imports and exports (1980–2014)

Source: Authors' elaboration on WTO data

Table 12.4 Top 10 Agri-food and seafood importers Worldwide, 2013

Country	Imports US$ billions	Top suppliers and market share		
		1	*2*	*3*
United States	127.4	Canada	Mexico	**China**
China	118.0	United States (22.6%)	Brazil (19.1%)	Australia (7.3%)
Germany	106.8	Netherlands	France	Italy
Japan	76.5	US	**China**	Canada
Netherlands	71.5	Germany	Belgium	Brazil
United Kingdom	68.8	Netherlands	France	Ireland
France	64.9	Spain	Netherlands	Belgium
Italy	54.8	Germany	France	Spain
Belgium	42.0	Netherlands	France	Germany
Russia	39.7	Brazil	Germany	Ukraine

Source: Authors' elaboration on Euromonitor International, 2014

GI products in each other's territories (Tables 12.5a and 12.5b). The European list contains five cheeses, two olive oils, one ham, 1one salmon and 1one dried fruit. In terms of countries, France and the UK have three products each, while Italy and Spain have two. In parallel, the European Commission has examined and registered 10 Chinese food names with the last two Chinese names 'Pinggu da Tao' (peach) and 'Dongshan Bai Lu Sun' (asparagus) receiving protected status in the EU as geographical indication products (European Commission, 2013).

These 10 Chinese names have been added to the more than 1,000 names of agricultural products and foodstuffs, which are already protected in the EU.

Agricultural policies in a nutshell

A historical overview of China highlights the high importance given to agriculture by Chinese policymakers since the proclamation of the People's Republic of China in 1949. In this Chapter, only some aspects of the Chinese policy will be taken into consideration.

Being self-sufficient to meet domestic demand for cereals and avoid having to resort to massive imports has always been the main concern of the government.

On 28 June 1950 Liu Shaoqi (刘少奇) implemented the **first agricultural reform** (土改, *tŭgăi*), called 'land to the tiller' (耕者有其田 *gèngzhěyŏuqítián*) addressed to all the non-farmland owning farmers (about 70% of the 500 million people in the countryside). It increased the fragmentation of agricultural land and lead to the consequent difficulty of extensive cultivation. Just three years after this land reform, the plan for collectivization of land, aimed at setting up a new production structure based on collectively owned companies, was adopted. Land ownership passed to communities, and farmers were forced to sell to the State surplus wheat production at prices and quantities set by the government (Lin, 1992).

The new Chinese countryside arrangement (in 1956, 90% of farmers were enrolled in socialist cooperatives) seemed to give new impetus to agricultural

Table 12.5a Ten renowned European products registered in the official AQSIQ* Chinese GI register

Country	Number of products registered	Designation (and type of product)
France	3	Comté (cheese); Pruneaux d'Agen/Pruneaux d'Agen mi-cuits (dried fruits); Roquefort (cheese);
United Kingdom	3	Scottish Farmed Salmon (fish); West Country Farmhouse Cheddar (cheese); White Stilton Cheese/Blue Stilton Cheese (cheese)
Itay	2	Grana Padano (cheese); Prosciutto di Parma (ham);
Spain	2	Priego de Córdoba (oil); Sierra Mágina (oil)

*General Administration of Quality Supervision, Inspection and Quarantine of the People's Republic of China
Source: Authors' elaboration on European Commission, 2013

Table 12.5b Ten renowned Chinese products protected in the EU

Type of product	Designation
Fruits	Pinggu Da Tao (peach); Guanxi Mi You (honey pomelo); Shaanxi ping guo (apple);
Vegetables	Dongshan Bai Lu Sun (Asparagus); Jinxiang Da Suan (garlic);
Fish/meat	Yancheng Long Xia (Crayfish) ;Lixian Ma Shan Yao (ham)
Other	Zhenjiang Xiang Cu (rice vinegar); Longjing cha (tea); Longkou Fen Si (noodles)

Source: Authors' elaboration on European Commission, 2013

production which recorded an annual increase of 3.5% (compared with the level of production in 1952) in cereals thanks to the adoption of the 'grain first' policy (以粮为纲, *yǐliángwèigāng)* (Zanier, 2010).

After the first five-year plan (五年计划, *wǔniánjìhuà*), the Chinese leadership began a new strategy, known as the 'Great Leap Forward' (大跃进, *dàyuèjìn*). The object was to 'produce more, more quickly and at a better price' (Bergère, 2000: 110) to allow China within 15 years to overtake the United Kingdom (赶上 英国十五年, *gǎnshàngyīngguóshíwǔnián*). However, agricultural production, in 1960, reached only 144 million tons, down 26.4% compared to 1958. This failure was due to a combination of factors: the shift in labor force from agriculture to the steel industry and to the construction of great hydraulic works, the 'Four pests campaign' that led to the extermination of sparrows and to the spread of insects and different pests, and a series of natural disasters that swept China in the late 1950s.[10] Only in 1965, was there a resumption of production to levels achieved before the Great Leap Forward (Bergère, 2000). The decline in production was compounded by the diffusion of distorted statistics which were used to decide the amount of grain to be exported in the period between 1958 and 1960, jeopardizing the self-sufficiency of the country. In 1960 the shortage turned into famine and the per capita consumption of cereals fell by 23.7%, going from 204 kg in 1957 to 156 kg in 1960 (Bergère, 2000) causing millions of deaths (Brown, 1995).

In 1978, a new era of reform began, with economic liberalization implemented by Deng Xiaoping (邓小平) after the death of the leader, Mao Zedong (毛泽东). Two major new features were introduced: the household responsibility system and township and village enterprises (OECD, FAO, 2013). Thanks to the first of these features, between 1981 and 1982, about 90% of farm families became responsible for a plot of land, which was previously publicly owned but was leased to families for longer and longer periods of time (Zanier, 2010). The second innovation, known by the acronym TVE or Township and Village Enterprises (乡镇企业, *xiāngzhènqìyè*), led to a significant increase in agricultural production, so that China returned to exporting cereals and agricultural income tripled between 1979 and 1985.

At the beginning of the 1990s China entered international markets: in 1993–1994 the country's exports increased by 60%, and the amount of foreign investments were greater than in all fourteen previous years (Zanier, 2010). The entry into the WTO in 2001 and the abolition of import duties significantly increased imports of agricultural goods (Fuller et al., 2001; Sun, 2016). As previously mentioned, in 2008 China became a net food importer (Cao et al., 2013).

In 2006, an agricultural tax that had been levied for millennia was abolished, bringing savings to farmers of over US$ 21 billion (Ni, 2013). As well as eliminating taxes, over the years the government has allocated an increasing share of its financial resources to agricultural subsidies. The following are the four main typologies of subsidies:

1   Grants for the improvement of seeds (良种补贴, *liángzhǒngbǔtiē*). These are in place since 2002 to promote the use of new and improved varieties of cultures, accelerating their use and, since 2009, they have been extended to the whole country with regards to rice, wheat, cotton and corn (Ni, 2013).
2   Direct payments to producers of cereals (粮食直补, *liángshízhíbǔ*). This policy was adopted in 2004 with the aim of reversing the drop in cereal production registered during the previous six years. The stated objective of this measure is to increase the production of cereals, promoting self-sufficiency in the country.
3   Subsidies for the purchase of agricultural machinery (购置补贴, *gòuzhìbǔtiē*). The objective is to promote the mechanization of agriculture so as to increase productivity. The stated goal is to achieve 70% mechanization of farming methods (DuPont, 2013).
4   Generic grants to inputs (农资综合补贴, *nóngzīzònghébǔtiē*). This measure was adopted starting in 2006 because of continuing fluctuations in prices of agricultural inputs including fertilizers and gasoline.

Immediately after entering the WTO, the Chinese authorities started to strengthen the policy of supporting market prices to sustain the income of farmers and encourage production. This policy, however, has triggered rising home market prices that, combined with the appreciation of the Chinese currency, have eroded the competitiveness of Chinese agricultural goods on the international market (OECD, FAO, 2013). A second effect was the increase in imports of foreign products available at lower prices and therefore more competitive with Chinese produce. Although China is expected to become the world's largest producer of rice and wheat, and occupies second place in world production of corn and buckwheat, the export of cereals (including barley, corn, millet, rice, rye, oats, sorghum, wheat and cereal blends) has gradually decreased from 19 million tons in 2002 to only 1.5 million in 2013.

Thanks to the extensive program of reforms initiated by the government during the decade 2004–2014, grain production has recorded steady growth year after year, enabling the country to achieve the so-called 'Grain Miracle' (Zhang, 2013). Production has increased by 29% from 469 million tons in 2004 to 607 million in 2014.

Recently, the National Development Plan for the period 2011–2015, the most recent plan (issued in March 2011), has policies to boost domestic consumption, improve living standards, develop the western and central regions and protect the environment.[11]

With regards to the food industry, the plan points out food safety as a main concern. With many food safety scandals in the past few years, the government has included policies to address this issue. The overall focus is on improving agricultural production and attracting foreign technology.

Main constraints

According to Aquastat (2014), China has renewable internal freshwater resources of about 2,000 cubic meters per capita, above the UN definition of water scarcity of 1,000 cubic meters per person (Figure 12.14).

China's water resources are not distributed equally: the dry northern and western desert provinces receive only 20% of the country's rainfall. In addition, due to inevitable population growth, climate change, increasing urbanization and the many activities that require water resources, per capita availability is continuously decreasing and demand for water is outstripping supply. As a result, in urban areas the share of population with access to safe drinking water is decreasing (Figure 12.15).

Agriculture and energy (mainly the coal industry) are the two largest consumers of China's freshwater reserves (Figure 12.16), accounting for nearly 90% of all the water used in China.

Agriculture and the coal industry are concentrated in China's North, where the average water per capita availability is only around 200 cubic meters. Therefore, although four-fifths of the country's water resources are located in the South of the country, two-thirds of the cultivated land is in the arid North (Hanjira et al., 2008). To solve this unequal distribution, since 2002 China has been working on a mega-project to bring water from the moisture-rich South to the arid North. Nevertheless, simply supplying more water will not solve the underlying problems.

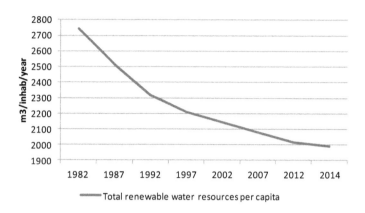

Figure 12.14 Total renewable water resources per capita

Source: Authors' elaboration on Aquastat data, 2014

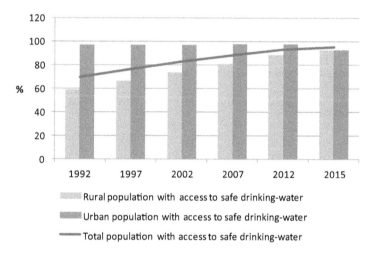

Figure 12.15 Population with access to safe drinking water

Source: Authors' elaboration on Aquastat data, 2014

In 2010, China's Communist Party Central Committee and State Council prom-ulgated a 'Three Red Lines'[12] (*santiao hongxian* 三条红线) policy intended to establish clear and binding limits on water usage, efficiency, and quality. In early 2012, the State Council announced that the 'Three Red Lines' policy would limit total national water consumption to less than 700 billion m³ per year, amount-ing to approximately three-quarters of China's total annual exploitable freshwater resources. In addition, the policy attempts to increase irrigation use efficiency.[13] The People's Republic of China's (PRC) 12th Five-Year Plan (2011–2015)

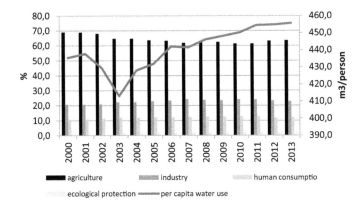

Figure 12.16 Water use

Source: Authors' elaboration on Chinese Statistical yearbook, 2014

focuses on water conservation and environmental protection as national priorities. China's leadership acknowledges in this plan that there is much to be done to limit pollution and secure adequate supplies of energy and water for growing northern and western cities. China's major cities, for example, are retrofitting their sewage treatment systems to recycle wastewater for use in washing clothes, flushing toilets, and other grey-water applications. Major industrial plants are required by the Water Law, initially enacted in 1988 and updated in 2002, to show that there is adequate water in the region to supply new factories before they are allowed to build (Circle of Blue, 2013).

Soil pollution is another crucial issue and a possible constraint on agriculture and food supply.

According to Cui and Kattumuri (2011), a study on soil pollution commissioned in 2006 by the government shows that industrial and urban effluent and waste as well as the massive use of fertilizers and pesticides have affected about one-fifth of Chinese agricultural land and have caused a loss of about 10 billion kg/year of crops. This loss becomes even more important considering that arable land is steadily decreasing.

Climate change can also play a critical role in determining the country's ability to maintain the viability of agricultural production. The frequency and intensity of adverse weather events, such as droughts in the North and Northeast and floods along the Yangtze river, have increased in the last fifty years as well as the relentless advance of desertification that affects about 666,700 hectares, of which about 200,000 hectares are arable land (Cui and Kattumuri, 2011).

Aware of these constraints, China, since the first decade of the 2000s, has progressively tried a new and alternative way to achieve a secure source of food supply by resorting to outward foreign direct investment (FDI) in agriculture (Smaller et al., 2012). Since 2001, the FDI flow in agriculture has gradually

242   M. Bruna Zolin and Matilde Cassin

increased US$ 5 billion in 2012). Since 2007 foreign investment in the primary sector has often taken the form of the so-called 'land grabbing': acquisitions (by purchase or rental) of large-scale land for farming, conducted by public actors (States) or private (companies) that usually have an average duration of 30 to 99 years (Zolin and Luzi, 2013).

In relation to China as an outward investor country, according to the Land Matrix, total Chinese land investment amounted to more than 1.206 million hectares with 65 agreements signed from 2001 to 2014 (Table 12.6).[14] More than 414,000 hectares (34% of the total) are domestic investments within national borders. Approximately 792,000 hectares are concentrated in some favorite target

Table 12.6 China's land investments (2014)

Target countries	Number of contracts signed	Investment on land in ha (contracts signed only)	Average size of investments (in ha)	Purpose of investments
Asia	**43**	**695,089**	**16,165**	
Cambodia	19	192,706	10,142	Non food agricultural commodities (11), Food crops (3), Agri unspecified (3), Wood and fibre (1), Tourism (1)
China	**8**	**414,054**	**51,757**	Food crops (7), other (1)
Laos	15	48,329	3,222	Non food agricultural commodities (12), Industry (2), Wood and fibre (1)
Philippines	1	40,000	40,000	Biofuels
Africa	**18**	**163,704**	**9,095**	
Angola	3	21,500	7,167	Food crops (3)
Benin	2	4,800	2,400	Biofuels, food crops
Cameron	1	10,120	10,120	Food crops
Congo	1	100,000	100,000	Biofuels
Nigeria	2	5,300	2,650	Food crops
Sierra Leone	4	6,820	1,705	Food crops (4)
Sudan	1	10,000	10,000	Biofuels, food crops
Uganda	2	4,540	2,270	Food crops (2)
Tanzania	2	624	312	Food crops, biofuels, wood and fibre
Europe	**1**	**2,000**	**2,000**	
Bulgaria	1	2,000	2,000	Food crops
South America	**3**	**345,400**	**115,133**	
Argentina	2	333,000	166,500	Food crops
Bolivia	1	12,400	12,400	Food crops
Total	**65**	**1,206,193**	**5,123**	–

Source: Authors' elaboration on Land Matrix data, 2015

areas: Asia occupies first place (57.6% of total), followed by Latin America (28.6% of total) and Africa (13.6% of total).

The deal gives the investor not only the right to cultivate the land, but also gives access to natural resources, water and minerals. Establishing the precise number of agreements signed is not simple. These contracts, are often negotiated with local governments for the use of land under concession for a length of time, followed by the deployment of one or more production sites. For the Chinese side, that should ensure a transfer of technical knowledge – with benefits for local people (especially in the poorest countries) – having the ability to export 'strategic' agricultural products to China at favorable prices. Although in theory local people should benefit from this Chinese presence, there have been numerous protests: Chinese companies are in fact accused of appropriating the land of poor local farmers, who, once dispossessed of their belongings, would not have the chance to be taken on as employees in the new Chinese factories that only employ Chinese labor.

The 'Chinese colonization' involves not only land, but also the acquisition of large foreign agribusiness empires: the so-called 'dragon-head' enterprises, (龙头企业, *lóngtóuqĭyè*) are in fact encouraged to expand their global presence through acquisitions of companies in key areas of the world food industry, thus challenging the hegemony of the great American groups such as Cargill and Monsanto.

Concluding remarks

China is the world's largest consumer market for food and beverages but is also a net importer of food. If the rate of food expenditure tends to decrease as income goes up, food expenditure in absolute values increases: in the period 2000–2010, it increased from 2,000 yen per capita in 2000, to almost 5,000 in 2010 for urban consumers. In the long term, China's demand for food imports will inevitably grow (Cao et al., 2013). The Chinese food industry is profiting from this development, but China is thus facing problems relating both to food security and to food safety.

As far as food security is concerned, the biggest advances in China's productivity, resulting from an (often excessive) application of fertilizer, has polluted land and groundwater with nitrates and caused toxic 'red tides' of algal blooms and the eutrophication of lakes and rivers.[15] Moreover, Chinese agricultural productivity is affected by the scarcity of natural resources (land and water) and the supply of arable land is not adequate to meet Chinese food security. To counteract land limitation, China has progressively tried a new and alternative way to find a secure supply by resorting to outward foreign direct investment (FDI) in agriculture. Asian countries are the favorite target of this new policy: the acquisitions, not only gives the investor the right to cultivate the land, but also gives access to natural resources, water and minerals. Conflict with local populations are increasing as they identify these investments as a violation of human rights.

Climate change can also play a crucial role in determining the country's ability to reach self-sufficiency.

Meanwhile, two growing food safety concerns are illegal additives to food and contamination by toxic industrial waste. China's connections to global agricultural markets are also having important effects on food supply and food safety within the country. Although the Chinese government has shown determination to reform laws, establish monitoring systems, and strengthen food safety regulation, weak links in implementation remain.

As a global problem, food safety affects public health, especially in countries with large populations, e.g. China. A 2011 survey (Zhang, 2013) reported that food safety was the most pressing issue for Chinese people, surpassing public security, traffic safety, medical safety, etc. Food contamination can occur at any step in the process from farm to table.[16] In addition, with rapid Chinese industrialization, the use of illegal additives and toxic industrial waste in food processing is a growing food safety problem.

Resourcefulness, technology, research, modernization, and sustainability are all factors, which China can and should focus on, as they will have a key role in determining the ability of China and of the world to feed their respective populations with safe food in the future.

Improved efficiency and productivity, the reform of land use rights, but also the policy of 'going out' or land investments are some of the plausible strategies that the country could improve on to avoid an inexorable stabilization or, at worst, a decline in domestic production, as well as taking into account the impact of climate change on agricultural commodities.

The Chinese food industry, on the one hand, is driven by the changing consumption habits of the Chinese population and favored by the market economy, which provides a huge platform for future development; while, on the other hand, it needs technological innovation and research, development investments and the enforcement of safety measures.

Appendix

Table 12.A Per capita income and expenditure of urban households

	1990	1995	2000	2010	2011	2012	2013
Per Capita Annual Income* (yuan)	1,516.2	4,288.1	6,295.9	21,033.4	23,979.2	26,959.0	29,547.1
Per Capita Annual Consumption** (yuan)	1,278.9	3,537.6	4,998.0	13471.5	15,160.9	16,674.3	18,022.6
Of which:							
Food	693.8	1,772.0	1,971.3	4,804.7	5,506.3	6,040.9	6,311.9
Clothing	170.9	479.2	500.5	1,444.3	1,674.7	1,823.4	1,902.0
Residence	60.9	283.8	565.3	1,332.1	1,405.0	1,484.3	1,745.1
Household Facilities and Articles	108.5	263.4	374.5	908.0	1,023.2	1,116.1	1,215.1
Transport and Communications	40.5	183.2	427.0	1,983.7	2,149.7	2,455.5	2,736.9
Education, Culture and Recreation	112.3	331.0	669.6	1,627.6	1,851.7	2,033.5	2,294.0
Health Care and Medical Services	25.7	110.1	318.1	871.8	969.0	1,063.7	1,118.3
Others	66.6	114.9	171.8	499.2	581.3	657.1	699.4
Consumption Expenditure index=100							
Food	54.2	50.1	39.4	35.7	36.3	36.2	35.0
Clothing	13.4	13.5	10.0	10.7	11.0	10.9	10.6
Residence	4.8	8.0	11.3	9.9	9.3	8.9	9.7
Household Facilities and Articles	8.5	7.4	7.5	6.7	6.7	6.7	6.7
Transport and Communications	3.2	5.2	8.5	14.7	14.2	14.7	15.2
Education, Culture and Recreation	8.8	9.4	13.4	12.1	12.2	12.2	12.7
Health Care and Medical Services	2.0	3.1	6.4	6.5	6.4	6.4	6.2
Others	5.2	3.2	3.4	3.7	3.8	3.9	3.9

* Per capita income measures the average income earned per person in a given area (city, region, country, etc.) in a specified year. It is calculated by dividing the area's total income by its total population

** Per capita consumption expenditure is the market value of all goods and services, including durable products (such as cars, washing machines, and home computers), purchased by households. It is calculated by dividing the area's total expenditure by its population

Source: Authors' elaboration on China Statistical Yearbook, 2014

Table 12.B Per capita income and expenditure of rural households

	1990	1995	2000	2010	2011	2012	2013
Per Capita Annual Income* (yuan)	**686.3**	**1,577.7**	**2,253.4**	**5,919.0**	**6,977.3**	**7,916.6**	**8,895.9**
Per Capita Annual Consumption** (yuan)	**374.7**	**859.4**	**1,284.7**	**3,859.3**	**4,733.4**	**5,414.5**	**6,112.9**
Of which:							
Food	155.9	353.2	464.3	1,313.2	1,651.3	1,863.1	2,054.5
Clothing	44.0	88.7	95.2	263.4	341.1	396.1	437.7
Residence	81.2	147.9	231.1	801.4	930.2	1,054.2	1,169.3
Household Facilities and Articles	30.7	68.1	74.4	233.5	308.6	341.4	384.5
Transport and Communications	8.4	33.7	93.1	461.1	547.0	652.8	795.8
Education, Culture and Recreation	31.3	102.4	186.7	366.7	396.4	445.5	485.6
Health Care	19.0	42.5	87.6	326.0	436.8	513.8	613.9
Others	4.3	23.1	52.5	94.0	122.0	147.5	171.6
Cash Consumption Expenditure index=100)							
Food	58.8	58.6	49.1	41.1	40.4	39.3	37.7
Clothing	7.8	6.9	5.7	6.0	6.5	6.7	6.6
Residence	17.3	13.9	15.5	19.1	18.4	18.4	18.6
Household Facilities and Articles	5.3	5.2	4.5	5.3	5.9	5.8	5.8
Transport and Communications	1.4	2.6	5.6	10.5	10.5	11.0	12.0
Education, Culture and Recreation	5.4	7.8	11.2	8.4	7.6	7.5	7.3
Health Care	3.3	3.2	5.2	7.4	8.4	8.7	9.3
Others	0.7	1.8	3.1	2.1	2.3	2.5	2.6

Source: Authors' elaboration on China Statistical Yearbook, 2014

Table 12.C Top 10 Chinese food and beverage companies

Company	Field of activities
No. 1. COFCO Group	Products and services in the agricultural sector and food industry in China
No. 2. Inner Mongolia Yili Industrial Group Co Ltd	Dairy company (processing and manufacturing of milk products, including ice cream, milk powder, milk tea powder, sterilized milk and fresh milk under 'Yili' brand)
No. 3. Shuanghui Group	Meat processing company (including pig raising, consumer meat products, flavoring products, and logistics)
No. 4. China Mengniu Dairy Co Ltd	Manufacturing and distribution company of dairy products and ice cream
No. 5. Bright Food (Group) Corp Ltd	Food and beverages company
No. 6. Hangzhou Wahaha Group Co Ltd	Non-alcoholic beverage producer
No. 7. Wuliangye Yibin Co Ltd	Alcoholic beverage company
No. 8. Tsingtao Breweries Co Ltd	Beer producer
No. 9. Kweichow Moutai Co Ltd	Producer of Maotai liquor, together with the production and sale of other beverages, food and packaging material
No. 10. Yurun Group Ltd	Meat supplier

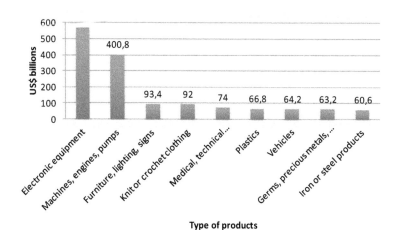

Figure 12.A Top 10 export products in 2014

Source: Authors' elaboration on data from www.worldstopexports.com/chinas-top-10-exports/1952

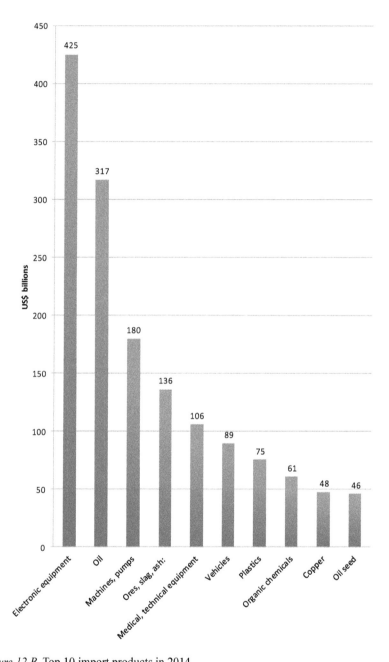

Figure 12.B Top 10 import products in 2014

Source: Authors' elaboration on data from www.worldstopexports.com/chinas-top-10-imports/4017

Notes

1 Some difficulties occurred when analyzing data regarding Chinese arable land size, because of discrepancies between data from different sources: the final decision was to use FAOSTAT data which provide a time series on this topic, even if they provide a lower figure than that reported by the Chinese government.

2 China began promoting the use of birth control and family planning with the establishment of the People's Republic in 1949, first on a voluntary basis and then, from 1980, mandatorily. Since 2013, there has been a gradual relaxation of China's family planning laws that already allowed minority ethnic families and rural couples whose firstborn was a girl to have more than one child. In 2015 China announced the intention to scrap its one-child policy, allowing all couples to have two children for the first time since draconian family planning rules were introduced more than three decades ago.

3 The GINI index measures the extent to which the distribution of income (or, in some cases, consumption expenditure) among individuals or households within an economy deviates from a perfectly equal distribution. A Lorenz curve plots the cumulative percentages of total income received against the cumulative number of recipients, starting with the poorest individual or household. The GINI index measures the area between the Lorenz curve and a hypothetical line of absolute equality, expressed as a percentage of the maximum area under the line. Thus a GINI index of 0 represents perfect equality, while an index of 100 implies perfect inequality.

4 During the National Video Conference on Permanent Basic Farmland Designation and Protected Agriculture Land Management, jointly organized by the Ministry of Agriculture and the Ministry of Land and Resources and held on 5 January 2015, the premier, Li Keqiang stressed that China must maintain its farmland above the minimum threshold of 120 million hectares, a 'red line' which must be observed. Furthermore, China must attach equal importance to the quantity and quality of farmland to ensure its food security and specific policies must be introduced for these purposes.

5 There are two protection levels: the first consists of high-quality farmland that cannot be converted to non-agricultural use in the long term; the second level consists of good-quality farmland that cannot be converted to non -agricultural use in the planned periods (usually five or 10 years) (Ding, 2003).

6 Hypermarkets: the major hypermarkets are Carrefour, Wal-Mart, Metro, Lotus, Auchan, and Tesco; Supermarkets: the major supermarkets are Lianhua, Wellcome, ParknShop, China Resources Vanguard and Suguo; Specialty Supermarket Stores and Boutique Stores: the major specialty supermarkets are City Shop Supermarket (Shanghai), City-Super, CRV Ole, BHG (Beijing Hualian Supermarket), Hisense Plaza in Qingdao, and Jin Bou Da in Zhengzhou); Convenience Stores: (such as 7-Eleven, Family Mart (Japan), ItoYokado (Japan), Sincere (Hong Kong), C-Store (Taiwan), and Lawson's (Sino-Japan JV); Online Sales: (one company, Taobao reportedly has a 75% market share at the moment); there are also traditional markets.

7 Per capita consumption expenditure is the market value of all goods and services, including durable products (such as cars, washing machines, and home computers), purchased by households. It is calculated by dividing the area's total expenditure by its population

8 In the first case the share of consumption on total income has been increasing over the years (54.6% in 1990, 68.7% in 2013); in the second the consumption share has been decreasing (from 84.3% in 1990 to 61% in 2013).

9 Less conspicuous than over the previous period (from 49.1% to 41.1% in rural areas and from 39.4% to 35.7% in urban areas).

10 The four pests to be eliminated were: rats, sparrows, flies, mosquitos.

11 The plan identifies seven strategic industries which are expected to benefit from special incentives and funding:

- Energy conservation and environmental protection
- Next generation telecommunications technology

- Biotechnology
- High-end equipment manufacturing
- New energy
- New materials
- Clean energy vehicles

12 It promotes 'the strictest system of water resource management', setting targets for total water use, water use efficiency, and ambient water quality for a number of benchmark years to 2030.
13 These headline policies are augmented by increased investment, including RMB 1.8 trillion in 2011–2015, primarily for irrigation infrastructure improvements, rural clean water delivery, and reservoir enhancements (More, 2013).
14 Source that collects data about the agreements involving agricultural land.
15 China was one of the earliest countries to use pesticides (Zhang, 2013) and though on the one hand, throughout China pesticides have killed crop pests, on the other hand, they have also poisoned farmers and consumers.
16 In China, the major harmful factors include toxic animals and plants (e.g. puffer fish and toadstools), pathogenic microorganisms (e.g. Salmonella and Vibrio Parahaemolyticus), and chemical contamination (e.g. pesticide and veterinary drug residues). For example, of 174 food safety incidents reported in 2012 in China, most were caused by toxic animals or plants (41.4%), followed by pathogenic microorganisms (32.8%), and chemical contamination (12.1%).

References

ANZ Agribusiness (2013). *Feeding the dragon: The modernization of China's food industry*, www.anzbusiness.com/content/dam/anz-superregional/AgricultureInsightsChina Food.pdf.
Bergère, M. C. (2000). *La Chine de 1949 à nos jours*. Paris: Armand Colin, III edition.
Brown, L. R. (1995). *Who Will Feed China? A Wake Up Call for a Small Planet*, The Worldwatch Environmental Alert Series. New York: Norton & Co.
Cao, L., Tian, W., Wang, J., Malcolm, B., Liu, H., and Zhou, Z. (2013). Recent food consumption trends in China and trade implications to 2020. *Australasian Agribusiness Review*, 21, 15–44. www.agri-food.info/review/2013/Cao_et_al.pdf.
China National Bureau of Statistics (2014). *China statistical yearbook*, www.stats.gov.cn/tjsj/ndsj/2014/indexeh.htm.
Circle of Blue (2013). *Scoping water and energy pollution Nexus in Urumqi and Qingdao for preparing PRC's Ministry of Environmental Protection Co-Control Program*, www.circleofblue.org/waternews/wp-content/uploads/2013/09/Water-Energy-Nexus-FinalReport_5.pdf.
Cui, S., and Kattumuri, R. (2011). *Cultivated land conversion in China and the potential for food security and sustainability*. Working Paper 35, Asia Research Centre, London School of Economics & Political, www.lse.ac.uk/asiaResearchCentre/_files/ARCWP35-CuiKattumuri.pdf, accessed 2 November 2014.
Ding, C. (2003). Land policy reform in China: Assessment and prospects. *Land Use Policy*, 20(2), 109–120.
Ding, C. (2007). Policy and praxis of land acquisition in China. *Land Use Policy*, 24(1), 1–13.
DuPont (2013). *China's insatiable appetite for change*. Fortune Global Forum, 6–8 June, Chengdu, China, http://www2.dupont.com/Media_Center/en_US/assets/downloads/pdf/DuPont_White_Paper_Food_Security_China.pdf, accessed 14 July 2014.

Euromonitor International (2014). *China in 2030: The future demographic*, www.euromonitor. com/china-in-2030-the-future-demographic/report.

European Commission (2012). *EU-China geographical indications – "10 plus 10" project is now complete*, http://europa.eu/rapid/press-release_IP-12-1297_en.htm?locale=en.

European Commission (2013). *Geographical-indications*, http://ec.europa.eu/trade/policy/ accessing-markets/intellectual-property/geographical-indications/

EUSME Centre (2015). *The food and beverage market in China*, www.eusmecentre.org. cn/report/food-beverage-market-china.

FAO (2013). *2000 World census of agriculture: Analysis and international comparison of the results 1996–2005*, www.fao.org/fileadmin/templates/ess/ess_test_folder/World_ Census_Agriculture/Publications/WCA_2000/Census13.pdf.

FAO (2015). *Status of the world soil resources*. Main Report, www.fao.org/3/a-bc599e.pdf.

FAO Aquastat (2014). *Water resources indicators*, www.fao.org/nr/water/aquastat/water_ res/index.stm.

FAOSTAT (2015). *Agri-environmental indicators*, http://faostat3.fao.org/download/E/*/E.

Fuller, F., Beghin, J., De Cara, S., Fabiosa, J., Fang, C., and Matthey, H. (2001). *China's accession to the WTO: What is at stake for agricultural markets?* CARD Working Papers. Paper 310, http://lib.dr.iastate.edu/card_workingpapers/310.

Hanjira, M. A., Mu, J., and Khan, S. (2008). *Water Management and Crop Production for Food Security in China: A Review*. Wagga Wagga: Charles Sturt University, Elsevier editions, http://bwl.univie.ac.at/fileadmin/user_upload/lehrstuhl_ind_en_uw/lehre/ss11/ Sem_Yuri/Agr-water.pdf.

Huang, J., Jun, Y., Xu, Z., Rozelle, S., Li, N. (2007). Agricultural trade liberalization and poverty in China. *China Economic Review*, Volume 18, Issue 3, 2007, 244–265, ISSN 1043-951X, http://www.sciencedirect.com/science/article/pii/S1043951X07000120

IMF (2015). *World Economic Outlook*, www.imf.org/external/pubs/ft/weo/2015/01/pdf/ text.pdf.

Lam, H. M., Remais, J., Fung, M. C., Xu, L., and Sun, S. S. M. (2013). Food supply and food safety issues in China. *The Lancet*, 381(9882), 2044–2053. *Issues in China*. Iran J Public Land matrix, www.landmatrix.org/en/

Lee, M., Park, D., and Ramayand, A. (2016). *How growth deceleration in the People's Republic of China affects other Asian economies. An empirical analysis*. ADB economics working paper series n. 484, www.adb.org/sites/default/files/publication/183899/ ewp-484.pdf.

Li, T. (2014). The Celestial Empire goes urban. *Brics Business Magazine*, www.bricsmagazine. com/en/articles/the-celestial-empire-goes-urban.

Lin, J. Y. (1992). Rural reforms and agricultural growth in China. *The American Economic Review*, 82(1).

Liu, X., Wang, X., and Xin, X. (2012). Did agricultural technological changes affect China's regional disparity? *China Agricultural Economic Review*, 4(4), 440–449. doi:10.1108/17561371211284803.

More, S. (2013). *Issue brief: Water resource issues, policy and politics in China*, www. brookings.edu/research/papers/2013/02/water-politics-china-moore.

Ni, H. (2013). *Analisi delle politiche di supporto all'agricoltura cinese*, Report No. 47, International Centre for Trade and Sustainable Development (ICSTD), www.cicos. agri.gov.cn/Upload/Files/NewsAttatches/2353/china_paper_v4.-.201351511010.pdf, accessed 1 November 2014.

OECD, FAO (2013). *Agricultural Outlook 2013–2022: Highlights*, www.oecd.org/site/ oecd-faoagriculturaloutlook/highlights-2013-EN.pdf, accessed 22 July 2014.

Park, A. (2009). *Agricultural development in China: Lessons for Ethiopia*, http://users. ox.ac.uk/~econstd/Brief_Park%20_rev_pdf.

Ren, T. (2008).*China agriculture: Challenge and countermeasures*, https://sustainablede-velopment.un.org/content/documents/ren_5may_agriculture.pdf.

Smaller, C., Wei, Q., and Yalan, L. (2012). *Farmland and water: China invests abroad.* IISD Report, International Institute for Sustainable Development, www.iisd.org/ pdf/2012/farmland_water_china_invests.pdf.

USDA (2015). *Gain report. China – Peoples Republic of food service – hotel restaurant institutional HRI food service sector annual report*, ain.fas.usda.gov/Recent GAIN Pub-lications/Food Service – Hotel Restaurant Institutional_Guangzhou ATO_China – Peo-ples Republic of_2–10–2015.pdf.

WenJun Zhang, FuBin Jiang, and JianFeng Ou (2011). *Global pesticide consumption and pollution: With China as a focus.* Proceedings of the International Academy of Ecology and Environmental Sciences.

WTO (2015). *Statistics, trade and tariff data*, www.wto.org/english/res_e/statis_e/statis_e. htm. Xiwen, C. (2006). Conflicts and problems facing China's current rural reform and development, Chapter 4 in: Dong X.-y, Song S., and Zhang X. (eds.), *China's Agricul-tural Development.* Aldershot: Ashgate Publishing Limited

Zanier, V. (2010). *Dal grande esperimento alla società armoniosa, trent'anni di riforme economiche per costruire una nuova Cina.* Milano: Franco Angeli.

Zhang, H. (2013). *Behind China's "Grain Miracle": More than Meets the Eye?* RSIS Com-mentaries No. 028/2013, S. Rajaratnam School of International Studies, Nanyang, www. rsis.edu.sg/wp-content/uploads/2014/07/CO13028.pdf, accessed 13 November 2014.

Zhao, G. (1986). *Man and Land in Chinese History: An Economic Analysis.* Stanford: Stanford University Press.

Zolin, M. B., and Luzi, L. (2013). Unexpected and growing interest in land investments? The Asian case, in: Andreosso O'Callaghan, B., Jaussaud, J., and Zolin, M. B. (eds.), *Economic Integration in Asia Towards the Delineation of a Sustainable Path.* Basing-stoke: Palgrave MacMillan, 78–98.

13 Food security, food safety and pesticides

China and the EU compared[1]

M. Bruna Zolin, Matilde Cassin, Ilda Mannino

Introduction

Pathogens, weeds, and pests cause significant crop losses worldwide, thus presenting a barrier to the achievement of global food security (Pretty and Bharucha, 2015).

In order to avoid losses and to feed the population, humans started fighting pests a long time ago. The use by ancient Sumerians of sulfur compounds to kill insects in 2500 BC is the earliest record of insect pest control. In the 1930s the trend of synthesizing new compounds, e.g. DDT, increased, but the real 'Revolution' happened in the 1950s and early 1960s, with the development of chemical synthetic pesticides and fertilizers presented as the answer to world hunger and the way to achieve food security.

If the use of pesticides has been key to the significant increase in per capita food availability and meeting the growing population needs, the consumption of pesticides and fertilizers has direct consequences on the environment in terms of water pollution, soil productivity damage, loss of insects and other animals, and on human health, in terms of chemical risk to farmers, workers in pesticides industries and consumers, related to their handling and application on crops. Furthermore, pesticide residue in food (the traces pesticides leave in treated products) represents a risk if it exceeds certain limits, raising food safety issues.

With a population projected to reach above 9 billion people by 2050 (FAO projections), food needs are expected to constantly increase and the main challenge will be to achieve global food security, ensuring, at the same time, food safety (FAO, 2013). This goal could be achieved by promoting sustainable and safe agricultural production methods and valorising agricultural outputs. First of all, this should mean a reduction in pesticide use.

Different countries have different pesticide regulations. They include limits for pesticide residue on food, product registration requirements and pesticide use restrictions. The certification schemes adopted in different countries are varied, playing key roles in terms of pesticides, food trade and consumption.

The main objective of this Chapter is to explore the relationship between food security and food safety, pointing out the role played in this relationship by

DOI: 10.4324/9781315102566-16

pesticides and focusing on the case studies of two key actors, the EU and China. Accordingly, the Chapter firstly outlines the international framework on pesticide use and the legal framework in the EU and in China, then analyzes pesticide global markets and finally addresses related concerns. Furthermore, the comparison between these various legal frameworks will allow the identification of challenges and possible future developments in terms of food security and safety in food trade relationships between the EU and China.

Pesticide international framework

The UN, WTO, FAO and WHO represent the main international institutions involved in policy formulation highlighting the impact of pesticide use on agriculture, human health, but also on food and trade and ruling on their use and trade.[2]

There are more than 250 multilateral environmental agreements (MEAs) and about 20 of these can affect trade. For our purposes, two multilateral environmental agreements should be mentioned. The Rotterdam Convention, dated 1998, entered into force in February 2004. It is based on the Prior Informed Consent (PIC) procedure for certain hazardous chemicals and pesticides in international trade.[3] The Stockholm Convention, dated 2001, on Persistent Organic Pollutants (POPs), entered into force in May 2004.[4] The former applies to banned or severely restricted chemicals and to severely hazardous pesticide formulations (listed in Annex III to the Convention), facilitating information exchange about these products, providing for a national decision-making process on their import and export and disseminating these decisions to members. The latter applies to POPs, chemicals (including several pesticides) that remain intact in the environment for long periods, become widely distributed geographically, accumulate in human tissue and have a harmful impact on human health or on the environment. It defines the criteria and procedures to identify these kinds of chemicals and establishes prohibitions and restrictions on the manufacture, use and trade of them.

It is also appropriate to remember a third agreement, the Basel convention (1989), related to the previous two, dealing with the management and disposal of the substances regulated by the Stockholm and the Rotterdam Conventions when they become waste, thus representing a relevant reference for pesticide legislation in the context of managing obsolete products.

These three MEAs have legal autonomy but in 2011 a Joint Executive Secretariat was established.

The WTO is the leading political and legal institution responsible for (free and fair) trade among states. Among the factors it takes into account is food safety related to the traded products and in this context pesticides are considered. The level of risk and harm associated with pesticide use was defined by the Recommended Classification of Pesticides by Hazard and approved by the WTO in 1975, distinguishing between the more and the less hazardous forms of each pesticide on the basis of the toxicity of the technical compound and of its formulations.

The WTO Agreement on the Application of Sanitary and Phytosanitary Measures (SPS), which entered into force in 1995, governs trading practices at the international level, in order to protect human, animal or plant life or health. According to the agreement, all WTO members have to adopt[5] sanitary (relating to human and animal health) and phytosanitary (relating to plant health) measures[6] to ensure that food is safe for consumers, and to prevent the spread of pests or diseases among animals and plants. These measures have to be defined using international standards, guidelines and recommendations. With regards to food safety issues, members have to take into consideration the standards established by the Codex Alimentarius Commission (FAO-WHO Codex Alimentarius international food standards, including 51 codes of practices, 73 guidelines and 212 standards) and with regards to plant health, the standards and guidelines developed by the International Plant Protection Convention[7] (IPPC) Secretariat (FAO-IPPC International Standards for Phytosanitary Measures – ISPMs).[8] Sanitary and phytosanitary measures apply to domestically produced food or local animal and plant diseases, as well as to products coming from other countries: member states are obliged to comply with the control, inspection and approval procedures called for in the agreement, especially as regards tolerances for contaminants in agricultural products. There are a large number of animal and plant diseases and pests that, given their ability to spread and because of the economic losses they cause, are considered to pose a high risk. Consequently, they deserve special attention in international agricultural trade operations. The control and eradication of such diseases and pests are essential in order to improve agricultural health in the affected countries, and to avoid exclusion from trade with those countries free of same (IICA, 1998). More specifically, exporting countries are obligated to guarantee that the sanitary and phytosanitary certificates they issue comply with the requirements imposed by an importing country, and must make special efforts to strengthen their export certification services. These measures may result in restrictions on trade or in discrimination between countries: the WTO recognizes, however, that the need to safeguard public policy interests (such as in health, safety and the environment) requires exceptions to the application of trade rules.

Among existing voluntary tools addressing pesticide management it is worth mentioning the FAO-WHO International Code of Conduct on Pesticide Management, which provides a framework guiding public and private stakeholders on best practices in managing pesticides throughout their lifecycle (FAO-WHO, 2014).[9] In this document, great attention has been paid to Integrated Pest Management (IPM), an ecosystem approach to crop production and protection that combines different management strategies and practices, i.e. biological control, mechanical control, cultural control and chemical control, to grow healthy crops and minimize the use of pesticides. The Code of Conduct presents IPM as a tool to reduce pesticide use and improve yields, food quality and income for farmers.[10] Since 2007 highly hazardous pesticides are a special focus area for the FAO in implementing the Code of Conduct (WHO, 2010).

Legal framework: the EU and China

The European Union

Policies and legislation on pesticides were first introduced at EU level in 1979, with the Council Directive prohibiting the placing on the market and use of plant protection products containing certain active substances.[11]

The European approach in the field of pesticides was strengthened with the 1992 reform of the CAP (Common Agricultural Policy) that integrates environmental issues in agricultural processes (European Commission, 2007). Particularly significant is Regulation (EC) No 396/2005 of the European Parliament and of the Council of 23 February 2005 on maximum residue levels (MRL) of pesticides in or on food and feed of plant and animal origin (amending Council Directive 91/414/EEC), i.e. the highest level of pesticide residue that is legally tolerated when pesticides are applied correctly (Good Agricultural Practice). The regulation aims at limiting the exposure of consumers at the end of the food chain. Furthermore, monitoring compliance with MRL makes it possible to assess whether professional users have implemented the good agricultural practices set out in the authorizations for plant protection products granted by the member states (ENDURE, 2010).

On 12 July 2006 the European Commission adopted the thematic strategy on the sustainable use of pesticides ('the Strategy'). Its roots are in the 6th Environmental Action Program (6th EAP), that includes coherent and integrated strategies on the sustainable use of pesticides.

The year 2009 was quite important for legislation on pesticides: Regulation (EC) No 1107/2009 of the European Parliament and of the Council of 21 October 2009 concerning the placing of plant protection products on the market was introduced (European Parliament and Council of the EU, 2009a).[12] It followed Directive 2009/127/EC of the European Parliament and of the Council of 21 October 2009, amending Directive 2006/42/EC with regard to machinery for pesticide application (European Parlament and Council of the EU, 2009b).

Directive 2009/128/EC, establishing a framework for Community action to achieve sustainable use of pesticides (Sustainable Use Directive – SUD), was adopted in 2009. This Directive establishes the obligation for member states to adopt National Action Plans (NAPs) to reduce risks and the impact of pesticide use by encouraging the development and introduction of Integrated Pest Management and of alternative approaches or techniques in order to reduce dependency on the use of pesticides (European Parlament and Council of the EU, 2009c). The key provisions introduced by the directives are:

1   Training of all professional users, distributors and advisors;
2   Restriction of sales of pesticides to professional users holding a certificate;
3   Information and awareness-raising of the general public on the risks and the potential effects of pesticides for human health, non-target organisms and the environment, and on the use of non-chemical alternatives;

4   Regular calibrations and technical checks of the pesticide application equipment of professional users;
5   Prohibition of aerial spraying, except in a few special cases;
6   Specific measures to protect the aquatic environment and drinking water (pesticides not classified as dangerous for water, low-drift equipment, mitigation measures for buffer-zones, etc.);
7   Restriction on the use of pesticides in specific areas like public parks, sports, school and recreation grounds;
8   Introduction of measures to promote low-pesticide input pest management, giving priority to non-chemical methods. This includes integrated pest management as well as organic farming. The general principles of integrated pest management should be implemented by all professional users from 1 January 2014;
9   Harmonized risk indicators shall be established.

It is worth mentioning the *White Paper on Food Safety* (European Commission, 2000) establishing that the driving force of the EU approach towards food sanitation is that market access is not granted to unsafe products, a principle that must apply 'whether the food is produced within the European community or imported from third countries'.

China

More recent is the history of pesticide legislation in China, where the Regulation on Pesticide Administration introduced in 1997 and amended in 2001, also known as the Regulation on the Control of Agrochemicals, represents the first comprehensive legislative and regulatory framework to manage pesticides in the country. It states that all the pesticides produced in China or imported to China must be submitted for registration. The Regulation also requires production licensing which means pesticide production in China must obtain a production license or approval document. On 29 November 2001, the Regulation was revised to meet the requirements of the WTO, which China joined that year. The Chinese government began revising its Regulations on Pesticide Administration, in 2010. The Legislative Affairs Office of the State Council published the draft of the revised regulation on its website – www.chinalaw.gov.cn – in 2011 but the process is still ongoing. The related local governments and departments also established relevant rules and regulations to comply with the 'Regulation on Pesticide Administration'. Every province, municipality directly under the central government and autonomous administration regions issued their own local 'Regulations on Pesticide Administration' (USDA, 2016).

In 2007, the Chinese government issued six new regulations to enhance pesticide management aiming at regulating pesticide names, label requirements and registration procedures (Yang, 2007). Early in 2008, the Chinese government released a well-enforced ban on the production, distribution and use of five highly-toxic organo-phosphorus pesticides (Methamidophos, Parathion, Parathion-methyl,

Monocrotophos and Phosphamidon), which represented nearly 60% of the total domestic pesticide market.[13]

The Chinese Ministry of Agriculture (MOA) launched on 17 March 2015 a campaign for zero growth of fertilizer and pesticide consumption by 2020. The target of the MOA is to achieve an over 40% fertilizer use efficiency rate and pesticide use efficiency rate by 2020, an increase of 7% and 5% respectively over 2013, and to achieve zero growth of fertilizer and pesticide consumption.[14]

The Food Safety Law (2009, revised in 2015) is also relevant, emphasizing the importance of agro-product quality and safety and underlining a transformation of the agricultural development mode, promoting standard, ecological, large-scale and brand-building approaches to production, and also, bringing production sources under control. It regulates, among others, the formulation of standards for food safety, establishing that they must also include limits on such pollutants as invasive organisms, pesticide residue, veterinary drug residue, biotoxins and heavy metals, and other materials endangering human health, contained in food, food additives, and food-related-products (Bian, 2012).

It is also worth mentioning two Acts indirectly related to pesticide issues: the Provisions on Organic Product Certification Management (5 November 2004) regulate the production, processing, trade and certification of organic products; the Regulations for the Implementation of Organic Products Certification (1 June 2005), ensure the validity of organic certification and the consistency of certification procedures and management. Since the 1980s the Chinese government has paid attention to the sustainable development of agro-ecosystems and began to develop a green food industry in 1990. After developing over two decades, the Chinese green food industry has reached a significant size and is expanding rapidly (Lin et al., 2010), thanks to different certification standards and systems.

The pesticide market

Pesticide supply

The global agrochemicals market is an oligopolistic market, dominated by a few big players: the world's five largest companies producing pesticides (based on revenue in 2013) are multinationals headquartered in different countries.[15]

According to Greenpeace research (2008), these five leading companies control three-quarters of the world's pesticide market and nearly two-thirds of the commercial seed market (Table 13.1). The largest company, Syngenta, is also the third largest seed company; Monsanto, is also the world's largest seed company and Bayer is the seventh largest seed company (PAN Europe, 2013). The number of active ingredients sold by these companies are 512, with 47% of these classified as dangerous for the environment and for health.

The concentration of power in a small number of companies and, as a consequence, their ability to set prices and determine varieties available, has been and is a cause of concern among farmers. Furthermore, some of these giants have

Table 13.1 Leading countries and leading 5 global agrochemical multinational companies based on revenue in 2013 (US$ millions)

Country	Company	Rank	Typology
Germany	Bayer	2	Chemical and pharmaceutical company
	BASF	3	Chemical company
Switzerland	Syngenta	1	Seed and agrochemicals company
USA	Dow Chemical	4	Chemical, advanced materials, agricultural science, plastic company
	Monsanto	5	Agricultural biotechnologies company

Source: Authors' elaboration Seeking Alpha, 2013

agreed to merge with their competitors in the future (such as Bayer and Monsanto, Syngenta and China National Chemical Corporation, Dow Chemical and DuPont). The EU has expressed concerns that these mergers could very likely lead to higher prices for consumers as well as creating high barriers to market entry (Neumeister, 2014).

According to the 2015 Annual Review on the Global Agrochemical Industry (Agropages, 2015), the European market, in terms of active ingredient volume was estimated at 639.4 KT in 2011 and is expected to reach 741.9. KT by 2018. Europe is the second largest market for herbicides and it is expected to reach more than US$ 15 billion in revenue by 2018.

Currently, pesticide production tends progressively to be concentrated in Asian countries (Table 13.2), and, more specifically in China. China's compound annual growth rate is expected to grow by 5.1% (globally 2.7%) between 2014–2019. The Chinese production of pesticides in 2011 was more than 2.6 million tons (compared to 0.2 million tons in 1991). Production surpassed consumption in 2007 and since 1994 Chinese pesticide exports have exceeded imports (Zhang et al., 2011).

According to the China Crop Protection Industry Association, in 2014 the list of the top 10 Chinese pesticide companies is led by Zhejiang Wnyca Chemical, which produces glyphosate, followed by Nutrichem Company Limited (its products primarily include herbicides and safeners, insecticides and acaricides, fungicides, plant growth regulators), Nanjing Red Sun Co., Shandong Weifang Rainbow Chemical (producing a variety of products from herbicides to insecticides), Zhejiang Jinfanda Biochemical (glyphosate pesticide and chemical intermediate products), Hubei Sanonda (acephate, paraquat, glyphosate, dipt), Jiangsu Yangnong Chemical (producing a large variety of products from herbicides to insecticides), Sichuan Leshan Fuhua Tongda Agro-Chemical Technology, Zhejiang Zhongshan Chemical Industry Group and Jiangsu Lianhe Chemical Technology. These 10 companies in 2014 registered total annual sales of more than 30 billion Yuan.[16] Considering the top 100 list, in 2014 the Chinese agrochemicals companies achieved total sales of more than 100 billion Yuan, up 9% year on year (Agropages.com, 2015).[17]

Table 13.2 Worldwide agrochemicals revenue markets
share by region in 2012

Region	Revenue share %
Asia	41,3
Latin America	17
North America	15,4
Europe	7,8
Other	18,5

Source: Authors' elaboration on Seeking Alpha, 2013

Pesticide consumption and trade

The worldwide production and consumption of pesticides have been increasing in parallel with human population and crop production (Figure 13.1).

In 2012 the worldwide consumption of pesticides was about 3.3 million tons (active ingredients). The trend from 1990 shows an overall increase (about 2 million tons from 1991 to 2012) although frequent fluctuations occurred over time.[18] Analyzing the percentages of the main pesticides used, it can be observed that (Figure 13.2) 48% are herbicides, 26% fungicides, 18% insecticides and others account for 8%. Since the 1990s herbicides have become the most used pesticide (their utilization was about 20% of total pesticides in 1960 compared to 48% in 2012), with the aim of enhancing agricultural intensification and productivity. Consequently, the proportion of insecticides and fungicides have declined (Zhang et al., 2011).

Glyphosate has become the most used pesticide by volume due to the decrease in price and a higher share of reduced tillage, where glyphosate replaces ploughing as a weed control measure (Greenpeace, 2015b). Globally, agricultural glyphosate use has risen almost 15-fold since the so-called 'Roundup Ready', genetically engineered glyphosate-tolerant crops were introduced in 1996, rising from 51 million kg (113 million pounds) in 1995 to 747 million kg (1.65 billion pounds) in 2014.[19] The largest segment (72%) of glyphosate used in the last 40 years was applied in the last decade. The major glyphosate manufacturer, Monsanto, has typically not competed directly or solely on price; instead it has been successful in holding or expanding market share by selling higher-price Roundup herbicides together with the purchase of Monsanto herbicide-tolerant seeds (Benbrook, 2015).

The Americas register 50% of world consumption, followed by Europe (30%) and Asia (16%).[20] China, the USA, France, Brazil and Japan are the largest pesticide producers, consumers or traders in the world (Zhang et al., 2011). Use of pesticides has risen in developing countries and the fastest growing markets are in Africa, Asia, South and Central America and the Eastern Mediterranean. Although developing countries use only 25% of the pesticides produced worldwide, they experience 99% of the deaths related to pesticide use. This is because the use of pesticides tends to be more intensive and unsafe, and regulatory, health and education systems are weaker in developing countries (WHO, 2008).

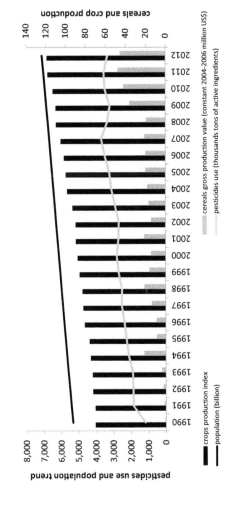

Figure 13.1 Pesticide use, population growth and crop production compared: 1990–2012

Source: Authors' elaboration on FAOSTAT data, 2015

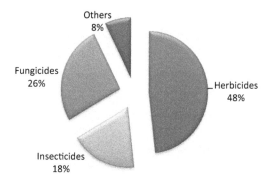

Figure 13.2 Main types of pesticides used worldwide in 2012
Source: Authors' elaboration on FAOSTAT data, 2015

According to FAOSTAT data (2015), the highest intensity of pesticide utilization is registered in China (17.8 tons of active ingredients per 1,000 ha) and in the
countries of South America. In the EU the values range from a minimum of 0.75
tons per 1,000 ha in Romania and Sweden to a maximum of 8.75 tons per 1,000
ha in the Netherlands.

In the EU, in 2013, the main consumer countries were Spain, France, Italy and
Germany.[21] Since 1991 the number of pesticide active ingredients in the EU has
decreased by about 50% and currently about 500 active ingredients are authorized
compared to about 650 in 2004 (Neumeister, 2014).

China was one of the earliest countries to use pesticides and it is today the
world's largest producer and exporter in terms of quantity as well as the second largest consumer of pesticides, using alone half of pesticides worldwide
(Pretty and Bharucha, 2015). The Chinese consumption of pesticides in 2011
was equal to 1.8 million tons (compared to 0.76 million tons in 1991), with
diversification across the country: the maximum values are registered in southern China, due to the warm and humid weather that favors pests' diffusion.
However, the highest pesticide application dosage (measured as kg of active
ingredients per ha of cultivated land) is located in the South-East of China,
more specifically in Hainan, Fujian, Guandong, Jiangxi and Zhejiang (from 32
to 65 kg/ha) (Li et al., 2014).

As far as pesticide trade is concerned, according to FAOSTAT data, from 2000,
China's pesticide exports with the rest of the world have been greatly increasing,
passing from an overall value of US $500 million to almost US $4.5 billion in
2014. (Figure 13.3).

The EU's pesticide trade with the rest of the world is increasing both for exports
and imports, which show similar trends and overall value, even if exports exceed
imports (Figure 13.4).

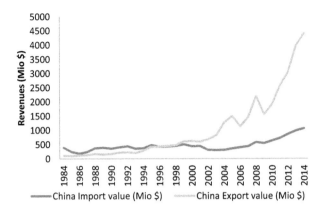

Figure 13.3 China's pesticide imports and exports with the rest of the world
Source: Authors' elaboration on FAOSTAT data

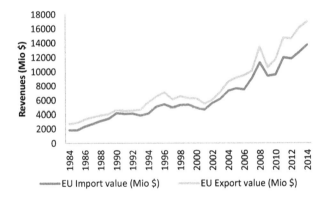

Figure 13.4 EU's pesticide imports and exports with the rest of the world
Source: Authors' elaboration on FAOSTAT data

Focusing on the pesticide trade between the EU and China, data shows that, on the one hand, the value (Figure 13.5) of the EU's exports to China (equal to €154 million in 2015) exceeds the value of imports (equal to €117 million in the same year) but, on the other hand, considering the quantity of imported and exported pesticides it can be observed that, since 2010 (Figure 13.6), the EU's imports from China (298,000 tons in 2015) exceed exports (218,000 tons in 2015). This result highlights the higher value added of European products.

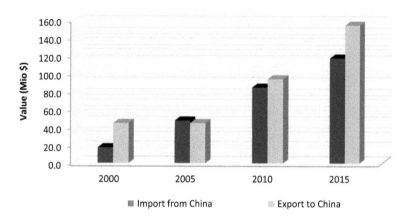

Figure 13.5 Pesticides: EU imports from China and EU exports to China (value)
Source: Authors' elaboration on Eurostat – Comext database data

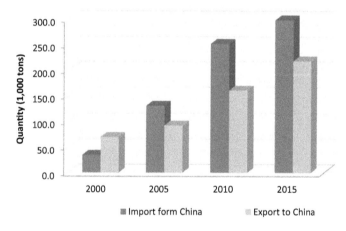

Figure 13.6 Pesticides: EU imports from China and EU exports to China (quantity)
Source: Authors' elaboration on Eurostat – Comext database data

Food trade: the EU and China

China and the EU's economic relationship has been continuously increasing in importance over the years. As far as total goods trade is concerned, in 2015, China was the EU's largest trade partner for imports and the second largest partner for exports. Also, EU trade with China shows that, while EU imports of goods from China (amounting to more than €350 billion in 2015, compared to €130 billion in 2004) are higher than exports (about €170 billion in 2015, compared to €50 billion in 2004), the EU is a net food exporter to China: in 2015, exports of agricultural products (in € million) were double that of imports. Moreover, considering EU agri-food exports, China was the second largest EU partner after the USA (with more than €10 billion), and considering EU agri-food imports, China ranked fourth largest, after Brazil, the USA and Argentina (Table 13.3). On the whole, primary goods represent 10% of the total goods exported from the EU to China and 3% of the total goods imported from China. These quite low percentages are compensated by the high image value of these kind of products (European Commission, 2016). Food safety is one of the major causes of conflict in the exchange relationship between the EU and China (Schibler, 2014).

The top five agri-food products exported (Table 13.4) from the EU to China (12.6% of the total agri-food exported) are infant food, with a constantly increasing value (+48% solely between 2014 and 2015), followed by raw hides and skins (11.4%), offal and animal fats (9.8%), pork meat (9.0% and with a growth rate between 2014–2015 equal to +117%) and wine, cider and vinegar (8%).

As far as imports from China are concerned (Table 13.5), vegetables rank first, processed vegetables and fruits rank third and tropical fruits fourth (representing more than 27% of the total agri-food imports altogether). These data are of special interest to this Chapter, considering that vegetables and fruits may contain pesticide residue, more than other agricultural products. Among the top five imported products, offal and animal fats (second, 9.4%) and wood and silk (fifth, 6.4%) are also listed.

Concerns related to pesticide use

Pesticide residue in food represents a risk to human health if they exceed certain limits. Pesticides can also produce environmental pollution. Pesticide contamination is rarely due to a single substance but to a mix of substances as Greenpeace research (2015a) shows.[22]

Table 13.3 EU top agri-food importers and exporters by regions, 2015

Rank	Top importers (region and country)	Value € millions (EU exports)	% extra EU	Rank	Top exporters	Value € millions (EU imports)	% extra EU
1	**North America**		15	1	**Latin America**		
	USA	19,407			Brazil	13,203	11.7
					Argentina	5,756	5.1
2	**Asia**		8	2	**North America**		
	China	10,342					
	Japan	5,354			USA	11,986	10.6
3	**Europe**		5.9	3	**Asia**		
	Switzerland	7,670			China	5,150	4.5
	Russia	5,569					

Source: Authors' elaboration on EC- DG Agriculture and rural development AGRI-FOOD TRADE STATISTICAL FACTSHEET European Union – China

Table 13.4 Top 5 EU Agri-food exports to China, 2011–2015 (€ million value)

Rank	Product	2011 € million value	2012 € million value	2013 € million value	2014 € million value	2015 € million value	Share in all Agro 2015 (%)	Change 2014–2015 (%)
1	**Infant foods and other cereals**	318	522	740	877	1 299	12.6	48.1
2	**Raw hides, skins and fur skins**	808	997	1 256	950	1 179	11.4	24.1
3	**Offal, animal fats and other meats**	431	605	668	723	1 011	9.8	39.8
4	**Pork meat**	211	361	446	431	935	9.0	116.9
5	**Wine, cider and vinegar**	697	769	666	655	828	8.0	26.4

Source: Authors 'elaboration EC- DG Agriculture and rural development

Table 13.5 Top 5 EU Agri-food imports from China, 2011–2015 (€ million value)

Rank	Product	2011 € million value	2012 € million value	2013 € million value	2014 € million value	2015 € million value	Share in all Agro 2015 (%)	Change 2014–2015 (%)
1	**Vegetables**	597	505	527	514	542	10.5	5.4
2	**Offal, animal fats and other meats**	551	564	493	482	486	9.4	0.8
3	**Processed vegetable & fruits**	490	520	444	404	485	9.4	20.0
4	**Tropical fruits**	221	213	279	321	398	7.7	24.0
5	**Wood and silk**	318	285	330	308	330	6.4	7.1

Source: Authors 'elaboration EC- DG Agriculture and rural development

Moreover, farmers and workers in the pesticide industry and exterminators of house pests can be exposed to pesticides' negative effects, often as a consequence of improper or careless handling (Fait et al., 2001). Every year thousands of farm workers experience short- and long-term effects of pesticide poisoning.[23]

The above mentioned issues are found in both the EU and in China.

The European legislative framework provides an annual pesticide monitoring program (aimed at analyzing pesticide residue on food), carried out by EU member states plus Iceland and Norway. In 2013, 80,967 samples were analyzed for 685 pesticides. Of the samples, 68.2% originated from the EU and two European Free Trade Association (EFTA) countries (Iceland and Norway) and 27.7% of the samples were from products imported from third countries. For 4.1% of the cases the origin of the products was not reported. The analysis shows that:

- 97.4% of the samples analyzed fell within the legal limits;
- 54.6% were free of detectable residue;
- 1.5% of samples clearly exceeded the legal limits.[24]

Among the samples from EU/EEA countries, 57.6% were free of measurable residue, and 1.4% contained residue that exceeded the legal limits.[25] The percentage of samples from Iceland and Norway free of detectable residue was 46.2%, with 5.7% clearly exceeding legal limits (ESFA, 2015).

By the end of 2009, more than 26,000 pesticides had been registered in China (Li et al., 2014) and from 2012, the Chinese food standards system includes 2,319 pesticides residue limits, involving 322 types of pesticides (Wu and Zhu, 2014). Research shows that in China crop pollution and pesticide residuals in crop products are frequent, with consequential damages in terms of yield and quality of products and of human health. A study conducted on fruits and vegetables collected from Xiamen in China from October 2006 to March 2009, demonstrated that 37.7% of the samples contained pesticide residue: pak choi cabbage, legumes, and leaf mustard were the commodities in which pesticide residue were most frequently detected, with 17.2%, 18.9% and 17.2% of the samples exceeding the maximum residue limits (MRLs), respectively (Chen et al., 2011). A 2013 Greenpeace East Asia investigation revealed that traditional Chinese herbal products being exported to Europe and North America are laced with toxic cocktails of pesticide residue, many of them exceeding levels considered safe by food and agriculture authorities (Greenpeace, 2015a).[26] Greenpeace China, furthermore, conducted an analysis of pesticide residue in China's markets (located in Beijing, Shanghai and Guangzhou), showing that 89% of the samples contained pesticides and 20% contained illegal or highly toxic pesticides (Zhang et al., 2011).

Coupling food security and food safety

Integrated Pest Management

Food safety, nutrition and food security are inextricably linked. This calls for alternative methods to reduce pest damage while avoiding the cost and negative outcomes associated with synthetic pesticides (Pretty and Bharucha, 2015) and Integrated Pest Management is often proposed as a solution (Bajwa and Kogan, 2002). The modern IPM concept is defined by the FAO as 'the careful consideration of all available pest control techniques and subsequent integration of appropriate measures that discourage the development of pest populations and keep pesticides and other interventions to levels that are economically justified and reduce or minimize risks to human health and the environment' (FAO – WHO, 2014: 4). Thus, IPM aims to maintain pest damage at economically acceptable levels while protecting the environment and human health.

Since the 1970s entomologists and ecologists have urged the adoption of IPM for pest control and, as highlighted by Parsa et al., (2014), IPM has become the dominant crop protection paradigm.

The overview of EU legislation highlights the great effort made to withdraw poisonous active ingredients from the European market (Lefebvre et al., 2014). Of great interest is the recent approach of the EU, which, as underlined by Lamichhane et al. (2016: 148), 'creates an opportunity to build a common IPM framework in agriculture, based on sustainable crop protection approaches that are flexibly adapted for cropping systems, changing pest pressures, changing climatic conditions and regional agronomic practices'. In particular, as already mentioned, Directive 2009/128/EC establishes the obligation to implement the IPM principles for all professional users starting from 1 January 2014. Great importance is given to the training of all professional users, distributors and advisors. Time will tell if it is effective in promoting IPM in the EU, where this approach is not yet broadly implemented (Movses, 2015).

As underlined by Wang et al. (2003), the development of IPM in China was a gradual, but continuous process, which had already started in the 1950s. A big boost to IPM was given by the first Nationwide Conference on Integrated Pest Control for Crop Diseases and Insect Pests held in Shaoguan City, Guangdong Province, in 1974. Since 1983, the Chinese government have funded IPM Technique Research Projects as one of the State Key Research Programs in four successive state five-year plans, testifying to the importance it gives to these solutions. The 40-plus years IPM experience in China gave ample proof that this strategy can decrease pesticide use without lowering crop yields, and help to improve farmers' income and protect the environment (Yang et al., 2014). On the other hand, the conventional assumption that pesticide use and yields are positively correlated is showing weakness. Recent studies carried out by Pretty and Bharucha (2015) on over 85 IPM projects report that at least half of the pesticides used in Asia and Africa do not need to be used. At the same time, they show that IPM can deliver substantial reduction in pesticide use coupled with increased yields.

According to these results, IPM seems to be the right solution to achieve a sustainable intensification in agriculture, but its adoption should involve a majority of farmers. In the case of China we are talking about the enormous number of smallholder farmers, who characterize Chinese agriculture, where the average farm size according to Yang et al. (2014) is less than 0.5 ha.

As underlined by Pretty and Bharucha (2015: 174) 'IPM is much more than just a simple resource-conserving technology. As with other forms of sustainable intensification, techniques of IPM are knowledge-intensive' and therefore requires training of farmers. The need for 'training and education of farmers, extension workers and policy-makers to deliver new information in the developing countries' was mentioned by Zeng (1993) already in 1993 as key for IPM implementation. Considering the case of China, training that many smallholders is not an easy task and requires ad hoc policies and support.

Policies are broadly considered as a fundamental means to promote IPM adoption, as shown by the reports on declining growth in pesticide use in China due to the implementation of IPM and related policies – mainly focused on the banning of highly poisonous pesticides – and the use of low volumes of more toxic pesticides (Peshin and Zhang, 2014). Yet IPM adoption remains low as well as the reduction of pesticide use (Pretty and Bharucha, 2015).

Last but not least, it has to be considered that IPM must adapt to changing ecological and economic conditions. As well described by Pretty and Bharucha (2015: 173), 'pests, diseases, and weeds evolve, new pests and diseases emerge (sometimes because of pesticide overuse), and pests and diseases are easily transported or are carried to new locations (often where natural enemies do not exist)'. In addition to these, the new challenges introduced by climate change to pest management have to be considered.

Food quality certification schemes in the EU and in China

Food safety should encourage the promotion of agricultural food obtained from low pesticide agriculture. From this perspective the definition of adequate product quality certification systems is extremely useful, as well as the mutual recognition of these systems among different states.

As far as the European Union is concerned, an inventory compiled for the European Commission (Aretè, 2010) counted 441 quality schemes for agricultural products and foodstuffs marketed in the EU. The main requirements are provided by Regulation (EU) No. 1151/2012 on quality schemes for agricultural products and foodstuffs and by the European guidelines on certification schemes. There are also a number of optional quality terms, and separate rules on organic farming (Council Regulation (EC) No. 834/2007). Since 1 July 2010, producers of packaged organic food have been required under EU law to use the EU organic logo. Furthermore, at national or local level, many European countries have adopted labels for certifying the use of Integrated Pest Management methods.

Certification schemes for agricultural products and foodstuffs in the EU provide assurance that certain aspects of the product or its production method, as laid down in a specification, have been observed. They cover different kinds of initiatives that function at different stages of the food supply chain, ranging from compliance with compulsory production standards to additional requirements relating to environmental protection, animal welfare, organoleptic qualities, 'Fair

Trade', etc. These schemes and their labels help producers/groups of producers to better market their products, protecting them from misuse or falsification of a product name.[27]

In particular, three EU schemes known as GIs (Geographical Indications) promote and protect names of quality agricultural products and foodstuffs, attributable to a specific origin.[28]

Over the past few years, China has reviewed and issued thousands of new food safety and hygiene standards mainly because of continuous food scandals and rising consumer concerns. Most notably, in 2015 China's revised Food Safety Law came into effect.

In China there are both food safety standards (mandatory) and food quality standards (voluntary), that explicitly refer to pesticide residue. The main ones are analyzed below.

As far as mandatory tools are concerned, QS (Quality Supervision) are standards that guarantee the food has passed the necessary quality and safety tests; GMP (Good Manufacturing Practice) is a quality assurance which ensures that products are consistently produced and controlled according to the quality standards appropriate to their intended use.

Furthermore, various voluntary tools and labels exist and in particular it is worth mentioning:

(1) 'Pollution-free products', which are unprocessed or primary edible products whose producing area environment, production processes and product quality meet the related national standards and norms, and obtaining the certificate after accreditation, are allowed to use the pollution-free agricultural products logo. The standards to be fulfilled are related to pesticide residue, veterinary drug residue, hazardous substances, water, soil and air quality in the producing area.

(2) 'Green food', is a Chinese eco-certification scheme for food, created in 1990. It consists of a set of voluntary standards, including environmental quality standards, packaging and labeling standards, inputs control standards, as well as product quality standards. The Green Food standards cover a wide range of products including crop production, livestock, aquaculture and beverages among others. It certifies both the production process and the outcome. Two categories of green food, AA and A, are defined by it. AA green food is the standard used for organic food. 'A' green food is of a higher standard than normal food but lower than AA green food or organic food (Bian, 2012): it is produced with a controlled and reduced use of pesticides, together with a testing regime for pesticide residue. These kinds of products are easily recognizable thanks to the green logo which can readily be seen on a variety of food items in Chinese supermarkets. The Green Food label is also recognized abroad and in particular in Finland (Europe), Canada and Australia. China's export of Green Food standards is an example of the Golden Rule – those with the gold make the rules – and demonstrates that China now has the purchasing power to impose its own eco-standards, and foreign producers have

the motivation to meet and seek Chinese eco-certification (Paull, 2008). In 2011 more than 7,000 Chinese farms had a Green Food certification, more than 16,000 products carried a Green label and the domestic sales of Green food labeled products amounted to RMB 313.4 billion, with US$ 2.3 billion exports (Sustanability map, 2012).

(3) 'Organic products', are products grown without the use of conventional pesticides, artificial fertilizers, GMO, etc. (Zhou and Jin, 2013). In more detail, Chinese organic farming officially started to be promoted in 1989 with the aim of addressing environmental concerns and later to meet the requirements of foreign markets and to make Chinese products more marketable in other countries. Indeed, most of the early development of Chinese organic agriculture was driven by export opportunities in the European Union and United States, and later in Japan. National regulations on organic agriculture were first introduced in the early 2000s and the most recent one was applied in 2005, when compulsory organic standards and supervision systems were introduced and, as a consequence, all organic products, including imports, must comply with the national rules and standards (International Trade Centre, 2011).

Concluding remarks

Food security and safety (in terms of quantity and quality) are global strategic objectives. It might seem that the goal of food security is inconsistent with the one of food safety: global population growth and the increase in food needs have resulted in a broad use of pesticides to control pests in producing food; furthermore, globalization and changes in consumption patterns have made a vast amount of food goods available which make the food chain a complex system, with increasing food scandals and fraud and risks to human health.

A large part of these risks is related to pesticide use, which has consequences both in terms of the environment and health. The increasing use of these chemicals, under the adage, 'if little is good, a lot more will be better' (Aktar et al., 2009) has generated risks in terms of environmental pollution and the health of humans and other life forms. In particular, a health impact can result from indirect exposure, via their residue in agricultural products and drinking water, or from direct exposure, in the case of industrial workers producing plant protection products and farmers applying them.

Consumers from food importer countries are more vulnerable and more likely to eat less healthy foods, and many states have adopted strong legislation on food safety, and control the use of pesticides and their trade. This is, for instance the case of the EU, but also of China, which has been introducing stricter laws over the last decades.

It is appropriate that public authorities pay particular attention to ensure food safety. Considerable progress has been made but commitment and international cooperation is still necessary. Trade has played an important role in bringing to development common rules and specific legislation in this field, as highlighted by the Chinese case analysis.

On the other hand, food safety needs to be coupled with food security and a further growth in terms of food production will be needed in order to feed the increasing population.

The adoption of sustainable production methods based on integrated pest management, in order to reduce the use and negative effects of pesticides, and the definition (and recognition among different states) of adequate product quality certification systems, could play a fundamental role in matching food security and food safety aims. The findings outlined in this Chapter show that both China and the EU are on this path and that they have been promoting IPM methods and certification schemes for food and agricultural products. What is still missing is a greater mutual recognition of labels, which could also support the marketing of these products abroad.

A big challenge for broadening the implementation of sustainable agriculture in China is to train and create the right capabilities in the large number of small-holder farmers forming the Chinese agricultural system. However, Peshin and Zhang (2014) report that growth in pesticide use is declining in China due to the implementation of IPM and related policies, but also because of the use of low volumes of more toxic pesticides.

The definition of common international strategies, measures, guidelines, codes of conduct, etc., in relation to negative environmental and human impacts of pesticide use is very important. It is appropriate that international organizations (UN, WTO, FAO, WHO) will continue to promote sustainable paths. On the supply side, international organizations may involve large multinational pesticide companies. In terms of demand, the same organizations and national public authorities could properly raise consumer awareness about the importance of sustainable farming systems and quality certification. The benefits would be huge for the world's population with a medium-long term positive impact. In this regard, the cases of China and the European Union are extremely important and interesting. As mentioned previously, domestic food regulations may hinder and limit international trade, but multilateral mechanisms can resolve potential trade conflicts (Roberts and Unnevehr, 2005), and food safety plays a key role in the food trade relationships between the EU and China.

Notes

1 This research was largely based upon work supported by the EUCLID project – EU-China Lever for IPM Demonstration. The project has received funding from the European Union's Horizon 2020 research and innovation program under grant agreement No 633999.
2 The World Trade Organization, Food and Agriculture Organization and World Health Organization are all organizations of the United Nations.
3 In 1989 the PIC procedure was jointly introduced for the first time by the FAO and UNEP as a voluntary tool within the Code of Conduct on the Distribution and Use of Pesticides and in the London Guidelines for the Exchange of Information on Chemicals in International Trade. These two instruments were developed and promoted voluntarily, respectively by the FAO and UNEP in the mid-1980s to ensure that governments had the necessary information to enable them to assess the risks of hazardous chemicals and to take informed decisions on their future import.

4 Signed by 152 countries. It entered into force in the EU in February 2005 and in China in November 2004.

5 Countries are allowed to set their own standards, but they must be based on science.

6 These sanitary and phytosanitary measures can take many forms, such as requiring products to come from a disease-free area, inspection of products, specific treatment or processing of products, setting of allowable maximum levels of pesticide residue or permitted use of only certain additives in food.

7 The FAO International Plant Protection Convention (IPPC) is the main international agreement related to pests control and management. It promotes cooperation in plant protection, with the aim to prevent the spread and introduction of plant pests and to adopt appropriate measures for their control. The IPPC was adopted in 1951 and it has been amended twice, most recently in 1997; this last revision aimed to incorporate phytosanitary concepts, adapting the convention to the WTO Sanitary and Phytosanitary Measures (SPS) Agreement

8 Including standards on pest risk analysis, requirements for the establishment of pest-free areas, and others which give specific guidance on topics related to the SPS Agreement.

9 In 2013 the fourth version was approved. The first one was dated 1985.

10 Articles 1.7; 3.7; 3.8; 3.9; 5.1 and 8.1 are dedicated or related to IPM.

11 Over the years, it evolved considerably, culminating in the adoption of Directive 91/414/EEC concerning the placing of plant protection products on the market, followed by Directive 98/8/EC on the placing of biocidal products on the market. According to this legislation all pesticides need to be evaluated and authorized before they can be placed on the market (EU, 2007).

12 Repealing Council Directives 79/117/EEC and 91/414/EEC.

13 Furthermore, the law on Agricultural Products Quality and Safety (2006) includes clauses on pesticide use and agricultural products quality and safety (Standing Committee of the Tenth National People's Congress of the People's Republic of China, 2006).

14 The efficiency rate has to be measured as the quantity of fertilizer (or pesticides) needed to get the maximum economic yield with minimum inputs.

15 The total revenues of the top five companies in 2013 is equal to more than US$ 37 billion (Seeking Alpha 2013).

16 About US$ 4.5 billion.

17 More than US$ 15 billion.

18 This could be due to lack of data for some countries in some years.

19 Monsanto brought glyphosate to market in 1974 under the trade name Roundup. 'Roundup Ready' are those crops genetically modified to tolerate herbicides glyphosate.

20 The total per continent has been calculated summing data (FAOSTAT database) for each country comprised in the continent, but data were not available for some countries.

21 It is impossible to conduct a European pesticide use trend analysis over many years because of the different reporting systems and timing utilized by the member states. Eurostat statistics assess pesticide use by the amounts of pesticides sold but the data are not homogeneous as they are not available for many countries in some years.

22 This is important because the cocktail effects of mixtures of pesticides are not routinely assessed.

23 Short- term (acute) effects may include stinging eyes, rashes, blisters, blindness, nausea, dizziness, headaches, coma, and even death. Some long-term health effects are delayed or not immediately apparent such as, infertility, birth defects, endocrine disruption, neurological disorders, cancer (Farmworker Justice, 2013). Some research refers to Parkinson's disease and Alzheimer's disease, depressive and anxiety disorders and death due to mental disturbance (Zhang et al., 2009).

24 MRL excesses for unprocessed products were most frequently noted in 2013 for guava, lychees, passion fruit, tea leaves, okra, basil, parsley, spinach-type vegetables, turnips, papaya, cassava, leafy vegetables and pomegranates. Processed products most

frequently exceeding legal limits were wild fungi, tea leaves, peas with pods, peppers, herbal infusions, tomatoes, beans with pods, pomegranates, table grapes, rice, grapefruit and rye.

   With regards to European countries, the highest percentages of residue exceeding the legal limits were found in products from Bulgaria, Portugal and France.

25 The remaining 41% contained residue but within the legal limits.

26 In total, 36 samples of Chinese herbal products collected from Germany, France, Italy, the Netherlands, the UK, the US and Canada were tested. It was found that 32 samples contained three or more kinds of pesticides. For example, samples of honeysuckle collected from Canada and Germany had 24 and 26 types of pesticides respectively; 17 samples showed residue of pesticide classified by the World Health Organization as highly or extremely hazardous. Some 26 samples showed pesticide residue levels that exceeded what the European authorities consider the maximum level for safety (MRLs).

27 In particular, the EU schemes known as Geographical Indications (GIs) promote and protect names of quality agricultural products and foodstuffs, attributable to a specific origin. To protect these products, the EU has signed various multilateral and bilateral agreements.

28 To protect these products, the EU has signed various multilateral and bilateral agreements. Among these initiatives, it is worth mentioning the project '10 plus 10' (European Commission, 2012) started in July 2007. The EU and China formally adopted the protection of 10 agriculture GIs in each other's territories. With regard to European products as Geographical Indications in China and as part of the so-called '10+10' project', the list shows five cheeses, two oils, one ham, one salmon and one dried fruit. In parallel, the European Commission has examined and registered 10 Chinese food names with the last two Chinese names 'Pinggu da Tao' (peach) and 'Dongshan Bai Lu Sun' (asparagus) receiving protected status in the EU as Geographical Indications (European Commission, 2013).

References

Agropages.com (2015). *Annual review- global agrochemical industry's 10 focuses of attention*, http://news.agropages.com/News/NewsDetail – -16903.htm.

Aktar, M. W., Sengupta, D., and Chowdhury, A. (2009). *Impact of pesticides use in agriculture: Their benefits and hazards*, www.ncbi.nlm.nih.gov/pmc/articles/PMC2984095/

Aretè (2010). *Inventory of certification schemes for agricultural products and foodstuffs marketed in the EU Member States*, http://ec.europa.eu/agriculture/quality/certification/inventory/inventory-data-aggregations_en.pdf.

Bajwa, W. I., and Kogan, M. (2002). *Compendium of IPM Definitions (CID)- What Is IPM and How Is It Defined in the Worldwide Literature?* IPPC Publication No. 998. Corvallis: Integrated Plant Protection Center (IPPC).

Benbrook, C. M. (2015). *Trends in glyphosate herbicide use in the US and globally*, https://enveurope.springeropen.com/articles/10.1186/s12302-016-0070-0.

Bian, Y. (2012). *An overview of Chinese law on food safety*, www.academia.edu/4342793/An_Overview_of_Chinese_Law_on_Food_Safety.

Chen, C., Qian, Y., Chen, Q., Tao, C., Li, C., and Li, Y. (2011). Evaluation of pesticide residues in fruits and vegetables from Xiamen, China. *Food Control*, 22(7), www.sciencedirect.com/science/article/pii/S0956713511000259.

ENDURE (2010). *Integrated pest management in Europe*, INRA, 132 pp, available at European Commission, 2005, Regulation (EC) No 396/2005 on maximum residue levels of pesticides in or on food and feed of plant and animal origin and amending Council

Directive 91/414/EEC, http://eur-lex.europa.eu/LexUriServ/LexUriServ.do?uri=OJ:L: 2005:070:0001:0016:en:PDF.

ESFA (2015). *Chemicals in food – overview of data collection reports*, www.efsa.europa. eu/sites/default/files/corporate_publications/files/chemicalsinfood15.pdf.

European Parlament and Council of the EU (2009a). *Regulation (EC) No 1107/2009 concerning the placing of plant protection products on the market and repealing Council Directives 79/117/EEC and 91/414/EEC*, http://eur-lex.europa.eu/legal-content/EN/ TXT/PDF/?uri=CELEX:32009R1107&from=EN.

European Commission (2000). *White Paper on Food Safety*, COM (1999)719 final, Brussels, 2000, para. 3.

European Commission (2007). *EU Policy for a sustainable use of pesticides. The story behind the strategy.*

European Commission (2016). *Update on the state of EU-China trade-related discussions.*

European Parlament and Council of the EU Commission (2009b). *Directive 2009/127/EC of the European Parliament and of the Council of 21 October 2009 amending Directive 2006/42/EC with regard to machinery for pesticide application*, http://eur-lex.europa.eu/ legal-content/EN/TXT/PDF/?uri=CELEX:32009L0127&from=EN.

European Parlament and Council of the EU Commission (2009c). *Directive 2009/128/EC establishing a framework for Community action to achieve the sustainable use of pesticides*, http://eur-lex.europa.eu/LexUriServ/LexUriServ.do?uri=OJ:L:2009:309:0071: 0086:en:PDF.

Fait, A., Iversen, B., Tiramani, M., Visentin, S., Maroni, M., and He, F. (2001). *Protecting workers' health series n° 1: Preventing health risks from the use of pesticides in agriculture*, edited by International Centre for Pesticide Safety, www.who.int/occupational_health/ publications/en/oehpesticides.pdf.

FAO (2013). *The state of the world's land and water resources for food and agriculture, Managing systems at risk*, www.fao.org/docrep/017/i1688e/i1688e.pdf.

FAOSTAT (2015). *Statistical yearbook*, www.fao.org/docrep/018/i3107e/i3107e.PDF.

FAO-WHO (2014). *The international code of conduct on pesticides management*, www.fao. org/fileadmin/templates/agphome/documents/Pests_Pesticides/Code/CODE_2014Sep_ ENG.pdf.

Farmworker Justice (2013). *Exposed and ignored. How pesticides are endangering our nation's farmworkers*, www.farmworkerjustice.org/sites/default/files/aExposed percent20and percent20Ignored percent20by percent20Farmworker percent20Justice percent20singles percent20compressed.pdf.

Greenpeace (2008). *The dirty portfolio of the pesticides industry*, www.greenpeace.org/eu-unit/ Global/eu-unit/reports-briefings/2009/3/dirty-portfolios-of-pesticides-companies.pdf.

Greenpeace (2015a). *Pesticides and our health*, www.greenpeace.org/eu-unit/Global/eu-unit/reports-briefings/2015/Pesticides percent20and percent20our percent20Health_ FINAL_web.pdf.

Greenpeace (2015b). *Europe's pesticide addiction – how industrial agriculture damages our environment*, www.greenpeace.org/international/Global/international/publications/ agriculture/2015/Europes-Pesticide-Addiction.pdf.

IICA (1998). *The ten commandments of the sanitary and phytosanitary agreement of the World Trade Organization*, www.fao.org/ag/againfo/resources/documents/Vets-l-2/7eng.htm.

International Trade Centre (ITC) (2011) Organic Food Products in China: Market Overview, xii, 36 pages (Technical paper) Doc. No. SC-11-196 available at http://www. intracen.org/uploadedFiles/intracenorg/Content/Publications/Organic-food-products-in-China-market-overview.pdf

Lamichhane, J. R., Aubertot, J-N., Begg, G., Nicholas, A., Birch, E., Boonekamp, P., Dachbrodt-Saaydeh, S., Grønbech Hansen, J., Støvring Hovmøller, M., Jensen, J. E., Nistrup Jørgensen, L., Kiss, J., Kudsk, P., Moonen, A.-C., Rasplus, J.-Y., Sattin, M., Streito, J.-C., and Messean, A. (2016). Networking of integrated pest management: A powerful approach to address common challenges in agriculture. *Crop Protection*, (89), 139–151.

Lefebvre, M., Langrell, S., and Gomez-y-Paloma, S. (2014). Incentives and policies for integrated pest management in Europe: A review. *Agronomy for a Sustainable Development*. doi:10.1007/s13593-014-0237-2.

Li, H., Zeng, E. Y., and You, J. (2014). *Mitigating pesticides pollution in China requires law enforcement, farmer training and technological innovation*, www.ncbi.nlm.nih.gov/pubmed/24753037.

Lin, L., Zhou, D., and Ma, C. (2010). Green food industry in China: Development, problems and policies. *Renewable Agriculture and Food Systems*, 25(1), www.cambridge.org/core/journals/renewable-agriculture-and-food-systems/article/green-food-industry-in-china-development-problems-and-policies/42E6FFE21007FF781280192E2D02A054.

Movses, G., and Micheli, M. A. (2015). *Study on the implementation of the provisions of the sustainable use directive on integrated pest management: Experience of eleven member states of the European Union*, http://graduateinstitute.ch/files/live/sites/iheid/files/sites/ctei/users/Mattia/Study percent20on percent20IPM_Final.pdf.

Neumeister (2014). *Corporate science fiction – a critical assessment of a Bayer and Syngenta funded HFFA report on neonicotinoid pesticides*, www.greenpeace.de/sites/www.greenpeace.de/files/publications/20131028-corporate-science-fiction.pdf.

PAN Europe (2013). *Is the pesticide industry really serious about their slogan?* www.pan-europe.info/old/Resources/Briefings/PANE percent20- percent202013 percent20-percent20Is percent20the percent20Pesticide percent20Industry percent20really percent20serious percent20about percent20their percent20slogan.pdf.

Parsa, S., Morse, S., Bonifacio, A., Chancellor, T. C. B., Condori, B., Crespo-Perez, V., Hobbs, S. L. A., Kroschel, J., Ba, M. N., and Rebaudo, F. (2014). Obstacles to integrated pest management adoption in developing countries. *Proceedings of the National Academy of Sciences of the USA*, 111, 3889–3894.

Paull, J. (2008). The Greening of China's Food - Green Food, Organic Food and Eco-Labelling, *Sustainable Consumption and Alternative Agri-Food Systems Conference* (SUSCONS), Liege University, Arlon, 27–30 May, available at http://www.orgprints.org/13563

Peshin, R. M., and Zhang, W. J. (2014). Integrated pest management and pesticide use, in: Pimentel, D., and Peshin, R. (eds.), *Integrated Pest Management, Pesticide Problems*, Vol. 3, Springer Netherlands.

Pretty, J., and Bharucha, Z.-P. (2015). Integrated pest management for sustainable intensification of agriculture in Asia and Africa. *Insects*, 6, 152–182.

Roberts, D., and Unnevehr, L. (2005). Resolving trade disputes arising from trends in food safety regulation: The role of the multilateral governance framework. *World Trade Review*, 4, www.cambridge.org/core/journals/world-trade-review/article/resolving-trade-disputes-arising-from-trends-in-food-safety-regulation-the-role-of-the-multilateral-governance-framework/85F0BCBA01FD62F96951556D20FB47F6.

Schibler, A. (2014). The issue of food safety in EU-China food trade relations. *EU-China Observer*, (4), Department of EU International Relations and Diplomacy Studies, College of Europe.

Standing Committee of the Tenth National People's Congress of the People's Republic of China (2006). *Law of the People's Republic of China on Quality and Safety of Agricultural Products* http://www.npc.gov.cn/englishnpc/Law/2008-01/02/content_1387986.htm

Sustainability Map (2012). Standars China Map, http://www.standardsmap.org/quick-scan ?standards=189&origin=China

USDA (2016). *China food and agricultural import regulations and standards – narrative FAIRS country report*, http://gain.fas.usda.gov/Recent percent20GAIN percent20Publications/Food percent20and percent20Agricultural percent20Import percent20Regulations percent20and percent20Standards percent20- percent20Narrative_Beijing_China percent20- percent20 Peoples percent20Republic percent20of_12–30–2015.pdf.

Wang, Z.-Y., He, K.-L., Zhao, J.-Z., and Zhou, D.-R. (2003). Integrated pest management in China, in: Karim, M., Maredia, D., and Dakouo, D. (eds.), *Integrated Pest Management in the Global Arena*.

WHO (2008). *Children's health and the environment*, www.who.int/ceh/capacity/Pesti cides.pdf.

WHO (2010). *The WHO recommended classification of pesticides by hazard and guidelines to classification: 2009*, www.who.int/ipcs/publications/pesticides_hazard_2009.pdf?ua=1.

Wu, L., and Zhu, D. (2014). *Food Safety in China: A Comprehensive Review*. Boca Raton: CRC Press.

Yang, P. Y., Zhao, Z.-H., and Shen, Z.-R. (2014). Experiences with implementation and adoption of integrated pest management in China, in: Peshin, R., and Perimentel, D. (eds.), *Integrated Pest Management, Experiences With Implementation, Global Overview*, Vol. 4. Berlin: Springer.

Yang, Y. (2007). *Highlights of pesticide laws and regulations in China*. A China Environmental Health Project Fact Sheet, www.wilsoncenter.org/sites/default/files/pesticidelaw.pdf.

Zeng, S. (1993). Sustainable agriculture and integrated pest management in China. *Ciba Found Symp.*, 177, 228–232.

Zhang, W. J., Jiang, F., and Ou, J. (2011). Global pesticide consumption and pollution: With China as a focus. *Proceedings of the International Academy of Ecology and Environmental Sciences*, www.iaees.org/publications/journals/piaees/articles/2011-1(2)/Global-pesticide-consumption-pollution.pdf.

Zhang, W. J., Stewart, R., Phillips, M., Shi, Q., and Prince, M. (2009). *Pesticide exposure and suicidal ideation in rural communities in Zhejiang province, China*, www.who.int/ bulletin/volumes/87/10/08-054122/en/

Zhou, J., and Jin, S. (2013). *Food safety management in China: A perspective from Food Quality Control System*, eBook. Singapore:World Scientific Publishing Co.

14 Assessing the trade potential between China and the EU

In the agricultural sector

Bernadette Andreosso-O'Callaghan
and Li Junshi

EU-China trade and economic relations

In the framework of global economic integration, trade and economic relations between the EU and China have become an inescapable issue from both a political and an economic perspective. This is in part because, after its accession to the World Trade Organization (WTO) in 2001, China became a key trade member in the global trade system and its influence has become stronger and stronger.

Since China and the then European Economic Community (EEC)[1] officially established diplomatic relations in 1975, EU-China trade and economic relations started to develop more formally with the signing of trade agreements and with the launch of bilateral dialogues covering more than 50 sectors. With Deng Xiaoping's opening-up policy and the successive ensuing reforms and with China's accession to the WTO, trade activities and economic cooperation between the two entities have increased drastically and a special type of relationship has evolved into what is now known as the 'EU-China Strategic Partnership'. Initiated in 2003, this Strategic Partnership is based on exploring mutual benefits whilst respecting different national conditions in both regions. Since then, EU-China trade and economic relations have been developing through cooperation and opposition and there still is a big potential for developing wider and deeper relations in terms of trade and economic cooperation.

Being a key exporter and importer worldwide, the EU is also a leading investor and recipient of foreign direct investment as well as the biggest aid donor in the world.[2] China has become the EU's first import partner and second export partner (European Commission, 2016). On the other hand, the EU as a whole is China's number one trading partner. After China became a member of the WTO in 2001, its importance as a trading partner of the EU has increased as shown in Table 14.1. According to EUROSTAT figures, the share of EU exports and imports to/from China has increased from 4.0% in 2002 to 9.7% in 2016 and 9.6% in 2002 to 20.2% in 2016 respectively. As can be seen from Table 14.1, the rising level of economic integration – through trade – between the two partners has only been slightly jeopardised by the 2008 GFC. To some extent, China has been playing some role in helping the EU recover from the crisis. According to International Monetary Fund (IMF) forecasts released after the beginning of the crisis (IMF,

DOI: 10.4324/9781315102566-17

Table 14.1 Trade Flows between the EU and China (excluding Hong Kong) 2001–2016 (€ Million)

Year	Exports	Imports	Balance	Share of China in EU exports (%)	Share of China in EU imports (%) Andreosso and LI Trade between China and EU
2001	–	–	–	–	–
2002	35,101.6	90,418.9	−55,317.3	4.0	9.6
2003	41,476.6	106,578.9	−65,102.3	4.8	11.4
2004	48,382.0	129,202.7	−80,820.7	5.1	12.6
2005	51,748.9	161,007.7	−109,258.8	4.9	13.6
2006	63,695.6	195,816.2	−132,120.6	5.5	14.3
2007	71,823.3	233,862.9	−162,039.6	5.8	16.1
2008	78,300.5	249,102.1	−170,801.6	6.0	15.7
2009	82,421.0	215,274.1	−132,853.1	7.5	17.4
2010	113,453.8	283,931.0	−170,477.2	8.4	18.5
2011	136,414.8	295,055.3	−158,640.5	8.8	17.1
2012	144,227.0	292,121.9	−147,894.9	8.6	16.2
2013	148,115.1	280,149.8	−132,034.7	8.5	16.6
2014	164,622.7	302,148.8	−137,526.1	9.7	17.9
2015	170,357.2	350,639.9	−180,282.7	9.5	20.3
2016	170,115.6	344,655.7	−174,540.1	9.7	20.2

Source: Eurostat, Extra–EU trade by partner, Luxembourg.

2012), 90% of future economic growth would be generated outside Europe, and China would take one third of the growth.

A first remark on the general trade relations between the EU and China is the imbalanced nature of the relationship, with a persistent trade deficit suffered by the EU, although some of this deficit is explained by the role of EU firms producing in China and re-exporting back to the EU, given the high import content of Chinese exports. Another and related remark is the huge trade potential that EU firms could explore and exploit (and vice versa). As the biggest economy within the group of emerging economies, China has a very large population representing potentially a vast domestic demand with a new big group of affluent consumers growing. Estimates from Crédit Suisse (2016) put the number of the middle class individuals as high as 109 million individuals in 2016. As one of the EU's important markets, the Chinese food market is being shaped increasingly as one of the largest and most profitable markets in the world. This results mostly from increasing living standards, as well as from a higher sophistication of consumers aware of food safety issues. Developments have been such that Chinese food conglomerates have emerged in the generalised race of 'land grabbing'.

The EU-China economic relationship has been a prevalent topic of interest in academic circles either from the viewpoint of the economic or political disciplines.

As the second largest economy and the biggest trading nation in the world, China stands out as a main trade and economic partner for the EU, leading to an increasing number of studies that shed light on the bilateral trade and economic relationship.[3] The existing literature on EU-China trade and economic relations focuses mostly on the following three aspects:

(1) Policy working papers from European official departments.

For example, a recent publication (European Parliament, 2015) by the policy department of the European Parliament has analyzed EU-China trade and economic relations in depth including the role of China in world trade, the EU's global commercial strategy of China as well as the development path of the EU-China partnership.

(2) Analyses on general EU-China trade and economic relations from different theoretical and disciplines angles.

In particular, Algieri (2002) clarifies that the EU Commission's agenda, rights and obligations are embedded in the European Union's external economic relations from an institutional point of view. Qiu (2004) points out that differences and contradictions still exist in EU-China relations beyond their political and economic differences. Andreosso-O'Callaghan and Nicolas (2007) examine the EU-China economic relationship from the perspective of complementarity and opposing forces between the two regions. Luo (2007) explains from a legal viewpoint, that the legal capacity of China for dealing with foreign trade barriers is being built up by engaging the private sector actively and by mobilizing the resources of the domestic industries. In addition, China's new trade policy utilizes more effectively the WTO rules. Men (2012) investigates the reasons why the EU-China relationship is fraught with so many problems and he tries to identify the reasons of these problems; then he goes on to analyze whether the relationship can be maintained despite these increasing problems through analyzing the differences between the EU and China from different perspectives such as history and economic development. Xin (2014) finds that not enough effort has been deployed from both sides through his analysis: of the driving forces behind China's trade surplus with the EU; of the situation of bilateral trade disputes; as well as of the issue of the 'Market Economy Status'. Xin (2013) also points out that it would be counterproductive to develop an EU-China Comprehensive Strategic Partnership if the EU does not clarify its strategic position towards China. Li et al. (2012) examine the degree of structural change in China's trade with the world especially with the EU during the 1996–2008 period. Lu et al. (2014) figure out that the EU and China have close trade relations in goods, especially from the perspective of intra-industry trade of manufacturing industrial products; the paper also highlights that trade imbalances between the EU and China arise from trade in machinery and transport equipment and other manufacturing goods. In addition, there exists a myriad of trade and investment barriers to EU-China interactions, including both tariff and non-tariff obstacles.

(3) Papers based on the implications for further development of the EU-China trade relations.

Huang (2010) formulates the implications for the future of EU-China trade relations based on analysing the current situation of EU-China trade disputes within the WTO framework. Zhang (2015) proposes the development of a trade relation which is based on analyzing the conditions of the development of trade, and especially on the limitation factors for developing trade relations between the two regions. Maher (2016) clarifies and examines the issues that have hindered the development of the EU-China relationship and points out that those issues are holding the greatest potential for a future expansion in the relationship.

Analysing the status quo of EU-China trade and economic relations and seeking methods and solutions for building up a more comprehensive and stabilized trade and economic relationship, which would ultimately boost economic growth in both regions, is a priority in academic-based studies. Much more scarce is nevertheless the literature related to the EU-China economic relationship when confined to the agricultural sector. The ensuing section will thus narrow down the scope of EU-China trade and economic relations, by looking at agricultural trade between China and the EU.

The EU-China agricultural trade relationship

After a brief review of the literature, this section first looks at the strength of the agricultural trade relationship and then it assesses the potential for further trade in this sector. Some policy recommendations will conclude the section.

Literature review

With regard to the existing literature on EU-China agricultural trade relations, there are less studies than on the general trade and economic relations between the two regions. However, some of the existing literature is very topical and has a profound significance for further research in this area. Early papers on this issue encompass those of Wang (1997) and of Colby et al. (2000) who illustrate that after China's entry into the WTO, freer trade would stimulate Chinese demand for food products. Schmidhuber (2001) points out that Chinese consumer demand for imported goods would be stimulated by competitive EU exports in the Chinese market from both a quality and a price dimension after significant tariff reductions. Saunders et al. (2005) comprehensively analyze the agricultural trade policy reforms from three dimensions which are WTO negotiations, Common Agricultural Policy (CAP) reform, and China's WTO accession. The impact of agricultural reforms on the EU, China and New Zealand are also analyzed by these authors. Peng (2006) uses the case of peanuts trade as an example to illustrate the fact that it is necessary for China to take adequate measures to counteract technical barriers from the EU. Niemi and Huan-Niemi (2007) find out that absolute prices will not follow big changes for Chinese agricultural imports; however, because of price competition, relative price changes will have a significant effect on the export market shares of EU firms. In addition, China's imports of agricultural products from the EU do not lead to big changes due to the reduced tariff in the background of trade liberalization but a rapid income growth will play an important role on the quantity of China's agricultural imports. The authors note that the emerging middle class has an increased appetite for imported food products and that their tastes are changing and include more western-style food products. At a meso-economic level, Fischer et al. (2007) find that there is a big export potential for the EU spirit industry to China. Yue et al. (2010) use a Gravity Model to analyse the impact of the EU's new food safety standards on China's tea exports and the results show that the new food safety standards have a strong impact on the tea exporters of the world; in this vein, China's tea exports did actually decrease, as the theoretical results would predict. Gai and Fan (2008) point out that China has less agricultural products presenting a competitive advantage compared to the EU and therefore that a key point for China is to improve its competitive advantages in its agricultural sector. Sun and Reed (2010) evaluate the Free Trade Agreements (FTAs) effects on agricultural trade in terms of trade creation and trade diversion effects. The paper finds that the formation of the EU-15 and EU-25, the ASEAN-China preferential trade agreement, and the Southern African Development Community agreements all have positive effects on agricultural trade growth among their members. Guo et al. (2011) study the short-term and long-term impact of significant economic events on China-Germany agri-food products trade and the authors find a sharp decrease of China's agri-food exports to Germany because of the 2008 crisis while Germany's exports to China in 2009 were not affected by the crisis as much. Goetz and Grethe (2010) investigate the relevance of the EU entry price system (EPS) for China's exports of apples and pears to the EU and the results show that the production of pears in China is more competitive than the production of apples with respect to the situation of the EU. Pawlak et al. (2016) find that agri-food products trade between the EU and China has grown significantly between 2008 and 2015, and that the EU trade balance position has shifted from being a net importer to becoming a net exporter.

It can be seen that the different studies that concentrate primarily on the effects of trade liberalization at both the bilateral or multilateral levels were published mostly after China's entry into the WTO. This chapter aims at building on the findings of Gai and Fan (2008) and going beyond the study by Pawlak et al. (2016) by refining the analysis in terms of trade potential.

Statistical analysis of EU-China agricultural trade

Data explanation

In order to conduct the analysis, we use several data relating to China only, to the bilateral agricultural trade relationship between China and the EU, and to the EU-China agricultural trade relationship at a refined product level.

The trade figures relating to China's exports and imports of agricultural products to the world from 2001–2015 were taken from the WTO statistics database and the agricultural products are defined following the Revision 3 of the Standard International Trade Classification (SITC) which correspond to SITC sections 0, 1, 2, 4 minus 27 and 28. The figures for 2016 were taken from the Ministry of Agriculture of China (MOACOM). For the bilateral agricultural trade relationship (EU – China), data are drawn from two sources. EU figures are from the UN COMTRADE database in line with the Harmonized System (HS) Classification. The agricultural products included are those covered under chapter 1 to chapter 24 of the HS Classification excluding chapter 50 (silk), chapter 51 (wool, fine or coarse animal hair; horsehair yarn and woven fabric), and chapter 52 (cotton).[4] The figures for China are from Chinese official monthly export and import reports which are released by the Ministry of Commerce of China Department of Foreign Trade. It should be noted that the method of product classification is not clarified, which presents a limitation of our study. Lastly, the trade figures at the product level are used to analyze the agricultural products trade potential (and complementarity) existing between the EU and China. The agricultural products are chosen from HS chapter 1 (live animals); chapter 2 (meat and edible meat offal); chapter 4 (dairy produce etc.).[5] The total amount of agricultural products for the study encompass up to nearly 90 different types of agricultural products. The limitation of this set data is that the figures for 2016 are not available from either the UN COMTRADE database or from Eurostat.

Data analysis

Since China Joined the WTO in 2001, the scale of bilateral trade in the agricultural sector has been expanding. By 2010, China had become the world's fifth largest agricultural trade nation (MOFCOM, 2010). As Table 14.2 shows, both agricultural exports from and imports into China to the world have increased year by year since 2001. However, this rising trend does not show a remarkable growth when compared with its total trade growth after China's accession to the WTO. It can be seen indeed that the share of agricultural trade in China's total trade actually decreased after 2002. It can further be inferred that China's agricultural trade still has a big development potential. With regard to the bilateral agricultural trade between China and the EU, Table 14.3 shows that in general, exports from the EU-27 are smaller than China's exports to the EU in this specific sector in line with the general trade deficit suffered by the EU vis-à-vis China although the former trend has changed since 2013 as noted earlier.

China is one of the main agri-food trade partners of the EU whereas it is the second export destination after the USA and the fourth importer of the EU after Argentina in extra-EU agri-food trade in 2006. According to EU data (European Commission, 2017), the main agricultural export product categories in 2016 from the EU to China were: infant food and other cereals, flour, starch or milk preparations (16% in value terms of the total EU agri-food exports to China); fresh, chilled and frozen pork meet (15%); fresh, chilled and frozen offal, animal fats and other meats (12% of EU-27 agricultural exports to China). The top

Table 14.2 Share of China's agricultural trade products in its total trade from 2001 to 2016 (in US$ million)

Year	Exports of agricultural products	Imports of agricultural products	Total agricultural trade	Total exports of China	Total imports of China	Total Chinese trade	Share of ag. trade in the total (%)
2001	16626	20125	36751	266098	243553	509651	7.21
2002	18796	21848	40644	325596	295170	620766	6.55
2003	22158	30482	52640	438228	412760	850988	6.19
2004	24121	42279	66400	593326	561229	1154555	5.75
2005	28711	45189	73900	761953	659953	1421906	5.2
2006	32542	51653	84195	968978	791460.87	1760438.9	4.78
2007	38862	65369	104231	1220060	956115	2176175	4.79
2008	40883	76617	117500	1430693.1	1132567	2563260.1	4.58
2009	40883	76617	117500	1201611.8	1005923.2	2207535	5.32
2010	51607	108260	159867	1577754.3	1396244	2973998.3	5.38
2011	64613	144724	209337	1898381.5	1743486.6	3641868.1	5.75
2012	66204	156835	223039	2048714.4	1818405	3867119.4	5.77
2013	70188	165476	235664	2209004	1949989.5	4158993.5	5.67
2014	74497	170107	244604	2342292.7	1959234.7	4301527.4	5.69
2015	72532	159733	232265	2273468.2	1679564.5	3953032.7	5.88
2016	72990	111570	184560	2097440	1587480	3684920	5.01

Sources: (1). For 2001–2015, China's exports and imports of agricultural products figures are from the WTO Statistics database; figures for 2016 are from The Ministry of Agriculture of China (MOA); (2). Figures on total exports and imports of China from 2001–2015 are from the National Bureau of Statistics of China, whereas the 2016 figures are from the Ministry of Commerce of China (MOFCOM).

Table 14.3 Bilateral Agricultural Trade between EU27 and China from 2001 to 2016 ($ Million)

Year	EU27		China	
	Export to China	Import from China	Export to EU	Import from EU
2001	957.881	2791.320	2184.042	–
2002	1086.365	2728.951	1801.332	–
2003	1172.328	3483.973	2361.594	–
2004	1790.260	4090.204	2650.848	–
2005	2274.354	5178.489	3531.173	2006.649
2006	2613.886	6147.619	4418.664	2142.956
2007	3384.383	7642.166	5479.114	2801.582
2008	3827.758	8572.452	6438.403	3707.700
2009	3946.150	7253.996	5756.058	3881.652
2010	5377.879	9105.299	6857.161	4881.542
2011	8107.249	10291.418	8104.142	7012.901
2012	9049.904	9098.820	7549.079	8363.662
2013	10988.617	9197.175	8050.778	10209.271
2014	11289.008	9275.982	8432.080	10953.610
2015	12611.338	8410.688	8120.664	13230.966
2016	13253.740	7643.030	7411.608	12796.625

Sources: (1) The trade figures of EU27 with China from 2001 to 2015 have been calculated by the authors according to the figures from UN Comtrade; EU27 trade figures for 2016 with China are from Eurostat Comext. (2) China's trade figures are gathered from monthly reports released by the Ministry of Commerce of China.

three imports product categories in 2016 were fresh, chilled and dried vegetables (€623 million, or 12% of total the EU agri-food imports from China); preparations of vegetables, fruit or nuts (€474 million, or 9%); fresh, chilled and frozen offal, animal fats and other meats (€444 million, or 9%) (European Commission, 2017).

With the help of a statistical analysis, the next section will analyse the trade potential existing between the EU-27 and China in the agricultural sector.

Assessing the trade potential

EU- China agricultural trade relations are very promising even though agricultural products trade represents a small amount of total EU-China trade; the negotiations on agricultural trade liberalization within the WTO framework coupled with the successive European Common Agricultural Policy (CAP) reforms as well as the specific and strategic importance of this sector for both sides, provide further scope for agricultural products trade between the EU and China (Gai and Fan, 2007). Consequently, Chinese demand for high quality western food increases. The gap between rising demand and Chinese production will be filled by imports but demand is also restricted by a number of factors such as high prices. Therefore, there is an opportunity for EU producers and exporters in this potentially growing market of China.

A thorough analysis of trade trends for the 90 or so agricultural product categories shows that there is a remarkable trade potential in eight product categories (for the EU) and in another 8 (different) products for China. These are shown in Tables 14.4 and 14.5. The selection of these products is based on the analysis of trade trends of both regions, first vis-à-vis the rest of the world. This is done as follows: the products for which China has a trade surplus vis-à-vis the world for two or more of the three selected years (2001, 2008 and 2015) that correspond to a trade deficit of the EU vis-à-vis the world for the same years are selected and categorised as areas of trade potential expansion for China and are represented in Table 14.5 (vice versa for the case of the EU-27 in Table 14.4.). The correspondence between trade surplus on the one hand and trade deficit on the other suggests the existence of a trade complementarity between the two countries. When reviewing the share of each selected product in the bilateral trade, one comes to the conclusion that these 16 products are already traded on a bilateral basis, albeit to a marginal extent; therefore, an improvement in the China-EU trade relationship would facilitate trade expansion in meat, dairy produce, etc. for the EU in particular. Conversely, China would gain EU market shares in fish, vegetables and fruits among others.

These results lead to a number of observations. First of all, the 16 product areas are only the most obvious areas of bilateral trade potential between the two partners; indeed, trade expansion in these areas would not entail structural problems in either region since a deficit, say in the EU, would be compensated for by a surplus emanating from China. These are therefore the areas of trade complementarity. It follows obviously that there might be a small element of trade diversion, an issue which is however beyond the scope of this study. It implies also that there are other product areas with a bilateral trade potential, but these areas

Table 14.4 Potential agricultural products areas of trade expansion for the EU (2001, 2008 and 2015)

Commodity Code	Product name	2001	2008	2015
2	Meat and edible meat offal	S	S	S
4	Dairy produce, birds' eggs; natural honey; edible products of animal origin, not elsewhere specified or included	S	S	S
10	Cereals	S	D	S
17	Sugars and sugar confectionery	S	S	S
19	Preparations of cereals, flour, starch or milk; pastrycooks' products	S	S	S
22	Beverages, spirits and vinegar	S	S	S
24	Tobacco and manufactured tobacco substitutes	D	S	S
51	Wool, fine or coarse animal hair; horsehair yarn and woven fabric	S	S	S

Key: S (trade surplus); D(trade deficit)

Table 14.5 Potential agricultural products areas of trade expansion for China (2001, 2008 and 2015)

Commodity Code	Product name	2001	2008	2015
3	Fish and crustaeans, molluscs and other aquatic invertebrates	S	S	S
5	Animal originated products; not elsewhere specified or included	S	S	S
7	Vegetables and certain roots and tubers; edible	S	S	S
8	Fruit and nuts; edible; peel of citrus fruit or melons	S	S	D
9	Coffee,tea, mate and spices	S	S	S
16	Meat, fish or crustaceans, molluscs or other aquatic inverteberates; preparations thereof	S	S	S
20	Preparations of vegetables, fruit, nuts or other parts of plants	S	S	S
52	Cotton	S	S	S

Key: S (trade surplus); D (trade deficit)

would be more problematic since they might include products for which both the EU and China have a comparative advantage. Second, availing of increased trade potential implies a policy change in both countries. In China in particular, more effort needs to be deployed in improving the food safety system as argued for example by Connolly et al. (2016) as well as the quality of Chinese agricultural products on western markets (Dongwen et al., 2016). This entails renewed efforts in fostering productivity and efficiency in particular through technological change (Songqin et al., 2010). These qualitative elements are important to allow Chinese products become more sought-after on Western and in particular on the EU markets.

Conclusions

The China-EU agricultural relationship is a relatively unexplored area of research and the studies looking at, for example, the impact of trade liberalization at a refined level of statistical analysis are rare. This chapter aimed therefore at filling the gap in this area by looking at the issue of increased bi-lateral trade potential with the help of a descriptive statistical analysis at the third digit level of analysis. The findings show that there is a trade complementarity (defined as a long-term global deficit experienced by country B compensated for by a long-term global trade surplus by country A) in a number of products. These are for example: fish (crustaceans, molluscs), vegetables (and certain roots), as well as tea and coffee for China, all product areas in which China could increase its trade with the EU. From the EU standpoint, the obvious products that could be traded much more on the Chinese market are meat, dairy products, cereals, sugar and tobacco, among others.

The delineation of a trade potential is subordinated to a number of policies and the main issue faced by China is to improve the quality (in terms of food safety) of its agricultural exports. On the EU side, safety standards are ultimately the main non-trade barrier that can always be used to block or restrict imports as the example of tea shows (Yue et al., 2010). From China's viewpoint, the eight products highlighted in this study correspond nevertheless to 8 product areas where the EU has a persistent deficit on the global market. One expects therefore that increased trade flows in these product areas should lead to a 'win-win' situation.

Notes

1 The European Community (EEC), emanating from the Treaty of Rome in 1957 was renamed as the European Community (EC) and was incorporated into the European Union (EU) in 1993. In 2009, the EC ceased to exist within the wider EU framework.
2 The EU referred to in the ensuing part of this section is the EU-28 whereas the statistical analysis in Section 3 will refer to the EU-27, without the UK.
3 A recent project gathering a number of world experts in the area is for example the one led by Brennan and Murray (2015).
4 Note that agricultural products and agri-food products are used interchangeably in this study.
5 See the Appendix for a full list of the products used in the study.

References

Algieri, F. (2002). EU economic relations with China: An institutionalist perspective. *The China Quarterly*, (169), Special Issue: China and Europe since 1978: A European perspective, March, 64–77.

Andreosso-O'Callaghan, B., and Nicolas, F. (2007). Complementarity and rivalry in EU-China economic relations in the twenty-first century. *European Foreign Affairs Review*, 12(1), 13–38.

Brennan, L., and Murray, P. (2015). *Drivers of Integration and Regionalism in Europe and Asia: Comparative Perspective.* New York: Routledge.

Colby, H., Price, J., and Tuan, F. (2000). *China's WTO accession would boost U.S. Ag exports and farm income.* Agricultural Outlook, Economic Research Service/USD, AGO-269, March.

Connolly, A. J., Shaojing Luo, L., Woosley, M., Lyons, M., and Phillips-Connolly, K. (2016). A blueprint for food safety in China. *China Agricultural Economic Review*, 8(1), 129–147.

Crédit Suisse (2016). *Global Wealth Report 2016.* Zurich: Research Institute.

Dongwen, T., Na Hu, X. Wang, and Li Huang (2016). Trade margins, quality upgrading and China's agri-food export growth. *China Agricultural Economic Review*, 8(2), 277–298.

European Commission (2016). *Countries and regions: China* [online], http://ec.europea. eu/trade/policy/countries-and-regions/countries/china/.

European Commission (2017). *Agri-food trade statistical factsheet: European Union-China.* Directorate-General for Agriculture and Rural Development.

European Parliament (2015). *In-depth analysis: Trade and economic relations with China 2015* [online]. European Parliament, www.eesc.europa.eu/resources/docs/trade-and-economic-relations-with-china-2015.pdf.

Fischer, C., Schiefer, J., and Schornberg, S. (2007). *Study 6: Agriculture, study on the future opportunities and challenges in EU-China trade and investment relations 2006–2010*. Conferences and Studies, 15 February 2007, Directorate General for Trade, European Commission, Brussels.

Gai, Y., and Fan, S. (2007). China and the EU agricultural product trade relations and development countermeasures. *GD-HK-MO Market & Price*, 2007(9).

Gai, Y., and Fan, S. (2008). China-EU agricultural trade structure and competitive analysis. *GD-HK-MO Market & Price*, 2008(1).

Goetz, L., and Grethe, H. (2010). The entry price system for fresh fruit and vegetable exports from China to the EU- Breaking a fly on the wheel? *China Economic Review*, 21, 377–393.

Guo, Z., Feng, Y., and Tan, X. (2011). Short- and long-term impact of remarkable economic events on the growth causes of China-Germany trade in agri-food products. *Journal of Economic Modelling*, 28, 2359–2368.

Huang, Z. (2010). EU-China trade dispute in the WTO: Looking back to look forward. *Journal of Yearbook of Polish European Studies*, 13, 41–57.

International Monetary Fund (2012). *World Economic Outlook* (WEO) [press release], www.imf.org/external/pubs/ft/weo/2012/01/pdf/text.pdf.

Jyrki Niemi, and Ellen Huan-Niemi (2007). EU-China agricultural trade in relation to China's WTO membership. *International Food and Agribusiness Management Review*, 10(3), 41–62.

Li, L., Dunford, M., and Yeung, G. (2012). International trade and industrial dynamics: Geographical and structural dimensions of Chinese and Sino-EU merchandise trade. *Applied Geography*, 32(1), 130–142.

Lu, Z., Yan, T., and Deng, X. (2014). EU-China economic relations: Interactions and barriers. *Review of European Studies*, 6(4), 12–30.

Luo, Y. (2007). Engaging the private sector: EU-China trade disputes under the shadow of WTO law? *European Law Journal*, 13(6), 800–817.

Maher, R. (2016). The elusive EU-China strategic partnership. *International Affairs*, 92(4), 959–976.

Men, J. (2012). The EU and China: Mismatched partners? *Journal of Contemporary China*, 21(74), March, 333–349.

MOFCOM (2010). *The Report of Agricultural Products*. Beijing: Ministry of Commerce of the People's Republic of China.

Pawlak, K., Kolodziejczak, M., and Xie, Y. (2016). Changes in foreign trade in agri-food products between the EU and China. *Journal of Agribusiness and Rural Development*, 4(42), 607–618.

Peng, C. (2006). The influence and countermeasures of the technical barriers in the international agricultural products trade: Peanuts trade as a case study. *Theory Journal*, 2006(11), language: Chinese.

Qiu, Y. L. (2004). Sino-EU relations: The status quo and future. *Journal of World Economics and Politics*, 2004(10).

Saunders, C., Wreford, A., and Rasin, Shanika (2005). *An analysis of agricultural trade policy reforms and their impact on the EU, China and New Zealand*. Conference paper, New Zealand Agricultural and Resource Economics Society, Tahuna Conference Centre, Nelson, New Zealand, 26–27 August.

Schmidhuber, J. (2001). *Changes in China's agricultural trade policy regime: Impacts on agricultural production, consumption, prices, and trade*. China's Agriculture in the International Trading System, OECD, 21–49.

Songqin, J., Ma, H., Huang, J., Hu, R., and Rozelle, S. (2010). Productivity, efficiency and technical change: Measuring the performance of China's transforming agriculture. *Journal of Productivity Analysis*, 33(3), Special Issue on Agricultural Productivity Growth, 191–207.

Sun, L., and Reed, Michael R. (2010). Impacts of free trade agreements on agricultural trade creation and trade diversion. *American Journal of Agricultural Economics*, 92(5), 1351–1363.

Uprasen, Utai, and Andreosso-O'Callaghan, B. (2009). *Measuring the impact of protectionism on China: A CGE approach.* American Association for Chinese Studies 51st Anniversary Annual Conference, Rollins College Orlando, 16–18 October.

Wang, Z. (1997). *The impact of China and Taiwan Joining the World Trade Organization on U.S. and World Agricultrual.* Economic Research Service/USDA, Technical Bulletin No. 1858, Washington, DC.

Xin, C. (2013). New trends in EU's economic relations with China. *Journal of Global Economic Observer*, 1(1), May, 11–18.

Xin, C. (2014). China-EU trade and economic relations (2003–2013). *Journal of Global Economic Observer*, 2(1), 41–45.

Yue, N., Kuang, H., Sun, L., Wu, L., and Xu, C. (2010). An empirical analysis of the impact of EU's new food safety standards on China's tea export. *International Journal of Food Science and Technology*, 45, 745–750.

Zhang, J. (2015). Further promote the development of Chinese economic and trade relations with the European Union. *Economic Review*, 2015(1).

Appendix
Harmonized system classification of agricultural products used in the study

Chapter 1 (live animals); chapter 2 (meat and edible meat offal); chapter 4 (dairy produce etc.); chapter 6 (trees and other plants etc.); chapter 7 (vegetables and certain roots etc.); chapter 8 (fruit and nuts, edible; peel of citrus fruit or melons); chapter 9 (coffee, tea, mate and spices); chapter 10 (cereals); 12 (oil seeds and oleaginous fruits, etc.); chapter 15 (animal or vegetables fats and oils and their cleavage products etc.); chapter 16 (meat, fish or crustaceans etc.); chapter 17 (sugars and sugar confectionery); chapter 18 (cocoa and cocoa preparations); chapter 19 (preparations of cereals, flour, starch or milk; pastrycooks' products); chapter 20 (preparations of vegetables, fruit, nuts or other parts of plants); chapter 21 (miscellaneous edible preparations); chapter 22 (beverages, spirits and vinegar; chapter 23 (food industries, residues and wastes thereof; prepared animal fodder); chapter 24 (tobacco and manufactured tobacco substitutes); chapter 51 (Wool, fine or coarse animal hair; horsehair yarn and woven fabric); chapter 52 (cotton); chapter 53 (vegetable textile fibres; paper yarn and woven fabrics of paper yarn).

Index